nelson**science**
Chemistry

2nd EDITION

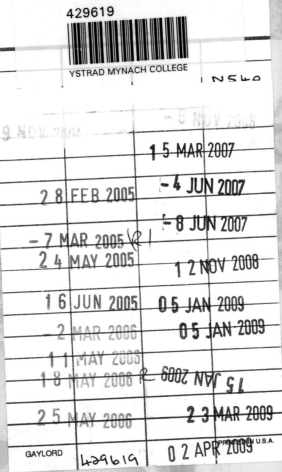

John Holman and **Phil Stone**

First published in 1995 by:
Thomas Nelson and Sons Ltd

Second Edition published in 2001 by:
Nelson Thornes Ltd
Delta Place
27 Bath Road
CHELTENHAM
GL53 7TH
United Kingdom

03 04 05 / 10 9 8 7 6 5 4 3 2

A catalogue record for this book is available from the British Library

ISBN 0 7487 6239 6

Typeset by TechSet Ltd
Printed and bound in Spain by Graficas Estella

N540
429619

Contents

To our readers

This book is about chemistry. It is about the materials the world is made from and how new materials can be produced. Studying chemistry helps you to understand how materials behave – whether they are in the kitchen, in your clothes or in a builder's yard. It helps us to understand how to make better materials, how to get the energy we need and how to protect the environment. Understanding chemistry is an important part of understanding the world around us.

How to use this book

The book is divided into eleven **sections** (A to K) and each section is split into **topics**: A1, A2 etc. Generally each topic consists of the main text (white background) together with:

Extensions (cream background). These take some of the ideas a bit further. Your teacher will advise you which ones to read. Some of them are specific case studies with thought-provoking questions at the end.

Activities (green background). These are things you can do yourself without any special equipment. Activities that can only be done in the laboratory are in a separate Teachers' Resource Pack (see below).

Questions (various backgrounds). These are designed to help you understand the topic and test your ability to recall and interpret information. Some of the questions invite you to put forward your own ideas.

In addition there are:
- Occasional special features which focus on particular issues and explore them in depth.
- A selection of GCSE exam questions at the end of the book.
- Instructions for practical work and investigations in a separate Teachers' Resource Pack (see below).

Key skills

There are certain things that you need to learn how to do. These are called **key skills**.
The main key skills are :

- **Application of number**: measuring things, doing calculations, interpreting information that has numbers in it.
- **Communication**: reading, writing essays and reports, making summaries, explaining things, giving talks and discussing topics.
- **Information and communications technology (ICT)**: using a computer to find information on the Internet, analysing data and presenting information by means of text, numbers and images (diagrams and graphs), using sensors with an interface linked to a computer to collect and process experimental data.

Other wider key skills are:
- **Working with others**: collaborating with other people in carrying out investigations and discussing issues.
- **Improving your own performance**: practising techniques, repeating experiments, perfecting your other skills.
- **Problem solving**: thinking up ways of investigating things, interpreting information gained by reading or from your own investigations.

From time to time you may be tested (assessed) on the three main key skills. Our book, and the accompanying Teachers' Resource Pack, will give you lots of opportunities for practising all the key skills.

Questions and activities that provide particularly good opportunities for developing ICT skills are marked like this:

Scientific enquiry

Scientific enquiry means the way scientists work and make discoveries. In the National Curriculum it is described as *Investigative Skills* and *Ideas and Evidence in Science*. Scientific Enquiry will underpin the whole of your chemistry course. In our book we give many examples of Ideas and Evidence in Science. Some of the examples are historical milestones in the history of chemistry, others focus on modern applications of chemistry.

We hope that by the time you finish your course you will not just know a lot of chemistry, but will understand what it means to be a chemist - and perhaps you may want to study chemistry further.

Other things to think about

Chemistry, like the rest of science, affects our lives in all sorts of ways. Here are some of them, and the questions they raise:

- **Spiritual and moral issues**: can we reconcile chemical discoveries with our beliefs?
- **European dimension**: how does chemistry relate to our being part of Europe?
- **Environment**: what part does chemistry play in tackling and solving the environmental problems that face society?
- **Citizenship**: can an understanding of chemistry help us to be good members of our communities?
- **Health and safety**: how does chemistry affect people's physical and mental well-being?

In our book we try to address all these issues in a variety of different contexts.

Teachers' Resource Pack

This pack contains:

- **Investigations and experiments** with instructions that can be photocopied and given to students, and separate notes for teachers and technicians.

- **Answers (with mark schemes) to the questions** in the textbook.
- **Explanations** of how the textbook can be used for fostering scientific enquiry (ideas and evidence) and key skills.
- **Enlarged versions of some of the diagrams** from the textbook, which can be photocopied and handed out to students.
- **Grids** showing how the textbook relates to your syllabus specifications and to the main key skills.
- **Support notes** on the Channel 4 television programmes.

Other books in the *Nelson Science* series

Nelson Science Biology by Michael Roberts and Neil Ingram, and *Nelson Science Physics* by Ken Dobson and Martin Roberts should help you to complete your understanding of science.

Website

The *Nelson Science* series has a website: www.nelsonscience.co.uk

The website contains a range of extra support for the book, including supplementary reading materials, useful links, and opportunities for feedback. The site is updated on an ongoing basis. Wherever you see the ICT icon (ICT) there will be useful ICT activities and suggestions provided at the corresponding point on the site.

Television programmes

Channel 4 have made a series of five programmes called *Science in Focus: the nature of scientific enquiry* which accompany the *Nelson Science* series. One of these, *Mendeléev's Dream*, links directly to section F of this book. *Mendeléev's Dream* describes how scientists, from the ancient Greeks onwards, tried to classify elements, and how Dmitri Mendeléev eventually came up with the Periodic Table.

Topics in the textbook that relate to the programme are marked with the Channel 4 logo:

The programmes are available as videos from Channel 4 by post from 4Learning, PO Box 100, Warwick CV34 6TZ; by telephone on 01926 436444; by fax on 01926 436446; by e-mail from 4learning.sales@channel4.co.uk; and via the Internet at www.4learning.co.uk/shop

Thanks

Many people have helped us produce this book. We are especially grateful to the other authors of the *Nelson Science* series, Ken Dobson, Martin Roberts, Michael Roberts and Neil Ingram.

Professor Bruce Gilbert of the University of York provided expert guidance, and we are also grateful to the following for their help.

Judith Bennett, University of York
Peter Borrows, CLEAPSS School Science Service
Professor Andrew Briggs, Department of Materials, University of Oxford
David Fielding, geology specialist
Professor Robert Fox, University of Oxford
Anna Grayson, geology specialist and broadcaster
Dan Harman, Grove Farm, Buckinghamshire
David Harris, the Aluminium Federation
Liz Hubbard, Chemical Industry Education Centre, University of York
John Moorhouse, Rhodia Eco Services
Omar Mukhtar, University of Bristol
William Stanton, geology specialist
Mike Taylor, science education consultant
Professor David Waddington, University of York
Mike Walton, Kemira fertilisers.

Good luck in your study of chemistry!

John Holman
Phil Stone
York, September 2001

A

Materials

A1

Changing substances

Chemistry is about what things are made of, and how we can change them.

Picture 1 The stages in making a clay pot.
(1) Shaping.

Picture 2 (2) Drying.

Picture 3 (3) Firing.

Think about the stages in making a clay pot. You take a lump of wet clay, then you change its shape so it's pot-like. If you don't like the result, you can easily reshape it. Once you have the shape you want, you let the wet clay dry. As it dries, it becomes hard, but quite crumbly. Even now you could reshape it: you would have to soak the dry clay in water to make it soft again.

When the clay is dry, you 'fire' the pot by heating it in a kiln. Now the clay changes a lot. Its colour changes, and it becomes much harder and no longer crumbly. No matter how long you soak it in water, it stays hard. In other words, *it has changed permanently*. Fired clay is a different substance from unfired clay.

POTTERY IS CHEMISTRY

Making a pot involves changing one substance into another. This is called a **chemical change** and it's what chemistry is all about. Notice these things about chemical changes.

- They involve making new substances
- They usually involve energy transfers
- They can usually be explained if we know the chemical formulas of the substances involved – the atoms it contains, and the way the atoms are arranged.

This last point is an important feature of chemistry, and we will come back to it many times in the book. You can find out in topic C7 about the changes that happen to the arrangement of atoms in clay when it is fired.

■ Who uses chemistry?

You do, I do – everyone does. Living things are constantly changing one substance to another, so life is all about chemistry.

Many people use chemistry as part of their work.

Cooks use chemistry all the time. They may not have studied chemistry like you, but they learn by experience how to control the changes that happen when food is cooked.

Farmers use chemistry when they decide how to neutralise acid soil, or how much fertiliser to use.

Doctors use chemistry, because everything that goes on in the human body involves chemistry.

Engineers use chemistry when they decide what materials to make things from.

People who have trained as chemists work in hospital laboratories, in breweries, in oil refineries, in food laboratories and in factories making everything from plastics to poppadums. Chemists do a particularly important job in protecting the environment from the effects of human activities.

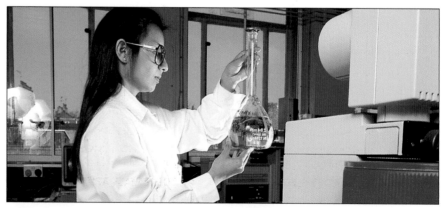

Picture 4 This chemist is checking the purity of a water sample.

MATTER AND SUBSTANCES

Matter is the name that scientists give to anything that has mass. You and I are made of matter; so is this book and so is the air you are breathing.

Scientists also use the word **substance**. This means a particular type of matter, which you can put a name to. Salt is a substance, and so is water. Light is not a substance, because it has no mass and so it isn't matter .

Chemistry involves studying the properties of substances. If you know the properties of a substance, you can say what it could be used for – and how it might be changed.

In a chemical change, one substance changes to another. Take charcoal, for example, which is nearly pure carbon. When this substance burns, it joins with oxygen in the air to form a new substance, carbon dioxide. We can summarise this change as

$$\text{carbon} + \text{oxygen} \rightarrow \text{carbon dioxide}$$

The substances on the left-hand side are the **reactants**. The **products** are on the right-hand side.

This summary is called a **word equation**. You can also write a summary using the formulas of the substances involved. This is called a **balanced equation**, and in this case it would be

$$C + O_2 \rightarrow CO_2$$

Picture 5 shows what this equation means in terms of atoms and molecules. There is more about equations in topic C3.

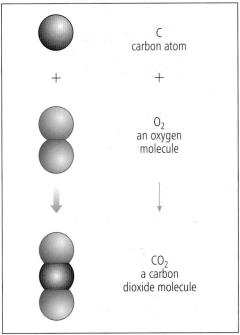

Picture 5 Carbon reacts with oxygen to give carbon dioxide.

■ Conserving mass

You cannot make matter out of nothing – nor can you destroy matter. In a chemical change, the total mass of all the matter involved stays the same before and after the reaction. This is called the **Law of Conservation of Mass**.

Look at Picture 6, for example. When you burn a match, it seems to lose mass. The ash has less mass than the original match. But the burning reaction involves gases too – and gases do have mass, even though they are difficult to weigh. You need to include the mass of the oxygen that reacts with the match, and the mass of all the gases formed in the reaction. You find that the total mass of the reactants (match and oxygen) is the same as the total mass of the products (ash, smoke and gases).

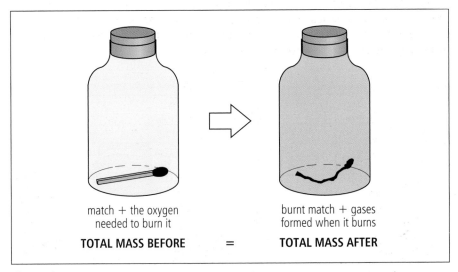

match + the oxygen needed to burn it		burnt match + gases formed when it burns
TOTAL MASS BEFORE	=	**TOTAL MASS AFTER**

Picture 6

Questions

1   Which of the following are substances?
    (a) water (b) sugar (c) electricity
    (d) alcohol (e) sound (f) oxygen.

2   Which of the following involve chemical changes? Remember – in a chemical change a new substance is formed.
    (a) burning wood (b) drying wet wood (c) turning wood to charcoal (d) slicing bread (e) turning bread to toast (f) burning gas (g) boiling water.

3   When magnesium burns, it gives out a bright white light and gets very hot. The magnesium turns into a white powder. Give two pieces of evidence that this is a chemical change.

Matter and materials

Matter is what the world is made of. This topic is about matter and how we can make use of it.

Picture 1   These drinks involve all three states of water – ice, water and water vapour.

THE STATES OF MATTER

There are three states of matter: solid, liquid and gas (picture 3). **Solids** have a fixed shape – think of an ice cube. **Liquids** have no fixed shape, but they take up the shape of their container and their volume is fixed – think of a litre of water. **Gases** have no fixed shape or volume. They spread out (**diffuse**) to fill all the available space – think of steam coming out of a kettle.

Gases are usually invisible, which makes it difficult to think of them as matter at all. But we know gases are a form of matter because they have mass. You can weigh gases – though their density is low, so they don't weigh much. A balloonful of air weighs about 5 g. A bedroomful of air weighs about 50 kg – as much as a small person!

Most substances can exist in all three states, depending on the temperature. Water is a solid (ice) below 0°C, a gas (steam) above 100°C and a liquid between these temperatures.

When we say 'water is a liquid', we mean that the substance scientists know as H_2O is a liquid at normal temperatures. 'Normal' temperature is around 20°C in Britain. But if you live in the Arctic it might be more sensible to say 'water is a solid', because it certainly is most of the time.

You can decide the normal state of a substance if you know its melting point and boiling point. For example, the element bromine has a melting point of $-7°C$ and a boiling point of 59°C. So at the 'normal' temperature of 20°C, bromine will be melted but not boiled. In other words it will be a liquid.

■ Changes of state

The state of a substance can be changed by heating or cooling (picture 2). Notice the words used to describe the changes of state shown in the picture.

You will see that liquids can be turned to gases by **boiling** and by **evaporating**. Liquids can evaporate even when they are cold. This is just as well, because we rely on water evaporating from wet clothes to get them dry.

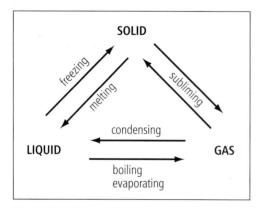

Picture 2   Changes of state.

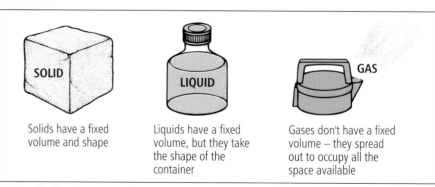

Solids have a fixed volume and shape

Liquids have a fixed volume, but they take the shape of the container

Gases don't have a fixed volume – they spread out to occupy all the space available

Picture 3   The three states of matter.

Subliming means turning directly from a solid to a gas, without melting to a liquid first. It is less common than other changes of state. Carbon dioxide sublimes (picture 4). If you cool carbon dioxide gas to about −55°C, it turns directly to a solid. If you allow the solid to warm up, it turns straight back to carbon dioxide gas, without melting. This makes the solid useful for keeping things like ice cream cool, and it is sometimes called 'dry ice'.

Air is a gas at normal temperature, but you can condense it into a liquid by cooling it to −194°C. You can even freeze it to make solid air if you cool it a bit further.

There is more about changes of state in topic C1 on the kinetic theory.

Look around you. What state of matter is the most common where you are at the moment? Unless you are reading this in the bath, it is likely to be the solid state. Admittedly there is a lot of invisible gas in the air around you, but the furniture, the building, your clothes and even you yourself are all in the solid state.

Picture 4 These vapour clouds are made by 'dry ice' – solid carbon dioxide. As the solid carbon dioxide turns to gas, it cools the air. This makes water vapour condense in clouds.

MATERIALS – MATTER FOR MAKING THINGS

The word 'material' has several meanings. We often use it to describe the fabrics used to make clothes. But to a scientist or an engineer, a material is a form of matter, normally solid, which is used to make things.

■ What kinds of material are used to make false teeth?

All kinds of materials can be used to make false teeth. You will probably think first of plastics – a white acrylic plastic is often used. Sometimes a ceramic, a kind of porcelain, is used instead of plastic. Metals are less common, although gold teeth are still popular with some people, and metals are often used for fillings. Fillings are also made using a special type of glass.

When you choose materials for a job, you have to make sure their properties are right. False teeth have a demanding job to do. They are constantly bathed in saliva, which is quite corrosive. The material chosen has to be hard, waterproof and unreactive, and preferably tooth-like in appearance. What's more, it has to be reasonably priced, which is why you don't see many gold teeth. Acrylic plastic is fine in all these ways.

Picture 5 George Washington's false teeth were made from hippopotamus bone.

THE RIGHT PROPERTIES FOR THE JOB

When you are considering a material for a particular purpose, you have to ask some basic questions.

ARE THE PHYSICAL PROPERTIES RIGHT?
Physical properties mean things like hardness, strength, density and melting point. If these properties are wrong, there is no chance of the material doing the job.

ARE THE CHEMICAL PROPERTIES RIGHT?
Chemical properties are to do with the chemical reactions of the material. Does it burn or corrode in air? Is it attacked by water or acid? These considerations are important if the material is to last and be safe.

IS THE PRICE RIGHT?
It's no use getting the properties of the material right if it costs a fortune.

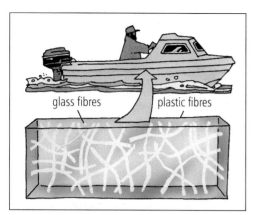

Picture 6 Glass-reinforced plastic: a composite material.

■ Composite materials – the best of both worlds

Sometimes you want a material that combines the properties of two different materials.

Glass-reinforced plastic is an example. It's used to make the body of things like boats and caravans which need to be light but strong. Plastic resin is light and quite strong, but it cracks easily. Glass fibres are also strong, and flexible. Glass-reinforced plastic has a plastic **matrix** with glass fibres embedded in it (picture 6). The glass fibres give the plastic extra strength so that it does not crack when it is bent or hit.

Glass-reinforced plastic is an example of a **composite material** – it contains two or more materials working together. Concrete is another composite, in which pieces of stone and gravel are embedded in a matrix of cement.

Questions

1 a What are the three states of matter?

  b What words are used to describe the following processes? (For example, the answer to (i) is 'melting'.)
    i) turning a solid to a liquid
    ii) turning a liquid to a gas
    iii) turning a gas to a liquid
    iv) turning a liquid to a solid
    v) turning a solid to a gas

  c What is formed when you carry out each of the following processes?
    i) Condensing steam
    ii) Subliming ice

2 What will be the state of each of the substances A–D at 20°C?
Substance A, melting point 1064°C, boiling point 3080°C.
Substance B, melting point 29°C, boiling point 669°C.
Substance C, melting point −112°C, boiling point −117°C.
Substance D, melting point −39°C, boiling point 357°C.

3 Here is a list of materials:
steel, earthenware, pottery, polythene, cotton, glass, concrete, wood, aluminium, Bakelite (a hard brown plastic which is difficult to melt)
Which material or materials would be suitable for each of the following uses?

If you think none of the materials is suitable, suggest a different one. In each case, give the reason for your choice.

  a the casing for an electric plug
  b a container for concentrated sulphuric acid
  c the lining for a furnace
  d a dustbin
  e the barrel of a pen
  f an air filter

4 Suppose you are planning a journey to the centre of the Earth in a self-propelled tunnelling machine. What special materials would be needed to build the machine?

Activities

A A survey of materials

ICT Make a list of at least 20 different objects and the material each is made from. The objects might be around your home, your school or any other place where a wide variety of different objects are to be found. Try to choose objects that are made from a single material, rather than complex objects like a radio that are made from lots of different materials.

Put your results in a table like the one below (two examples have been entered in the table to help you).

Object	Material it is made from
cup	china
paper clip	steel

Once you have collected your list, try to classify the materials in each of the following ways:

1 Natural or artificial materials.

2 Metal, ceramic, glass, plastic or fibre materials.

3 Materials that would or would not have been used a hundred years ago.

B Identifying materials

Suppose you are given a piece of a material that is painted black so you cannot tell its normal appearance. Plan the tests you would do on the material to decide whether it is metal, ceramic, glass, plastic or fibre. Remember, your tests must be safe.

Your teacher may give you some samples of materials to try out your tests on.

Choosing materials

Picture 1 Modern canoes are usually made from glass-fibre-reinforced plastic.

Table 1 gives some properties of different materials. Use the table to answer 1 to 4 below.

1 *Tennis racquets*
The frame of a tennis racquet needs to be strong and stiff, yet light. Traditionally, tennis racquet frames were made from wood, but to get a strong and stiff enough frame you have to use a lot of wood. This gives a thick, heavy frame. Nowadays racquets come in a number of different materials.

For each of the possible materials (a) to (d) below, list what you think are the advantages and disadvantages of the material for making tennis racquet frames.

a steel b aluminium c nylon
d carbon-fibre-reinforced plastic.

2 *Canoes*
At one time canoes were made of wood. Modern canoes are usually made from glass-fibre-reinforced plastic.

Explain why glass-fibre-reinforced plastic has largely replaced wood. Suggest one other material that might be used instead. Remember to bear cost in mind as well as properties.

3 *School chairs*
List the criteria that must be considered when choosing a material for making school chairs.

Now use these criteria to select the best material in the table for this purpose.

4 *Car bodies*
Most cars have bodies made from steel. What other materials in the table could be used instead? Are any of them ever in fact used? Why do you think steel continues to be much the most popular material for car bodies?

Table 1   Some properties of selected materials.

Material	Description	Density (kg/m³)	Strength (GPa)	Stiffness (GPa)	Cost
Steel	Grey metal which rusts readily unless protected	7800	1	210	Low
Aluminium	Silvery metal	2700	0.2	70	Low
Wood (spruce)	Brown fibrous material which rots unless protected	500	0.1	20	Low
Polythene	Plastic which can be given any colour	960	0.02	0.6	Low
Nylon	Plastic which can be given any colour	1100	0.08	3	Medium
Kevlar	Plastic or fibre which can be given any colour	1450	3	190	High
Glass-fibre-reinforced plastic	Plastic matrix containing glass fibres. Can be given any colour	1900	1.5	21	Medium
Carbon-fibre-reinforced plastic	Plastic matrix containing black fibres	1600	1.8	200	High

Elements – the building blocks for materials

Every substance on Earth is made from the same building blocks – the 92 elements.

Picture 1 Spoilt for choice.

Picture 2 When wood is heated, it decomposes to form carbon.

Have you every felt spoilt for choice? You go shopping and you can't decide what to buy from the enormous choice available? It's the same with clothes, food – and materials for that matter. There is an almost infinite selection of materials available, both natural and artificial.

Yet all this choice is built from fewer than a hundred chemical elements.

WHAT IS AN ELEMENT?

Iron and wood are both materials. Iron is an element, but wood is not. The difference is that wood can be turned into simpler substances, but iron cannot. If wood gets hot, it chars – it turns black on its surface. The wood has broken down (**decomposed**) and formed carbon, which is the black solid. But no matter what you do to the carbon, you cannot break it down any more. It is an element.

An element is a substance that cannot be broken down into any simpler substance.

Obviously, wood is not an element, because it can be broken down to give carbon (and other substances as well). On the other hand, iron is an element, because whatever you do to iron you cannot turn it into anything simpler.

There are 92 elements occurring in nature. Another 12 or so have been made artificially by scientists. Each element is given a **symbol** of one or two letters. For example, oxygen is O and chlorine is Cl. There is a full list of all the elements and their symbols in the Data Section.

The 92 elements range from reactive gases like chlorine to unreactive metals like gold. All these different elements can be classified according to their various properties. One simple way is to classify them as metals or non-metals. A very important classification system is the Periodic Table (topic F1).

WHAT IS A COMPOUND?

Consider water. For centuries scientists believed this familiar substance to be an element. We now know that water can be decomposed to form hydrogen and oxygen, which means it isn't an element. On the other hand, hydrogen and oxygen cannot be decomposed any further, so they are elements. Hydrogen and oxygen are combined together in water, and water is a **compound** of hydrogen and oxygen.

A compound is a substance made by chemically combining two or more elements.

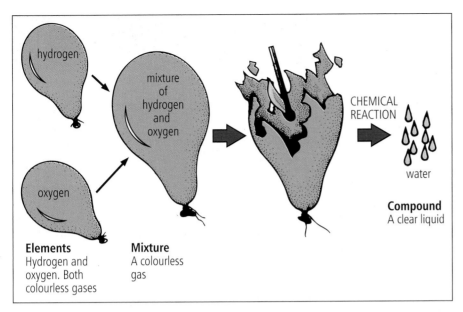

Picture 3 A mixture of elements is different from a compound made by combining them.

Combining elements to form a compound is different from simply mixing them together (picture 3). When you make a mixture you get something that still looks like the starting substances, just mixed together. But a compound usually has *completely different* properties from the elements it is made from.

Salt is a good example. If you melt salt, then pass electricity through it, the salt decomposes. You get a green gas called chlorine and a soft metal called sodium. Both these substances are elements because you cannot break them down any further. But you can easily make them combine together again by warming the sodium with the chlorine, when you get salt again. Salt is a compound of sodium and chlorine; its chemical name is sodium chloride.

As you can see from picture 4, the compound sodium chloride has very different properties from the elements sodium and chlorine. You would be very unwise to eat either of these elements, but sodium chloride is an essential part of your diet.

Combining sodium and chlorine to form sodium chloride is an example of **synthesis** – building up simple substances into more complicated ones. Synthesis is the opposite of decomposition.

■ Names and formulas of compounds

The chemical name of a compound often tells you which elements it contains. The name sodium chloride tells you the compound contains the elements sodium and chlorine. The ending **-ide** shows the elements are combined together, not just mixed. A chemical name like 'sodium chloride' is more useful to a scientist than a common name like 'salt' because it tells you what elements are present.

Some compounds have names ending in -**ate**. This usually means that oxygen is present as well as the other two elements. For example, copper sulphate contains copper, sulphur and oxygen.

Every compound has a **formula** which tells you the elements that it is made from. The formula of sodium chloride is NaCl – Na and Cl are the symbols for sodium and chlorine. The formula of water is H_2O, which tells you it contains the elements hydrogen (H) and oxygen (O). The number 2 tells you there is twice as much hydrogen as oxygen.

You can find out more about formulas in topic C2.

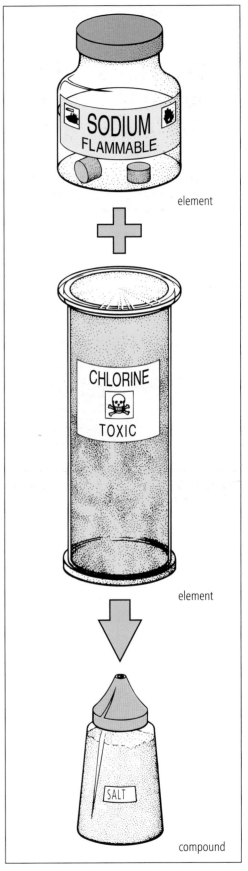

Picture 4 Sodium chloride (salt) is very different from the elements it is made from.

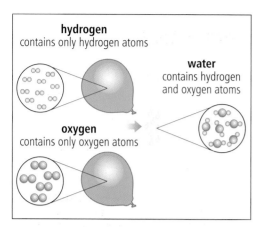

Picture 5 Elements contain only one type of atom.

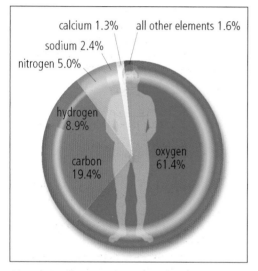

Picture 6 The main elements in the human body, and their percentages by mass in the body.

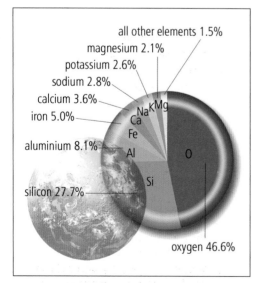

Picture 7 The most abundant elements by mass in the Earth's crust.

HOW CAN YOU TELL AN ELEMENT FROM A COMPOUND?

It isn't always easy to decide whether a substance is an element or a compound. You certainly can't tell just by looking at the substance. You can do experiments to see if the substance can be broken down into anything simpler, but even this isn't always easy.

The sure way to decide is to find out what kind of atoms the substance is made from. Everything is made of atoms (topic C2), and there are 92 different kinds of atom – one for each of the 92 different elements. **An element contains only one type of atom**. For example, hydrogen contains only hydrogen atoms, oxygen contains only oxygen atoms.

Compounds contain at least two different kinds of atom. For example, water contains hydrogen atoms and oxygen atoms (picture 5). Sugar is a compound of carbon, hydrogen and oxygen (formula $C_{12}H_{22}O_{11}$). It contains three different kinds of atoms – carbon, hydrogen and oxygen.

If you know the formula of a substance, you can tell straight away whether it is an element or a compound. You just look at the formula and decide how many different elements are present.

ELEMENTS IN YOUR BODY

Everything is made of elements, and your body is no exception. Picture 6 shows the proportions of different elements in the human body. These elements do not occur on their own in the body. They are combined together as compounds – thousands of different ones.

You can see that nearly 95% of the mass of the body is made up of just four elements – oxygen, carbon, hydrogen and nitrogen. More than half the mass of the human body is water, so it's not surprising that there is so much hydrogen and oxygen. Apart from water, the main compounds in the body are proteins, fats and carbohydrates (topic H5).

Fats and carbohydrates are made from carbon, hydrogen and oxygen, while proteins also contain nitrogen. So you can see why these four elements are so abundant in the body.

We get the elements our bodies need from the food we eat. That's why it is important to eat a balanced diet that will provide all the elements you need in roughly the right proportions. Elements like copper and zinc are only present in tiny amounts, but they are still vital for good health. They are known as trace elements.

ELEMENTS IN THE EARTH

The elements we need for our diet start off in the Earth and in its atmosphere – and eventually end up there again. The same is true for every one of the elements we use for making houses, clothes, furniture, fuels, medicines and other necessities. All the raw materials we need to keep life going come from the Earth. To be more exact, they come from the Earth's atmosphere, oceans and crust. The Earth's crust is the thin layer of rock, about 50 km deep, on the surface.

Picture 7 shows the eight commonest elements in the Earth's crust. There are 92 elements to be found on Earth altogether, but these eight account for more than 98% by mass of the Earth's crust. The remaining 84 make up only 1.5%. What is more, the two most abundant elements, oxygen and silicon, make up almost three-quarters of the mass of the Earth's crust.

Picture 8 These strata get their colours from elements such as iron, which are abundant in the Earth's crust.

Very few of the elements in the Earth are uncombined. Most occur combined with one another as compounds. Most of the oxygen and silicon in the Earth are combined together in rocks. Sand is almost pure silicon oxide. Clays also contain silicon and oxygen, together with aluminium, which is the third most abundant element after silicon and oxygen.

Iron is the fourth most abundant element, and most of it is combined with oxygen as iron oxide, also called iron ore. Calcium, the fifth most abundant element, is mostly combined with carbon and oxygen as calcium carbonate, the compound in chalk and limestone.

Topic D1 has more about the storehouse of raw materials to be found in the Earth.

Topic D1 has more about the storehouse of raw materials to be found in the Earth.

Activities

A Elements in your food

Look at the tables of ingredients on a range of foods and drinks. Tables of ingredients are found on the label or package.

Use these tables of ingredients to make a list of elements present in the foods.

In some cases elements may be mentioned by name. Most of the ingredients that are mentioned will be compounds, though. Try to work out what elements are present in as many of these compounds as you can. Use information given in this topic and in other parts of the book.

Compare your list of elements with the elements shown in picture 6. Which elements from picture 6 do not appear on your list? Suggest reasons why.

B Explaining about elements

The idea of elements and compounds is quite difficult to understand. Often the best way to see if you understand something is to try and explain it to another person.

Find someone who does not know much science. It might be a neighbour or a relative. Try to explain to them the difference between an element and a compound.

Afterwards, get them to tell you how well you did. Try to find out how much they really understand. You could test their understanding by getting them to do some of the questions at the end of this topic!

Questions

When answering these questions, you can get information about elements from table 1 in this topic, and from of the Data Section.

1 The formulas of several substances are listed below:

(a) CH_4 (b) $CuSO_4$ (c) Zn (d) $CaCO_3$
(e) Fe (f) Cu (g) MgS (h) $AlCl_3$
(i) $NaNO_3$ (j) H_2 (k) HBr (l) S_8
(m) $C_6H_{12}O_6$ (n) He, (o) V_2O_5
(p) $BaCl_2$ (q) Ag.

For each substance:
   i) say whether it is an element or a compound;
   ii) name the elements that it contains.

2 a Explain what is meant by the terms i) synthesis and ii) decomposition.

b Each of the word equations below describes a chemical reaction. For each reaction, say whether it is an example of i) synthesis or ii) decomposition.
   1. mercury oxide → mercury + oxygen
   2. carbon + oxygen → carbon dioxide
   3. aluminium + sulphur → aluminium sulphide
   4. calcium carbonate → calcium oxide + carbon dioxide
   5. potassium chlorate → potassium chloride + oxygen
   6. iron + chlorine → iron chloride

3 What elements are present in each of the following compounds? In each case, give the name and symbol of each element present:

a hydrogen bromide
b magnesium sulphide
c magnesium sulphate
d aluminium iodide
e potassium nitrate
f zinc fluoride
g tin chromate
h gallium arsenide

4 a Use picture 6 to list the elements in the human body in order of abundance, most abundant first.

b Use picture 7 to list the elements in the Earth's crust in order of abundance, most abundant first.

c Would you expect the two lists in (a) and (b) to match up in any way? Do they in fact?

Lavoisier's elements

Antoine Lavoisier was a great French scientist. He was born in 1743 and became a civil servant. But he also developed an interest in science and he was especially good at very accurate experimental work. This helped him to make discoveries which other scientists missed because their results were not accurate enough.

Lavoisier was executed in 1794 by French revolutionaries because he had been a tax-collector. After his death a colleague said, 'It only took them an instant to cut off his head, and a hundred years may not produce another like it.'

In 1789 Lavoisier published a book called *Traité Elementaire de Chimie*. It explained his ideas about burning and the air and it changed people's thinking about chemical reactions. In fact, many people say this book marked the beginning of chemistry as a subject in its own right.

One of the important ideas Lavoisier put forward in this book was the idea of elements, which he called in French *substances simples*. He listed 33 things that he thought were elements. The list as it appeared in his book is shown in table 1.

Use table 1 to answer question 1.

1 Use your knowledge of French, plus guesswork, plus (as a last resort) a French dictionary, to translate into English all the names in the middle column (the one headed 'Noms nouveaux').

Check and correct your answer to question 1 using table 2 on page 13. Use the corrected table to answer the remaining questions.

2 Two of the things in Lavoisier's table of elements are not even substances. Which two?

3 Of the remaining substances, five are not in fact elements, but compounds. Which five? Use the table of elements in the Data Section to help you if necessary.

4 For each of the five substances you have mentioned in your answer to 3, find out the proper chemical name. For example, the proper chemical name for lime is calcium oxide. You may have to use an encyclopaedia or an advanced chemistry book to find them all.

5 Why do you think Lavoisier thought that these five compounds were elements?

Noms nouveaux.	Noms anciens correspondans.
Lumière.........	Lumière.
	Chaleur.
	Principe de la chaleur.
Calorique.........	Fluide igné.
	Feu.
	Matière du feu & de la chaleur.
	Air déphlogistiqué.
Oxygène.........	Air empiréal.
	Air vital.
	Base de l'air vital.
	Gaz phlogistiqué.
Azote............	Mofete.
	Base de la mofete.
Hydrogène.......	Gaz inflammable.
	Base du gaz inflammable.
Soufre..........	Soufre.
Phosphore........	Phosphore.
Carbone..........	Charbon pur.
Radical muriatique.	Inconnu.
Radical fluorique..	Inconnu.
Radical boracique..	Inconnu.
Antimoine........	Antimoine.
Argent..........	Argent.
Arsenic..........	Arsenic.
Bismuth..........	Bismuth.
Cobolt..........	Cobolt.
Cuivre..........	Cuivre.
Etain...........	Etain.
Fer............	Fer.
Manganèse.......	Manganèse.
Mercure.........	Mercure.
Molybdène......	Molybdène.
Nickel..........	Nickel.
Or............	Or.
Platine.........	Platine.
Plomb.........	Plomb.
Tungstène.......	Tungstène.
Zinc...........	Zinc.
Chaux..........	Terre calcaire, chaux.
Magnésie........	Magnésie, base du sel d'Epsom.
Baryte..........	Barote, terre pesante.
Alumine........	Argile, terre de l'alun, base de l'alun.
Silice...........	Terre siliceuse, terre vitrifiable.

Substances simples qui appartiennent aux trois règnes & qu'on peut regarder comme les élémens des corps.

Substances simples non métalliques oxidables & acidifiables.

Substances simples métalliques oxidables & acidifiables.

Substances simples salifiables terreuses.

Table 1   Lavoisier's table of elements.

6 Suppose you could go back in time and talk to Lavoisier. Write down what you would say to him to explain that lime is not an element. What might his reply be? You can write your answers in English if you like.

7 Give five elements that are not included in Lavoisier's table. Why do you think he failed to list them?

Table 2 Translations into English of Lavoisier's list of elements. Only the 'Noms nouveaux' (new names) are shown here.

Light	Tin
Heat	Iron
Oxygen	Manganese
Nitrogen	Mercury
Hydrogen	Molybdenum
Sulphur	Nickel
Phosphorus	Gold
Carbon	Platinum
Chlorine*	Lead
Fluorine*	Tungsten
Boron	Zinc
Antimony	Lime
Silver	Magnesia
Arsenic	Barytes
Bismuth	Alumina
Cobalt	Silica
Copper	

*Lavoisier actually confused chlorine and fluorine with their oxides, but this can be ignored as far as this exercise is concerned.

Picture 1 Antoine Lavoisier.

When were the elements discovered? ICT

Find the list of elements in the Data Section (table 1). The list includes the dates when each element was discovered. Use these dates to carry out this exercise.

1 Count the total number of elements that had been discovered by each of the following dates:
(a) 1700,   (b) 1750,
(c) 1800,   (d) 1850,
(e) 1900,   (f) 1950,
(g) the present.

2 Using your results from 1, plot a graph showing the total number of elements discovered (vertical axis) against date.

3 Why were relatively few elements discovered after 1900?

4 Why were relatively few elements discovered before 1700?

5 What was the peak time for discovering elements? Suggest a reason why this was such an active time.

6 In the second half of the nineteenth century, scientists became very interested in classifying elements by grouping them together.

a Why do you think they became so interested in it at that particular time?

b What is the name of the grouping system that they eventually came up with?

Different kinds of mixtures

Most of the materials around us are not pure elements or compounds, but mixtures. In this topic we look at the different kinds.

IS IT PURE?

We like our food to be pure, but if it was really pure in the way that chemists understand the word, food would actually be rather boring.

When people use the word 'pure', they usually mean 'not mixed with anything else'. 'Pure orange juice' contains only the juice of oranges, with no additives. But in chemistry the word 'pure' means more than this. **A pure substance is a single substance on its own**.

Elements and compounds are pure substances, but mixtures are not. To a chemist, orange juice isn't really pure because it is a mixture of many different substances such as water, sugars, vitamins and acids. That's why it tastes so nice. Any one of these pure substances on its own would taste much less interesting.

Practically all the things we eat are mixtures. Usually they contain many different compounds mixed together.

The last topic looked at elements and compounds. We saw that compounds are very different from the elements they contain. But a mixture resembles the substances it contains. The properties of a mixture are a kind of average of the properties of the substances in it. So a mixture of sugar and water is both sweet and wet.

Table 1 sums up the differences between compounds and mixtures. Notice that an important property of mixtures is that they can be separated into their component parts. The separation of mixtures is covered in the next topic, topic A5.

Table 1 Comparing compounds and mixtures.

Compounds	Mixtures
Consist of a single substance	Consist of two or more substances
Properties are very different from the elements in them	Properties are similar to the substances making up the mixture
Can only be separated into elements by a chemical reaction	Often quite easily separated
The amount of the elements in the compound are fixed	The amounts of the different substances in the mixture can vary

Picture 1 'Pure' orange juice: is it really pure?

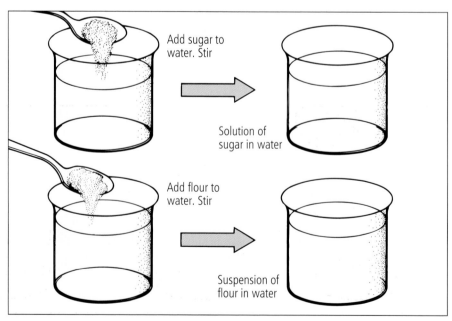

Add sugar to water. Stir

Solution of sugar in water

Add flour to water. Stir

Suspension of flour in water

Picture 2 The difference between a solution and a suspension.

MIXTURES OF SOLIDS AND LIQUIDS

When you shake a solid with a liquid, the solid sometimes disappears into the liquid. The solid has **dissolved**, and the result is a **solution**. Sugar forms a solution in water and many drinks contain sugar dissolved in water.

Not all solids form solutions in liquids. If you add flour to water, the flour does not dissolve, no matter how much you stir. The flour stays **suspended** in the water, and eventually it settles out. The flour forms a suspension in water. Picture 2 shows the difference between a solution and a suspension.

Sometimes you get a **gel** when you mix a solid with a liquid. The solid makes a kind of network which traps the liquid so it cannot flow freely. The result is a semi-solid which can move around, but not as freely as a liquid.

The jelly you sometimes eat for pudding is a gel made from water and a protein called gelatine. The kind of gel you put on your hair is made from water and an oil. Starch forms a gel when you heat it with water.

Picture 3 This tasty gel is a mixture of protein and water.

MIXTURES OF LIQUIDS

When you add one liquid to another, the two liquids sometimes dissolve in each other so they form a single layer. The liquids are **miscible**. Alcohol and water are miscible – if they were not, alcoholic drinks like whisky would separate into two different layers.

But some pairs of liquids are **immiscible**. When you add them together, they form two different layers. Oil and water are like this. If you have ever mixed a 'French dressing' from oil and vinegar, you will know that the oil floats on top of the watery vinegar. These liquids are immiscible. Picture 4 shows the difference between miscible and immiscible liquids.

Immiscible liquids will mix together better if you can break down one of the liquids into tiny droplets. The droplets of one liquid float suspended in the other liquid, so they do not separate out into different layers. This kind of mixture is called an **emulsion**. Picture 5 shows the idea. Unlike pure liquids, emulsions are cloudy (opaque) so you cannot see through them. To make an emulsion, an **emulsifier** is used to stop the droplets joining together to form a separate layer.

Cream is an emulsion. It has tiny droplets of butterfat floating in water. If you churn the cream around a lot, the drops of fat join together and you get butter.

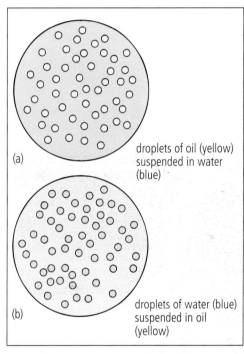

(a) droplets of oil (yellow) suspended in water (blue)

(b) droplets of water (blue) suspended in oil (yellow)

Picture 5 In an emulsion, droplets of one liquid are suspended in another liquid.

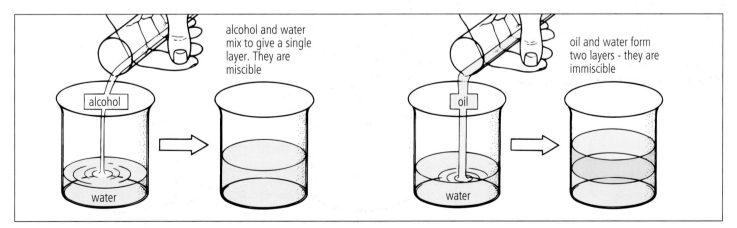

alcohol and water mix to give a single layer. They are miscible

alcohol

water

oil and water form two layers - they are immiscible

oil

water

Picture 4 Miscible and immiscible liquids.

Picture 6 Mayonnaise and salad cream are emulsions of oil and vinegar. In mayonnaise the oil is broken up into tiny droplets which float suspended in the watery vinegar. The emulsifier used in traditional mayonnaise is egg yolk.

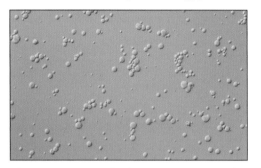

Picture 7 Cream under the microscope. Notice the droplets of fat suspended in the water.

Picture 8 Gases can mix with liquids to form a solution or a foam.

Many cosmetics are emulsions too. Hand creams and foundation creams are usually emulsions of oil in water. Oil helps prevent skin from getting dry, but if you use oil on its own it makes the skin feel greasy. An emulsion of oil in water feels much nicer.

Some cosmetics are an emulsion of water-in-oil, rather than oil-in-water – picture 5 on the previous page shows the difference. Cold cream and cleansing cream are water-in-oil emulsions. If you feel their texture you will notice they feel oilier than oil-in-water emulsions like hand cream.

MIXTURES OF GASES AND LIQUIDS

What happens when you add a gas to a liquid? You do this every time you shake or stir some water – a little air always gets added to the water. When you blow into a drink through a straw you are adding air to the drink.

It may seem that the gas just bubbles through the liquid and comes out again. But in fact, some of the gas actually dissolves in the liquid. It disappears into the liquid and forms a **solution**. Fizzy drinks are solutions of carbon dioxide in water, with a bit of sugar and flavouring also dissolved to make them taste interesting.

Fizzy drinks like cola and beer often have a frothy 'head' on top. This is a different kind of gas–liquid mixture, called a **foam**. The gas is not dissolved in the liquid, but has formed tiny bubbles in it (picture 8). Unlike pure liquids, foams are usually opaque because the bubbles of gas scatter the light. This is why the water in a waterfall looks white instead of transparent.

Eventually, the tiny bubbles in a foam join together to form bigger bubbles, and these escape from the foam. The foam collapses. Some foams last for a very long time – they are stable. If you whip egg white with air you get a stable white foam. If you then heat the foam in an oven, the liquid egg white dries out and solidifies. You now have a solid foam: meringue.

Bread is a solid foam, with bubbles of carbon dioxide gas trapped in the solidified dough. Plastics are often made as solid foams: sponge and foam rubber, for example.

Table 2 Important types of mixtures.

Name	Description	Example
Solution of solid in liquid	Transparent solution of solid dissolved in liquid	Sea water, sugar in water
Suspension of solid in liquid	Cloudy mixture of solid particles suspended in liquid	Muddy river water, flour in water
Gel	Jelly-like mixture of solid and liquid	Fruit jelly, cold custard
Solution of two miscible liquids	Single transparent liquid layer	Vodka (alcohol and water), petrol–oil mixture
Emulsion of two immiscible liquids	Cloudy mixture containing tiny drops of one liquid suspended in the other liquid	Milk, skin cream
Solution of gas in liquid dissolved in liquid	Transparent solution of gas	Soda water
Foam of gas in liquid	Many tiny bubbles of gas trapped in liquid	Washing lather, shaving foam
Solid foam of gas in solid	Many tiny bubbles of gas trapped in solid	Sponge cake, expanded polystyrene

A SUMMARY OF DIFFERENT KINDS OF MIXTURES

Table 2 summarises the important kinds of mixtures that have been mentioned here. Notice that each mixture has two parts, or **phases**, which may be solid, liquid or gas.

Notice too that there are several kinds of solutions: solid-in-liquid, liquid-in-liquid and gas-in-liquid. In a solution, the two phases are *completely* mixed, so that they become a single liquid phase. In other types of mixtures, such as suspensions, emulsions and foams, the two phases are separate. But one phase may be broken up into such tiny particles, bubbles or droplets that you can only see them with a microscope.

Picture 9 Custard is made from cornflour and milk. Cornflour contains starch. The long starch molecules form a network which traps water, forming a gel. The more cornflour you use, the thicker the gel.

Activity

Looking for emulsions

Many food products are emulsions. They contain emulsifiers to make oil and water mix. You can often spot emulsifiers in the ingredients lists on the food package. Emulsifiers have E numbers beginning with 4.

Have a look in your food cupboard for food products that are emulsions. List at least 10. For each one, list the emulsifier(s) it contains.

Questions

1   Explain, in your own words, the difference between a compound and a mixture. Use as examples (i) the compound iron sulphide (FeS), and (ii) a mixture of iron filings and powdered sulphur.

2   David and Susan were looking at a jar of honey. The label said 'Pure Honey'. David said, 'That means it's natural honey, with nothing else added.' Susan said, 'It isn't really pure. It's a mixture of lots of different substances.' Who was right? Explain your answer.

3   Look at the following list of substances. Classify each one as a pure substance or a mixture: salt, sugar, tap water, distilled water, coal, carbon, soil, copper, brass, oxygen, air, sodium hydroxide, sodium hydroxide solution.

4   Use table 2 to decide what type of mixture each of the following contains. In some cases there may be more than one type of mixture present: expanded polystyrene, margarine, bubble bath, golden syrup, whipped cream, mud, marshmallow, ice cream, dilute sulphuric acid (hint: pure sulphuric acid is a liquid).

5   'Instant whip' desserts are sold as a powder in a packet. You add the powder to milk. Then you beat the mixture with a food mixer and leave it to set for a few minutes. It becomes a kind of frothy milk jelly.

   a   Name three types of mixture that are present in the dessert when it is ready to eat.

   b   Name two ingredients the powder is likely to contain.

A5

Separating mixtures

In the kitchen and in the laboratory, we often need to separate mixtures.

To separate mixtures, a cook might use a sieve, a tea strainer or simply a jug. Scientists need to separate mixtures too, and they often use similar apparatus to cooks. The equipment used depends on the type of mixture being separated.

SEPARATING SOLIDS FROM LIQUIDS

The method that you use depends on whether or not the solid dissolves in the liquid.

■ Separating an insoluble solid from a liquid

Tea leaves don't dissolve in tea. You use a tea strainer to separate them. This is a kind of **filtration**. But if you can't be bothered to use a tea strainer, you just drink the tea and the leaves stay behind in the bottom of the cup. This is a kind of **decantation** – pouring the liquid off from the solid.

When you carry out filtration in the laboratory, you use the apparatus shown in picture 2. The filter paper has tiny holes that let the liquid through, but these holes are too small for the solid particles. The clear liquid that runs out of the filter is called the **filtrate**. The solid that is left behind is called the **residue**.

Sometimes **centrifugation** is used instead of filtration (picture 3). The suspension of solid in liquid is poured into a tube, then spun round very fast in a centrifuge. This forces the solid to the bottom of the tube. The liquid can then be easily poured off (decanted) from the solid.

Centrifugation is used in dairies to separate milk from cream. This is possible because milk is denser than cream.

Picture 1 A filter is used to separate the grains from coffee. Coffee grains are smaller than tea leaves so a filter is used instead of a simple strainer.

■ Separating a soluble solid from a liquid

Suppose you are marooned on a desert island. You need fresh water to drink. How will you get it?

To get pure water from a salty solution, you need to use **distillation**. You boil the solution, and water comes off as steam. The steam is then cooled in a condenser, to give liquid water again. The liquid water is collected as the distillate. Picture 4 shows the equipment that you would use in the laboratory. What kind of equipment might you use on a desert island? (See question 2.)

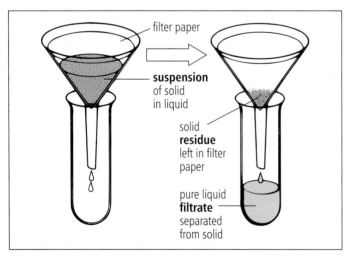

Picture 2 Filtration.

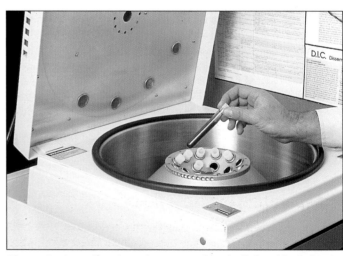

Picture 3 A centrifuge is used to separate blood cells from blood plasma.

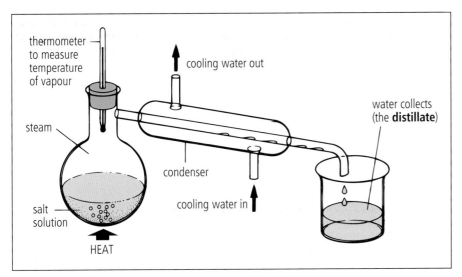

Picture 4 Simple distillation.

Distillation can be used whenever you want to separate and collect the liquid part (the solvent) from a solution.

Sometimes the part of the solution you want is the solute, not the solvent. For example, suppose your desert island already had a supply of fresh water. Then you would only need the salt from the sea water, not the water itself. There would be no need to collect the steam and condense it – you could just let the steam escape into the air. This is called **evaporation** (picture 5).

During evaporation, you boil the solution and let the solvent vapour escape into the air. The solid part (the solute) is left behind, usually in the form of small crystals. It has **crystallised**. If you want larger crystals, you don't boil all the solvent off. You leave some of it behind, and let it evaporate slowly. This allows the crystals to grow gradually, so they grow bigger in the end.

Making toffee involves evaporation. You make a solution of sugar in water, plus a bit of butter and other things to make it taste interesting, then you evaporate off the water. If you evaporate *all* the water away, you get a hard, brittle toffee. If you leave some of the water, you get a softer toffee, more like fudge.

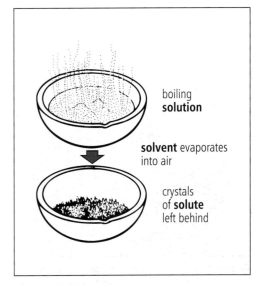

Picture 5 Evaporation.

SEPARATING LIQUIDS FROM ONE ANOTHER

The method that you use depends on whether or not the two liquids mix.

■ Separating immiscible liquids

When you roast a joint of meat, a watery gravy oozes out of the meat. Fat also melts and runs out of the meat. The fat floats on the watery gravy, because fat and water are immiscible. This makes the two quite easy to separate. You can spoon the melted fat off the gravy.

In the laboratory, immiscible liquids are separated using a **separating funnel,** as shown in picture 6.

■ Separating miscible liquids

Alcohol and water mix completely with one another. You cannot use a separating funnel on them, because they form a single layer. To separate these two liquids, you must use distillation.

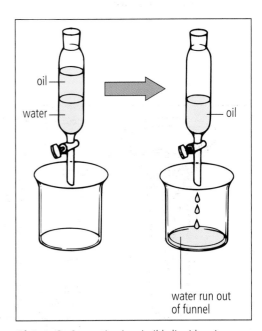

Picture 6 Separating immiscible liquids using a separating funnel.

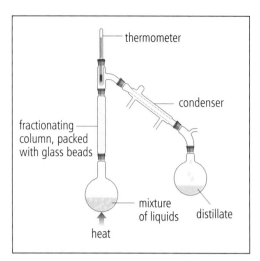

Picture 7 Fractional distillation. The fractionating column makes the two liquids separate better than in simple distillation. Vapour from the more volatile liquid reaches the top of the column and distils over into the condenser. Vapour from the less volatile liquid condenses on the glass beads and runs back down.

Picture 8 Chromatography is used to check the urine of a patient to see if he or she has a rare disease.

Simple distillation is shown in picture 4. To separate miscible liquids, a special form of distillation is often used, called **fractional distillation** (Picture 7). The different liquids have different boiling points. When the mixture is boiled, the vapours of the two liquids boil off at different temperatures. They can be condensed separately.

A different kind of fractional distillation is used to separate the fractions in crude oil. Details of the process are given on page 181.

CHROMATOGRAPHY: A SPECIAL WAY OF SEPARATING MIXTURES

Suppose you have bought a green food colouring to make coloured icing for a cake. The green colouring might be made of a single green dye, or a mixture of a blue dye and a yellow dye. You could use chromatography to find out which it is.

Picture 9 shows the simplest type of chromatography – **paper chromatography**. The dyes separate because some dyes prefer to stick to the paper, but others prefer to dissolve in the solvent. The dyes that prefer the solvent travel further up the paper.

Chromatography is very useful for separating small amounts of substances in a mixture, to find out what these substances are. It is often used in hospitals. For example, chromatography might be used to find out whether sugar is present in a person's urine. This would help the doctor to know whether the person has diabetes.

The substances being separated by chromatography do not necessarily have to be coloured. Colourless substances can be made to show up by spraying the paper with a **locating agent**. The locating agent reacts with each of the colourless substances to form a coloured product which shows up.

TESTING THE PURITY OF A SUBSTANCE

Chemists often need to know if a substance is pure. For example, medicines must be tested for purity before they are sold. Impurities might harm the patient.

Chromatography can be used to see if a substance is pure. If it's pure, a single spot will show up on the chromatogram. But if it is impure, there will be several spots.

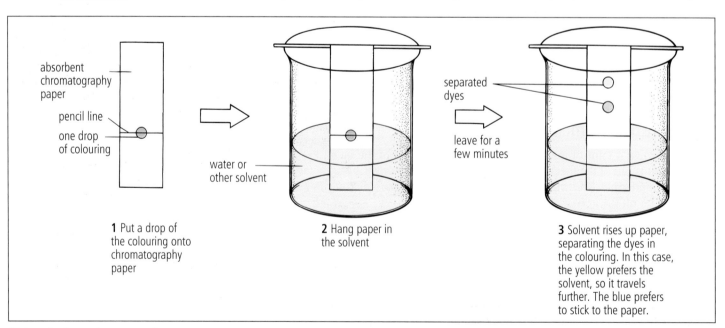

Picture 9 Paper chromatography.

Another way of testing a substance's purity is to measure its **melting point** or **boiling point**. The melting points and boiling points of most elements and compounds are known accurately. They can be found in data books. If a substance is not pure, its melting point or boiling point will be different from the known, accurate value. For example, pure water boils at 100°C. But if the water contains impurities, such as salt, the boiling point is higher.

The melting point of a mixture depends on its composition. Often the melting point of the mixture is lower than the melting points of its components. For example tin melts at 232°C and lead melts at 328°C. However, a mixture containing 64% tin and 36% lead melts at only 183°C. This easily melted mixture is called **solder**.

Questions

1 For (a), (b) and (c), write a sentence containing each of the words, to make the meaning of the words clear:

   a   filtration, filtrate, residue.

   b   distillation, distillate, residue.

   c   evaporate, crystallise.

2 You are cast away on a desert island. There is a stream with fresh water, but it is very muddy. There is sea all round. You hunt around and manage to find the following: some newspaper, a saucepan, a kettle, several tumblers, a knife, some wire, an empty plastic lemonade bottle and a short piece of copper piping. You also have a box of matches.

   Draw diagrams to show how you would obtain:

   a   clean water from the muddy river water

   b   fresh water from the sea water

   c   salt from the sea water

3 In 'dry cleaning', a special solvent is used to dissolve grease and dirt from clothes. A dry-cleaning machine is basically a washing machine that uses this solvent instead of water. After use, the solvent is dirty. The dirty solvent cannot be thrown away: it is expensive and it would cause pollution.

   What method could be used to recover pure, clean solvent from the dirty solvent? How could this method be built into the working of a dry-cleaning machine?

4 What method would you use to get:

   a   pure water from ink?

   b   copper sulphate crystals from a solution of copper sulphate in water?

   c   petrol from a mixture of petrol and oil?

   d   salt from a mixture of salt and sand?

Separating air

Many of the gases in air are very useful. Separating the gases from one another is an important industrial process, called the **fractional distillation** of liquid air.

Air is liquefied by cooling it and compressing it. The liquid air is then allowed to warm up. At a temperature of –194°C it begins to boil. The different gases of the air boil at different temperatures (picture 1). They can be collected separately as they boil off. *Industrial gases from air* on page 29 gives more information about what the gases are used for.

Picture 2   An air separation plant. Notice the tower used for fractional distillation.

1   The fractional distillation of liquid air uses different equipment from that shown in picture 7 on page 20. In what ways would the equipment be different, and why?

2   Fractional distillation is also used to separate crude oil into fractions (see page 181). In what ways is the fractional distillation of liquid air different from that of crude oil?

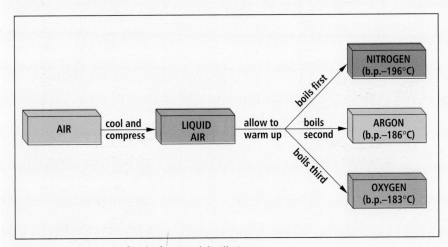

Picture 1   Separation of air by fractional distillation.

B

Air and water

What's in the air?

Air is a vital resource – a mixture of very useful gases. And it's free!

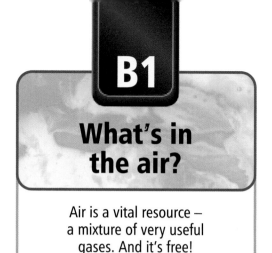

Picture 1 Most of the air is nitrogen. When you breathe, it goes in and out of your lungs unchanged.

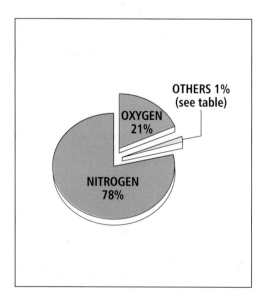

OTHERS 1% (see table)

OXYGEN 21%

NITROGEN 78%

Picture 2 The composition of air.

If you rest all day today, you will breathe in about 15 000 litres of air. If you take exercise you'll need quite a lot more.

Air isn't just vital for humans. It is needed by most living things, and for everyday happenings such as burning and rusting. And it's an important raw material for manufacturing industrial gases.

THE COMPOSITION OF AIR

The mixture of gases that surrounds the Earth is called the **atmosphere**. The Earth is very unusual among planets, because it has an atmosphere containing oxygen.

Experiments show that air is 21% oxygen. The rest is mainly nitrogen (picture 2). Table 1 gives the most important gases in dry air.

Table 1 The composition of dry air. In practice, air also contains water vapour.

Gas	Percentage by volume
Nitrogen, N_2	78.03
Oxygen, O_2	20.99
Argon, Ar	0.93
Other noble gases (neon, helium, krypton, xenon)	0.002
Carbon dioxide, CO_2	0.03
Hydrogen, H_2	0.001

Nitrogen is a very unreactive gas.

Oxygen is the most reactive gas in the air. When you breathe, it passes from the air in your lungs into your bloodstream, and is carried to the cells of your body. There is more about oxygen in topic B2.

Argon and the other noble gases are almost completely unreactive (see topic F7).

Carbon dioxide is only present in small amounts, but it is very important to plants, which use it in photosynthesis (see topic I3).

Some of the important uses of these gases are described in *Industrial gases from air* on page 29.

Water vapour is also present in air. The quantity of water vapour varies according to the weather.

HOW THE ATMOSPHERE AND OCEANS FORMED

■ The Earth's first atmosphere

The first gases in the Earth's atmosphere came from deep inside the young Earth, through volcanoes. This first atmosphere was very different from today's. Scientists believe that it consisted mainly of carbon dioxide (CO_2) and water vapour (H_2O), with smaller quantities of nitrogen (N_2) and other gases.

■ The atmosphere gradually changes

Picture 3 shows how the original atmosphere changed as the Earth cooled down. Notice that the oxygen in the atmosphere was formed by plants, through **photosynthesis**. There is more about photosynthesis in topic I3.

■ How did nitrogen build up in the atmosphere?

The gases coming out of volcanoes contain small quantities of nitrogen, and this gradually built up in the atmosphere over millions of years. The volcanic gases also contain small quantities of ammonia, NH_3. Gradually, this ammonia was converted to nitrogen gas by bacteria in the soil. That is where the nitrogen in today's atmosphere came from. Some of the ammonia was converted to soluble nitrogen compounds, which fertilise the soil.

■ Recycling the atmosphere

The processes that created the atmosphere are still going on. The composition of the atmosphere is kept roughly in balance by the carbon cycle (topic I3).

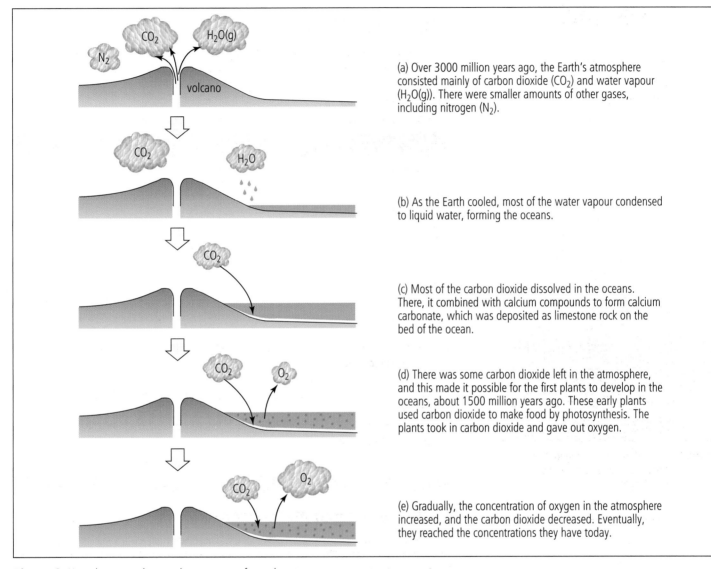

(a) Over 3000 million years ago, the Earth's atmosphere consisted mainly of carbon dioxide (CO_2) and water vapour ($H_2O(g)$). There were smaller amounts of other gases, including nitrogen (N_2).

(b) As the Earth cooled, most of the water vapour condensed to liquid water, forming the oceans.

(c) Most of the carbon dioxide dissolved in the oceans. There, it combined with calcium compounds to form calcium carbonate, which was deposited as limestone rock on the bed of the ocean.

(d) There was some carbon dioxide left in the atmosphere, and this made it possible for the first plants to develop in the oceans, about 1500 million years ago. These early plants used carbon dioxide to make food by photosynthesis. The plants took in carbon dioxide and gave out oxygen.

(e) Gradually, the concentration of oxygen in the atmosphere increased, and the carbon dioxide decreased. Eventually, they reached the concentrations they have today.

Picture 3 How the atmosphere and oceans were formed.

Questions

1 List the five most abundant gases in the air, in order of abundance

2 a Suppose air was 78% oxygen and 21% nitrogen instead of the other way round. What differences would this make to the world?

  b Table 1 shows only the most abundant gases in air. But other gases are present in tiny amounts. Suggest four gases you might expect to be present apart from the ones in the table.

3 Look at picture 3. Answer these two questions in your own words.

  a Why is there much less water vapour today than there was when the first atmosphere formed?

  b Why is there much less carbon dioxide in the atmosphere today than there was when the first atmosphere formed?

4 The planet Venus has an atmosphere that is over 90% carbon dioxide. The temperature on the suface of Venus is 477 °C. Why do you think Venus's atmosphere has never formed oxygen in the way that the Earth's has?

5 Plants have removed most of the carbon dioxide from the Earth's original atmosphere, and replaced it with oxygen. However, over the last 100 years the concentration of carbon dioxide in the atmosphere has begun to increase again. Find out why, and why this is worrying some scientists. Topic I3 will help you.

Oxygen, oxides and oxidation

Oxygen is the reactive part of the air.

OXYGEN
- a colourless gas with no smell
- about the same density as air
- dissolves in water slightly
- reacts with many substances to form oxides
- helps fuels to burn
- relights a glowing splint

Picture 2 Some properties of oxygen.

Testing for oxygen

Oxygen relights a glowing splint. Ordinary air contains oxygen, but not enough to make a glowing splint relight. To test for oxygen, light a wooden splint, then blow out the flame so the splint is just glowing and smouldering. Put it in a test-tube of gas and if the splint catches fire again (picture 3), it is a positive test for oxygen.

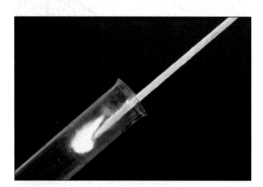

Picture 3 Oxygen makes a glowing splint re-ignite.

Picture 1 Oxygen is used to remove impurities in steel by oxidising them.

Have you flown in an airliner? If so, you will probably have heard the cabin crew explaining the emergency oxygen masks. These are used for breathing if the plane accidentally becomes depressurised. Passengers are always reminded to put out cigarettes before using the mask. A wise precaution because, like all fuels, tobacco burns much more fiercely in pure oxygen than in air!

Some of the properties of oxygen are shown in picture 2. One of the most important things about oxygen is the way it helps things to burn. Unlike air, oxygen has no unreactive nitrogen to 'thin it out'. If a substance burns in air, it will burn much better in oxygen.

WHAT HAPPENS WHEN ELEMENTS BURN IN OXYGEN?

In the experiment on the next page you can see how various elements burn in oxygen, and what the products are like. Picture 4 shows the method, and table 1 gives the results for some elements.

Here are some key points about the reaction of elements with oxygen. Check them against the results in table 1.

- When elements burn in oxygen, they form **oxides**. Oxides contain the element combined with oxygen. For example

$$\text{magnesium} + \text{oxygen} \rightarrow \text{magnesium oxide}$$
$$\text{carbon} + \text{oxygen} \rightarrow \text{carbon dioxide}$$

- *Metals* form solid oxides. These oxides are bases (topic G2). They give alkaline solutions if they dissolve in water.
- *Non-metals* form oxides which are solid, liquid or gaseous. These oxides are acids.

Some elements form oxides which can behave like both a base and an acid: they are described as **amphoteric**. Elements which form amphoteric oxides have some characteristics of metals and some of non-metals. Aluminium is an example of such an element.

Oxygen encourages many substances to burn – not just elements. This can be very useful, for example in the oxy-acetylene torches used to cut and weld metals. Some of the major uses of oxygen are described in *Industrial gases from the air* on page 29.

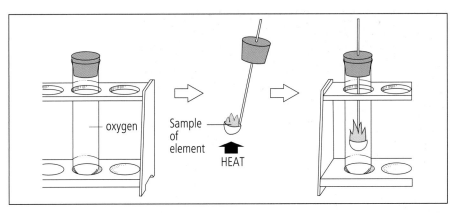

Table 1   How different elements react with oxygen.

Element	How it reacts	Product	Effect of adding product to water, then testing with indicator
Sodium	Burns vigorously with yellow flame	White solid (sodium oxide, Na_2O)	Dissolves, alkaline solution
Magnesium	Burns vigorously with bright white flame	White solid (magnesium oxide, MgO)	Dissolves slightly, weakly alkaline solution
Sulphur	Burns with bright blue flame	Colourless gas (sulphur dioxide, SO_2)	Dissolves, acidic solution
Carbon	Burns with bright red glow	Colourless gas (carbon dioxide, CO_2)	Dissolves slightly, weakly acidic solution

OXYGEN AND OXIDATION

When a substance combines with oxygen, we say it has been oxidised. Oxidation reactions are very common.

Burning (topic I2) is rapid oxidation. For example, natural gas is mainly methane, CH_4. When methane burns, it is oxidised to carbon dioxide and water.

$$methane + oxygen \rightarrow carbon\ dioxide + water$$
$$CH_4 + 2O_2 \rightarrow CO_2 + 2H_2O$$

Respiration is a slower, more controlled kind of oxidation. Living organisms use it to get energy from foods like glucose.

$$glucose + oxygen \rightarrow carbon\ dioxide + water$$
$$C_6H_{12}O_6 + 6O_2 \rightarrow 6CO_2 + 6H_2O$$

Sometimes food oxidises when you don't want it to. Fats turn rancid because they are oxidised to nasty-tasting substances. Antioxidants are added to fatty foods to stop this happening.

Rusting is the slow oxidation of iron.

$$iron + oxygen \rightarrow iron\ oxide$$
$$2Fe + 3O_2 \rightarrow 2Fe_2O_3$$

Notice that in all these reactions, oxides are formed.

■ The oxidation of hydrogen

The oxidation of hydrogen is one of the simplest and most famous oxidation reactions.

$$2H_2(g) + O_2(g) \rightarrow 2H_2O(l)$$

The reaction occurs very readily – in fact it is explosive. A mixture of hydrogen and oxygen can explode dangerously. Until 1937, airships were filled with hydrogen, the lightest of all gases. But since the Hindenburg disaster (picture 5) they have been filled with helium, which is much safer.

Testing for hydrogen

If you hold a flame over the mouth of a test-tube full of hydrogen, you hear a small explosive 'pop'. The pop is often squeaky-sounding, because the gas in the test tube resonates like a miniature organ pipe. This 'squeaky pop test' is a simple way to identify hydrogen gas.

Picture 5   The German airship Hindenberg was filled with hydrogen. It burst into flames as it arrived in New York in May 1937.

REDUCTION – THE OPPOSITE OF OXIDATION

In some chemical reactions, oxygen is *removed* instead of being added. This is called reduction. For example, iron is manufactured from iron oxide, Fe_2O_3. To turn Fe_2O_3 to Fe, you need to take away the oxygen. This is done by heating the iron oxide in a blast furnace with carbon monoxide (topic E3). The carbon monoxide, CO, takes away the oxygen and gets oxidised to carbon dioxide, CO_2. The iron oxide is reduced to iron (picture 6).

Whenever oxidation happens, reduction must also happen. If something is gaining oxygen, something else must be losing it. The two processes together are called **redox**.

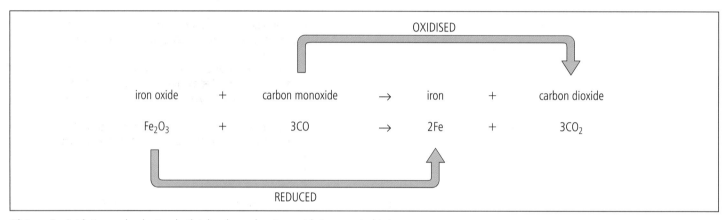

Picture 6 Oxidation and reduction both take place when iron oxide is converted to iron.

Questions

1 Consider the elements aluminium, phosphorus (a yellow waxy solid) and zinc.

a Which would burn more readily in oxygen than in air?

b Which would form an oxide when heated in oxygen?

c Which would form an oxide which gives an acidic solution in water?

2 Look at the following reactions. In each case, say whether the element that is underlined has been oxidised or reduced.

a <u>sulphur</u> + oxygen → sulphur dioxide

b magnesium + <u>carbon</u> dioxide → magnesium oxide + carbon

c <u>iron</u> + copper oxide → iron oxide + copper

d <u>NO</u>$_2$ + SO_2 → NO + SO_3

3 Space rockets carry liquid oxygen.

a What is it used for?

b Why is liquid oxygen carried, rather than oxygen gas?

c What are the safety hazards involved in using liquid oxygen?

4 The test for oxygen is to see if it relights a glowing splint. Why does a splint relight in oxygen?

Industrial gases from air

Table 1 Information about three important gases manufactured from air: oxygen, nitrogen and argon.

Gas	Approximate cost of the gas bought in cylinders	Amount of gas used in UK (tonnes per day)	Major uses of the gas
Oxygen	£1 per cubic metre (volume measured at atmospheric pressure)	11 000	In steel making – used to remove impurities from iron by oxidising them In hospitals – for patients with breathing difficulties For divers and high altitude climbers – as a breathing gas For welding – an 'oxy-acetylene' flame is hot enough to melt metal For treating sewage – oxygen helps micro-organisms to break down harmful materials
Nitrogen	£1 per cubic metre	4000	For freezing – liquid nitrogen is so cold (−196 °C) it can be used to freeze food and biological material in order to preserve them As an unreactive atmosphere – nitrogen is used as a cheap, unreactive gas 'blanket' to stop things reacting with air (for example, in petrol storage tanks and food packaging)
Argon	£5 per cubic metre	300	As an unreactive atmosphere – an inert gas 'blanket' to stop reaction with air (for example, inside light bulbs and in welding)

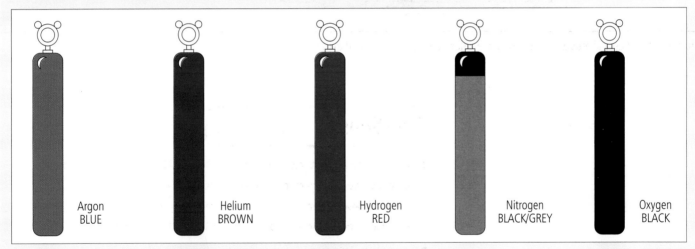

Picture 1 Gas cylinders are colour-coded according to their contents.

Use the information in table 1, and any other things you know, to answer these questions.

1 Which of the uses of oxygen depend on the fact that it is needed by living things?

2 Which of the uses of oxygen depend on the fact that it is needed for fuels to burn in?

3 Nitrogen and argon can both be used to provide an unreactive atmosphere. For what kind of uses might argon be more suitable than nitrogen? For what kind of uses might nitrogen be more suitable than argon?

4 Liquid nitrogen is used to freeze food, but liquid oxygen and liquid air are never used for this purpose. Why?

5 Compare the costs of nitrogen, oxygen and argon. Try to account for any differences and similarities.

6 Compare the amounts of nitrogen, oxygen and argon used each day. Try to account for the differences.

7 Industrial gases have to be transported from the manufacturing plant to the user. Small quantities are transported in cylinders, carried in lorries. Larger quantities are transported in the liquid form, in tankers. What safety problems do you think there might be in transporting the gases? How might these problems be overcome?

Corrosion and rusting

Rusting costs Britain about £6000 million a year. What causes rusting, and how can it be prevented?

Picture 1 Rusting steam engine in a scrapyard.

In the 3 or 4 seconds it takes you to read this sentence, Britain will have lost about 40 kg of iron and steel. It will have turned to rust. Forty kilograms is enough to make four bicycles!

Rusting is a form of **corrosion**. Corrosion is the reaction of metals with air, usually forming an oxide. Metals usually corrode faster if they are wet. If the air contains acid pollutants, such as sulphur dioxide, corrosion happens much faster.

Corrosion is a **chemical reaction**. When a metal corrodes, it changes into a new substance, and it is very difficult to change it back.

When a metal corrodes it loses its shine. If the corrosion is bad the metal may break. When iron or steel corrode, it is called rusting. Under the right conditions, iron corrodes fast, even though it is a relatively unreactive metal.

WHAT HAPPENS WHEN IRON RUSTS?

Picture 3 shows an investigation into the conditions needed for rusting. The experiment shows that, for rusting to occur, two things must be present: air and water. The iron is oxidised by the air, forming iron oxide:

$$\text{iron} + \text{oxygen} \rightarrow \text{iron oxide}$$
$$2Fe + 3O_2 \rightarrow 2Fe_2O_3$$

The iron oxide then reacts with water to form hydrated iron oxide – which is rust. ('Hydrated' means the iron oxide has water combined with it.) The rust is brittle and it swells up and flakes off as it is formed. The surface of the iron is then exposed to more air and water, and so the rusting goes on. The rusting occurs even faster if the water contains impurities like salt.

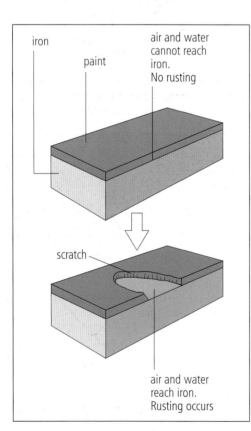

iron

paint

air and water cannot reach iron. No rusting

scratch

air and water reach iron. Rusting occurs

Picture 2 Paint protects iron from rusting, but only until it is scratched.

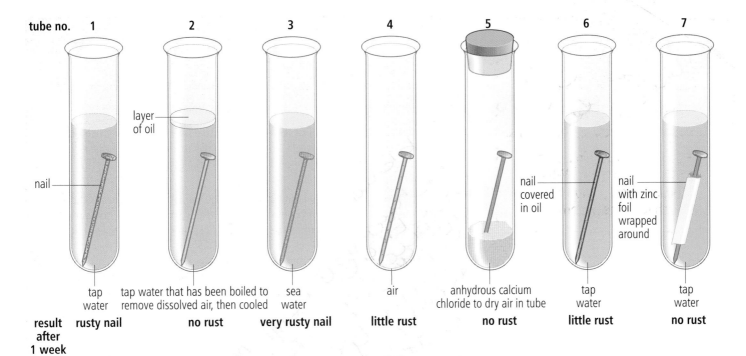

tube no.	1	2	3	4	5	6	7
	tap water	tap water that has been boiled to remove dissolved air, then cooled	sea water	air	anhydrous calcium chloride to dry air in tube	tap water	tap water
result after 1 week	rusty nail	no rust	very rusty nail	little rust	no rust	little rust	no rust

Picture 3 Investigating the conditions needed for rusting. Use the results to answer Question 1 at the end.

HOW CAN YOU STOP IRON RUSTING?

Iron and steel are used more than any other metal, because they are strong and cheap. But they have to be protected from rusting somehow. There are several methods.

STOP AIR AND WATER REACHING THE SURFACE OF THE IRON
This is most commonly done by covering the surface with paint (picture 2). But if the paint gets scratched, the iron starts to rust. The iron may also be **plated** with another metal, such as tin or chromium. The trimmings on bicycles and cars are sometimes chromium-plated, to stop them rusting and to make them look nice.

COAT THE IRON WITH A MORE REACTIVE METAL
Zinc is most commonly used (see picture 4). Zinc is more reactive than iron, so the oxygen in the air reacts with the zinc instead of the iron. The zinc is 'sacrificed' to protect the iron. Zinc-plating is often used to protect things like dustbins that are kept outdoors. The iron is said to be galvanised. Picture 5 shows another example.

MIX THE IRON WITH ANOTHER METAL TO MAKE AN ALLOY
Mixing iron with chromium or nickel makes an alloy which does not rust. It is called stainless steel, and it is used to make cutlery among other things. Unfortunately, these metals are expensive, so stainless steel costs quite a lot more than iron or ordinary steel.

Some rust-protection methods are cheaper than others. The method that is chosen depends on the value of the item being protected. More is given about this in the exercises on page 33.

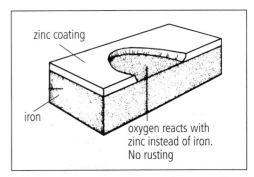

Picture 4 Zinc protects iron from rusting – even if the zinc layer is scratched.

Picture 5 Coating steel helps prevent rust. The lorry is being zinc coated.

■ Why do some metals stay uncorroded?

Some metals stay shiny and uncorroded even when they are exposed to air and water. This is for one of two reasons.

1. The metal is very unreactive so it does not react with air or water. Gold is an example.

Or

2. The metal reacts with air, but forms a protective layer of oxide which stops any more corrosion. Aluminium is an example (picture 6). Aluminium is in fact a rather reactive metal, but once its tough oxide coat is formed, the metal is protected from further attack.

This is also how stainless steel works. Iron oxide is brittle and flaky and does not protect the metal from further corrosion. But if the iron is mixed with a metal like chromium, the chromium forms a tough layer of chromium oxide that protects the iron.

The oxide layer on aluminium can be made thicker by *anodising*. The piece of aluminium is used as the anode in an electrolysis cell. This builds up the thickness of the oxide layer making the aluminium even more corrosion-resistant.

pure aluminium exposed to air	aluminium reacts with air to make a tough invisible thin layer of oxide	oxide coat protects aluminium from further attack by air

Picture 6 Why aluminium doesn't corrode

Activity

A rusting survey

Do a survey to see what things are affected by rust. You could look around your home and garden, your local streets and/or your school. Make a note of:

1 The object that has rusted.

2 Its situation (outdoors/indoors, wet/dry, etc.).

3 Any rust protection it has been given.

4 Any parts that have rusted particularly badly.

In each case, try to decide why rusting has occurred.

Questions

1 Look again at the experiment shown in picture 3.

   a Why is the water in tube 2 covered in a layer of oil?

   b Why does tube 5 have a stopper in?

   c What form of rust-protection is represented by tube 7?

   d In tube 6 the nail is protected by oil. This is a cheap form of protection, but it doesn't last long. Why not?

   e For each tube, explain the results.

2 Suppose each of the metal articles in the following list were left outside: an iron nail, a galvanised iron dustbin, a bright new penny, aluminium foil, a stainless steel knife.

   a Which would corrode quickly?

   b Which would corrode slowly?

   c Which would not corrode at all?

3 a Why is the steel hull of an ocean-going ship especially likely to rust?

   b Blocks of zinc are often bolted to a ship's hull. Why do you think this is?

   c A small child dropped an iron nail into a kettle. The nail was only discovered weeks later by the child's parent, but it had hardly rusted at all. A similar nail dropped in the garden pond rusted badly in 2 days. Explain the difference.

4 Which methods are normally used to protect the following from rusting: (a) wheelbarrows, (b) bicycle handlebars, (c) pins and needles, (d) car bodies, (e) a surgeon's scalpel, (f) food cans?

5 Picture 7 shows an experiment that was set up to investigate how much air is used up in rusting. After one week, the water had risen a fifth of the way up the tube. Explain why.

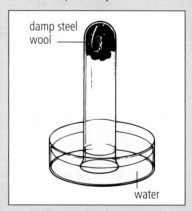

Picture 7 How much of the air is used up during rusting?

Which kind of rust protection?

Table 1 gives a comparison of some different methods of rust protection.

1 Why does zinc plating give better protection than chromium plating? (Look at table 2, which lists some metals in order of reactivity.)

> **Table 2** Some metals listed in order of decreasing reactivity.

> aluminium, Al
> zinc, Zn
> chromium, Cr
> iron, Fe
> tin, Sn
> gold, Au

2 What metal in table 2 might give even better protection than zinc?

3 Why does painting on top of rust give only poor protection?

4 What method would be suitable for each of the following situations? Give your reason in each case. If you can think of a different method, not in the table, then say so.
  a To protect a steel pencil sharpener.
  b To protect steel railings on a cross-channel ferry.
  c To protect steel scissor blades.
  d To protect iron gutters on a house. They were painted once, but they are starting to get rusty.
  e To protect a steel bridge over a motorway.
  f To protect a secondhand car whose doors have started rusting.

Table 1

Method	Protection given appearance	Finished	Relative cost
Zinc plating	Very good	Dull silvery	Medium
Chromium plating	Good	Bright, shiny	High
Painting (after sandblast cleaning)	Fairly good	Colour of paint	Medium
Painting (after ordinary cleaning)	Fair	Colour of paint	Medium/low
Painting on top of rust	Poor	Colour of paint	Low

Picture 1 Iron is galvanised (coated with zinc) to prevent it rusting.

Car exhaust systems

Your car exhaust has rusted badly. It has a large hole in it and is making a terrible noise. You have to buy a replacement system, and you have a choice of two types.

An ordinary steel system. This is guaranteed to last 2 years before it is rusted through again. It costs £110.

A stainless steel system. This is guaranteed to last the lifetime of the car. It costs £240.

1 Which system is cheaper in the long run?

2 What factors will you consider before you decide which system to buy?

3 Only about 10% of car owners in Britain buy stainless steel exhausts. Why do you think this is?

4 Exhaust systems rust faster than any other part of a car. Why is this, do you think?

Picture 1

5 Exhaust systems cannot be protected from rusting by painting. Why?

6 What is stainless steel? Why does it rust more slowly than ordinary steel?

7 Ordinary steel exhausts are made from steel coated with aluminium. How does the aluminium help slow down rusting?

How pure is the air?

Human activities release many polluting gases into the atmosphere. In this topic we look at their effects, and how they can be controlled.

Picture 1   Motor vehicles are the most serious source of air pollution.

Air pollution isn't new. The earliest humans cooked on wood fires which produced nasty polluting gases. People have been polluting the air ever since humans arrived on Earth. It's just that there are many more people on Earth now. More people means more homes, more industries and more motor vehicles – and more air pollution.

The problem is, all gases **diffuse** – that is, they spread out as much as possible. So any gases we release spread all through the atmosphere. Some of the gases released by human activities are fairly harmless, but others can have damaging effects on the environment.

Two effects are particularly serious. Let's look at them in turn.

ACID RAIN

Some air pollutants are acidic gases, particularly sulphur dioxide, SO_2, and nitrogen dioxide, NO_2. These gases are formed when fuels are burned, especially in car engines and in power stations. Sulphur dioxide is also formed naturally, for example by the breakdown of natural products made by seaweeds in the oceans. After they have been released into the air, SO_2 and NO_2 may react with other gases in the air, and with rain water. For example, sulphur dioxide reacts with oxygen to form sulphur trioxide:

$$\text{sulphur dioxide} + \text{oxygen} \rightarrow \text{sulphur trioxide}$$
$$2SO_2 \quad + \quad O_2 \quad \rightarrow \quad 2SO_3$$

The sulphur trioxide then reacts with rainwater to form sulphuric acid:

$$\text{sulphur trioxide} + \text{water} \rightarrow \text{sulphuric acid}$$
$$SO_3 \quad + \quad H_2O \quad \rightarrow \quad H_2SO_4$$

Reactions like this make rain water become acidic. Acid rain has a pH of between 5 and 2. In some extreme cases, the water is as acidic as vinegar. Picture 2 sums up the formation of acid rain.

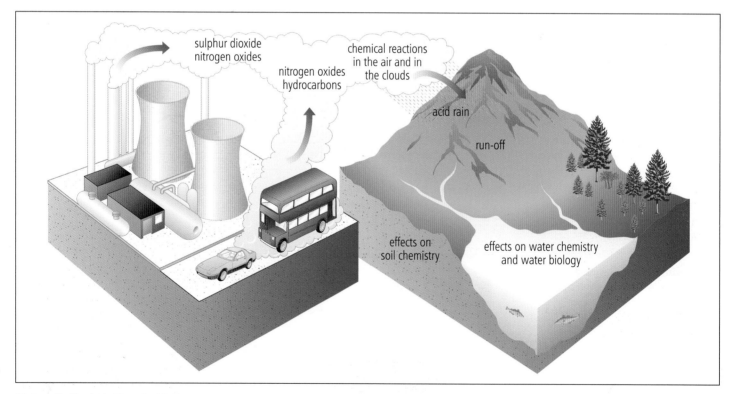

Picture 2   The formation of acid rain.

When acid rain falls into streams and lakes, it makes them acidic and this may kill water life, including fish. Fish are dying in lakes in Scandinavia, probably because of acid rain. The people there believe most of the acid gases come from industries in Britain, carried hundreds of miles on the wind. In Britain, limestone rocks help to neutralise the acid, but Scandinavia has very little limestone.

Acid rain may also help cause the death of trees in forests in Europe, particularly in Germany. It also damages buildings and other structures. It corrodes metals, and wears away the stonework on buildings.

It is not easy to control acid rain. Scientists do not yet understand all the complicated chemical reactions that cause it. Sulphur dioxide is certainly involved. A lot of sulphur dioxide is produced by coal-burning power stations. The sulphur dioxide could be removed from the chimney gases by special equipment, but this is expensive (see *Pollution and power stations* on page 39). Another cause is the nitrogen oxides produced in car engines, and this can be controlled by careful engine design.

THE GREENHOUSE EFFECT AND GLOBAL WARMING

A garden greenhouse keeps plants warmer than they would be outside. It does this because the glass traps some of the Sun's radiation energy.

In a similar way, the atmosphere helps keep the Earth warm. It does this by trapping some of the Sun's radiation that would otherwise escape. This is just as well. Without this **greenhouse effect** the average surface temperature of the Earth would be about 33 °C lower than it is, −18 °C instead of a nice comfortable 15 °C.

Some gases are better than others at keeping the Earth warm. Oxygen and nitrogen are not very effective, but carbon dioxide is very good. Picture 3 shows how carbon dioxide warms the atmosphere by the greenhouse effect.

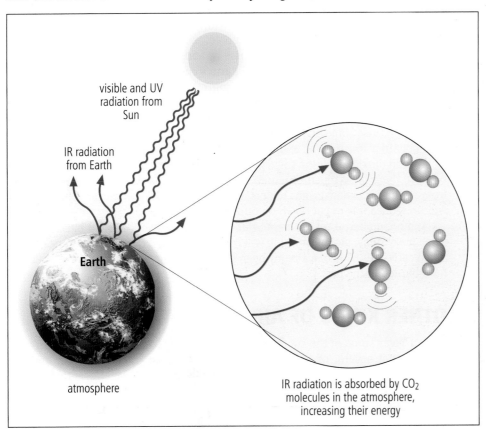

visible and UV radiation from Sun

IR radiation from Earth

Earth

atmosphere

IR radiation is absorbed by CO_2 molecules in the atmosphere, increasing their energy

Picture 3 Why carbon dioxide is a greenhouse gas. The Earth absorbs visible and ultraviolet (UV) radiation from the Sun. The Earth re-emits this radiation as infrared (IR). Infrared radiation is absorbed by CO_2 molecules, making them vibrate faster and increasing their energy. The energy is passed on to other molecules in the atmosphere, making the atmosphere hotter.

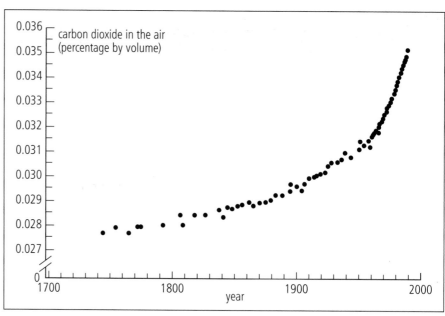

Picture 4 How the concentration of carbon dioxide in the air has changed since 1700.

Carbon dioxide is such a good 'greenhouse gas' that there may be a problem. Scientists are concerned that human activities are putting so much *extra* carbon dioxide into the atmosphere that the Earth is overheating. The problem is known as **global warming**.

Whenever fossil fuel, are burned, carbon dioxide is released into the atmosphere. Altogether, we release about five thousand million tonnes of carbon dioxide into the air every year (picture 4). Scientists believe that by the year 2020 the concentration of carbon dioxide in the atmosphere will have doubled from its level in 2000.

The average temperature of the Earth is already showing a small increase. In the past 100 years the average temperature in the USA has increased by about 2 °C. It is estimated that if the amount of carbon dioxide in the atmosphere doubles, the average temperature of the Earth will rise by about 3 °C. This may not sound a lot, but it will make a big difference to the Earth's climate.

Some of the effects of global warming could be good. In places with good rainfall, farmers will be able to grow bigger crops. But there will be more droughts (picture 5). The level of the sea will rise. This is because water expands when heated, and also because some of the ice at the poles will melt. This will bring floods to low-lying countries like Holland and Bangladesh – and also to low-lying parts of Britain.

Carbon dioxide isn't the only 'greenhouse gas'. But it is the most serious one, because there is so much of it – so much that there is no chance of removing it from all the car exhausts, gas boilers and other places it pours from. The only way we can reduce it is to cut down on our use of fossil fuels.

And remember, it takes time to put things right. Even if we cut back on using fossil fuels today, global warming will continue for many years. This is because so much carbon dioxide has already been put in the atmosphere from fossil fuels we have burned in the past.

OTHER KINDS OF AIR POLLUTION

Table 1 gives some of the substances that are major sources of air pollution. You can see that several of these air pollutants can help cause acid rain and the greenhouse effect. These are *long-range* pollutants: they have effects that are felt over long distances.

Carbon monoxide (CO) and smoke are more *local* pollutants. Their effects are felt mainly near the place where they are produced.

Picture 5 The drowned village of Mardale in the Lake District was exposed when the water level in Haweswater reservoir fell during the drought of summer 1995.

Table 1   Major air pollutants

Air pollutant	Man-made source	Effects	Possible methods of control
Sulphur dioxide (SO_2)	Burning fossil fuels	Causes acid rain (see above)	Remove sulphur from fuels before burning. Remove sulphur dioxide from chimney gases of power stations
Nitrogen oxides (NO, NO_2, N_2O)	Vehicle exhausts, burning of fuels	Help cause acid rain and photochemical smog	Fit catalytic converters to vehicle exhausts. Modify engines to run on a weaker mixture of fuel and air
Carbon dioxide (CO_2)	Burning fuels	Causes greenhouse effect, affecting Earth's climate (see above)	Burn less fossil fuels
Carbon monoxide (CO)	Burning fuels, vehicle exhausts, cigarette smoke	Poisonous to animals, including humans	Ensure vehicle engines are well maintained. Prevent cigarette smoking
Hydrocarbons	Vehicle exhausts, burning fuels	Help cause acid rain and photochemical smog	Fit catalytic converters to vehicle exhausts. Modify engines to run on a weaker mixture of fuel and air
Smoke	Burning fuels	Damages lungs; reduces photosynthesis of plants	Use smokeless fuels. Make sure engines and burners have plenty of air to burn fuel efficiently
Chlorofluorocarbons (CFCs)	Aerosol propellants, refrigerators	Destroy ozone in the ozone layer which protects Earth from ultra violet radiation. Also contribute to the greenhouse effect	Use different substances as aerosol propellants and refrigerants

■ Destroying the ozone layer

Ozone, O_3, is an unstable form of oxygen. It is a very reactive gas. When it is formed near the Earth's surface, in the part of the atmosphere called the **troposphere** it can cause nasty pollution problems.

But further up in the atmosphere, ozone does a *useful* job. There is a very thin layer of ozone about 20–40 kilometres above the Earth, in the part of the atmosphere called the **stratosphere**. This layer acts as a kind of sunscreen. It filters out some of the harmful ultraviolet radiation from the Sun (picture 6). If this radiation reaches Earth it can cause sunburn and even skin cancer.

In 1984, scientists discovered that a large 'hole' had developed in the ozone layer above Antarctica. If this 'hole' spreads to more populated parts of the Earth, there could be serious results for people's health.

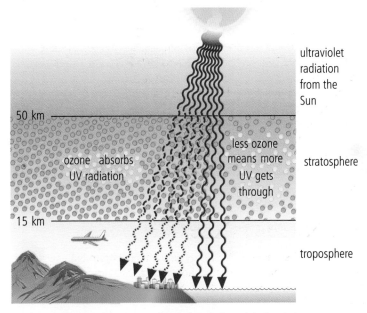

ultraviolet radiation from the Sun

50 km

ozone absorbs UV radiation

less ozone means more UV gets through

stratosphere

15 km

troposphere

Picture 6   Ozone in the stratosphere absorbs harmful ultraviolet radiation before it reaches us on Earth.

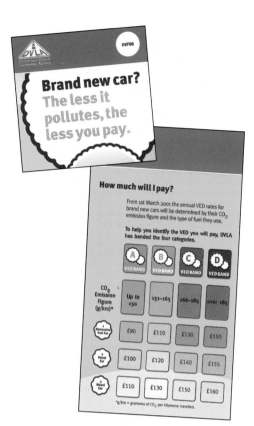

Picture 7 Taxation is one way of controlling pollution. This leaflet explains how the government's Vehicle Exise Duty (VED) – or tax disc – gets more expensive the more pollution your car causes.

Scientists have discovered that the damage to the ozone layer is caused by chemical compounds called chlorofluorocarbons, or CFCs. These compounds are used as refrigerants and as propellants for aerosols. CFCs are very stable and unreactive, and they stay in the atmosphere for a long time. Over the years they slowly diffuse upwards through the troposphere until they reach the stratosphere. Here they react with ozone, and destroy it.

Many countries have now agreed to stop using the harmful types of CFCs. But even if all use of CFCs is stopped at once, the ozone layer will go on being destroyed for at least 20 years, because of all the CFCs that are already in the atmosphere. It is a problem that will be with us for a long time yet.

CONTROLLING AIR POLLUTION

Pollution of the atmosphere is one of the most serious threats to our future. If problems like global warming get out of control, they could have disastrous effects on life on Earth.

Controlling air pollution means controlling the release of pollutant gases. Most of these gases come from the burning of fossil fuels. So there are two important ways to control air pollution:

1 Burn less fossil fuels.
2 Remove the gases before they get into the atmosphere.

In the long run, the best way is the first. But burning less fossil fuels means sacrifices. To put it bluntly: would you be prepared to go without a car of your own to help reduce global warming?

The second approach, removing pollutant gases before they reach the atmosphere, can be expensive. You can fit a catalytic converter to remove pollutant gases from car exhausts, but each converter costs several hundred pounds. You can fit units to power stations to remove acid gases, but a unit for a large power station costs about £200 million. In the end, it is we, the consumers, who pay these costs. Is it worth it?

Activities

A Persuading the public to pay petrol tax

Imagine you work for the government's Ministry of Transport. You are senior press officer for the Minister. The government has decided to increase the tax on petrol, so people will use cars less and reduce pollution. The government has said it will use the money raised from the tax to build new railways.

You know the new tax will be unpopular, but the Minister has to persuade people that it makes sense.

The Minister has asked you to write a press release to send to newspapers explaining the policy.

ICT Draft the press release. It should be no more than 500 words.

B Taxing pollution

Picture 7 shows a leaflet produced by the government. It explains a policy for taxing cars according to how much pollution they produce. Vehicle Excise Duty (VED) is the cost of the 'tax disk' that every car must display. You pay VED once a year.

a Look at the row of figures for petrol cars. Why do different petrol cars produce different CO_2 emission figures?

b Look at VED band A. Why are diesel cars taxed at a higher rate than petrol cars?

c Give an example of an 'alternative fuel' that a car might use. Why is this kind of car taxed at a lower rate than a petrol car?

d What effect do you think the government is hoping this pollution taxing policy will have?

e Do you think the policy will have a big effect? Explain your answer.

C How aware are the public about air pollution?

Carry out a survey of people's awareness of air pollution. You could ask questions like

● What polluting gases do you think are released by your car, your home and your place of work?

● What harmful effects do you think these gases have on the environment?

● How could you cut down the release of these gases?

You could try asking your family, neighbours or teachers in your school.

D What are your local pollution problems?

ICT Find out about the particular air pollution problems in your neighbourhood. What are the major sources of pollution in the area? You could ask your family and neighbours or use local newspapers or websites.

Questions

1 Consider the various air pollutants mentioned in this topic.
   a Which are produced by burning fossil fuels?
   b Which are produced by motor vehicles?
   c Which are produced by nature as well as by human activities?
   d Which do you think could be most easily controlled?
   e Which do you think will be most difficult to control?

2 Many important air pollutants are oxides.
   a List the air pollutants mentioned in this topic that are oxides.
   b Suggest a reason why oxides are more common air pollutants than, say, sulphides or chlorides.
   c The oxides that pollute the air are non-metal oxides, not metal oxides. Suggest a reason why.

3 Air pollution is a global problem. It can only be controlled if all the countries of the world agree to do something about it.
   a Why is this?
   b Some countries cause more air pollution than others. What factors decide how much air pollution a particular country produces?
   c Name four countries that you think are major polluters of the air.

4 You are Minister for the Environment. You have decided that new laws must be passed to control air pollution. You realise that it is impossible to remove pollution completely, but you want to cut it down as much as possible.

   What new laws will you make? How will you enforce the laws, and check they are being obeyed?

5 What special air pollution problems would you expect in the following places?
   a near a coal-fired power station
   b near an airport
   c near a farm
   d near a steel works

Pollution and power stations

Sulphur dioxide is a serious air pollutant which helps cause acid rain.

Fossil fuels like coal and oil contain small amounts of sulphur. When these fuels are burned, the sulphur is oxidised to sulphur dioxide.

Coal-fired power stations are a major source of sulphur dioxide in Britain. They account for nearly half of the sulphur dioxide produced by human activities each year. So cutting down the sulphur dioxide from power stations can do a lot to control acid rain.

There are several possibilities for cutting down the sulphur dioxide from power stations.

● Build nuclear power stations to replace coal-fired ones.

● Use coal with only a small amount of sulphur in it. This low-sulphur coal would have to be imported from abroad, because coal from British mines contains quite a lot of sulphur.

● Remove the sulphur from the coal before burning it. This is difficult and expensive.

● Remove the sulphur dioxide from the chimney gases after the coal has been burned, but before the gases can escape. The equipment needed to do this is expensive to fit, but it produces calcium sulphate. Calcium sulphate can be used to make plaster for the building industry.

1 For each of the four possibilities, say what you think are the advantages and disadvantages of using this method to control sulphur dioxide. Which method would you choose?

2 All these different methods cost money. Where should this money come from? Who will pay in the end for removing sulphur dioxide?

Picture 1

Getting water supplies

Water supplies are vital to all our lives. In this topic we look at where water comes from and how it is purified.

Picture 1   The water works at Hampton near London.

Picture 2   Cooling towers in a power station. Cooling water does not have to be as pure as tap water.

Today you will use about 180 litres of water—about two bathfuls. That's the average amount used per person in Britain every day.

Industry also uses huge amounts of water. About 50 000 litres are used in the manufacture of one car, and it takes about 350 litres of water to make 1 litre of beer! The water is used for cooling, washing out bottles and vats, and so on.

Some of the water needed by industry doesn't have to be very pure. A large power station uses around 200 000 litres of cooling water an hour (picture 2). It is usually taken straight from rivers or the sea.

But when we turn on our taps, we expect something purer than river or sea water to come out.

SUPPLYING CLEAN WATER

In Britain, most of our water comes from rivers and lakes, and from underground wells called **aquifers**. Before the water can be used, it must be purified. Picture 3 shows the main stages in the purification of river water.

In the reservoir, some of the impurities sink to the bottom. The water then goes through filters made of sand and gravel.

Next, a small amount of chlorine is added to the water to kill any bacteria left in it. This is important, because bacteria carried in water can cause epidemics of diseases like typhoid and cholera. Fluoride may also be added to the water if there is not enough naturally present. Fluoride in the water helps prevent tooth decay.

The purified water is finally pumped to storage reservoirs. From here it flows by gravity to the homes and factories where it is used.

To a scientist, the word 'pure' has a special meaning. A pure substance is a single substance, with nothing else at all mixed with it. Although tap water looks pure, it is really a solution. It has gases like carbon dioxide and oxygen dissolved in it. It also contains dissolved solids, which may make the water 'hard' (topic G5).

And in spite of purification, the water may still contain impurities like nitrates and aluminium which could be harmful to health. There is more about this in topic B7.

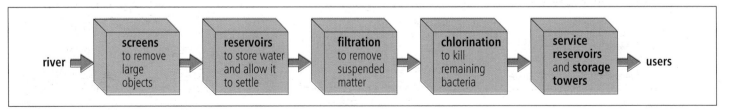

river → **screens** to remove large objects → **reservoirs** to store water and allow it to settle → **filtration** to remove suspended matter → **chlorination** to kill remaining bacteria → **service reservoirs** and **storage towers** → users

Picture 3   The main stages in the purification of water.

THE WATER CYCLE

After we have used water, it passes into sewers and on to sewage works. Here it is purified and returned to the sea or rivers so it can be used again. This recycling is part of a much bigger cycle called the water cycle. Without the water cycle we would soon run out of the fresh water we need.

Picture 4 summarises the water cycle. About 97% of the world's water is in the oceans. The sun keeps evaporating water from the oceans, and this goes into the atmosphere. Water vapour condenses into drops, which collect in clouds. Eventually the water falls back to earth as rain or snow.

We rely on this cycle to keep us supplied with fresh water. But the cycle is affected by changes in climate. Scientists believe the world's climate is getting warmer because of the 'greenhouse effect' (page 35).

If the climate gets warmer, more water vapour will stay in the atmosphere instead of falling to earth as rain. This could lead to droughts.

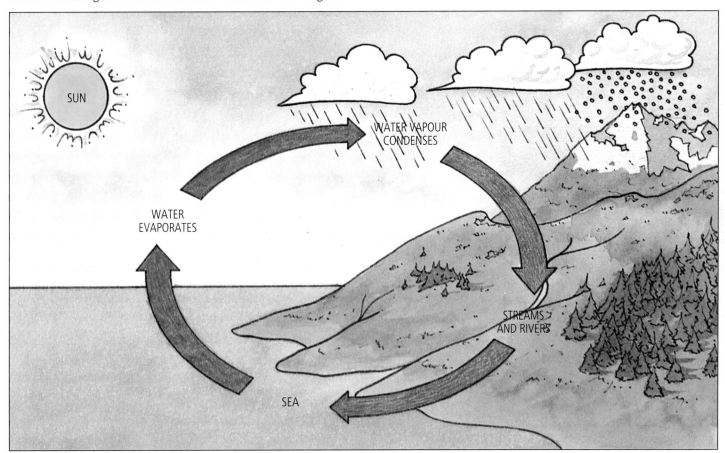

Picture 4 The water cycle.

Questions

1 Look at the water purification process in picture 3.

  a At which stage is each of the following removed? Bacteria, fish, suspended clay particles

  b Even after the purification process, the water is still not completely pure. Why?

  c Water can be made very pure by distillation. Why don't the water companies distil the water supply?

2 Describe the water cycle. Begin your description 'The sun evaporates water from the sea ...'

3 Assume each person in your family uses 180 litres of water a day.

  a i) How much water is used by the whole family per day?

    ii) How much water is used by the whole family per year?

  b Find out how much your family pays for its water supply each year. To do this you will need to look at some water bills.

  c Use parts (a) and (b) to work out the cost per litre of the water used by your family. How does it compare with the cost per litre of (i) milk and (ii) petrol?

Water and solutions

Water is an excellent solvent. In this topic we look at solutions.

Picture 1 The Dead Sea in Israel is a concentrated solution of salt. It quickly crystallises in the hot sun.

How often do you drink a glass of plain water? Most people prefer to take their water in a flavoured form—as tea, lemonade, beer or whatever. All these drinks are over 95% water, but they get their taste from substances that are dissolved in the water.

WHAT ARE SOLUTIONS?

When you add sugar to water and stir, the sugar disappears. It has **dissolved** in the water. We say that sugar is **soluble** in water. The mixture of sugar and water is called a solution. In this solution, the water is the **solvent**—the liquid part. The sugar is the **solute**—the substance dissolved in the solvent (picture 3). A solution that has a lot of solute in a certain volume of solvent is **concentrated**. A **dilute** solution has only a little solute in a certain volume.

If you go on adding sugar to water, the solution gets more and more concentrated. Eventually no more will dissolve, and the solution is **saturated**.

Suppose you leave a saturated solution in an open container such as an evaporating basin. The water slowly evaporates. When there isn't enough water left to dissolve the solute, the solute comes out of solution, forming crystals. It **crystallises**.

If you add flour to water and stir, the flour *doesn't* disappear. You can still see it, suspended in the water. We say that flour is **insoluble**.

Have a go at question 1 to check that you understand the meaning of these key words to do with solutions.

Sometimes, when you mix two solutions together, a chemical reaction takes place and a new substance is formed. If this new substance is insoluble, it comes out of solution as a **precipitate**. Picture 4 shows an example. There is more about **precipitation** in topic G4.

Picture 2 A solution of copper sulphate. Water is the solvent; copper sulphate is the solute.

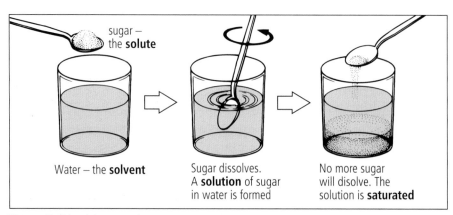

sugar – the **solute**

Water – the **solvent**

Sugar dissolves. A **solution** of sugar in water is formed

No more sugar will dissolve. The solution is **saturated**

Picture 3 Dissolving sugar in water.

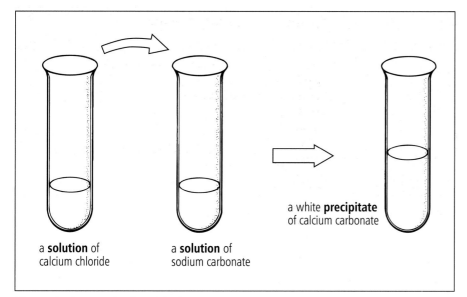

Picture 4 An example of precipitation.

LOOKING AT SOLUBILITY

Water is an excellent solvent, and many different substances will dissolve in it. We rely on water as a solvent whenever we eat, drink or wash. All living things need water in which to dissolve their supplies of food, oxygen and other essentials.

Sometimes, water's solvent properties can be a nuisance. As water runs over the rocks and soil it dissolves substances which may make the water **hard**. Hard water prevents soap lathering well, and it forms solid deposits called **fur** in kettles and pipes. There is more about hard water in topic G5.

Harmful waste substances from industry and agriculture may get dissolved in waterways, making them **polluted**. You can read more about this in topic B7.

Table 1 The solubility of some substances in water. The figures show the mass of the substance that will dissolve in 100 g of water at 25 °C.

Substance	Solubility
Salt (sodium chloride)	36
Sand	0
Sugar	211
Alcohol (ethanol)	infinite
Oxygen	0.0041
Carbon dioxide	0.144

Some substances dissolve in water better than others. Table 1 compares the solubility of a few common substances. Picture 5 explains what we mean by 'solubility'. Notice that the table includes two gases, carbon dioxide and oxygen. Gases can be soluble in water, just like solids can.

Notice too that the table includes alcohol which, like water, is a liquid. Alcohol and water always mix, whatever the proportions of each. That is why the solubility of alcohol in water is described as 'infinite'.

The solubility of a substance depends on the temperature. Solids are usually more soluble at higher temperatures—sugar dissolves better in hot water than in cold.

Testing for water

It is not always easy to tell if a liquid has water in it. Solutions and suspensions often look different from clear, colourless water. In any case, water is not the only clear, colourless liquid.

To find out if a liquid has water in it, we carry out the **cobalt chloride test**.

Cobalt chloride crystals are normally pale pink. They are hydrated, which means they contain water as part of the crystal structure. But if you heat pink cobalt chloride crystals gently to drive off water, they become anhydrous and turn deep blue. Adding water to the blue form of cobalt chloride turns it back to pale pink. Often this test is done using paper that has been soaked in cobalt chloride solution and allowed to dry.

So, to test if a substance contains water, you add it to the blue form of cobalt chloride. If it turns pink, water is present.

A similar test for water uses **anhydrous copper sulphate**, which is white. When water is added to white anhydrous copper sulphate, it turns blue.

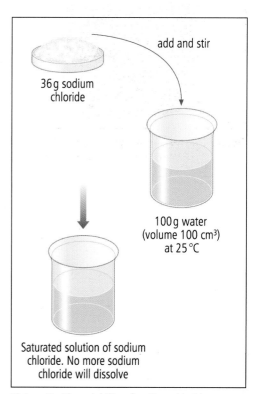

Picture 5 The solubility of sodium chloride at 25 °C is 36 g per 100 g of water.

HOW DOES SOLUBILITY CHANGE WITH TEMPERATURE?

Picture 6 shows how the solubilities of two different solids change over a range of temperatures. The lines on the graph are called **solubility curves**. The lines show the maximum mass of solid that will dissolve in 100 g of water at a particular temperature, to give a saturated solution.

You can see from the graph that the solubility of potassium nitrate is about 10 times as great in water at 100°C as at 10°C. The solubility of potassium chloride also increases with increasing temperature but not as much. In general, all solids become more soluble with increasing temperature.

■ Using solubility curves

Here are some examples of how solubility curves can be used.

Example 1: What mass of potassium nitrate will dissolve in a litre of water at 40°C?
The graph in Picture 6 tells us that the solubility of potassium nitrate at 40 °C is about 65 g per 100 g of water. One litre of water weighs 1000 g, so it would dissolve ten times as much as this.

The mass which dissolves in 1 litre is 10 × 65 g = **650 g**

Example 2: What is the minimum mass of water which will be needed to dissolve 75 g of potassium chloride at a temperature of 70 °C?
From the graph, the solubility of potassium chloride at 70 °C is about 50 g per 100 g of water.

If 50 g of potassium chloride just dissolves in 100 g of water, 75 g will dissolve in 75/50 × 100 g of water = **150 g** of water.

■ Crystallisation

When a saturated solution of potassium nitrate is cooled, crystals of solid potassium nitrate are formed. This is because the solubility decreases when the temperature is reduced. We can use the solubility curve to work out what mass of solute comes out of solution.

Example 3: A saturated solution of potassium nitrate in 100 g of water is cooled from 90°C to 30°C. What mass of solute crystallises?
The solubility of potassium nitrate per 100 g of water is:

205 g at 90 °C and **45 g** at 30 °C

Mass of solute which crystallises on cooling from 90 °C to 30 °C

= **(205–45) g** = **160 g**

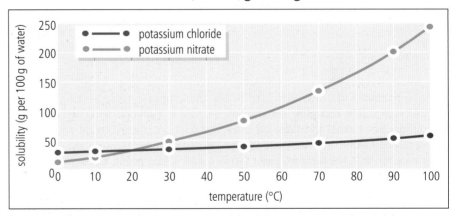

Picture 6 Solubility curves for potassium chloride and potassium nitrate. The solubility is measured as grams of solid dissolved in 100 g of water.

WHAT ABOUT GASES?

Unlike a solid, the solubility of a gas in a liquid *decreases* when the temperature rises. Air dissolves reasonably well in *cold* water. You may have noticed that gas bubbles appear when you heat a beaker or saucepan of water, long before the water reaches its boiling point. This is because the air becomes *less* soluble as the temperature rises, so the gas comes out of solution.

This has important results for organisms which live in water. At higher temperatures, less oxygen can dissolve in the water, which makes it harder for organisms to survive.

Industry needs huge volumes of water for use as a coolant. Water which has been used for cooling is often discharged into rivers and other water sources. This can result in thermal pollution of the water and threatens the survival of water life.

Picture 7 The air which is dissolved in the water in this aquarium provides a supply of oxygen for the fish.

WATER ISN'T THE ONLY SOLVENT

We use water, together with detergents, to do most of our washing, because water is so cheap and abundant.

But sometimes you send clothes to be 'dry cleaned' instead of washed. Dry cleaning uses solvents without any water in them—**non-aqueous solvents**. You may have used a non-aqueous solvent such as alcohol or white spirit to remove ball-pen stains or to get paint off brushes. Non-aqueous solvents generally dissolve grease and oil better than water does. But they are less good at dissolving substances, such as sugar and salt, that dissolve well in water.

A dry-cleaning machine is like a washing machine, but it uses a non-aqueous solvent instead of water. Because the solvent is expensive, it is distilled and re-used instead of being thrown away like the water from a washing machine (picture 8). Dry-cleaning solvents can often remove stains that won't dissolve in water—and they are less likely to make the clothes shrink.

Picture 8 A dry cleaning machine.

Questions

1 Answers these questions to check that you understand the key words about solutions and solubility.

  a Sea water is a solution.
    i) What is the solvent in sea water?
    ii) Name one solute in sea water.

  b Soda water (fizzy water) is a solution. What is the solute in soda water?

  c What happens to a saturated solution when some of the solvent evaporates?

  d Which of the following are soluble in water: sand, salt, alcohol?

2 Try to explain the following observations.

  a Ordinary fountain pen ink 'runs' if you spill water on the page. But ball-pen ink doesn't run with water.

  b Water alone will not remove a greasy stain from clothing, but alcohol will.

  c If you catch a fish in a stream and put it in a jar of water, it survives for quite a long time if the jar is kept cool. But if you let the jar get warm, the fish soon dies.

  d The sea is salty, but inland lakes are not.

3 The following questions are about dry cleaning.

  a What happens in a dry-cleaning machine?

  b Is dry cleaning really 'dry'? Explain.

  c Petrol dissolves grease and oil, but it is never used in dry cleaning. Suggest a reason why.

  d When you take clothes home from the dry cleaner in a car, you are advised to have a window open. Why do you think this is?

Use the solubility curve of potassium chloride in picture 6 to help you answer questions 4 and 5.

4 a What is the solubility of potassium chloride at 75 °C?

  b What mass of potassium chloride would dissolve in 250 g of water at this temperature?

  c At 90 °C, what is the minimum volume of water which dissolves 300 g of potassium chloride?

5 A student made an unsaturated solution containing 50 g of potassium nitrate dissolved in 100 g of water at 40 °C.

  a The student cooled the solution from 40°C. At what temperature would the solution begin to crystallise?

  b What mass of solid would crystallise when the solution is cooled from 40°C to 20°C?

6 a Use the data in table 2 to plot solubility curves for potassium chlorate(V), $KClO_3$, and sodium chloride, NaCl.

  b At what temperature are the solubilities of potassium chlorate and sodium chloride equal?

Table 2

Temperature (°C)	Solubility (g per 100 g)	
	$KClO_3$	NaCl
10	5.1	35.8
30	10.1	36.2
50	18.5	36.8
70	30.2	37.6
90	46.0	38.6

  c Use the data to suggest a way of obtaining pure potassium chlorate from a sample which has been contaminated by a small quantity of sodium chloride.

How pure is the water?

In this topic we look at some of the ways water can become polluted and dangerous to life.

On 6 July 1988 a lorry load of aluminium sulphate was accidentally tipped into the water supply in the Cornish town of Camelford. Before the mistake had been discovered, people were complaining of sickness and some people's hair had turned green. There is more about this on page 50.

A safe, unpolluted water supply is essential to good health. Unpolluted water is even more important to aquatic organisms, which spend all their life surrounded by the liquid.

WHAT'S THE PROBLEM?

There are two general ways that water can become harmful through pollution.

1   The oxygen dissolved in it gets used up

This happens when algae and bacteria grow in the water so fast that they use up most of the oxygen. This is usually because the water has become polluted with sewage or other substances, such as fertilisers from fields, that encourage bacteria to grow. This is called **eutrophication**.

2   Harmful substances get into the water

Harmful substances may poison organisms which live in the water or drink it. These substances may come from industries, farms or homes. Some of them may be **biodegradable** – they can be broken down by living organisms. This is good, because it means that the harmful substances do not stay around too long.

■ What are the major water pollutants?

Let's look at some of the most serious pollutants of rivers, lakes and oceans.

Sewage

This is produced wherever humans live and work. Sewage is rich in organic substances which can act as fertilisers. They encourage algae and bacteria to grow and cause eutrophication. In 1950, the River Thames at London was so polluted with sewage that there were no fish left in it. Since then, the dumping of sewage has been controlled, and fish have returned (picture 3). There is more about this on page 50.

Picture 1 The water looks pure, but is it?

Picture 2 The polluted water of the River Seine near Paris.

Picture 4 The 'Thames Bubbler' bubbles oxygen into polluted river water.

Nowadays in Britain, most sewage is purified before it is allowed into waterways. But in some places raw, untreated sewage is still pumped into the sea.

Fertilisers are used in large amounts on modern farms. They can get washed down through the soil by rain, and they end up in streams and rivers. Like sewage, fertilisers cause eutrophication and encourage algae and bacteria to grow.

Fertilisers which contain nitrates are particularly bad, because nitrates are very soluble in water. They also get into drinking water supplies (see below).

Pesticides are used on farms and can also end up in water supplies. Pesticides are designed to kill pests, particularly insects, which eat the crops. Unfortunately they are often poisonous to other organisms as well – including humans.

The best way to control pollution by pesticides is to use less of them and control pests in some other way. Another approach is to develop pesticides that are relatively harmless to innocent organisms.

Detergents get into the water from homes and factories. Most detergents are biodegradable, so they get broken down reasonably quickly. But if a lot of detergent gets into a river, it may cause foaming and it may poison aquatic organisms.

Industrial waste is sometimes pumped into waterways from factories. There are many different kinds of waste, but what matters is whether it is harmful to life. Common industrial pollutants include acids and alkalis and compounds of poisonous metals.

There are laws about how much harmful waste can be pumped into rivers in Britain, but they are sometimes broken. Accidental leakages also sometimes happen.

Oil may get spilt into the sea from refineries or leaking oil tankers. Oil floats on water, so the oil may end up on beaches. It may get on the feathers of sea birds, so they can't fly.

Are rivers now too clean for fish to survive?

The rivers of Britain are in crisis. One expert fears salmon could be heading for extinction while others are shocked by the rapidly falling numbers of coarse fish such as roach.

The dramatic decline is sure to affect the fragile ecology of rivers and put at risk the future of angling – which is enjoyed by three million Britons…

On the Witham, in Lincolnshire, fish stocks have plunged by 66 per cent in 15 years. Other rivers such as the Great Ouse at Bedford, the Wye at Hereford and Monmouth and the Swale in North Yorkshire suffer similar problems. The NFA [National Federation of Anglers] says the water in all the affected rivers has become "very clear" in the past five years. Prime suspect is the water industry which has spent nearly £9billion cleaning them up, particularly by reducing sewage pumped into them.

The Trent is now so clean, also thanks to the decline in heavy industry pollution, that it is now a tap water source. The NFA suspects this may have deprived young roach of their "suspended solids" diet and left them unable to survive the winter. The NFA's Rodney Cauldron said: "The river seems to be chemically clean but biologically dead."

Yet there are growing numbers of fish in once polluted rivers such as the Mersey, Tyne and Yorkshire's Don. An Environment Agency spokesman said: "Cleaner rivers are resulting in a shift towards fewer, larger fish, bringing the return of native crayfish, water voles, otters and a diverse fish population."

Salmon are also in decline. The catch in England and Wales last year was 20 per cent down on 1997, which was 40 per cent down on 1996. TV journalist and angler, Jeremy Paxman, said yesterday: "There is a crisis concerning the stocks of salmon and sea trout…"

Picture 3 An article that appeared in *The Express*, 5th May 1999

Picture 5 To get big wheat crops a lot of fertiliser has to be used, and this can pollute water supplies.

Picture 6 Oil spills from tankers are a pollution hazard. This dead fish is among oil-coated rocks off Shetland, following a tanker accident in 1993.

Picture 7 Poisonous blue-green algae may flourish in water polluted with nitrates.

When these kinds of spillages happen, detergents have to be used to try and make the oil mix with the sea water so it is dispersed. Unfortunately, the detergents themselves may also be harmful to life.

HOW SAFE IS THE DRINKING WATER?

Before it reaches our taps, water is purified to make it safe for drinking. It is impossible, though, to get all the impurities out of the water. In any case, some impurities, like calcium compounds, are useful because they make the water taste better and they may even be good for your health.

But there are some impurities left in the water that may be harmful to health.

Nitrates get into the water from the fertilisers used on farmland. Nitrates contain the NO_3^- ion, and they are very soluble in water. This makes it difficult to remove them.

The trouble is that nitrate takes a long time to reach the water supply after it has been put on the fields as fertiliser. It can take up to 40 years for the nitrate to work its way down through the soil and into the aquifers – the underground reservoirs which feed the water supply. So even if farmers cut down on the use of nitrate fertilisers now, the problem will still be with us for several decades.

Aluminium gets into water from several sources. Soil is full of aluminium compounds, and these may dissolve in rain water, particularly if the rain is acidic.

Aluminium sulphate is sometimes added at the water treatment works, to help make cloudy water clear. Some excess aluminium sulphate is often left over, dissolved in the water (see *Trouble with aluminium* on page 50).

Aluminium ions may also get into water in tiny amounts from aluminium kettles and saucepans, especially when they are used to cook acidic foods like fruit.

So what's the problem with aluminium? Until recently it was considered to be fairly harmless, but doctors now believe that aluminium ions may be harmful in a number of ways.

Aluminium has been linked with Alzheimer's disease, which results in loss of memory and odd behaviour in some old people. People with Alzheimer's disease often have abnormally large amounts of aluminium compounds in their brains. This doesn't prove that aluminium causes the disease, but it is enough to make us suspicious.

■ Cleaning up the water

Stopping pollution always costs something. As consumers, we want all our drinking water to have safe levels of aluminium ions and nitrate ions. This means that in some areas the water companies will have to spend more on purifying the water. Or they may have to find new, purer sources of water.

All this costs money, and in the end we, the consumers, pay. And it's not easy to decide what is a 'safe' amount of an impurity, whether it's aluminium, nitrate or other harmful substances like pesticides. It's impossible to get the water completely pure. We have to decide what we can afford, and what we are prepared to put up with.

Picture 8 Tiny amounts of aluminium get into food from cooking utensils.

Activities

A Looking at local water

Choose a river near to your home. Find out whether any industries use the river, either as a source of water or for discharging waste.

Try to find out what the water is used for, and what kind of waste is discharged.

B Looking at mineral water

Collect the labels from bottles of mineral water. If all the class collect labels, you will get a good selection.

Use the labels to compare what substances are dissolved in the different brands of mineral water. Are all the dissolved substances good for health?

Questions

1 Here are three sources of water pollution: (a) homes, (b) farms, (c) industries. For each one of these, list two pollutants that it might produce.

2 a Why is it important to living things that oxygen dissolves in water?

   b What is the effect of sewage on the concentration of oxygen dissolved in the water? Explain why this effect occurs.

3 Three neighbours are having a conversation about the purity of drinking water.

   Mr Jenkins says, 'I want my drinking water to be completely pure. I'm not prepared to put up with any impurities in it.'

   Mrs Johnson says, 'It's impossible to remove all the impurities from the water.'

   Mr Ahmed says, 'Water is like everything else. You get what you pay for.'

   Which of these people do you agree with? Why? What further points would you want to make yourself?

4 Thermal pollution may occur when warm water is pumped into a river or other body of water. This sometimes happens near power stations.

   a Why do power stations produce warm water?

   b What problems might be caused by thermal pollution?

Trouble with aluminium

Lowermoor waterworks in Cornwall treats drinking water for the nearby town of Camelford. The water coming into the works is rather acidic, so lime (calcium hydroxide) is added. The water is also quite cloudy due to suspended clay particles. Aluminium sulphate is added to make the particles clump together so they can be filtered off.

The aluminium sulphate is normally kept as a solution in a special storage tank. On 6 July 1988 a driver delivered fresh supplies of aluminium sulphate solution. Instead of putting the solution in the storage tank, he pumped 20 tonnes of it straight into the water supply by mistake.

Picture 1 shows what happened to the concentration of aluminium ions in the water over the next few days. As a result of this accident, the water also became much more acidic. This made copper from pipes and boilers dissolve in the water.

People were soon complaining of sickness, curdling milk and nasty tasting water. Some people noticed that the water coming out of the taps was blue, and some people's hair went green.

When they discovered the problem, the water engineers flushed out the mains into nearby rivers. As a result, 30 000 fish were killed.

Fortunately, the level of aluminium returned to normal before long (see picture 1). However, in 1999, medical researchers reported that some local people had suffered long-term brain damage as a result of the incident.

1 Why are the following added to the water at the treatment works?

   (a) lime

   (b) aluminium sulphate

2 Explain in your own words how the excess aluminium ions got into the drinking water.

3 Aluminium compounds are colourless. Why, then, did the water turn blue and some people's hair turn green?

4 Aluminium sulphate is added to water as part of its normal treatment, but normally very little of this aluminium ends up in the drinking water. Suggest a reason why.

5 Apart from water treatment, how else can aluminium ions get into the water supplies?

6 No people were killed as a result of this accident, but it killed thousands of fish. Why were the fish more vulnerable?

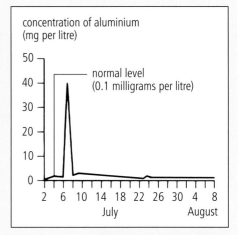

Picture 1 The variation in the concentration of aluminium ions in the Camelford water supply in July and August 1988. The recommended maximum is 0.2 milligrams per litre.

Cleaning up the Thames

Picture 1 shows the concentration of dissolved oxygen in different parts of the River Thames. The three graphs show how the concentration has changed since 1895.

1 In which of the three periods was the oxygen concentration at its lowest? Suggest a reason why.

2 Look at the graph for 1981. Whereabouts in the Thames was the oxygen concentration lowest? Explain why the concentration was higher (i) upstream and (ii) downstream of this point.

3 The figures for the concentration of dissolved oxygen are given as '% saturation'. What do you think this means?

4 Between 1835 and 1974 no salmon were caught in the River Thames near London. Today salmon is one of 70 species of fish that can be caught. Explain.

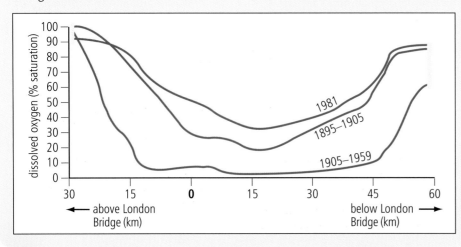

Picture 1 The concentration of dissolved oxygen in different parts of the River Thames, at different times since 1895.

Examining the water

Table 1 shows the results of an examination of water supplies carried out by the Anytown Water Company.

Table 1

Anytown Water Company   Water Analysis Report
Location   High Street Anytown   Date   20 May 2000

Bacteriological

Colony Count (per ml 37 °C, 24 h)   3

Physical

Appearance	Clear	Conductivity at 20 °C (μS/cm)	536
Taste	Normal	Temperature (°C)	14
pH Value	7.13	Odour	Nil

Chemical (concentration in mg/litre)

Carbonate Hardness ($CaCO_3$)	255	Total Residual Chlorine	0.15
Non-Carbonate Hardness ($CaCO_3$)	27	Total Hardness ($CaCO_3$)	282
Calcium (Ca^{2+})	108	Free Residual Chlorine	0.12
Magnesium (Mg^{2+})	3.1	Carbonate (CO_3^{2-})	153
Sodium (Na^+)	8.2	Sulphate (SO_4^{2-})	12
Potassium (K^+)	1.1	Chloride (Cl^-)	16
Iron (Fe^{3+})	0.02	Nitrate (NO_3^-)	21
Aluminium (Al^{3+})	0.01	Fluoride (F^-)	0.1
Copper (Cu^{2+})	0.02	Phosphate (PO_4^{3-})	0.13
Lead (Pb^{2+})	0.03	Silica (SiO_2)	–
Zinc (Zn^{2+})	0.01	Free Carbon Dioxide (CO_2)	33

Table 2 shows the European Union's guidelines for water purity. **Guide level** means the recommended safe concentration. **Maximum admissible concentration** means the highest concentration allowed.

Use the analysis report in table 1, together with the guidelines in table 2, to answer these questions.

1 An easy question to start you off! How many milligrams of magnesium are present in each litre of Anytown water?

2 The tables give figures for the concentrations in water of metals like magnesium, iron and aluminium. Yet none of these metals dissolve in water. Explain.

3 Which metallic element is present in the Anytown water in greatest concentration?

4 Use the water analysis report to decide whether the water is acidic, alkaline or neutral.

5 What do you think is meant by the 'colony count'?

Table 2   Water purity guidelines of the European Union (EU).

Substance present in the water	Guide level (mg/litre)	Max. admissible conc. (mg/litre)
Calcium (Ca^{2+})	100	
Magnesium (Mg^{2+})	30	50
Sodium (Na^+)	20	150
Potassium (K^+)	10	12
Iron (Fe^{3+})	0.05	0.2
Aluminium (Al^{3+})	0.05	0.2
Copper (Cu^{2+})	0,1	
Lead (Pb^{2+})		0.05
Zinc (Zn^{2+})	0.1	
Sulphate (SO_4^{2-})	25	250
Chloride (Cl^-)	25	
Nitrate (NO_3^-)	25	50
Fluoride (F^-)		1.5
Phosphate (PO_4^{3-})	0.2	5
Acid	pH 6.5–8.5	

6 Why might the conductivity of the water tell you something about its purity?

7 Compare the concentrations in the water analysis report (table 1) with the EU guidelines (table 2).

a Which substance in the Anytown water exceeds the EU guide level?

b Do you think it matters that the guide level is exceeded for this substance? Explain.

8 What other substances, not mentioned in the water analysis report, might be present in the water?

What are things made of?

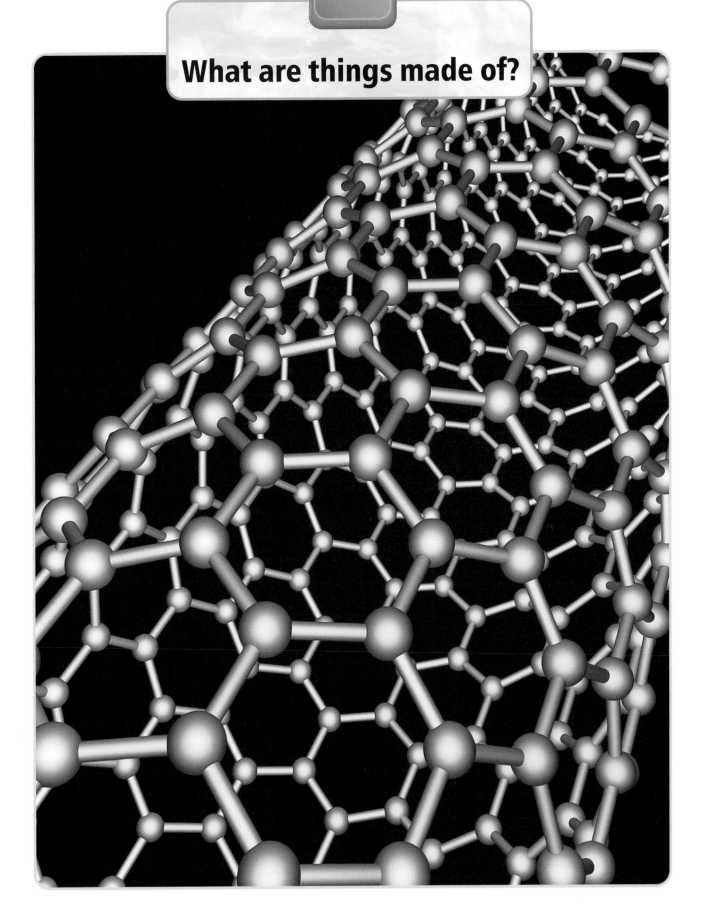

Particles on the move

We can use the kinetic theory to explain many of the things that happen around us.

Picture 1 'An experiment on a bird in the air pump', by Joseph Wright of Derby, painted in 1768.

Picture 1 shows a famous painting of an eighteenth century science demonstration. The demonstrator has put a bird in a glass sphere, then pumped the air out. This cruel experiment shows that, although we cannot see air, it exerts pressure.

We can explain air pressure and many other familiar things using the **kinetic theory**.

WHAT IS THE KINETIC THEORY?

The kinetic theory says that matter is made of tiny particles that move all the time. Let's look at the main points of the theory.

- **All matter is made up of tiny, invisible, moving particles. (These particles are actually atoms, molecules and ions: see topic C2.)**
- **The particles move all the time. The higher the temperature, the faster they move.**
- **Heavier particles move more slowly than light ones at a given temperature.**

USING THE THEORY TO EXPLAIN THE STATES OF MATTER

A good scientific theory can be used to explain things. It can be used as a model – a mental model, rather than the kind of model you build. The kinetic theory is a good model because it explains lots of things – particularly concerning the states of matter. Also, very usefully, it helps us predict things.

▇ Gases, liquids and solids

The kinetic theory explains the difference between gases, liquids and solids.

In a **gas**, the particles are widely spaced. They are free to move anywhere. They move very fast, colliding with each other and with the walls of the container (picture 3a).

Picture 2 How does the smell reach your nose?

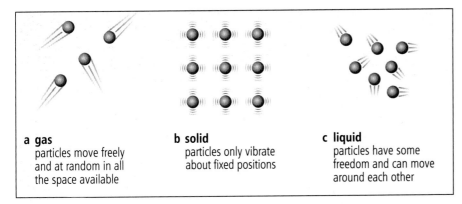

a gas
particles move freely
and at random in all
the space available

b solid
particles only vibrate
about fixed positions

c liquid
particles have some
freedom and can move
around each other

Picture 3 What happens when a solid melts.

In a **solid**, the particles are strongly attracted to each other. There are bonds between the particles. This holds them close together (picture 3b). The particles are arranged in a regular way, which explains why many solids form regular crystals. The particles in a solid have very little freedom of movement. They are in fixed positions, and all they can do is vibrate. They can't move all over the place like the particles in a gas.

In a **liquid**, the situation is somewhere between a solid and a gas. The particles are quite close together, but they attract each other more weakly than in a solid. The particles have more freedom of movement than in a solid (picture 3c).

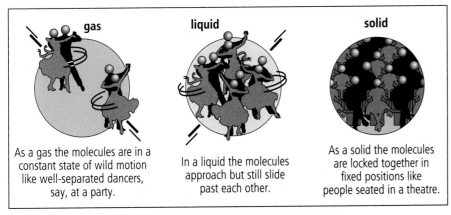

gas

As a gas the molecules are in a
constant state of wild motion
like well-separated dancers,
say, at a party.

liquid

In a liquid the molecules
approach but still slide
past each other.

solid

As a solid the molecules
are locked together in
fixed positions like
people seated in a theatre.

Picture 4 Another way of illustrating the states of matter.

■ Changes of state

Why do substances change state when they are heated or cooled?
We can use the kinetic theory to explain these changes (picture 6).

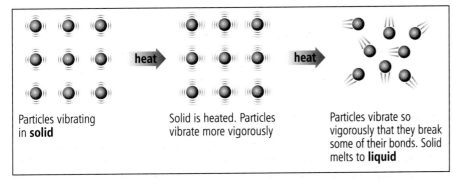

Particles vibrating
in **solid**

heat ▶ Solid is heated. Particles
vibrate more vigorously

heat ▶ Particles vibrate so
vigorously that they break
some of their bonds. Solid
melts to **liquid**

Picture 6 What happens when a solid melts.

Gases have mass

Gases may feel light, but like all matter they do have mass. Picture 4 shows an experiment you can do to find the mass of a gas.

The mass of a certain volume of gas depends on its density – and some gases are denser than others. A litre of hydrogen has a mass of less than 0.1 g, but the mass of a litre of air is about 1 g. A balloon filled with hydrogen rises in the air because hydrogen is less dense than air.

The air in your bedroom probably has a mass of about 50 kg, assuming the volume of the room is 50 m³. This may be similar to your own mass!

Some gases are very dense. A litre of xenon, one of the noble gases, has a mass of about 5 g. A balloon filled with xenon would drop to the floor very quickly!

Picture 5 shows how you can measure the mass of a gas.

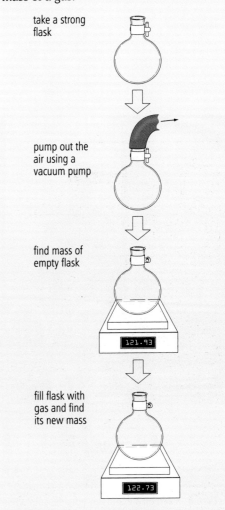

take a strong
flask

pump out the
air using a
vacuum pump

find mass of
empty flask

121.93

fill flask with
gas and find
its new mass

122.73

Picture 5 Finding the mass of a gas.

When a solid is heated, the particles vibrate faster and faster until they break away from their fixed positions. The solid has melted to a liquid. Melting a solid needs energy. The extra energy is sometimes called **latent heat**. The energy is needed to break the bonds holding the particles together, and pull the particles apart. We give the solid energy by heating it.

If you go on heating the liquid, the particles are given more energy and move faster and faster still. Eventually the faster ones break away completely from each other. The liquid is becoming a gas. Turning a liquid to a gas needs energy to break bonds between particles. You can feel the energy change as you stand wet and shivering beside a swimming pool (picture 8). As the liquid water on your body evaporates, it takes the energy it needs from your skin and you feel cold. This is also why sweating keeps you cool. Sweat evaporates from the skin, taking energy away from it.

Liquids evaporate slowly when they are cool. But when you heat the liquid, more and more of the particles get enough energy to break away. Eventually so many particles are escaping that bubbles of gas form in the liquid. The liquid is *boiling*.

The opposite happens when a gas turns to a liquid and a liquid turns to a solid. In these changes, energy is *given out*.

Refrigerators use the energy changes involved in changes of state. A special fluid called a refrigerant circulates around the fridge (picture 7).

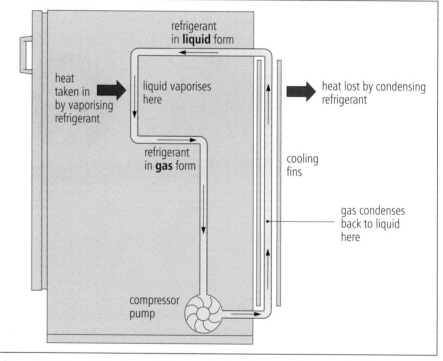

Picture 7 How a refrigerator works. The overall effect is to move heat from the fridge compartment and out of the back.

When the inside of the fridge starts getting warm, a thermostat makes the pump switch on – you can hear the pump as a humming or whirring sound. The pump compresses the refrigerant so it condenses to a liquid. This gives out energy, and the refrigerant gets hot. There are special cooling fins at the back of the fridge to let it cool down again. The liquid refrigerant circulates in pipes inside the fridge, where it turns back to a gas. This takes in energy, so the inside of the fridge gets cool.

Table 1 sums up the energy changes involved in different changes of state. The energy changes involved when water changes state are very important in deciding the weather.

Picture 8 Even on a warm day you feel cold when you are wet. The water takes heat from your body as it evaporates.

Table 1 Energy changes and changes of state.

Change of state	Energy change involved	Why the energy change occurs
Solid → liquid (melting)	Heat taken in	Energy needed to break bonds between particles in solid
Liquid → gas (boiling, evaporating)	Heat taken in	Energy needed to break bonds between particles in liquid
Liquid → solid (freezing)	Heat given out	Energy given out as particles bond together in solid
Gas → liquid (condensing)	Heat given out	Energy given out as particles bond together in liquid

Picture 10 When a gas dissolves in a liquid it seems to disappear – but it reappears when the pressure is released.

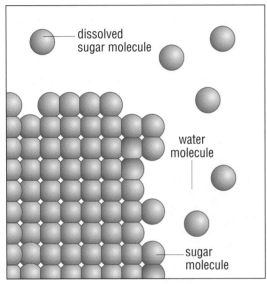

Picture 9 What happens when sugar dissolves in water.

WHAT ELSE CAN THE KINETIC THEORY EXPLAIN?

■ Dissolving

When you stir sugar into water, the sugar dissolves and seems to disappear. But it's still there, because you can taste its sweetness when you drink the water. Picture 9 shows how we can explain this using the kinetic theory. When a solid dissolves, it seems to disappear because its particles get spread out between the particles of the liquid. The same sort of thing happens when a gas dissolves in a liquid (picture 10).

■ Diffusion

Baking bread has a delicious smell. If bread is being baked in the kitchen, you can soon smell it all round the house. Particles of gas are released from the bread and they spread or **diffuse** around the house. All gases diffuse to fill the space available to them – even dense gases like bromine (picture 11).

The kinetic theory says that gases contain particles that are free to move anywhere. So it's not surprising that gases diffuse. The particles do not care where they go, so sooner or later they are bound to fill up all the space available.

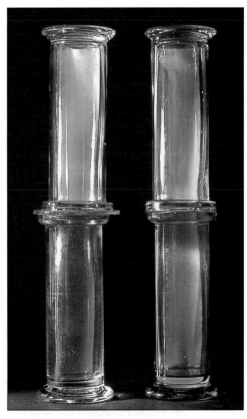

Picture 11 Bromine vapour diffuses to fill a gas jar.

Picture 12 Diffusion makes the colour and flavour of the tea spread through the hot water.

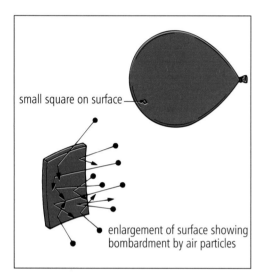

Picture 14 How a gas exerts pressure.

small square on surface

enlargement of surface showing bombardment by air particles

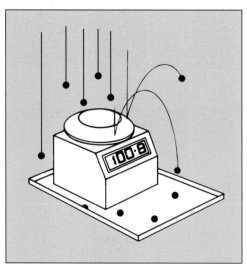

Picture 15 Ball-bearings are poured onto the pan of a weighing machine. How does this experiment model gas pressure?

Dense gases like bromine and carbon dioxide diffuse more slowly than lighter gases like hydrogen. The denser gases have heavier particles which move more slowly. Have you noticed that a balloon filled with a light gas such as hydrogen or helium deflates more quickly than a balloon filled with air? The balloon rubber has tiny holes through which the gas particles slowly diffuse. The lighter hydrogen particles move faster, so they get through the holes more quickly.

It's not only gases that can diffuse. Diffusion occurs in liquids too. You are using diffusion every time you make a cup of tea (picture 12).

Look at the experiment shown in picture 13. When water is added, the copper sulphate starts to dissolve. Particles of blue copper sulphate diffuse into the water. At first the copper sulphate is more concentrated at the bottom of the jar. But gradually the particles spread throughout the water, until the concentration is the same everywhere. This illustrates an important point about diffusion: **diffusion involves the movement of particles from a region of higher concentration towards a region of lower concentration**.

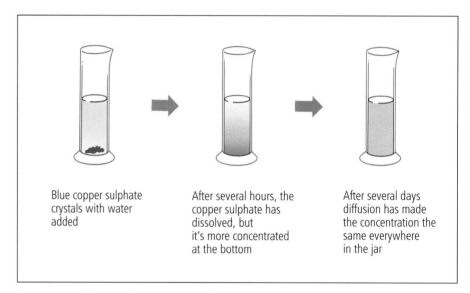

Blue copper sulphate crystals with water added

After several hours, the copper sulphate has dissolved, but it's more concentrated at the bottom

After several days diffusion has made the concentration the same everywhere in the jar

Picture 13 Diffusion of copper sulphate in water.

Diffusion is very important in all living things. Diffusion makes it possible for oxygen to get into your blood from your lungs. A special kind of diffusion, called osmosis, helps water move in and out of the cells of plants and animals.

■ Gas pressure

Think of gas inside a balloon. The gas particles move around at random. They constantly collide with each other, and with the walls of the balloon. Every square millimetre of the balloon is battered by millions and millions of tiny particles every second (picture 14).

Each particle is too small to have much of an effect on the balloon wall by itself. But the constant battering by millions of particles adds up to a steady force on each square millimetre, and this is what we call pressure. (Pressure = force/area.) Picture 15 shows a simple experiment that models the way a gas exerts pressure.

■ Brownian motion

This is covered in the exercise *Dr Brown and Dr Einstein* on page 60.

■ Expansion

When you heat things, they get bigger. In other words, they **expand**. Solids don't expand very much. Even so, bridge builders have to take precautions against the expansion that occurs on a hot summer's day. Liquids expand a bit more than solids, and we use this in thermometers (picture 16). Gases expand a lot when heated.

Why do things expand? Think of what happens to a solid when it is heated. The particles stay in the same fixed positions, but vibrate faster. This makes them nudge their neighbouring particles so they move over a bit (picture 17). The more the solid is heated, the more the particles nudge each other, and the more the solid expands.

Many other properties of matter can be explained using the kinetic theory. You can try explaining some in the questions at the end of the topic.

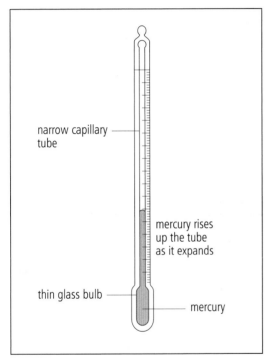

narrow capillary
tube

mercury rises
up the tube
as it expands

thin glass bulb

mercury

Picture 16   A thermometer uses the expansion of a liquid to measure the temperature. Why is the capillary tube narrow? Why is the glass bulb thin?

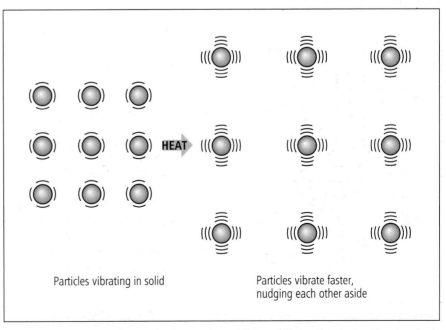

Particles vibrating in solid

HEAT

Particles vibrate faster, nudging each other aside

Picture 17   Why a solid expands when it is heated. (The expansion is exaggerated quite a lot.)

Questions

1 a State the main points of the kinetic theory.

b Use the kinetic theory to explain each of the following. Use diagrams to illustrate your answers.
  i) Liquids turn to gases when they are heated.
  ii) Gases diffuse to fill all the space available.
  iii) When a solid dissolves in a liquid, the solid seems to disappear.
  iv) When a solid is heated it expands.

2 The kinetic theory can be used to explain many of the properties of matter. Try to explain each of the following. Use diagrams to illustrate your answers.

a Washing dries better on a warm day than on a cold one.

b Washing dries better if it is spread out than if it is squashed up.

c Gases remain gases, no matter how much they are heated.

d Solids are usually hard, but liquids are soft.

e An air-filled balloon slowly goes down over the course of a week or two, even if the neck is securely tied.

f A balloon goes down faster on a warm day than on a cold one.

g Gases can easily be compressed, but solids and liquids are very difficult to compress.

3 Here are some more things to try and explain using the kinetic theory. Some of them are quite hard.

a Some solids, such as sugar, dissolve in water. Others, such as sand, do not dissolve.

b 1 g of liquid water occupies a volume of 1 cm^3. But 1 g of water vapour, which contains the same number of particles, occupies about 1700 cm^3.

c If a piece of gold and a piece of silver are pressed together for several years, a few atoms of silver pass into the gold, and a few atoms of gold pass into the silver.

d Gases expand more than solids when they are heated.

e Washing dries better on a windy day than on a still day.

4 Look at picture 10. It shows a bottle of fizzy drink before and after opening. Use diagrams to show how the particles of carbon dioxide ('fizz gas') and water are arranged before and after.

5 Look at picture 12. It shows tea being made. Use the kinetic theory to explain some of the following questions about tea making. Use the terms 'water particles' and 'tea flavour particles' in your answer.

a How does the tea flavour get out of the tea leaves and into the water?

b Why does tea get stronger the longer it is left in the pot?

c Why is it important that the water is as hot as possible?

d Why does it help to give the tea a stir in the pot?

6 a When onions are being cooked, you can soon smell them around the house. It has been estimated that the particles responsible for onion-smell travel at the speed of a jet plane. Why, then, does it take some minutes for the smell to spread?

b Why don't the gases in the Earth's atmosphere diffuse away into space?

Dr Brown and Dr Einstein

This exercise is about Brownian motion. Before you go any further, you should see Brownian motion for yourself. If was first observed using pollen grains, but you can see it most easily in smoke. You will probably use apparatus like that shown in picture 1. You should see the tiny particles of smoke dancing and jigging round, as shown in picture 2.

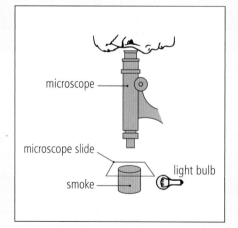

Picture 1 Looking for Brownian motion.

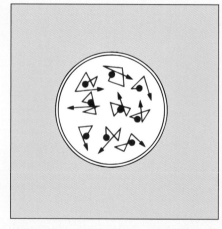

Picture 2 Smoke particles in Brownian motion.

Brown discovers, Einstein explains.

In 1827, a Scottish biologist called Robert Brown was studying pollen grains. He used a microscope to examine pollen grains suspended in water. To his surprise, he noticed that the tiny grains were constantly jiggling around in a completely random way. He explained what he saw by saying that the pollen grains were alive, and moving of their own accord.

In 1905, the great scientist Albert Einstein was 26 years old. In that year he did three pieces of work, all three of them good enough to win a Nobel Prize.

One of Einstein's papers gave an explanation of Brownian motion, using the kinetic theory. Einstein suggested that the motion happens because the

Picture 3   Robert Brown discovered Brownian motion.

Picture 4   Albert Einstein.

grains of pollen are bombarded by tiny fast-moving molecules of water. He even worked out how fast the motion should be, and his calculations matched what was actually observed.

At that time there were still some scientists who did not believe that atoms and molecules actually existed. Einstein's work on Brownian motion was a real breakthrough because it convinced even the doubters that atoms and molecules exist.

Imagine Brown met Einstein....

In this exercise you are going to act an imaginary discussion between Robert Brown and Albert Einstein. (Of course, they never actually met because Brown made his discovery over 50 years before Einstein was even born.)

Brown and Einstein would have had different theories about why Brownian motion occurs. Each would have argued for his theory. When scientists disagree on a theory, there is only one thing they can do. They suggest new experiments to test the theory.

Organising the exercise

There are several ways you could organise this exercise. One is to work in groups of four. Two of you will take the part of Brown, and two will be Einstein. The stages are as follows.

Stage 1. Brown speaks for 2 minutes. He describes what he has seen, and explains his theory that the grains move because they are alive.

Stage 2. Einstein speaks for 2 minutes. He describes his theory to explain why the grains move.

Stage 3. Brown speaks for 2 minutes. He gives his reaction to Einstein's theory, and explains why he does not believe it.

Stage 4. Einstein speaks for 2 minutes. He gives his reaction to what Brown has just said.

Stage 5. Brown speaks for 2 minutes. He suggests a new experiment that will test Einstein's theory.

Stage 6. Einstein speaks for 2 minutes. He suggests a new experiment that will test Brown's theory.

Preparing what you will say

You need to decide how you will present your theory. It would be a good idea to use diagrams. You also need to decide what experiment you will suggest in stage 5 or 6.

These notes may help you.

Brown's theory. Brown believes the grains move because they are alive. After all, pollen is produced by living plants. Being a biologist, he has often seen microscopic organisms jiggling around under the microscope.

Try to get yourself into Brown's way of thinking. The idea of atoms and molecules seems strange to Brown. They are so small that it's impossible to see them, and there is no evidence that they actually exist. In his time, the ideas of atoms and molecules was much less well known than it is today.

Einstein's theory. Einstein believes that the grains move because they are being bombarded by fast-moving molecules of water. The pollen grains may look small, but they are far bigger than the invisible molecules of water. Nevertheless, the water molecules move so fast that they can jolt the pollen grains when they collide with them. Picture 5 illustrates the theory.

After you have finished your presentation, discuss how it went.

Were the arguments convincing?

Were the ideas for new experiments good? Would they test the two theories conclusively? What results would you expect from the experiments?

Would Brown's theory have explained Brownian motion in smoke? Would Einstein's theory?

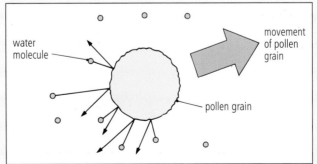

Picture 5   How Einstein explained Brownian motion.

Atoms, molecules and ions

The particles of matter come in three types.

Picture 1 The sea, a mixture of many different particles, but mostly water molecules and sodium and chloride ions.

Ask a person in the street if they have heard of atoms and molecules. They probably will have, and they'll probably be able to give you a rough idea of what atoms are.

The idea of atoms seems obvious to us today (picture 2). Yet as recently as the beginning of this century there were still some scientists who refused to believe that matter was made of atoms. There is more about this in the exercises on page 60.

In topic C1 we look at the kinetic theory, which says all matter is made of 'particles'. But what are these particles? There are three types: atoms, molecules and ions.

WHAT ARE ATOMS?

The word 'atom' comes from a Greek word meaning 'unsplittable'. Scientists used to think atoms are the smallest particles of matter, and could not be split into anything smaller. We now know that atoms *can* be split (topic J4), but in ordinary life you can think of atoms as the simplest particles.

Elements (topic A3) are made of only one type of atom. Iron contains nothing but iron atoms, and oxygen contains nothing but oxygen atoms. There are 92 different types of atom which occur naturally, one for each of the 92 naturally occurring elements. Each element has its own symbol. There is a full list of elements and their symbols in the Data Section.

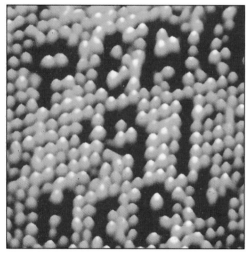

Picture 2 Today, scientists can not only take pictures of atoms: they can write messages in them. In this picture, atoms have been removed to write the message.

WHAT ARE MOLECULES?

Atoms can join together in groups. These atoms are held together by **chemical bonds**. These groups, which may be large or small, are called **molecules**. One of the commonest molecules contains two hydrogen atoms and one oxygen atom (picture 3). We can represent this as a **formula**, H_2O. It's a molecule of water, of course.

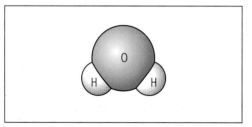

Picture 3 A water molecule.

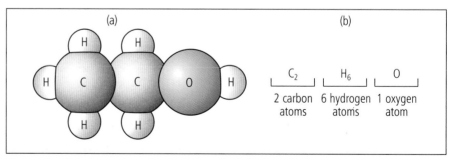

Picture 4 (a) A picture of a molecule of ethanol; (b) the formula of ethanol.

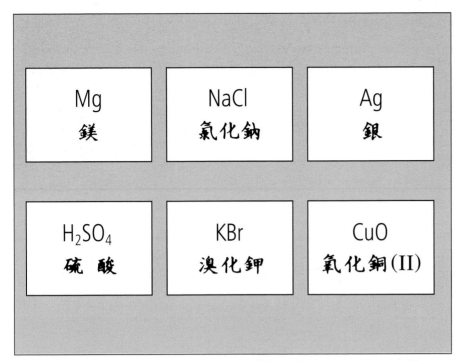

Picture 6   How good is your Chinese? These are labels from chemicals. Translate the Chinese names into English.

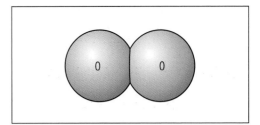

Picture 5   A molecule of oxygen, O_2.

A chemical formula shows the types and numbers of atoms in a molecule. The numbers are written after the symbols, as subscripts. Picture 4 shows a molecule of ethanol, also called alcohol, and its formula.

Molecules can be very simple, like water (H_2O) or carbon dioxide (CO_2). They can also be more complex, like octane (C_8H_{18}) or glucose ($C_6H_{12}O_6$). Some biological molecules are very complicated. For example, chlorophyll, which gives leaves their green colour, has the formula $C_{51}H_{72}O_4N_4Mg$!

Molecules of elements

The substances we have mentioned so far contain atoms of at least two different elements. This means they are *compounds* – two or more elements joined together. But molecules are also formed by some elements on their own.

Picture 5 shows a molecule of oxygen. This is the normal form in which oxygen exists, so we write the formula of oxygen as O_2, not O. Several of the gaseous elements form **diatomic** molecules like this. Thus nitrogen is N_2, hydrogen is H_2 and chlorine is Cl_2.

A molecule of sulphur contains eight sulphur atoms, so the formula of sulphur is S_8. Picture 8 shows different ways of representing a molecule of water.

State symbols

Ice, steam and liquid water are the same substance, but in different states. All three have the same formula, H_2O, which could be confusing. To show the state of a substance, we use state symbols alongside the formula.

(s)   means a substance in the solid state
(l)   means a substance in the liquid state
(g)   means a substance in the gaseous state
(aq) means a substance in the aqueous state – dissolved in water.

So ice is $H_2O(s)$, steam is $H_2O(g)$ and liquid water is $H_2O(l)$. A solution of glucose in water is $C_6H_{12}O_6(aq)$.

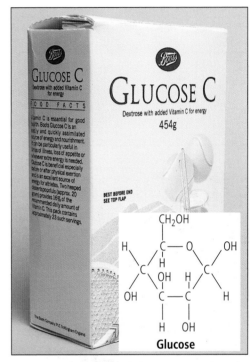

Picture 7   The formula of glucose is $C_6H_{12}O_6$. Each molecule of glucose contains 6 carbon atoms, 12 hydrogen atoms, and 6 oxygen atoms.

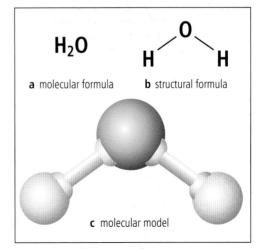

Picture 8   Different ways of representing a molecule of water. See also picture 3 on page 83.

Table 1 Some common ions.

Name	Formula
Sodium ion	Na^+
Magnesium ion	Mg^{2+}
Aluminium ion	Al^{3+}
Copper ion	Cu^{2+}
Zinc ion	Zn^{2+}
Chloride ion	Cl^-
Bromide ion	Br^-
Oxide ion	O^{2-}
Sulphide ion	S^{2-}
Nitrate ion	NO_3^-
Sulphate ion	SO_4^{2-}
Ammonium ion	NH_4^+

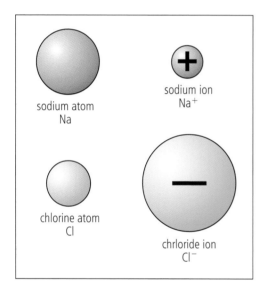

Picture 9 Atoms and ions.

sodium atom
Na

sodium ion
Na^+

chlorine atom
Cl

chrloride ion
Cl^-

WHAT ARE IONS?

An ion is a particle with an electric charge on it. Picture 9 shows atoms and ions of sodium and chlorine. You can see that the **atoms** of sodium and chlorine have no electric charge – they are **neutral**. The sodium ion has a positive charge on it: it is a **positive ion**. The chloride ion has a negative charge on it: it is a **negative ion**. (You can find out in topic J6 where ions get their charges from.)

Table 1 gives some examples of ions. Notice that the metals like sodium and aluminium form positive ions, and the non-metals like chlorine and oxygen form negative ions. This follows a general rule:

Metals form positive ions and non-metals form negative ions.

You can see from table 1 that ions may contain more than one type of atom. For example the nitrate ion contains a group of one nitrogen atom and three oxygen atoms, with a minus charge on the group. You can also see that an ion may have more than one unit of charge. For example, a sodium ion has one positive charge, a magnesium ion has two and an aluminium ion has three. The formula of an ion shows both the atoms it contains and the charge on the ion. Thus the formula of an aluminium ion is Al^{3+}.

◼ Ions in compounds

Look at picture 9. The sodium ion has a + charge and the chloride ion has a − charge. You would expect these two oppositely charged ions to attract one another. This is what happens in the compound sodium chloride, commonly known as salt. It consists of Na^+ and Cl^- ions holding each other together in a regular arrangement called a lattice (picture 10). More about ionic lattices in topic C7.

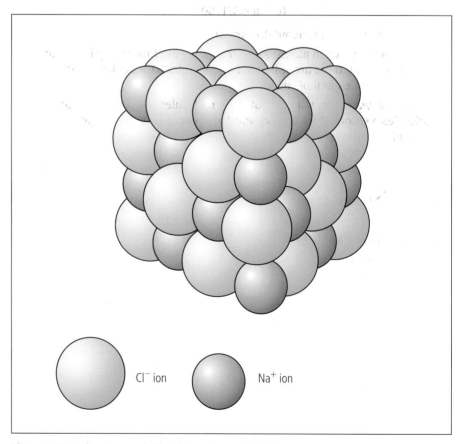

Cl^- ion Na^+ ion

Picture 10 Sodium ions and chloride ions in a crystal lattice.

Oppositely charged ions pack together in this way because opposite charges attract. But you couldn't pack ions of like charge together – they would repel each other and fly apart. So substances that contain ions are always compounds, with at least two different types of ion – a positive and a negative.

Sometimes the formula of an ionic compound shows the charges on the ions, but sometimes these are left out. For example, the formula of sodium chloride is sometimes written as Na^+Cl^-, but more commonly as just NaCl.

THE STRUCTURE OF SUBSTANCES

The formula of a substance shows the types and number of atoms or ions it contains. But the formula doesn't say anything about the way these atoms are joined together: the **structure** of the substance. It's useful to know the structure of a substance because it helps to explain its properties. To see the structure you need diagrams like picture 7, showing the structure of glucose, and picture 10, showing the structure of sodium chloride.

The structure of substances is covered in detail in topic C6.

HOW BIG ARE ATOMS, MOLECULES AND IONS?

Atoms, molecules and ions vary a lot in size, but they are all very, very small.

- The smallest atom is the hydrogen atom. It is about 10^{-10} metres (0.000 000 0001 m) across.

To measure these very small particles, we use a unit called the nanometre (nm).

$$1 \text{ nm} = 10^{-9} \text{ m} = 1/1000\,000\,000 \text{ m}$$

A hydrogen atom measures about 0.1 nm across.

- Compared to hydrogen atoms, sugar molecules are moderately large – about 1 nm across. But there are still about 10^{19} (10 000 000 000 000 000 000) molecules in one grain of sugar!

- A glass of water contains about 10^{25} molecules. If you could count five molecules a second it would take you 10 million million million years to count them all.

Activity

Do people believe in atoms?

Try asking ordinary people some questions to see if they believe in atoms and understand what atoms are. Try asking parents, relatives, neighbours – anyone as long as they are not expert scientists!

Here are some questions you could ask. Try to think of more.

1 Suppose you had a very powerful microscope. What do you think you would see if you magnified a piece of iron as much as possible?

2 Suppose you take a piece of iron and cut it in half, then in half again and so on. Could you go on doing this for ever (assuming you had a small enough knife!)?

3 Have you heard of atoms? Do you know what they are? What about molecules?

4 How big do you think molecules are? How many molecules do you think there are in a glass of water?

Questions

1 Explain in your own words the difference between:

   a an atom and a molecule

   b an atom and an ion

2 Look at this list of formulas. Classify each as atom, molecule or ion:

   a SO_2 g Br^-

   b Fe   h N_2

   c H^+ i C_6H_6

   d CH_4 j CO

   e CO_3^{2-} k Co

   f He   l PO_4^{3-}

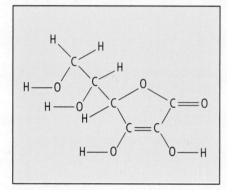

Picture 11   A molecule of vitamin C.

3 Vitamin C is an essential part of the human diet. Shortage of vitamin C causes a disease called scurvy. Picture 11 shows how the atoms are joined together in a molecule of vitamin C.

   a Which elements does vitamin C contain?

   b Write down the formula of vitamin C.

4 In A to D in picture 12, ○ represents an atom of oxygen and ● represents an atom of hydrogen. Choose from A to D the diagram that shows:

   i) hydrogen atoms and oxygen atoms

   ii) hydrogen molecules and oxygen molecules

   iii) water molecules

   iv) oxygen molecules and water molecules

5 Classify each of the substances E to I below as an element, a compound or a mixture.

Substance E contains three different types of molecules.

Substance F contains only one type of atom.

Substance C contains only one type of molecule. Each molecule of C contains two different atoms.

Substance D contains one type of positive ion and one type of negative ion.

Substance E contains molecules. Each molecule has two identical atoms joined together.

6 Write formulas, including state symbols, for each of the following. You'll find all the formulas you need somewhere in this topic.

   a gaseous carbon dioxide

   b solid carbon dioxide

   c molten iron

   d oxygen gas

   e a solution of chlorine in water

   f octane vapour

   g solid glucose

   h salty water

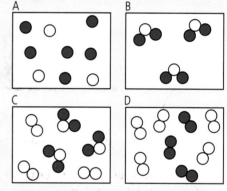

Picture 12

Ideas about atoms

The idea of everything being made of atoms has been around for a long time. But in 1808 John Dalton made a breakthrough.

Going back a bit

The ancient Greeks first thought of the idea of atoms, nearly 2500 years ago. They had no experimental proof for atoms, but they liked the idea because it explained many things about the world.

After the Greeks, the atomic theory was almost forgotten in Europe. But in India, the idea reappeared and was

improved. A thousand years ago, Indian scientists suggested that there are four 'elements' and that each of these has its own atoms. Other substances were made by combining these atoms together.

John Dalton's breakthrough

John Dalton was an English schoolteacher who lived near Manchester. He started teaching in the village school when he was 12! He taught himself science and became a professor in a Manchester college.

Like all good scientists, John Dalton observed things closely. He enjoyed walking in the countryside outside Manchester, and he became interested in the gases around him – air, marsh gas, carbon dioxide, water vapour. He began to think about what they are made from.

Between 1803 and 1808 John Dalton worked out an atomic theory which is the basis of the one we use today. Dalton used the results of his own experiments and those of the French scientist Antoine Lavoisier.

Picture 1 John Dalton.

Here are the key points about Dalton's theory.

- Every chemical element is made up of atoms of a unique type.

- All the atoms in a particular element are identical and have the same mass.

- Chemical compounds are made up of molecules. Molecules are made by joining together atoms.

- All the molecules in a particular compound are identical.

John Dalton invented symbols for the atoms of the elements. His symbols are shown in picture 2. He used these symbols to write formulas for compounds, some of which are shown in picture 3.

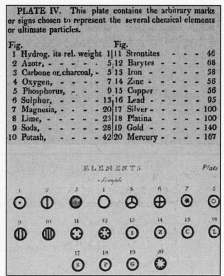

Picture 2 John Dalton's symbols for the elements.

Dalton was the first person to realise the importance of writing chemical formulas. Today we no longer use his symbols, but chemical formulas are still at the heart of chemistry. The first thing a chemist asks on hearing about a new substance is, 'What's its formula?'

1 In what way was John Dalton's atomic theory more scientific than that of the ancient Greeks?

What similarities are there between the ancient Indian atomic theory and John Dalton's theory? What differences are there?

3 Look carefully at Dalton's symbols for the elements in picture 2.

a There are numbers beside each element's name. What do you think they show?

b Are all the substances in the table really elements? If not, name the exceptions.

c Dalton only listed 20 of the 92 elements in his table. Suggest two reasons why he did not list them all. (It will help you to look in the Data Section.)

4 Look at Dalton's compounds in picture 3. For each compound:

a Rewrite Dalton's formula using modern symbols for the elements. Note that 'azote' is now called 'nitrogen';

b Give the formula we use for the compound today (you may need to look it up in the Data Section).

Which formulas did Dalton get wrong?

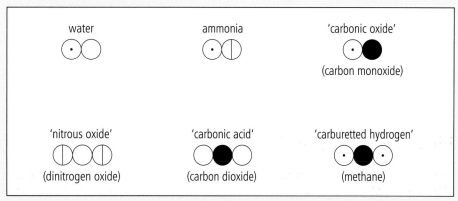

Picture 3 Some of John Dalton's formulas. (The modern names are shown in brackets.)

Picture 1 Methane is a very useful fuel. In this picture a hot, clean methane flame is being used in the manufacture of light bulbs.

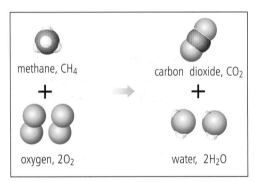

methane, CH_4

$+$

oxygen, $2O_2$

carbon dioxide, CO_2

$+$

water, $2H_2O$

Picture 2 The reaction of methane with oxygen, represented by models. Count up the different types of atoms on each side of the arrow, to check the equation is balanced.

源于碱法造纸、化学纤维、印染、制革、炼油等工业污水。天然水体中的无机悬浮物如粘土和各种矿物可以跟废水中的酸碱成分起化学反应而生成盐类。如：

$$H_2SO_4 + CaCO_3 \longrightarrow CaSO_4 + H_2O + CO_2$$

$$2NaOH + SiO_2 \longrightarrow Na_2SiO_3 + H_2O$$

自然环境对污染物都有一定的承受量，即环境容量。水体可以在它的环境容量范围以内，经过水体的物理、化学和生物的作用，使排入的一定数量的污染物质浓度降低，逐步恢复原有的水质，这个过程叫

Picture 3 Chemical equations are an international language.

Cuando al tener lugar la reacción la entidad representiva de un elemento presenta un balance negativo densidad electrónica, se dice que se ha oxidado; en caso contrario, que se ha reducido.

$$C + O_2 \rightarrow CO_2$$

En esta reacción, el carbono se oxida y el oxigeno se reduce.

Understand? Well, perhaps not all of it. But you probably worked out that this extract (from a Spanish chemistry book) is about the reaction of carbon with oxygen to form carbon dioxide.

Throughout the world, chemists use equations like this to describe reactions. It's a truly international language.

WHAT DO CHEMICAL EQUATIONS TELL US?

Picture 1 shows a well known reaction. When natural gas burns, it reacts with oxygen to form carbon dioxide and water. We can write a **word equation** to summarise the reaction:

methane + oxygen → carbon dioxide + water

The substances on the left-hand side are the **reactants**, and the **products** are on the right-hand side.

If we use the **formulas** of the substances instead of their names, we get a different kind of equation.

$$CH_4 + O_2 \rightarrow CO_2 + H_2O$$

This equation is an improvement on the word equation because it gives the formulas of the reactants and products. *But there is one thing wrong with it*. The numbers of atoms do not match up. There are four H atoms on the left and only two on the right. Likewise there are two O atoms on the left and three on the right. This is impossible, because atoms can't be created or destroyed in a reaction.

To put this right we need to look at the *amounts* of the different substances involved in the reaction. Experiments show that for every molecule of methane, *two* molecules of oxygen are used up, forming one molecule of carbon dioxide and two molecules of water. So we need to rewrite the equation like this:

$$CH_4 + 2O_2 \rightarrow CO_2 + 2H_2O$$

The figure 2 in front of the O shows there are two molecules of oxygen involved. Now the numbers of atoms are the same on each side. The equation is said to be **balanced**. Picture 2 shows the reaction using models.

A balanced equation like this tells us a lot. We can see not only what is formed in the reaction, but also the numbers of molecules involved.

Here is another example. You probably know that hydrogen burns in oxygen to form water. The equation for the reaction can be written as:

$$2H_2(g) + O_2(g) \rightarrow 2H_2O(g)$$

This tells us that two molecules of hydrogen combine with one molecule of oxygen to give two molecules of water. Notice that *state symbols* have been included, so we can tell the state of the reactants and products. What do you notice about the state of the water?

HOW TO WRITE BALANCED EQUATIONS

The only way to be sure of the balanced equation for a reaction would be to do experiments. First you need to carry out the reaction to find exactly what the reactants and products are. Then you need to find the numbers of each type of particle reacting.

But chemists write lots of equations, and it isn't possible to do experiments every time. Fortunately, if we know the reactions and products, we can find their formulas and *predict* the equation. Here are the rules for predicting balanced equations.

Rules for predicting balanced equations

STEP 1 Make sure you know what the reactants and products are.
Let's take as an example the burning of magnesium to form magnesium oxide (picture 4).

STEP 2 Write a word equation for the reaction.

$$\text{magnesium} + \text{oxygen} \rightarrow \text{magnesium oxide}$$

STEP 3 Write formulas for elements and compounds.
Remember that gaseous elements like oxygen are diatomic, so we must write O_2, not O. Our example is now:

$$Mg + O_2 \rightarrow MgO$$

STEP 4 Balance the equation.
There must be the same number of each type of atom on both sides. In the equation above there are two O atoms on the left, but only one on the right. To balance the number of O atoms, we need to double the amount of MgO:

$$Mg + O_2 \rightarrow 2MgO$$

But now there are two Mg atoms on the right, and only one on the left. So we need to double the amount of Mg on the left:

$$2Mg + O_2 \rightarrow 2MgO$$

The equation is now balanced, with equal numbers of each type of atom on each side.

Remember that *equations cannot be balanced by altering formulas*. This would create an entirely different substance. You can only balance equations by putting a number in *front* of a formula.

Picture 3   Burning magnesium in a sparkler. What is the equation for the reaction?

Questions

 ICT You will find a word processing application very useful for writing formulas and equations.

1   Propane, C_3H_8, is used as a portable fuel for homes. The following equation represents the burning of propane:
$$C_3H_8(g) + 5O_2(g) \rightarrow 3CO_2(g) + 4H_2O(g)$$

   a   Is propane a solid, a liquid or a gas?

   b   The normal state of water is liquid. Why is it not liquid in this equation?

   c   How many molecules of (i) propane, (ii) oxygen, (iii) carbon dioxide and (iv) water are involved in the reaction?

   d   How many atoms of (i) carbon, (ii) hydrogen and (iii) oxygen are there on (a) the left-hand side and (b) the right-hand side? Can you confirm that the equation is balanced?

2   Butane is present in camping gas. Here are a word equation and a balanced equation representing the burning of butane:

butane + oxygen →
carbon dioxide + water
$$2C_4H_{10}(g) + 13O_2(g) \rightarrow 8CO_2(g) + 10H_2O(g)$$

Write down three things that the balanced equation tells you which you could not find from the word equation.

3   Look at the equation below. Write in words everything that the equation below tells you about the reaction of carbon monoxide (CO) with oxygen.

$$2CO(g) + O_2(g) \rightarrow 2CO_2(g)$$

Write down two things that the equation does not tell you about the reaction.

4   The following equations are not balanced. Write them out and balance them.

   a $Zn + HCl \rightarrow ZnCl_2 + H_2$

   b $Na + H_2O \rightarrow NaOH + H_2$

   c $Fe + Cl_2 \rightarrow FeCl_3$

   d $C_5H_{10} + O_2 \rightarrow CO_2 + H_2O$

5   Write balanced equations for the following reactions. If there are any formulas you don't know, look them up in the Data Section.

   a   carbon + oxygen → carbon dioxide

   b   nitrogen + hydrogen → ammonia

   c   aluminium + oxygen → aluminium oxide

   d   sodium hydroxide + hydrochloric acid → sodium chloride + water

   e   hydrogen + chlorine → hydrogen chloride

6   Each of the following equations is incomplete. Fill in the blanks to complete them.

   a   One of the things that happens to iron when it rusts:
$$_____ + 3O_2 \rightarrow 2Fe_2O_3$$

   b   An important reaction in making fertilisers:

nitrogen + hydrogen → ammonia
$$_____ + 3H_2 \rightarrow 2NH_3$$

   c   The reaction that produces energy from glucose:

glucose + oxygen → carbon dioxide + water
$$C_6H_{12}O_6 + \_\_\_\_\_ \rightarrow \_\_\_\_\_ + 6H_2O$$

Weighing atoms

In this topic we see how to work out the quantities of substances formed in reactions.

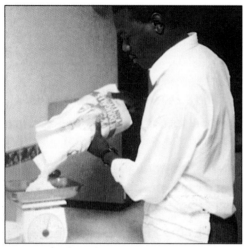

Picture 1 Weighing out the ingredients for a recipe helps make sure you get the right product.

Table 1 Relative atomic masses of some elements.

Element	Symbol	Relative atomic mass
aluminium	Al	27
bromine	Br	80
calcium	Ca	40
carbon	C	12
chlorine	Cl	35.5
copper	Cu	63.5
fluorine	F	19
gold	Au	197
hydrogen	H	1
iron	Fe	56
magnesium	Mg	24
nitrogen	N	14
oxygen	O	16
phosphorus	P	31
potassium	K	39
sodium	Na	23
sulphur	S	32
uranium	U	238
zinc	Zn	65

HOW CAN WE WEIGH ATOMS?

When you use a recipe, you have to measure out the amounts of ingredients. You usually *weigh* them out. Getting the quantities right is important: it helps you get the right product, and the right amount of it.

Chemical reactions are similar. Suppose you manufacture lime by heating limestone (topic D3). If you get an order for 1000 tonnes of lime, what mass of limestone should you heat? You need a kind of chemical recipe. The recipe you have to follow is the *balanced equation* for the reaction, which tells you the number of atoms and molecules involved.

Weighing out flour and sugar is easy enough, but how do you weigh atoms?

Finding the mass of atoms is tricky, because it's impossible to weigh such tiny things directly. But scientists have developed a method for finding the mass of atoms, called mass spectrometry (see page 75). Using this method, we find that the smallest atom, hydrogen, weighs just

$$0.000\,000\,000\,000\,000\,000\,000\,0017\,g \text{ or } 1.7 \times 10^{-24}\,g$$

Or to put it another way, you need getting on for a million million million million hydrogen atoms to make one gram! Even the heaviest atoms are only a hundred times heavier than this.

These numbers are so tiny that a new scale has to be used for measuring the masses of atoms. Instead of working in grams, we say how heavy an atom is compared with other atoms. In other words, we measure the masses of atoms *relative to one another*. This gives numbers that are much easier to handle.

■ Relative atomic masses

The basis of the **relative atomic mass scale** is the carbon atom, which is given a mass of exactly 12.

Relative atomic mass of C = 12.000

Other atoms are weighed relative to this. For example, the mass spectrometer shows that magnesium atoms are twice as heavy as carbon atoms. This means that the relative atomic mass of magnesium is twice that of carbon, which is 24 (picture 2).

In this way we can find the relative atomic masses of all the elements. Table 1 gives the relative atomic masses of some of the common ones, and there is a full list for all the elements in the Data Section.

Picture 2 Magnesium atoms are twice as heavy as carbon atoms, so the relative atomic mass of magnesium is twice that of carbon.

■ How heavy are molecules?

If you know the formula of a molecule, you can work out its **relative formula mass**. You just add up the relative atomic masses of all the atoms in the formula. For example, what is the relative formula mass of water, H_2O?

relative mass of two hydrogen atoms	$= 2 \times 1$
relative mass of one oxygen atom	$= 16$
∴ relative formula mass of water	**= 18**

By a similar calculation, the relative formula mass of carbon dioxide, CO_2, is $(12 + 16 + 16) = 44$. Try working out the relative formula mass of methane, CH_4.

Relative masses are very useful when you need to measure the right numbers of atoms for a chemical reaction.

COUNTING ATOMS

Let's take an example. Suppose you wanted to make some iron sulphide, FeS. This is easily done by heating iron and sulphur together.

$$\text{iron} + \text{sulphur} \rightarrow \text{iron sulphide}$$
$$\text{Fe} + \text{S} \rightarrow \text{FeS}$$

If you were manufacturing iron sulphide, you would want to do it as cheaply as possible. This means using exactly the right quantities of iron and sulphur, so none is left over and wasted.

The equation shows that one atom of iron combines with one atom of sulphur. To get a decent amount of iron sulphide, you will need very large numbers of atoms, but there must always be equal numbers of iron atoms and sulphur atoms. If you take a trillion atoms of iron, you will need a trillion atoms of sulphur. But how could the atoms be counted out? They are so small that counting them out one by one is impossible.

■ The chemist's counting unit

When people count out large numbers of small things, they often use a counting unit. If you buy nails in a hardware shop, you can't buy them singly. They are sold in units of ten, twenty, thirty and so on. And rather than count out the nails separately, the storekeeper might *weigh* them out (picture 3). If you know the mass of ten nails, you can work out the mass of, say, fifty, and weigh them out instead of counting.

Chemists count atoms by weighing, in the same way that storekeepers count nails by weighing. Atoms are far smaller than nails, so the counting unit is much larger. It is in fact

600 000 000 000 000 000 000 000 (6×10^{23}) atoms

This number is used because it turns out that

6×10^{23} atoms of any element have a mass equal to the relative atomic mass of the element in grams.

Some examples will help make this clearer. Using the relative atomic masses in table 1,

6×10^{23} atoms of carbon weigh 12 g
6×10^{23} atoms of hydrogen weigh 1 g
6×10^{23} atoms of oxygen weigh 16 g

The number 6×10^{23} is called the **Avogadro Constant**. This is in honour of the Italian scientist Amadeo Avagadro. The amount of substance that contains 6×10^{23} particles is known as one **mole**.

One mole of an element contains 6×10^{23} atoms. It has a mass equal to the relative atomic mass in grams.

Thus,
one mole of magnesium, Mg, weighs 24 g.
24 g of magnesium contains 6×10^{23} Mg atoms.
12 g of Mg is 0.5 mole, and this amount contains 3×10^{23} Mg atoms.
240 g of Mg is 10 moles, containing 60×10^{23} Mg atoms.

Picture 3 To save counting nails separately, the storekeeper can weigh them out.

Picture 4 This glass contains 18 g of water. This means it contains 6×10^{23} molecules.

If you know the mass of a substance, you can work out the number of moles it contains by dividing the mass by the mass of 1 mole.

$$\text{number of moles} = \frac{\text{mass in grams}}{\text{mass of 1 hole}}$$

The number of moles of a substance has a special name. It is called the **chemical amount**. Picture 5 shows how the chemical amount and the mass of a substance can be interconverted.

Counting molecules

Molecules are counted in just the same way as atoms. For example, the relative formula mass of water, H_2O, is 18. So one mole of water, containing 6×10^{23} H_2O molecules, weighs 18 g.

One mole of a compound contains 6×10^{23} molecules. It has a mass equal to the relative formula mass in grams.

USING MOLES

The mole is a very useful unit. We can use it to measure out known numbers of atoms just by weighing – we don't have to count them.

Let's go back to the example of iron reacting with sulphur to make iron sulphide.

$$Fe + S \rightarrow FeS$$

To make iron sulphide without any waste, we need to be able to weigh out equal numbers of atoms of iron and sulphur. Using relative atomic masses, we know that

56 g of iron contains 6×10^{23} Fe atoms
32 g of sulphur contains 6×10^{23} S atoms

So, to make the iron sulphide we would heat together 56 g of iron and 32 g of sulphur. This would provide equal numbers of iron and sulphur atoms. We would get 56 g + 32 g = 88 g of iron sulphide. If we wanted more or less than 88 g, we could scale the quantities up or down. But the mass of iron and the mass of sulphur must always be in the ratio 56 : 32.

Working out reacting masses

We can use moles to work out the masses involved in chemical reactions, *provided we know the balanced equation for the reaction*.

Look at this example. When you burn charcoal on a barbecue, this reaction takes place

$$\text{carbon} + \text{oxygen} \rightarrow \text{carbon dioxide}$$
$$\text{C} \quad \times \quad \text{O}_2 \quad \rightarrow \quad \text{CO}_2$$

This equation tells us that 1 atom of carbon reacts with 1 molecule of oxygen to form 1 molecule of carbon dioxide.

It also means that 1 *mole* of carbon reacts with 1 *mole* of oxygen to form 1 *mole* of carbon dioxide.

We know the mass of 1 mole of each of these substances: C = 12 g, O_2 = 32 g and CO_2 = 44 g. So these are the masses involved in the reaction.

C	+	O_2	$\rightarrow$	CO_2
1 mole		1 mole		1 mole
12 g		32 g		44 g

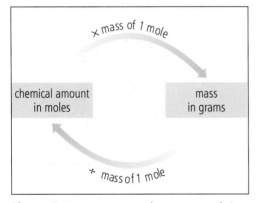

Picture 5 How to convert moles to mass, and vice versa.

In other words, every 12 g of charcoal you burn on the barbecue needs 32 g of oxygen – and makes 44 g of carbon dioxide (picture 6). Here are two more worked examples.

WORKED EXAMPLE 1 – MAKING LIME

Lime is calcium oxide, CaO. It has many uses, including neutralising acid soil. Lime is made by heating limestone, $CaCO_3$. Suppose you heated 100 tonnes of $CaCO_3$. What mass of CaO would you get (picture 7)?

The equation tells us the numbers of moles involved in the reaction. From this we can work out the masses.

$$\text{calcium carbonate} \rightarrow \text{calcium oxide} + \text{carbon dioxide}$$
$$CaCO_3 \rightarrow CaO + CO_2$$
$$\text{1 mole} \qquad \text{1 mole} \qquad \text{1 mole}$$

1 mole of $CaCO_3$ weighs $(40 + 12 + 3 \times 16) = 100$ g
1 mole of CaO weighs $(40 + 16) = 56$ g. So we can write

$$CaCO_3 \rightarrow CaO + CO_2$$
$$\text{1 mole} \qquad \text{1 mole} \qquad \text{1 mole}$$
$$\text{100 g} \qquad \text{56 g}$$

So the equation tells us that 100 g of $CaCO_3$ gives 56 g of CaO.

⇒ 100 tonnes of $CaCO_3$ gives 56 tonnes of CaO

So if you heated 100 tonnes of limestone, you would make 56 tonnes of lime, CaO.

Picture 8 Potters use chemical calculations to get the right quantities for the coloured glaze they use on a pot.

WORKED EXAMPLE 2 – MAKING ALUMINIUM

Aluminium has many uses, including making bicycles, saucepans and aeroplanes. It is made from an ore called bauxite. Purified bauxite is aluminium oxide, Al_2O_3. It is split up into aluminium and oxygen by electrolysis (see topic J1).

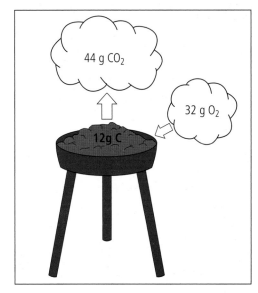

Picture 6 Burning carbon.

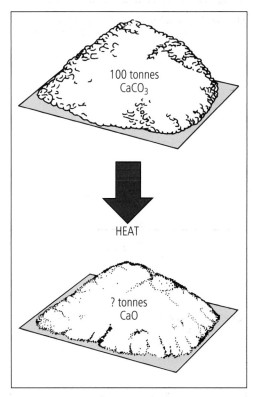

Picture 7 How much calcium oxide can you get from 100 tonnes of calcium carbonate?

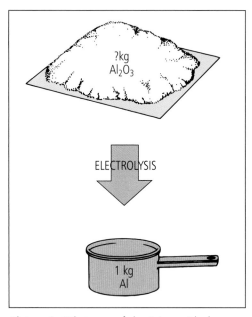

Picture 9 What mass of aluminium oxide do you need to make 1 kg of aluminium?

Here's the problem: what mass of aluminium oxide would you need if you wanted to make 1 kg of aluminium (picture 9)? Once again, the equation tells us the numbers of moles involved in the reaction, and hence the masses.

$$\text{aluminium oxide} \rightarrow \text{aluminium} + \text{oxygen}$$
$$2\,Al_2O_3 \quad \rightarrow \quad 4\,Al \quad + \quad 3O_2$$
$$\text{2 moles} \qquad \text{4 moles} \qquad \text{3 moles}$$

2 moles of Al_2O_3 weigh $2 \times (2 \times 27 + 3 \times 16) = 204$ g
4 moles of Al weigh $4 \times 27 = 108$ g. We can write

$$2\,Al_2O_3 \quad \rightarrow \quad 4\,Al \quad + \quad 3O_2$$
$$\text{2 moles} \quad \rightarrow \quad \text{4 moles} \qquad \text{3 moles}$$
$$\text{204 g} \qquad \text{108 g}$$

So the equation tells us that you can get 108 g of Al from 204 g of Al_2O_3.

$$\Rightarrow \text{you can get 1 g of Al from } \frac{204}{108} \text{ g of Al}$$

$$\Rightarrow \textbf{you can get 1 kg of Al from 1.89 kg of } \mathbf{Al_2O_3}$$

In other words, if you wanted 1 kg of aluminium, you would need to start with 1.89 kg of aluminium oxide.

Questions

 You will find a spreadsheet application helpful for several of these calculations.

Use table 1 to find the relative atomic masses you need to answer these questions.

1 a i) Which element in table 1 has the lightest atoms?

    ii) Which element has the heaviest atoms?

    iii) How many times heavier is the heaviest element compared with the lightest element?

  b How many times heavier is one sulphur atom compared with one oxygen atom?

  c How many hydrogen atoms make up the same mass as one sodium atom?

2 Work out the relative formula mass of each of the following

(a) hydrogen chloride, HCl (b) sulphuric acid, H_2SO_4 (c) carbon monoxide, CO (d) butane, C_4H_{10} (e) glucose, $C_6H_{12}O_6$.

3 What is the mass of 1 mole of each of the following?

(a) magnesium, Mg (b) sulphur dioxide, SO_2 (c) helium, He (d) oxygen, O_2 (e) chlorophyll, $C_{51}H_{72}O_4N_4Mg$.

4 a How many moles of carbon atoms are there in 12 g of carbon, C?

  b i) How many moles of carbon atoms are there in 3 g of carbon?

    ii) How many carbon atoms are there in 3 g of carbon?

    iii) What mass of hydrogen contains the same number of atoms as 3 g of carbon?

  c i) What is the mass of 3 moles of carbon?

    ii) How many carbon atoms are there in 3 moles of carbon?

5 Sulphur burns in air to form sulphur dioxide, SO_2 – one of the main gases responsible for causing acid rain. The object of this question is to find the mass of SO_2 formed when 8 g of S is burned.

$$S + O_2 \rightarrow SO_2$$
$$\underline{\hspace{2em}}\text{ moles} \qquad \underline{\hspace{2em}}\text{ moles}$$
$$\underline{\hspace{2em}}\text{ g} \qquad \underline{\hspace{2em}}\text{ g}$$

  a Fill in the blanks to show the numbers of moles of S and SO_2 involved in the reaction.

  b Fill in the blanks to show the masses involved in the reaction.

  c What mass of SO_2 is formed from 1 g of S?

  d What mass of SO_2 is formed from 8 g of S?

6 Iron is manufactured by reducing iron oxide, Fe_2O_3, in a blast furnace. The reducing agent is carbon monoxide, CO. The object of this question is to find the mass of Fe that could be produced from 16 tonnes of Fe_2O_3.

$$Fe_2O_3 + 3CO \rightarrow 2Fe + 3CO_2$$
$$\underline{\hspace{2em}}\text{ moles} \qquad \underline{\hspace{2em}}\text{ moles}$$
$$\underline{\hspace{2em}}\text{ g} \qquad \underline{\hspace{2em}}\text{ g}$$

  a Fill in the blanks to show the numbers of moles of Fe_2O_3 and Fe involved in the reaction shown in the equation.

  b Fill in the blanks to show the masses involved in the reaction.

  c What mass of Fe is formed from 1 g of Fe_2O_3?

  d What mass of Fe is formed from 16 g of Fe_2O_3?

  e What mass of Fe is formed from 16 tonnes of Fe_2O_3?

7 Ammonia is manufactured by the Haber Process. This involves the reaction of nitrogen with hydrogen.

$$\text{nitrogen} + \text{hydrogen} \rightarrow \text{ammonia}$$
$$N_2 + 3H_2 \rightarrow 2NH_3$$

What mass of (i) nitrogen (ii) hydrogen is needed to make 34 g of ammonia?

The mass spectrometer

Scientists measure the mass of atoms using a mass spectrometer. There are many different types but they all work on the same principle. Picture 1 shows a simplified diagram of a mass spectrometer. There are three main parts to any mass spectrometer (picture 2).

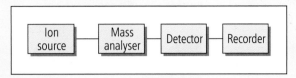

Picture 1 A block diagram of a mass spectrometer.

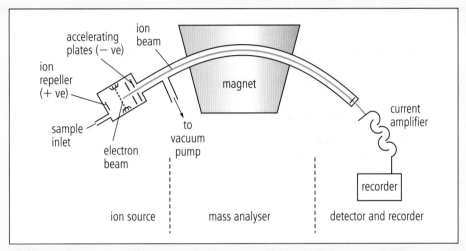

Picture 2 The parts of a mass spectrometer.

The ion source

1 A sample of the element is introduced into the spectrometer and vaporised.

2 The atoms of the gas are converted into ions by bombardment with high energy electrons. This bombardment knocks electrons out of the atoms to create positive ions.

3 The ions are accelerated out of the ion source by attraction to negatively charged plates.

The analyser

4 The ions pass into the analyser. Here they are deflected by the magnetic field created by an electromagnet. Lighter ions are deflected more than heavy ions. By altering the strength of the magnetic field, different ions are allowed to pass into the detector depending on their mass.

The detector and recorder

5 The detector produces a current when hit by the ions. This current is amplified and fed to a computer. The information collected by the computer can be displayed on screen or used to produce a printed copy called a mass spectrum. Picture 3 shows a mass spectrum. Each line corresponds to an ion of a particular mass. The more abundant the ion in the sample, the higher the line.

Inside is a vacuum to stop air molecules getting in the way.

We can use a mass spectrometer to:

- measure mass of atoms
- identify complex molecules. The molecules break into fragments which can be identified.

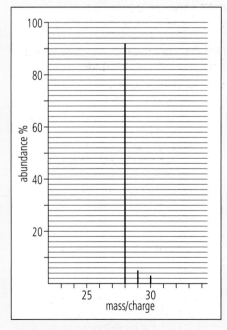

Picture 3 A mass spectrum.

Chemical calculations

We can use relative atomic masses to carry out many different kinds of chemical calculations.

Picture 1 Emeralds are the most expensive of all gemstones. They are made from the mineral beryl, formula $Be_3Al_2Si_6O_{18}$.

FINDING FORMULAS

Picture 1 shows emeralds. Emeralds are made from a mineral called *beryl*, formula $Be_3Al_2Si_6O_{18}$. But how do we know this is its formula?

Today there are many ways to find the formula of a substance, using instruments such as the mass spectrometer on the previous page. But most of the formulas we use were originally found by measuring the masses of the different elements in a compound. If we know the masses of the different elements present, we can work out the relative numbers of moles, and hence find the formula.

■ Finding formulas from reacting masses

WORKED EXAMPLE 1 – MAGNESIUM OXIDE

You may know the formula of magnesium oxide: it is MgO. Chemists first found this formula by burning magnesium and finding the mass of magnesium and oxygen that combine together.

For example, suppose we burn 0.24 g of magnesium, and we find that 0.40 g of magnesium oxide is formed. This means that 0.24 g Mg combines with (0.40 g – 0.24 g) = 0.16 g O. We can use these results to find the formula of magnesium oxide. The steps are:

1 **Find the masses of elements combined.**
2 **Find the numbers of moles of each element.**
3 **Find the simplest whole-number ratio of the number of moles.**

1 Find the masses of elements combined
    0.24 g Mg combine with 0.16 g O

2 Find the number of moles of each element
    Mg = 24, O = 16
    0.24 g Mg = 0.24/24 = 0.01 mol Mg
    0.16 g O = 0.16/16 = 0.01 mol O

3 Find the simplest whole-number ratio of the number of moles
    There are 0.01 mol Mg and 0.01 mol O
    ⇒ Simplest ratio = 1 : 1, so there is 1 mole of Mg for each 1 mole of O. So the formula is **MgO**.

Table 1 shows a simple way of setting out this calculation. Picture 2 illustrates the calculation in a different way.

Table 1 Finding the formula of magnesium oxide.

	Mg	**O**
Masses combined	0.24 g	0.16 g
Mass of 1 mole	24 g	16 g
⇒ Amount in moles	0.01	0.01
⇒ Simplest ratio	1	1
⇒ Formula	**MgO**	

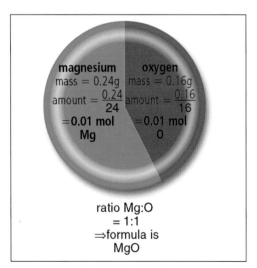

Picture 2 Finding the formula of magnesium oxide. The pie chart indicates the masses of Mg and O in the compound.

WORKED EXAMPLE 2 – PHOSPHORUS OXIDE

Phosphorus burns in air, producing clouds of white phosphorus oxide (picture 3). What is the formula of this oxide?

In an experiment to find out, 0.31 g of phosphorus was burned in plenty of air. It formed 0.71 g of phosphorus oxide.

We can use the results of the experiment to find the masses combined.

Mass of P = 0.31 g
Mass of O = (0.71–0.31 g) = 0.40 g

Table 2 shows the working. Notice that the ratio of the number of moles of phosphorus and oxygen is $0.01 : 0.025$. This simplifies to $1 : 2.5$, but we convert this to $2 : 5$ because it is not possible to have a half-atom of oxygen.

Empirical formula and molecular formula

In example 2, we found that the formula of phosphorus oxide is P_2O_5. The relative mass of P_2O_5 comes to $(2 \times 31 + 5 \times 16) = 142$. However, when we actually measure the relative molecular mass of phosphorus oxide, we find it is 284 – twice as much. This means that the actual formula of phosphorus oxide molecules must be $(P_2O_5)_2$, in other words P_4O_{10}.

The formula P_2O_5 is the *simplest* formula for phosphorus oxide. We call this the **empirical formula**. The formula of actual phosphorus oxide molecules is P_4O_{10} – we call this the **molecular formula**. It means that each molecule of phosphorus oxide contains 4 P atoms and 10 O atoms.

Once you know the empirical formula of a molecular substance, you can always find its molecular formula if you know the relative molecular mass. Here is another example.

Empirical formula of ethene (from experiments) = **CH₂**

M_r of ethene = 28   CH₂ has a M_r of 14

So **molecular formula** must be = (CH₂)₂ = **C₂H₄**

PERCENTAGE COMPOSITION

If we know the formula of a substance, we can find out the mass of each element in it. From this we can find its percentage composition by mass.

Worked example – ammonium nitrate

Ammonium nitrate is an important nitrogenous fertiliser – but what percentage of it is actually nitrogen?

The steps in the calculation are:

1 **Find the relative molecular mass of the compound.**
2 **Find the total relative mass of the element you are interested in.**
3 **Turn the mass of the element into a percentage of the total mass.**

1 Find the relative molecular mass of the compound
The formula of ammonium nitrate is NH_4NO_3, so its relative molecular mass is 80.

Table 2 Finding the formula of phosphorus oxide.

	P	O
Masses combined	0.31 g	0.4 g
Mass of 1 mole	31 g	16 g
⇒ Number of moles	0.01	0.025
⇒ Simplest ratio	2	5
⇒ Formula	P_2O_5	

Picture 3 Phosphorus burns to produce clouds of white phosphorus oxide.

Picture 4   At ordinary room temperature, 1 mole of any gas has a volume of about 24 dm³. This is about the volume of a large biscuit tin.

Picture 5   The numbers on a fertiliser bag tell you the proportions of nitrogen, phosphorus and potassium it contains.

Measuring volumes

In this book we use the cubic decimetre (dm³) for measuring volumes of gases and solutions. A cubic decimetre is also called a litre (l). For smaller volumes, we use the cubic centimetre (cm³).
1 dm³ = 1000 cm³.

Picture 6   This camping stove contains 190 g of butane, C_4H_{10}. What volume of carbon dioxide will be formed when all the butane burns (see question 11 on page 81)?

2   *Find the total relative mass of the element you are interested in*
NH_4NO_3 contains two N atoms, total relevant mass $2 \times 14 = 28$.

3   *Turn the mass of the element into a percentage of the relative molecular mass.*

$$\frac{\text{relative mass of N}}{\text{relative molecular mass of } NH_4NO_3} = \frac{28}{80} = 0.35 = \textbf{35\%}$$

So NH_4NO_3 is 35% N by mass.

CALCULATIONS WITH GASES

The volume of a mole of a gas

Many chemical reactions involve gases, and we often want to find the quantities of gases taking part. We could do this by working out the *mass* of gas involved, as shown in topic C5. But weighing gases can be tricky, and it is often easier to measure the *volume* of a gas instead.

Fortunately, there is a simple rule about the volume of gases.

One mole of a gas has approximately the same volume at a given temperature and pressure, whatever the gas.

What is this volume? It depends on the temperature and pressure, of course. At ordinary room temperature, **1 mole of a gas has a volume of about 24 dm³ (24 litres)** (picture 4).

This rule applies to *all* gases. This makes it easy to convert moles of gas into volumes, and volumes into moles. The general formula to use is

volume of gas in dm³ = amount of gas in moles × 24 dm³

We can use this handy piece of information to calculate the volumes of gases involved in reactions.

WORKED EXAMPLE: SULPHUR DIOXIDE FROM SULPHUR

Many fuels contain traces of sulphur compounds. This is a problem because the sulphur forms polluting sulphur dioxide when the fuel burns.

Suppose 8 g of sulphur burns. What volume of sulphur dioxide would be formed, measured at room temperature?

First, we need to work out the number of moles of sulphur dioxide formed. We can work this out from the equation for the reaction.

$$\begin{array}{ccccc}
\text{sulphur} & + & \text{oxygen} & \rightarrow & \text{sulphur dioxide} \\
S(s) & + & O_2\,(g) & \rightarrow & SO_2\,(g) \\
1\ \text{mole} & & 1\ \text{mole} & & 1\ \text{mole}
\end{array}$$

8 g sulphur = 8/32 = 0.25 mol sulphur
1 mole of S forms 1 mole of SO_2.
So 0.25 mol S forms 0.25 mol SO_2
0.25 mol SO_2 has a volume of 0.25 × 24 dm^3 = **6 dm³** at room temperature.

CALCULATIONS WITH SOLUTIONS

Many chemical reactions are carried out in solution. We normally measure out a solution by *volume*. To work out the volume of a solution involved in a reaction, we need to know its concentration.

■ The concentration of solutions

The **concentration** of a solution means the amount of solute dissolved in a certain volume of solvent. We normally measure concentration in moles per dm^3 (mol/dm^3). A solution of copper sulphate of concentration 1 mol/dm^3 contains 1 mole of $CuSO_4$ dissolved in 1 dm^3 of solution (picture 7). A solution of concentration 2 mol/dm^3 contains 2 moles of $CuSO_4$ in 1 dm^3 of solution.

Once we know the concentration of the solution, we can work out the amount of solute in a particular volume.

Amount in moles

= concentration of solution in mol/dm³ × volume of solution in dm³

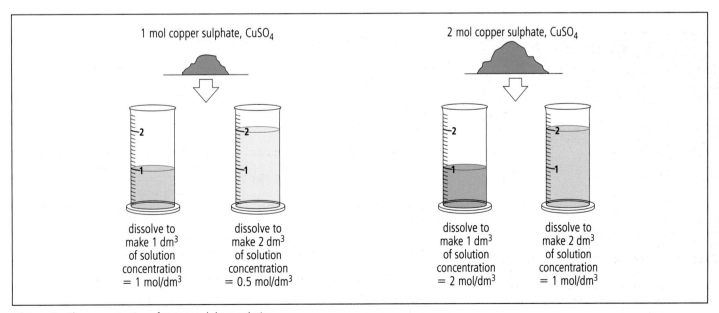

Picture 7   The concentration of copper sulphate solutions.

Picture 8   This analytical chemist is working out the results after carrying out a titration.

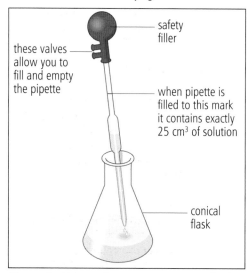

Picture 9   Using a pipette to measure out a fixed volume of solution. This pipette measures 25 cm³, but you can get pipettes of different volumes.

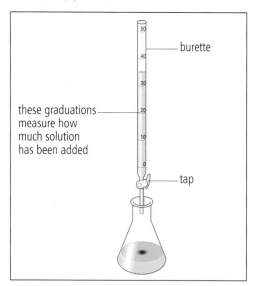

Picture 10   Using a burette to measure out a varying volume of solution. The burette is graduated in cubic centimetres.

WORKED EXAMPLE – HYDROCHLORIC ACID

The dilute hydrochloric acid used in school laboratories usually has a concentration of 2 mol/dm³. How many moles of HCl are there in 250 cm³ of this acid?

$$250 \text{ cm}^3 = 0.25 \text{ dm}^3$$

Amount in moles = concentration of solution in mol/dm³ × volume of solution in dm³
$$\Rightarrow \text{Amount in moles} = 2 \text{ mol/dm}^3 \times 0.25 \text{ dm}^3 = \mathbf{0.5 \ mol}$$

■ Titration

Vinegar contains ethanoic acid, CH_3COOH (sometimes called acetic acid). Suppose you wanted to work out the concentration of ethanoic acid in vinegar. You can take a solution of an alkali whose concentration you already know, and use a **titration** to find the volumes of acid and alkali that react together.

You can do a titration (picture 8) whenever you want to measure the reacting volumes of solutions.

First, you measure a fixed volume of one of the solutions into a conical flask. You do this using a **pipette** (picture 9).

Then you add an indicator to the solution in the conical flask. The indicator will change colour when the reaction between the two solutions is complete. Now you run the second solution from a **burette** into the conical flask (picture 10). You go on adding the solution from the burette until the indicator changes colour. This is called the **end-point**. You read off the volume of the solution in the burette at the end-point.

WORKED EXAMPLE 1: SULPHURIC ACID AND SODIUM HYDROXIDE

A student wanted to find how many moles of sodium hydroxide are needed to neutralise 1 mole of sulphuric acid.

She used a pipette to put 25 cm³ of sulphuric acid of concentration 0.1 mol/dm³ into a conical flask. She added an indicator. She filled a burette with sodium hydroxide solution of concentration 0.1 mol/dm³. She ran this solution into the conical flask until the indicator just changed colour. She read off the volume on the burette and found she had added 50.0 cm³ of sodium hydroxide solution.

Quantities used: 50.0 cm³ (0.05 dm³) of 0.1 mol/dm³ NaOH (aq)
25.0 cm³ (0.025 dm³) of 0.1 mol/dm³ H_2SO_4 (aq)

Amount in moles = concentration of solution in mol/dm³
× volume of solution in dm³

Amount of NaOH(aq) = 0.1 mol/dm³ × 0.05dm³ = 0.005 mol
Amount of H_2SO_4 (aq) = 0.1 mol/dm³ × 0.025 dm³ = 0.0025 mol

So 0.005 mol NaOH (aq) reacts with 0.0025 mol H_2SO_4 (aq)

So 2 mol NaOH (aq) reacts with 1 mol H_2SO_4 (aq)

WORKED EXAMPLE 2: FINDING THE CONCENTRATION OF A SOLUTION

A student wanted to find the concentration of a solution of hydrochloric acid, HCl. She decided to do a titration using a solution of sodium hydroxide, NaOH. The concentration of the NaOH was 0.2 mol/dm³.

The equation for the reaction of NaOH with HCl is:

$$NaOH + HCl \rightarrow NaCl + H_2O$$

She put 10 cm³ of the HCl in a flask and added a few drops of indicator. She added NaOH solution from a burette. She found 12 cm³ of NaOH were needed to neutralise the acid.

Volume of NaOH used $= 12\ cm^3 = 0.012\ dm^3$

Concentration of NaOH $= 0.2\ mol/dm^3$

Amount in moles $=$ concentration of solution on mol/dm^3
 $\times$ volume of solution in dm^3

Amount of NaOH used $= 0.012\ dm^3 \times 0.2\ mol/dm^3 = 0.0024\ mol$

1 mole of NaOH reacts with 1 mole of HCl

Amount of HCl reacted $= 0.0024\ mol$

$10\ cm^3$ of HCl contains $0.0024\ mol$

$1000\ cm^3$ HCl ($1\ dm^3$) contains $0.24\ mol$

Concentration of HCl $= 0.24\ mol/dm^3$

Questions

 You will find a spreadsheet application useful for several of these calculations.

You can find relative atomic masses in table 1 of the Data Section.

1 Find the empirical formulas of each of the following compounds from the experimental data given.

   a Sodium oxide. In an experiment, 2.3 g of sodium combined with 0.8 g of oxygen.

   b Silicon oxide. In an experiment, 1.4 g of silicon combined with 1.6 g of oxygen.

   c Iron chloride. In an experiment, 1 g of iron combined with 1.9 g of chlorine.

2 A chemist analysed a hydrocarbon X and found that X contained 43 g of C combined with 7.2 g of H.

   a Work out the empirical formula of the hydrocarbon X.

   b The relative molecular mass of X was found to be 42. What is the molecular formula of X?

3 a The molecular formula of glucose is $C_6H_{12}O_6$. What is the empirical formula of glucose?

   b What is the percentage by mass of C, H and O in glucose?

4 Look at picture 1. What is the percentage by mass of beryllium, Be, in beryl?

5 Urea is an important nitrogenous fertiliser. The formula of urea is CON_2H_4. What is the percentage by mass of nitrogen in urea? Compare your answer with the percentage of nitrogen in ammonium nitrate (see the worked example on page 78) and comment.

6 What is the volume, at ordinary room temperature and pressure, of each of the following?

   (a) $0.1\ mol\ CO_2(g)$, (b) $2\ mol\ CH_4(g)$, (c) $0.5\ mol\ NH_3(g)$, (d) $10\ mol\ N_2(g)$.

7 What is the number of moles of each of the following gases, measured at room temperature and pressure?

   (a) $1.2\ dm^3$ of $O_2(g)$, (b) $12\ dm^3$ of $CO(g)$, (c) $1\ dm^3$ of $H_2(g)$, (d) $100\ dm^3$ of He(g).

8 1 g of calcium carbonate ($CaCO_3$) is heated strongly. All the $CaCO_3$ decomposes.

   calcium carbonate $\rightarrow$ calcium oxide + carbon dioxide

   $CaCO_3(s) \rightarrow CaO(s) + CO_2(g)$

   What volume of carbon dioxide, measured at room temperature and pressure, would be formed?

9 $2.4\ dm^3$ of hydrogen (measured at room temperature and pressure) is burned in excess oxygen. What mass of water is formed?

10 You eat the equivalent of about 600 g of glucose a day. This glucose is used in respiration, and forms carbon dioxide.

   a Write the equation for respiration (look at page 218 if necessary)

   b Calculate the number of moles of carbon dioxide formed from 600 g of glucose.

   c Calculate the approximate volume of carbon dioxide you breathe out in a day.

11 Look at picture 6.

   a Write an equation for the complete combustion of butane to form carbon dioxide and water.

   b What volume of carbon dioxide, measured at room temperature and pressure, will be formed when all the 190 g of butane burns?

   c What volume of oxygen, measured at room temperature and pressure, will be needed to burn all the butane?

12 How many moles of

   a KOH are there in $1\ dm^3$ of KOH(aq) of concentration $0.5\ mol/dm^3$?

   b HCl are there in $100\ cm^3$ of HCl(aq) of concentration $2\ mol/dm^3$?

   c H_2SO_4 are there in $25\ cm3$ of H_2SO_4(aq) of concentration $0.1\ mol/dm^3$?

13 What volume of

   a HNO_3(aq) of concentration $2\ mol/dm^3$ contains 1 mol of HNO_3?

   b NaOH(aq) of concentration $0.1\ mol/dm^3$ contains 1 mol of NaOH?

   c NH_3(aq) of concentration $0.5\ mol/dm^3$ contains 0.001 mol of NH_3?

14 William was investigating citric acid, the acid found in lemons. He wanted to find how many moles of sodium hydroxide, NaOH react with 1 mole of citric acid.

   He made a solution of citric acid of concentration $0.1\ mol/dm^3$. He put exactly $10\ cm^3$ of this solution into a conical flask and added an indicator. He filled a burette with NaOH(aq) of concentration $0.1\ mol/dm^3$. He then titrated the citric acid with the NaOH(aq), and found that $30\ cm^3$ of NaOH(aq) were needed to reach the end-point.

   a What piece of equipment should William use to measure out exactly $10\ cm^3$ of citric acid solution?

   b How would he know when the end-point had been reached?

   c Use the results to work out how many moles of sodium hydroxide react with 1 mole of citric acid.

The structure of substances

Atoms join together to form structures. The properties of a substance depend on its structure.

Picture 1

Picture 2 Like scaffolding, atoms, molecules and ions form structures.

WHAT ARE STRUCTURES?

Sand and water are very different substances (picture 1). Why is the sand a hard and gritty solid, but water a liquid? It's because of their different structures.

Scaffolding is a structure (picture 2). The way it is joined together makes it strong and rigid – which is what you want when you're working 30 metres above the street.

In this topic we shall be looking at much smaller structures, made of atoms, molecules and ions. But the idea is the same. The way the structure is joined together decides the properties of the substance.

■ Working with models

Models are an essential part of science. Models help us to think about the way things work. The kinetic theory is a model – a mental model that explains a lot about the behaviour of matter.

In this topic we'll be looking at a different kind of model. To represent structures, we use **atomic** and **molecular models**. You can build these models yourself, as shown in pictures 3a and 3b. You can also show the models by drawings, as in pictures 3c and 3d.

Pictures 3a and 3c are the closest to the way we believe a water molecule really is. They are called **space-filling** models, because they show all the space that is occupied by oxygen and hydrogen atoms.

Picture 3b is called a **ball-and-stick** model. This kind of model is sometimes useful, because it shows the **bonds** that hold the atoms together. Picture 3d is a quick and simple way of drawing a ball-and-stick model.

A LOOK AT SOME STRUCTURES

Picture 3 shows single water molecules. In fact, water is made of vast numbers of these molecules. To understand the structure of water, we need to see how the molecules look when there are many of them together. Today, we know the structures of many substances, even though their atoms are far too small to see. They have been investigated using a method called **X-ray diffraction**. There is more about this method in *Believing without seeing* on page 87.

THE STRUCTURE OF WATER

Picture 4 shows how we think water molecules look in liquid water. Notice these points:

- We have used a space-filling model to represent the water structure.

- The water molecules are arranged in a fairly random way. This is typical of the situation in a liquid.

- *Within* a water molecule, the atoms are bonded strongly together. But *between* the molecules, there are no strong bonds to hold them together. It does not need much energy to separate the molecules completely and turn the liquid water to a gas – steam. Just a little heating is enough. In other words, water has a fairly low boiling point.

Water has a simple **molecular structure**. A simple molecular structure contains small molecules. Within the molecules, the atoms are held together by strong bonds. These are called **covalent** bonds, and there is more about them in topic J6.

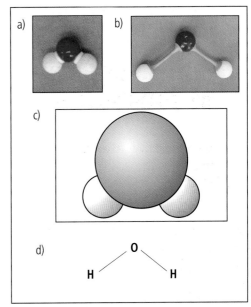

Picture 3 Different ways of showing a water molecule. Oxygen atoms are red, hydrogen atoms are white.
(a) Space-filling model built from a kit.
(b) Ball-and-stick model built from a kit.
(c) Space-filling drawing.
(d) Simple drawing.

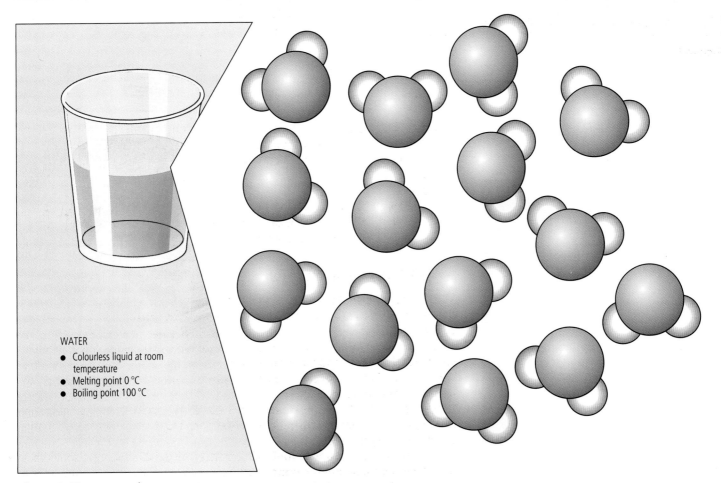

WATER
- Colourless liquid at room temperature
- Melting point 0 °C
- Boiling point 100 °C

Picture 4 The structure of water.

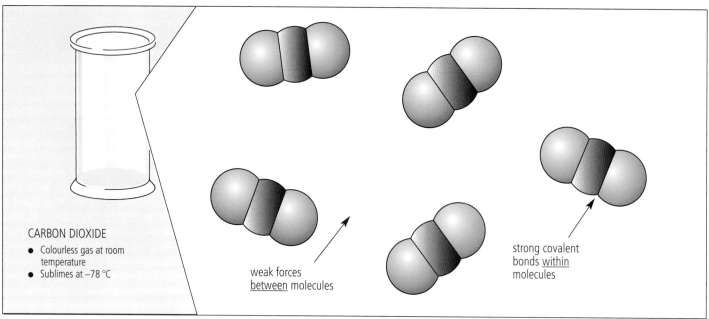

CARBON DIOXIDE
- Colourless gas at room temperature
- Sublimes at −78 °C

weak forces _between_ molecules

strong covalent bonds _within_ molecules

Picture 5 The structure of carbon dioxide. Carbon atoms are black, oxygen atoms are red.

But between the molecules there are only weak forces holding them together. This is illustrated in picture 5, which shows another substance with a molecular structure: carbon dioxide.

▇ The structure of sand

Sand is not at all like water. It feels hard and gritty and is difficult to melt. Judging from its properties, it has a different structure from water.

Before we can talk about the structure of sand, we need to know what sand is made of. Pure sand is mainly made of a mineral called **quartz**. Quartz is silicon oxide, SiO_2. It sometimes occurs as large crystals with beautifully regular shapes (picture 6). But more often it is found in a powdered state, which is sand.

Picture 7 shows the structure of quartz.

Notice these points about the structure.

- We have used a ball-and-stick model rather than a space-filling one. This is so you can see inside the structure clearly.
- The structure is very regular. Every Si atom (grey) is joined to four O atoms (red) by strong covalent bonds. Every O atom is joined to two Si atoms. This arrangement goes on continuously. It holds the Si and O atoms together in a strong, rigid structure – rather like scaffolding. This is why sand is so hard and difficult to melt. It needs a lot of energy to break apart the strongly bonded Si and O atoms.

The structure of sand, SiO_2, is called a **giant structure**. In a giant structure, the atoms are all strongly bonded together in a vast network that goes on indefinitely. Notice how different the structure of SiO_2 is from the simple molecular structure of CO_2 shown in picture 5. These two substances have a similar formula: the only difference is that one has Si atoms instead of C atoms. But their structures are completely different, and so are their properties. CO_2 is a simple molecular structure, SiO_2 is a giant structure. As a result, CO_2 is a gas, but SiO_2 is a hard solid.

Many of the rocks that the earth is made from are based on the SiO_2 structure in picture 7. These giant silicate structures make rocks hard and strong.

There are several different types of giant structure. Some contain atoms, some contain ions. We look in more detail at the different types in the next topic.

Picture 6 Crystals of quartz.

SAND (QUARTZ)

- hard, solid at room temperature
- melting point 1610 °C
- boiling point 2230 °C

Picture 7 The structure of quartz, SiO_2. Silicon atoms are shown in grey, oxygen atoms in red.

COMPARING SIMPLE MOLECULAR AND GIANT STRUCTURES

Both elements and compounds can have simple molecular or giant structures..

The strength of a structure is decided by the strength of the bonds in it. In a giant structure, the atoms are all bonded together strongly, and the structure is difficult to break up. This gives a strong substance that is difficult to melt or boil. The substance will be a solid, and probably hard, like SiO_2 in sand.

In a simple molecular structure, some of the bonds – the bonds *between* the molecules – are weak. This makes the structure weaker. It tends to fall apart more easily. This gives a substance that is easy to melt or boil – like water. The substance may be a gas or liquid at room temperature. If it is a solid, it is likely to be soft.

Table 1 summarises the main differences between simple molecular and giant structures.

Table 1 The main differences between simple molecular and giant structures.

	Description of structure structure	Typical properties of substances with this this structure	Examples of substances with
SIMPLE MOLECULAR	Small molecules held together by strong covalent bonds. Only weak forces between the molecules	<ul><li>low melting point and boiling point</li><li>often liquid or gaseous at room temperature</li><li>soft, if solid</li><li>do not conduct electricity</li></ul>	oxygen, O_2 chlorine, Cl_2 iodine, I_2 carbon dioxide, CO_2 water, H_2O
GIANT	Atoms or ions all strongly bonded together in a giant structure (see topic C7 for more details)	<ul><li>high melting point and boiling point</li><li>hard solids</li><li>sometimes conduct electricity</li></ul>	metals sand, SiO_2 diamond, C graphite, C calcium carbonate, $CaCO_3$

Picture 8 Agate, a form of silicon oxide. Impurities give it the blue colour. The giant structure makes agate very hard.

Activity

Building models

The best way to find out about structures is to build models. You will need a model kit for this activity: ball-and-stick models would be best.

1 *Start with carbon atoms only – as many as possible. If you share your atoms with others, you can make a bigger structure. Notice that the C atoms have four holes: this is because carbon forms four covalent* bonds. Use the 'sticks' to join the carbon atoms together. **Rules:** There should be a stick in every hole, and every atom should be joined to as many other atoms as possible.

What shape is your structure? Is it simple molecular or giant? Would you expect this form of carbon to be solid, liquid or gas? Find out the everyday name of the form of carbon you have built.

2 *Now build another structure using carbon and hydrogen atoms. Notice* that the H atoms have one hole: this is because hydrogen forms only one covalent bond. **Rules:** There should be a stick in every hole. C atoms must only be joined to H atoms, and H atoms must only join to C atoms. Go on joining the atoms together until you have used them all up.

What is your structure like? Is it simple molecular or giant? Would you expect this substance to be solid, liquid or gas? Find out the everyday name of the substance you have made.

Questions

1 Fill in the blanks in the passage below. You can use the following words or groups of words: **hardness, giant, low, covalent, melting point, high, continuously, small, weak, boiling point**.

The structure of a substance means the way its atoms, molecules or ions are joined together. The structure of a substance decides properties such as _____ (1) _____, _____ (2) _____ and _____ (3) _____

A simple molecular structure contains _____ (4) _____ molecules. The atoms in these molecules are held together by strong _____ (5) _____ bonds. But between the molecules, the bonds are only _____ (6) _____. This makes the molecules easy to break apart.

In a _____(7)_____ structure, all the atoms are bonded together strongly. The structure goes on _____ (8) _____. The atoms are difficult to break apart, and the structure is strong.

Substances with simple molecular structures tend to have _____ (9) _____ melting points and boiling points. Substances with giant structures tend to have _____ (10) _____ ones.

2 Picture 9 shows the structures of substances A to D.

a Classify each structure as giant or simple molecular.

b Which substance(s) would you expect to be hard solid(s)?

c Which substance is most likely to be a gas?

d Which substance or substances are elements?

3 From what you know of their properties, decide whether each of the following substances has a simple molecular or a giant structure.

a iron

b brick

c ice

d glass

e oil

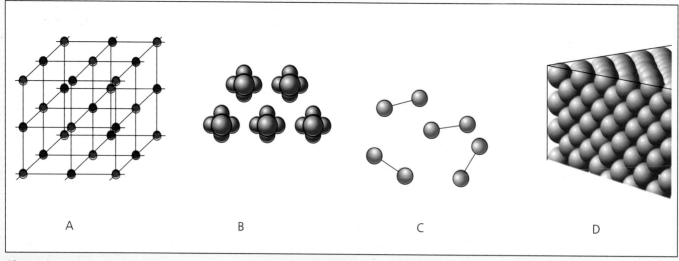

A   B   C   D

Picture 9

Believing without seeing

How do we know about the structure of materials? Why do we believe that the carbon atoms in diamond are arranged in the way shown in picture 3, page 89? Atoms are far too small to see directly, so structures cannot be found out just by looking!

Most of what we know about structures has been found out by **X-ray crystallography**. **X-rays** are a form of electromagnetic radiation with a shorter wavelength than ordinary light. Their short wavelength makes it possible to investigate very small structures and find out much more than you can with light. When you pass X-rays through a crystal, you get a pattern of light and dark spots, called a diffraction pattern. You can't see X-rays directly, but the pattern can be recorded on a photographic film. A crystal gives a particular **diffraction pattern**, depending on its structure. Picture 1 shows the diffraction pattern given by diamond.

Plenty to Bragg about

The method of X-ray crystallography was developed in 1912 by a father and son team of scientists, Sir William and Sir Laurence Bragg. Between them, they found a way to record diffraction patterns, then use them to work out how the atoms or ions are arranged in a crystal. They couldn't actually see how the atoms are arranged, but they found a way to work out the structure from the diffraction pattern. The Braggs

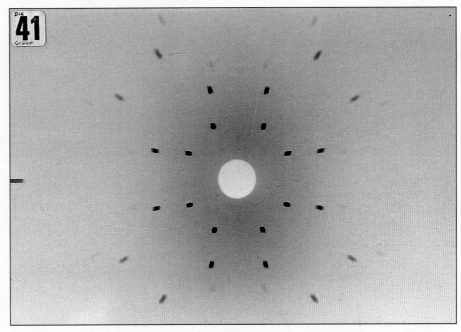

Picture 1 An X-ray diffraction pattern given by diamond.

worked out the structures of many substances, including diamond and sodium chloride. They both received Nobel Prizes for their work.

The method of X-ray crystallography is still used a great deal. It has been used to find the structures of very complex molecules, like proteins and DNA.

A very important piece of X-ray crystallography work was done by Dorothy Hodgkin during the Second World War. Penicillin became very important in the war for treating infected wounds. Scientists needed to know the structure of penicillin so they could make it synthetically. Dorothy Hodgkin used X-ray crystallography to find the structure of penicillin. She received the Nobel Prize in 1964, for her work on the structures of biological substances (picture 3).

1 We cannot see atoms, and we cannot see X-rays. Yet X-rays make it possible to 'see' how the atoms are arranged in diamond. Explain why.

2 Look at these three statements.

'We know the structure of diamond from X-ray crystallography.'

'We know what the surface of Mars is like from photographs taken by spacecraft.'

'I know what I look like because I've seen myself in the mirror.'

For each of these statements, say whether you think it is certain. Explain your answers.

3 Suppose you are Sir Laurence Bragg. You have just worked out the structure of sodium chloride from X-ray crystallography. Another scientist challenges you and says your structure is wrong. What further experiments could you do to show you are right?

Picture 3 This stamp celebrates Dorothy Hodgkin's achievements in science.

Picture 2 Dorothy Hodgkin.

Giant structures

Most of the materials we use have one of three types of giant structure.

Picture 1 Crystals grow in a definite, regular shape. The regular shape of these sugar crystals comes from the regular arrangement of the sugar molecules in them.

In a substance with a giant structure, the atoms or ions are all joined together strongly in a structure that goes on continuously. There are three different ways they can be joined, and these give three different types of giant structure: giant covalent, giant metallic and giant ionic.

In this topic we'll be looking at details of these different types of structure. We know these details from X-ray analysis experiments (see *Believing without seeing* on the previous page).

GIANT COVALENT STRUCTURES

The structure of sand, shown in the last topic, is a giant covalent structure. The atoms in the structure are joined together by strong covalent bonds.

▨ The structure of diamond

The great strength of giant covalent structures is shown perfectly in diamond. Diamond is a form of carbon, although it looks very different from the more common forms like charcoal and graphite. Apart from making beautiful gemstones, diamond is the hardest of all naturally occurring substances. This makes it useful for cutting glass and drilling into hard substances (picture 2).

Picture 3 on the next page shows the structure of diamond. Of course, this is only a tiny part of the structure. There are over 10^{20} atoms in even a tiny diamond. We've used a ball-and-stick model, so you can see clearly how the atoms are joined together. Every C atom is joined to four others in a regular tetrahedral arrangement. This regular, symmetrical arrangement makes the structure very difficult to break apart. To separate one C atom from the structure, you have to break four strong covalent bonds. No wonder diamond is so hard and so difficult to melt.

Like other giant covalent structures, diamond doesn't dissolve in water, because the atoms cannot be broken apart and spread among water molecules. And it doesn't conduct electricity, because there are no charged particles to carry the current.

▨ The structure of graphite

Graphite is a much commoner form of carbon than diamond. Pencil 'lead' is made from graphite. Like diamond, graphite has a giant covalent structure (picture 4 on the next page). But its properties are very different from diamond: graphite is soft and slippery, and it conducts electricity.

(a)

(b)

Picture 2 Both of these 'pencils' contain a form of carbon. (a) is diamond, (b) is graphite.

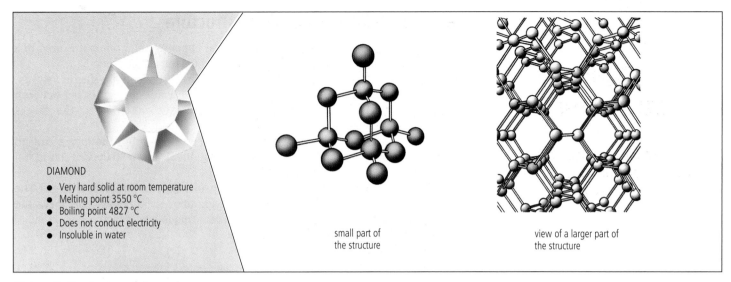

DIAMOND

- Very hard solid at room temperature
- Melting point 3550 °C
- Boiling point 4827 °C
- Does not conduct electricity
- Insoluble in water

small part of
the structure

view of a larger part of
the structure

Picture 3 The structure of diamond.

Picture 4 shows the structure of graphite. You can see it is made up of layers. Within each layer, every carbon atom is joined to three others by strong covalent bonds. This forms a pattern of interlocking hexagonal rings. The carbon atoms are difficult to separate from one another, so graphite, like diamond, has a high melting point.

However, the bonds *between* the layers are weak. The layers are able to slide easily over one another, rather like a pack of cards. This makes graphite soft and slippery. When you write with a pencil, layers of graphite flake off and stick to the paper.

Diamond and graphite are both forms of carbon, despite being very different. Different forms of the same element are called **allotropes**.

In 1990, scientists discovered a third allotrope of carbon, which they named buckminsterfullerene, formula C_{60}. It is a black solid, but it dissolves in organic solvents like hexane to give a red solution. The structure of C_{60} is shown in picture 5. Notice that, even though the molecules are quite big, this is not a giant structure, unlike the other two allotropes of carbon. Its melting point is much lower than for diamond or graphite.

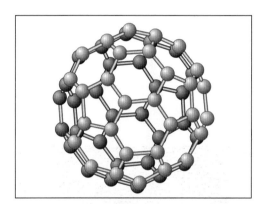

Picture 5 Buckminsterfullerene C_{60}, is the third allotrope of carbon. The molecules are sometimes called 'buckyballs'. Notice the arrangement of the C atoms, like the panels on a soccer ball.

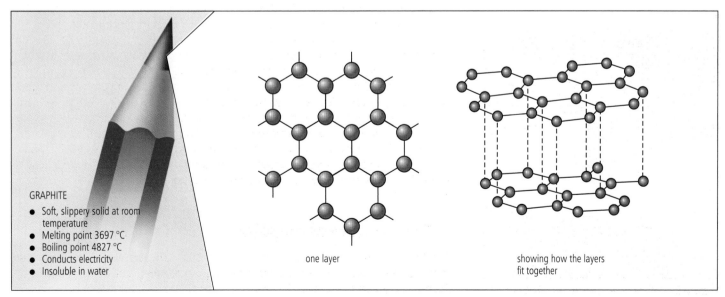

GRAPHITE

- Soft, slippery solid at room temperature
- Melting point 3697 °C
- Boiling point 4827 °C
- Conducts electricity
- Insoluble in water

one layer

showing how the layers
fit together

Picture 4 The structure of graphite.

▰ Clay: another giant layer structure

The pictures on page 2 show the changes that happen to clay when it is fired in a kiln. Before firing, it is soft and crumbly. After, it is hard and strong.

Clay has a giant layer structure (picture 6). The layers contain silicon, oxygen, aluminium and hydrogen atoms. When clay is wet, water molecules get between the layers and lubricate them so they can slide over one another. The clay is slippery and pliable.

When the clay dries, the water molecules evaporate and the layers can no longer slide over one another. But the layers can break apart. So the dry clay is still crumbly.

When dry clay is fired by heating it strongly in a kiln, the structure changes. The atoms in one layer join to atoms in the layers above and below. This locks the layers together, making the clay much harder. This is why a clay pot is so much harder and stronger after it has been fired.

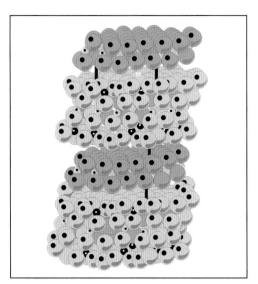

Picture 6 The giant layer structure of one form of clay.

GIANT METALLIC STRUCTURES

We look at the typical properties of metals in topic E1. Most metals are dense and hard, with high melting points. These are useful properties – in fact, without metals our civilisation would literally collapse. But *why* do metals have these special properties? It's because of their particular kind of giant structure.

You may not think of metals as being crystalline, but they are. An ordinary, shiny piece of metal doesn't show crystals. This is because the straight, regular edges of the crystals have been rubbed off by polishing. But if you **etch** the metal by dipping it in acid, the crystals show up and you can see them under the microscope. The crystals show that the metal has a regular structure – a giant metallic structure.

Picture 7 shows the typical metallic structure of copper. It's a space-filling model, and you can see how closely together the atoms of copper are packed. In fact, they are packed as close together as it is possible to be, and this is called a **close-packed** structure. Every atom has 12 other atoms touching it, and this is the maximum number possible. Try building a close-packed structure with model atoms in activity A. Picture 8 shows an example of a close-packed structure in a greengrocer's shop.

Picture 8 Greengrocers sometimes stack fruit in a close-packed structure.

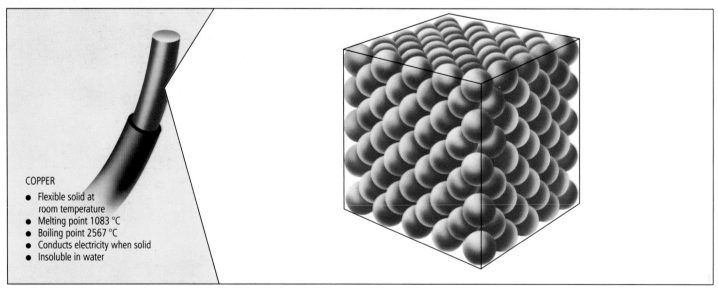

COPPER
- Flexible solid at room temperature
- Melting point 1083 °C
- Boiling point 2567 °C
- Conducts electricity when solid
- Insoluble in water

Picture 7 The structure of copper.

Metallic bonding

Most metals have a close-packed structure, and this accounts for their high density – lots of atoms are packed into a small space. But what holds them together? In a giant *covalent* structure, the atoms are held together by strong covalent bonds. This makes giant covalent substances hard, but brittle. When you try to bend the substance, it shatters. The covalent bonds have a fixed direction, and if you try to change that direction, they break.

Metals are different. They are malleable, not brittle – when you bend a piece of metal, it stays in its new shape, and does not shatter. Metals have a different kind of bond holding their atoms together, called a **metallic** bond. Metallic bonds are strong, but flexible so they don't break when the atoms are moved to a new position.

Here is how the metallic bond works. Metal atoms tend to lose electrons easily. In the solid metal, the atoms lose their electrons and become positive ions. The electrons, no longer held by the atoms, drift freely between the positive ions (picture 9). This structure is sometimes described as a 'lattice of positive ions in a sea of electrons'.

The electrons can move freely between the ions, which explains why metals conduct electricity well. When an electric current flows through a metal wire, the free electrons drift from one end of the wire towards the other. The free-moving electrons also help the metal conduct heat. Heating makes the free electrons jiggle around more energetically. They jostle their neighbours, passing on the energy.

Although the electrons are free, the metal ions themselves are packed together in a regular lattice. This explains why metals form regular crystals.

What happens when you bend a piece of metal?

A piece of metal contains many separate crystals, called **grains**. What would you see if you enlarged the grains so you could see the atoms in one layer of the structure? Picture 10 gives you an idea – there are in fact many more atoms than are shown here. When you apply a force to a metal, the layers of atoms can slip over each other (picture 11). When the layers slip in this way, the metallic bonds between them do not break, but re-form in their new position. So the metal does not shatter: it just takes its new, bent shape.

The slipping of one layer of atoms over another stops when the slip reaches the edge of a crystal grain. The smaller the grains, the shorter the distance that the slip can move. This means that metals with small grains are stronger and harder than metals with large grains.

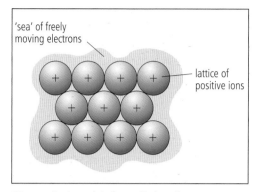

Picture 9 A model of metallic bonding.

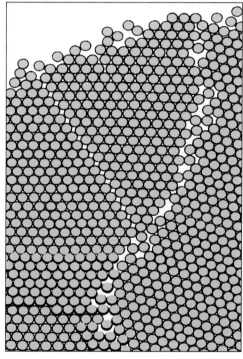

Picture 10 This represents the atoms in one layer of a metal structure. Look for the boundaries between the 'crystal grains'. Each crystal grain would actually contain far more atoms than shown here.

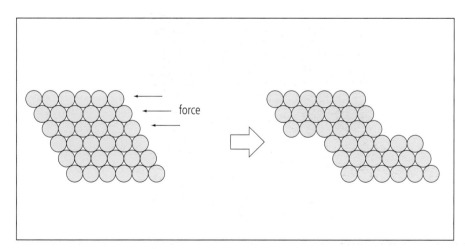

Picture 11 When you apply a force to a metal, the layers of atoms slip over one another.

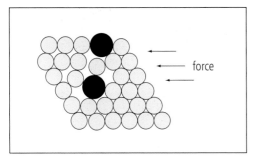

force

Picture 12 The arrangement of metal atoms in an alloy. The black circles are the larger atoms of a metal added to make an alloy.

The size of grains in a piece of metal can be altered by **heat treatment**. If you heat the metal to a high temperature and let it cool slowly, the grains increase in size. This is called **annealing**, and it makes the metal softer and easier to shape. If you heat the metal, then cool it quickly by plunging it into water, you get very small grains. This is called **quenching**, and it makes the metal hard but brittle.

Another way to make a metal harder is by adding a small amount of another metal, in other words making an alloy. Picture 12 represents what happens in an alloy. The different-sized atoms of the second metal disrupt the arrangement of atoms in the metal, making it difficult for the layers to slide over one another.

GIANT IONIC STRUCTURES

Giant ionic structures contain positive and negative ions. Topic J6 tells you more about how ions form. Every positive ion is next to a negative ion, and vice versa. The oppositely charged ions attract one another strongly, and this holds the structure together.

Picture 13 shows the structure of sodium chloride, common salt. Notice that the regular arrangement of Na^+ and Cl^- ions builds up into a cubic shape. This is why crystals of sodium chloride are cubic.

Giant ionic substances are difficult to melt, because of the strong bonds holding the ions together. The size of the ionic charge makes a difference to the melting point. Doubly charged ions like Mg^{2+} and O^{2+} attract each other more strongly than singly charged ions like Na^+ and Cl^-. Because of this, the melting point of MgO (2852 °C) is a lot higher than the melting point of NaCl (801 °C). Despite the strong bonds, ionic substances often dissolve in water. This is because water molecules have small electrical charges on them, and this charge attracts the charged ions.

Giant ionic substances do not conduct electricity when they are solid, because the ions are locked in the structure and cannot move. But when the ions are free

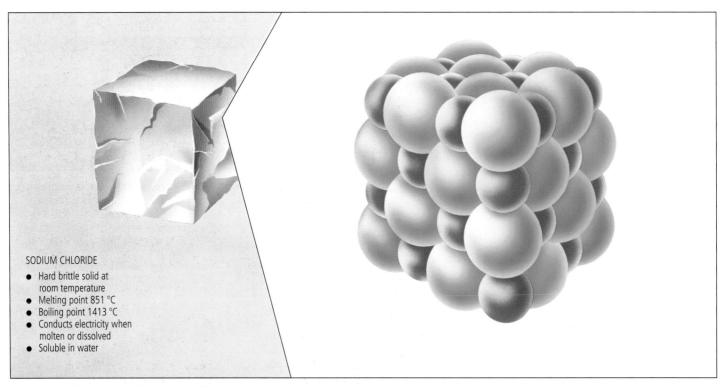

SODIUM CHLORIDE
● Hard brittle solid at room temperature
● Melting point 851 °C
● Boiling point 1413 °C
● Conducts electricity when molten or dissolved
● Soluble in water

Picture 13 The structure of sodium chloride.

to move, they can carry an electric current. So ionic substances conduct electricity when they are molten or dissolved in water. (More about the effect of electricity on ionic substances in topics J1 and J2.)

Many of the minerals found in the earth have giant ionic structures. Limestone ($CaCO_3$) is giant ionic. It is made up of Ca^{2+} and CO_3^{2-} ions. Picture 14 shows another example.

COMPARING THE DIFFERENT TYPES OF GIANT STRUCTURE

Table 1 compares the three different types of giant structure. Substances with giant structures may be elements (like carbon) or compounds (like sodium chloride). Table 1 in the Data Section gives the structures of the different elements.

Picture 14 Sapphire. It has a giant structure, made of aluminium ions and oxide ions. The blue colour is due to impurities. The strong bonds between Al^{3+} and O^{2-} make sapphire hard and difficult to melt.

Table 1 Comparing different giant structures.

	Description of structure	TYPICAL PROPERTIES			
		Melting and boiling point	Hardness	Solubility in water	Electrical conductivity
GIANT COVALENT	Atoms joined by covalent bonds	High	Hard but brittle	Insoluble	Do not conduct (except graphite)
GIANT METALLIC	Atoms joined by metallic bonds	Usually high	Usually hard, but malleable	Insoluble	Conduct when solid
GIANT IONIC	+ and – ions attracting one another	High	Hard but brittle	Often soluble	Conduct when molten or dissolved

Questions

1 Fill in the blanks in the passage below. You can use the following words or groups of words: **water, covalent, flexible, layer, attract, dissolve, strong, positive, negative, brittle, close-packed**.

A giant covalent structure contains a continuous network of atoms joined together by _____(1)_____ bonds. Substances with this kind of structure are hard but _____(2)_____, and difficult to melt. Diamond and graphite both have this kind of structure, but they are different because graphite has a _____(3)_____ structure.

A giant metallic structure contains atoms held together by metallic bonds. The atoms are usually _____(4)_____, with the maximum possible number of atoms fitted into the available space. Metallic bonds are _____(5)_____ but _____(6)_____, so metals are usually hard, but not brittle.

A giant ionic structure contains _____(7)_____ and _____(8)_____ ions arranged regularly. The oppositely charged ions _____(9)_____ one another strongly, so giant ionic

substances are usually hard, but brittle, and difficult to melt. Unlike other giant structures, they often _____(10)_____ in _____(11)_____.

2 Using your knowledge of giant structures, explain why

a Diamond is hard and brittle

b Iron is hard and malleable

c Sodium chloride does not conduct electricity when it is solid, but conducts when it is molten

d Crystals of sodium chloride always grow in a cubic shape.

3 Look at table 1 in the Data Section. This gives the melting points of different elements.

a Write down the symbols of all the elements whose melting points are below −200 °C.

b Write down the symbols of all the elements whose melting points are above 2000 °C. Now look at the structures of elements.

c What are the structures of each of the elements you wrote down in (a)?

d What are the structures of each of the elements you wrote down in (b)?

e Comment on your answers to (c) and (d).

4 Look at table 1 in the Data Section, giving the structures of different elements.

a What is the commonest type of structure among the elements?

b i) Write down the symbols of the elements that have giant covalent structures.

   ii) Now look at the Periodic Table of the elements in the Data Section. What do you notice about the position of elements with giant covalent structures?

c Why do no elements have giant ionic structures?

5 Sodium chloride (salt) and calcium oxide (lime) both have giant ionic structures. Sodium chloride contains Na^+ and Cl^- ions. Calcium oxide contains Ca^{2+} and O^{2-} ions. The melting points of these substances are: sodium chloride 801 °C, calcium oxide 2614 °C.

Explain why calcium oxide's melting point is so much higher than sodium chloride's, even though they both have the same type of structure.

D

Raw materials

Making things from raw materials

Manufacturing means turning raw materials into valuable things. But there are costs.

Look around you. Can you see anything that has *not* been manufactured?

Tables, walls, clothes, paints, food ... all have been manufactured in some way from raw materials. Most manufacturing processes use chemical reactions to convert raw materials into things that are more useful. We make bleach from salt, glass from limestone, fertilisers from air and computer chips from sand.

WHERE DO WE GET RAW MATERIALS FROM?

Picture 1 shows the major sources of the raw materials used by humans. We get raw materials from:

The Earth, which provides rocks, minerals and fossil fuels.
The air, which provides vital gases.
The sea, which provides water and minerals.
Living things, which provide food, clothing fibres and wood.

THE COST OF MANUFACTURE

Manufacturing involves turning raw materials into products that are more useful – and more valuable.

Take an example. The other day I bought a washing-up bowl which cost £2.50. The bowl is made from polythene. Polythene is manufactured from ethene, and ethene is manufactured from crude oil. The oil was the raw material needed to make the bowl. To make the bowl needed 5 kg of oil, which cost only £0.80. (Of course, the 5 kg of crude oil produced several other products as well as the polythene for the bowl.)

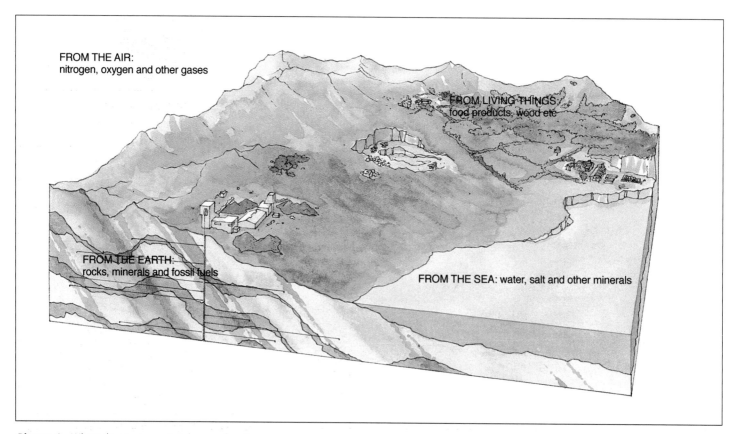

Picture 1 Where do our raw materials come from?

Turning the oil into a bowl has **added value** to the oil, as you can see from picture 2. The bowl is more valuable than the oil it came from – both in terms of its price and its usefulness. Which would you find more useful – a washing-up bowl or 5 kg of crude oil?

But you don't get the extra value without a cost. Picture 3 shows some of the costs that are involved in manufacturing things. All manufacturing processes need **energy** to drive them along. They need **people** to do the work. And they need **machines** and **buildings**. The cost of all these things make up the **economic cost** of the manufacturing process – the cost in money. But there is another cost to be counted.

■ The environmental cost

All manufacturing processes have some effect on the environment and on people's lives. This is a different kind of cost, but like the economic cost we need to keep it as low as possible. For every process, we have to consider:

People's health and safety, particularly the people who work in the factory or live nearby.
Pollution of the environment by the manufacturing process.
Damage to the landscape and to the habitats of wildlife.
Depletion of resources – using up fossil fuels and raw materials, especially those that are **non-renewable** and cannot be replaced.

These four factors make up the **environmental cost** of a product (picture 4). We will come back to them in other topics in this section.

When you buy a product, you always look to see its cost – its economic cost. Then you decide whether its value is worth the cost.

Try thinking of its environmental cost too. It's much less easy to find out, but it's just as important.

We'll come back to this idea in other topics in this section.

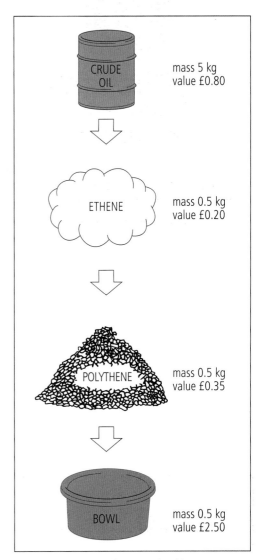

Picture 2 Adding value to crude oil by turning it into washing-up bowls.

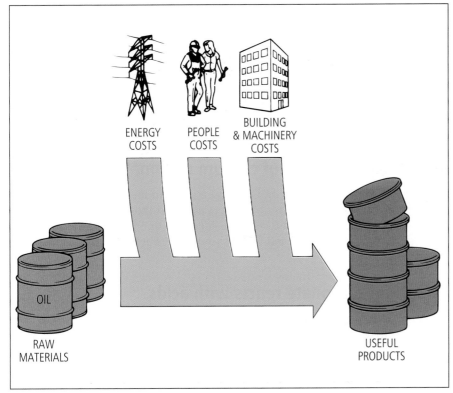

Picture 3 The main economic costs of manufacture.

Picture 4 The economic and environmental costs of a product.

Limestone

Limestone is one of the most valuable raw materials of all.

Picture 1 Limestone country in the Pennines.

Limestone gives us some of the most beautiful country in Britain. The Derbyshire Peaks, the Mendip Hills, the Sussex Downs, the Yorkshire Dales – all are made of limestone, or chalk, which is a form of limestone.

As well as giving beautiful countryside, limestone is a very useful raw material. And that means there are some difficult decisions to make when it comes to quarrying limestone.

THE PROPERTIES OF LIMESTONE

Limestone is calcium carbonate, $CaCO_3$. The calcium carbonate you find in the laboratory is a white powder, but limestone comes out of the ground in hard lumps. Some forms of limestone are hard enough to be used for building stone and aggregate.

Aggregate is crushed stone used in construction. Limestone aggregate is popular for making roads (picture 2). Some people feel it is a waste of limestone to use it for aggregate, because other rocks would do just as well.

■ Chemical reactions of calcium carbonate

We might be able to use other rocks as aggregate, but there is no substitute for limestone as a source of calcium carbonate. Calcium carbonate is one of the most important raw materials for the chemical industry. Understanding its chemical reactions helps you to understand its uses – and also why limestone scenery is so spectacular.

■ Calcium carbonate reacts with acids

All carbonates react with acid to give carbon dioxide, water and a salt. The carbonate 'fizzes' and dissolves when the acid is added. For example, with hydrochloric acid:

Picture 2 Limestone aggregate is used as the base for many roads, before the tarmac surface is laid on top.

calcium carbonate	+	hydrochloric acid	→	calcium chloride	+	carbon dioxide	+	water
$CaCO_3(s)$	+	$2\,HCl\,(aq)$	→	$CaCl_2(aq)$	+	$CO_2(g)$	+	$H_2O(l)$

In this reaction, the calcium carbonate neutralises the acid. Because of this property, the soil in limestone country is neutral or slightly alkaline. This is why such a variety of wild plants grow in limestone country.

Even weak acids will react with calcium carbonate. Ordinary rain water is very slightly acid, due to the carbon dioxide dissolved in it. The acidic rain slowly dissolves limestone:

$$\begin{array}{ccccccc}
\text{calcium} & + & \text{carbon} & + & \text{water} & \rightarrow & \text{calcium} \\
\text{carbonate} & & \text{dioxide} & & & & \text{hydrogencarbonate} \\
CaCO_3(s) & + & \underbrace{CO_2(g) \ + \ H_2O(l)}_{\text{in rain water}} & & & \rightarrow & Ca(HCO_3)_2(aq)
\end{array}$$

This has two results. One is that limestone gets slowly dissolved away, giving spectacular cliffs, valleys and underground caves (picture 3). This is one reason why limestone scenery is so impressive.

The other result is that water supplies collected in limestone country contain dissolved calcium hydrogencarbonate, which makes the water 'hard'.

The reaction of calcium carbonate with carbon dioxide and water is reversible – it can go backwards as well as forwards. This means that the dissolved calcium hydrogencarbonate can turn back into solid calcium carbonate:

$$Ca(HCO_3)_2(aq) \rightarrow CaCO_3(s) + CO_2(g) + H_2O(l)$$

This may happen very slowly in limestone caves, forming deposits of calcium carbonate called stalactites and stalagmites. Or it may happen quickly in your kettle, forming a deposit of calcium carbonate called 'fur'.

Picture 3 Limestone caves in France.

■ Using limestone as a base

Substances that neutralise acids are called **bases** (topic G2). Calcium carbonate is used as a base a great deal.

- *In agriculture.* Farmers sometimes use powdered limestone to neutralise acid soil.
- *To prevent acid air pollution.* Burning fossil fuels produces acidic gases, especially sulphur dioxide. Limestone can be used to neutralise these gases before they can get into the air and cause acid rain. Power stations can be fitted with equipment to pass the gases through limestone before they leave the chimney. The reaction forms calcium sulphate, which is used to make plaster for the building industry. A big power station needs 300 000 tonnes of limestone a year to neutralise all its gases.
- *To neutralise acidified lakes.* (See picture 4.)

Picture 4 Adding powdered limestone to an acidified lake.

Picture 5 Pouring concrete. Cement is made by heating limestone with clay. When cement is mixed with water, a slow chemical reaction takes place and the cement sets hard. If sand and stones are mixed with the cement, you get concrete.

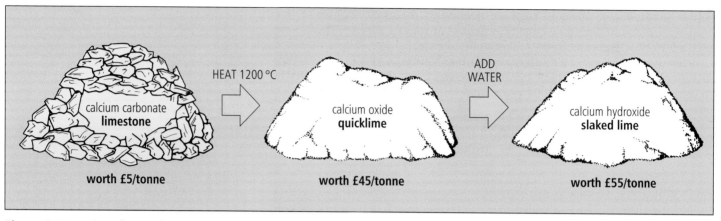

Picture 6 Converting calcium carbonate to calcium oxide and calcium hydroxide adds value. Why does the value increase so much more in the first stage than in the second?

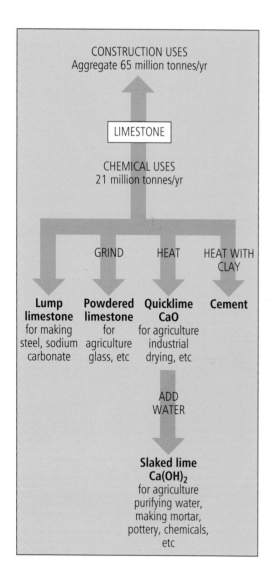

Picture 7 The uses of limestone.

Calcium carbonate decomposes when it is heated

Like other carbonates, calcium carbonate decomposes when it is heated strongly. Calcium oxide and carbon dioxide are formed:

$$\text{calcium carbonate} \rightarrow \text{calcium oxide} + \text{carbon dioxide}$$
$$CaCO_3(s) \rightarrow CaO(s) + CO_2(g)$$

This is an example of **thermal decomposition** – breaking down by heating.

Calcium oxide is also called 'lime'. It reacts vigorously with water to form calcium hydroxide, 'slaked lime'.

$$\text{calcium oxide} + \text{water} \rightarrow \text{calcium hydroxide}$$
$$CaO(s) + H_2O(l) \rightarrow Ca(OH)_2(s)$$

Both calcium oxide and calcium hydroxide are very useful chemicals. Calcium hydroxide is used as a cheap industrial alkali. Water companies use a lot of it to neutralise acid in water supplies. Farmers and gardeners use it to neutralise soil acidity.

A solution of calcium hydroxide in water is called **lime water**. When carbon dioxide is bubbled into this solution, calcium carbonate is formed as a milky precipitate. This is a common way of testing for carbon dioxide. (See page 219.)

$$\text{calcium hydroxide} + \text{carbon dioxide} \rightarrow \text{calcium carbonate} + \text{water}$$
$$Ca(OH)_2(aq) + CO_2(g) \rightarrow CaCO_3(s) + H_2O(l)$$

Adding value to limestone by heating it

You can carry out the thermal decomposition of calcium carbonate in the laboratory. Industrially it is done in big **lime kilns**. The temperature inside is about 1200 °C, and the kilns use enormous quantities of energy.

Picture 6 shows how value is added to limestone by turning it to calcium oxide. What do you think are the main economic costs in this process? (See question 3.) In *Making money from limestone* on page 102, you can try your hand at making money by making calcium oxide.

Picture 8 summarises the reactions of limestone that have been mentioned here.

THE ENVIRONMENTAL COST OF LIMESTONE

We couldn't do without limestone. Apart from the uses already mentioned, limestone is used to make cement, steel, glass and sodium carbonate (picture 7). All these things are vital to society. They cannot be made without a supply of pure limestone.

Limestone is very cheap to quarry out of the ground – there's lots of it, and it's near the surface. But there are environmental costs in extracting limestone. Picture 9 summarises the major ones. You can list them under the headings we have used before: people's health and safety; pollution of the environment; damage to the landscape; depletion of resources.

Limestone is one of the most useful of all raw materials. We have to balance its value to us against the cost to the environment of quarrying it. Find out more about this in *What could we use instead of limestone?* on page 103.

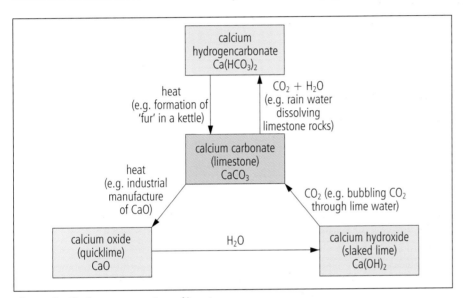

Picture 8   The important reactions of limestone.

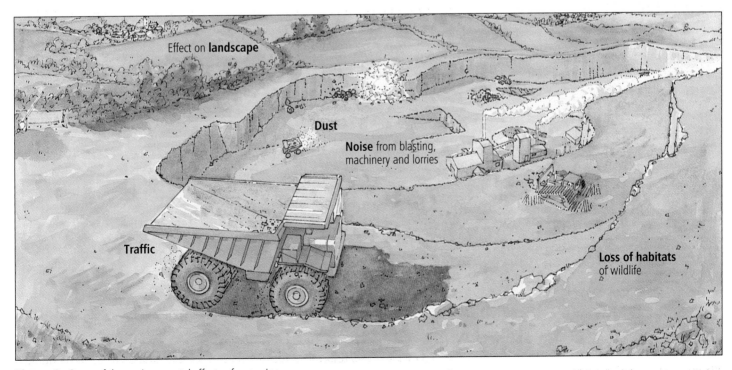

Picture 9   Some of the environmental effects of quarrying.

Questions

1 a What are the chemical names for (i) limestone, (ii) chalk, (iii) quicklime and (iv) slaked lime?

   b Write balanced equations for the reactions that occur when:
   (i) calcium carbonate is heated strongly; (ii) hydrochloric acid is added to calcium carbonate; (iii) water is added to calcium oxide; (iv) carbon dioxide is bubbled through lime water.

2 Dolomite is a rock. It is similar to limestone, but contains a mixture of magnesium carbonate and calcium carbonate instead of calcium carbonate alone. Magnesium is in the same family as calcium in the Periodic Table, and has similar properties to calcium.

   What products would you expect to be formed when dolomite is:
   (a) heated strongly; (b) reacted with hydrochloric acid?

3 Look at picture 6, showing how value is added to limestone by converting it to calcium oxide and calcium hydroxide.

   a Write down three types of cost that are involved in the first stage, turning calcium carbonate to calcium oxide. (Look back at picture 3, topic D1 if you are not sure.)

   b Which of these costs do you think adds most to the total cost of turning calcium carbonate to calcium oxide?

   c What is the cost of turning: (i) calcium carbonate to calcium oxide; (ii) calcium oxide to calcium hydroxide?

   d Why is the answer in (i) so much greater than the answer in (ii)?

4 Picture 9 on the previous page summarises the major environmental costs of quarrying limestone.

   a Suggest any other environmental costs, not shown on the picture, that you think are important.

   b List each of the costs under one of the four headings: People's health and safety; pollution of the environment; damage to the landscape; depletion of resources.

   c For each of the environmental costs, say whether you think it is: **A** a very significant cost, **B** a moderately significant cost or **C** a relatively insignificant cost.

5 a 50 g of calcium carbonate is heated strongly until it is completely decomposed.

   i) Write an equation for the reaction that occurs.

   ii) Calculate the mass of calcium oxide that is formed.

   b Suppose the calcium oxide formed in (a) is reacted with water.

   i) Write an equation for the reaction that occurs.

   ii) Calculate the mass of calcium hydroxide that is formed.

   (Ca=40; C=12; O=16; H=1)

Making money from limestone

In this practical activity you will put yourself in the place of an industrial manufacturer. You manufacture calcium oxide from calcium carbonate, and you have to do it as cheaply and efficiently as possible.

Your source of calcium carbonate will be a marble chip. When it is heated strongly, the hard marble chip will glow white hot and turn to powdery calcium oxide.

Here are the rules:

1 You must have a company name. Decide this before you start.

2 You can only use the following equipment: bunsen burner; heating mat; tongs; spatula; stand and clamp; eye protection; glass dish. You can have access to a weighing balance.

3 Safety rules: Eye protection must be worn. Do not handle calcium oxide or let it come into contact with your skin. The glass dish should not be heated.

EYE PROTECTION
MUST BE WORN

CORROSIVE
Calcium oxide

4 Your only source of calcium carbonate is a marble chip. You must weigh it, then scale up from grams into tonnes. (For example if it weighs 2.3 g, call its mass 2.3 tonnes.) You must pay for the chip (see the table for prices).

5 You have to pay for the energy you use. The charge for gas is given below.

6 You have to pay for the depreciation (wear and tear) on the equipment you use. This goes towards eventually replacing it (see table for charge).

7 You have to pay your own wages. The nationally agreed wage rates are given in the table.

8 When you have made your calcium oxide, you must separate it from unreacted calcium carbonate and put it on the glass dish. The glass dish must be weighed beforehand.

   You must take the calcium oxide to your teacher, who will weigh it, then test it to see it is genuine. You will be told how much it is worth.

 ICT 9 You must fill in a balance sheet like the one below.

Outgoings	
Mass of marble chip	tonnes
Cost of marble chip	£
Time for which gas was used	min
Cost of gas	£
Total time spent by all workers	hours
Total wages	£
Time for which equipment was used	min
Depreciation cost of equipment	£
Total cost	£
Income	
Mass of calcium oxide produced	tonnes
Value of calcium oxide produced	£
Net profit	£

Table of prices and costs (remember you have scaled up from grams to tonnes)

Marble chips (calcium carbonate)
    £7.50 per tonne
Calcium oxide
    £75 per tonne
Gas
    £3.00 per minute
Depreciation of equipment
    £1.50 per minute
Wages
    £7.50 per person per hour

What could we use instead of limestone?

Limestone is a popular raw material because it's cheap and versatile. Unfortunately, quarrying limestone damages some of the most attractive country in Britain. Could we use other rocks instead?

Dr William Stanton, a geologist who is an expert on limestone scenery, has compared the usefulness of limestone with other rocks. He asked geologists, civil engineers and others to award points to limestone and to other types of rocks as a measure of their value.

Table 1 compares the industrial value of limestone with other rocks. Note that the table is concerned with 'hard' limestone. This is the kind in the Mendip Hills, the Peak District and the Yorkshire Dales. This kind of limestone is particularly good for industrial use.

The numbers in the table give the 'score' for each rock, on a 1 to 5 scale.

Table 2 looks at the value of limestone and other rocks when they are left in place instead of being quarried.

Table 1 The industrial value of limestone and other rocks. The numbers give the score for each rock.

	Hard limestone	Granite	Hard sandstone
Cost of extraction	Low 5	High 2	Very high 1
How much wastage at the quarry?	Low 4	Medium 3	Very high 1
How good for aggregate?	Very good 5	Very good 5	Very good 5
Is it used as building stone?	Yes 2	Yes 3	Yes 2
Is it used as a chemical raw material?	Yes 5	No 0	No 0

Table 2 The value of limestone and other rocks if left in place.

	Hard limestone	Granite	Hard sandstone
Quality of landscape	Very varied 5	Good 4	Good 4
Variety of wildlife	Very varied 5	Limited 2	Limited 2
What is the soil like for agriculture?	Good (where present) 4	Poor 2	Poor 2
Value for recreation: walking, climbing, open spaces	Very good 5	Very good 5	Very good 5
Underground drinking water supplies	Plenty, very pure 4	None 0	Some 2

1. How scientific is this method for comparing the value of different rocks? Can you think of a more scientific way of doing it?

2. Use table 1 to summarise why there is a big industrial demand for hard limestone.

3. Use table 2 to summarise the arguments for preserving limestone countryside.

4. How far is it possible to satisfy the industrial demand for limestone and preserve limestone countryside?

5. Imagine the Minister for the Environment has asked you to report on how limestone countryside can be preserved. You have been told to take account of the country's industrial need for limestone. What recommendations will you make?

Picture 3 Sandstone cliffs in Dorset.

Picture 1 Limestone scenery in the Pennines.

Picture 2 Granite scenery in Dartmoor.

Ammonia and fertilisers

Nitrogenous fertilisers help plant to grow. This topic is about how fertilisers are manufactured.

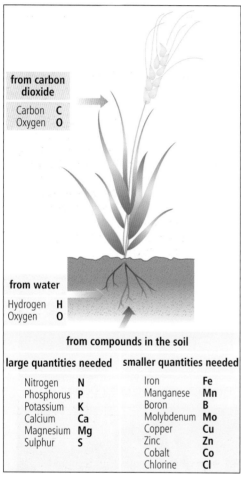

from carbon dioxide

| Carbon | C |
| Oxygen | O |

from water

| Hydrogen | H |
| Oxygen | O |

from compounds in the soil

large quantities needed		smaller quantities needed	
Nitrogen	N	Iron	Fe
Phosphorus	P	Manganese	Mn
Potassium	K	Boron	B
Calcium	Ca	Molybdenum	Mo
Magnesium	Mg	Copper	Cu
Sulphur	S	Zinc	Zn
		Cobalt	Co
		Chlorine	Cl

Picture 2   Elements which plants use and where they get them from.

AMMONIA, NH$_3$
- colourless gas
- pungent smell, toxic
- very soluble in water
- forms alkaline solution in water
- reacts with acids to form ammonium salts

Picture 3   The properties of ammonia.

Picture 1   Farmers need to think carefully and take advice on the amount of nitrogenous fertiliser to put on a crop.

Plants don't feed like animals do. Instead, they make carbohydrates, proteins and other biochemicals, starting with simple compounds that they get from air, water and the soil (picture 2).

But here's something rather odd. Nitrogen makes up 80% of the air and yet plants can't use it. On the other hand, carbon dioxide is only 0.03% of the air, and plants can use that.

The problem is that the nitrogen in the air is very unreactive. Plants need nitrogen in the form of soluble compounds they can take up through their roots. **Nitrogenous fertilisers** provide nitrogen in this form, and this topic is about the way chemistry can provide them.

There are two types of nitrogen compounds that plants can take up through their roots: ammonium compounds and nitrates. Ammonium compounds contain the **ammonium ion, NH$_4^+$**, and nitrates contain the **nitrate ion, NO$_3^-$**.

The modern fertiliser industry is based on one chemical more than any other: ammonia.

WHAT IS AMMONIA?

Ammonia is a smelly gas. You can smell it in some household cleaners and in old nappies and public lavatories. Picture 3 summarises the most important properties of ammonia.

■ Ammonia or ammonium?

Ammonia is a base – it neutralises acids. When ammonia neutralises an acid, it forms an **ammonium salt**. Ammonium salts contain the **ammonium ion, NH$_4^+$** (picture 4). For example, when ammonia solution reacts with nitric acid, ammonium nitrate is formed:

$$\text{ammonia} + \text{nitric acid} \rightarrow \text{ammonium nitrate}$$
$$NH_3(aq) + HNO_3(aq) \rightarrow NH_4NO_3(aq)$$

Ammonium nitrate is the most important of all the nitrogenous fertilisers. It's known as 'NITRAM'.

Notice the state symbols in the above equation: all the substances are in aqueous solution. Ammonia is very soluble in water, and in laboratory experiments we normally use ammonia solution rather than ammonia gas.

Ammonia reacts with other acids to give other ammonium salts. With sulphuric acid it gives ammonium sulphate, $(NH_4)_2SO_4$. With hydrochloric acid it gives ammonium chloride, NH_4Cl.

■ Testing for ammonia

There are two tests you can do to see whether a gas is ammonia.

1 Smell
Ammonia has a characteristic pungent smell. However, it is very strong-smelling and toxic, and you should only smell it very cautiously.

2 Effect on damp indicator paper
Ammonia is the only common gas that is alkaline. It turns damp indicator paper blue.

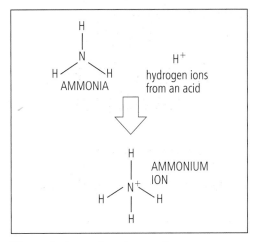

Picture 4 Ammonia and ammonium.

MANUFACTURING AMMONIA – THE HABER PROCESS

All nitrogenous fertilisers are based on ammonia, so it's vital to have a cheap way of making ammonia in bulk. The obvious way to do it is to combine nitrogen and hydrogen together:

$$\text{nitrogen} + \text{hydrogen} \rightarrow \text{ammonia}$$
$$N_2(g) + 3H_2(g) \rightarrow 2NH_3(g)$$

Unfortunately nitrogen is so unreactive that it doesn't combine with hydrogen under ordinary condition (see box alongside).

■ Haber's discovery

In 1908 Fritz Haber, a German scientist, discovered a way to make nitrogen and hydrogen combine. He did the trick by using conditions that often work in chemical reactions: high pressure, high temperature and a catalyst. Even then the reaction is reversible (see topic I9).

$$N_2(g) + 3H_2(g) \rightleftharpoons 2NH_3(g)$$

Under the conditions Haber used, only 8% of the hydrogen and nitrogen was converted to ammonia: the rest was left unchanged. Nitrogen and hydrogen really are reluctant partners.

■ Getting the best you can

Look at picture 5. It shows the percentage of ammonia you get by reacting nitrogen with hydrogen under different conditions. Judging from this graph alone, the best conditions would be a temperature of 350 °C and a pressure of 400 atmospheres. That would give you a 70% yield of ammonia – much better than Haber got. Indeed, you might do even better if you followed the trend of the graphs and used a higher pressure and a lower temperature.

But it isn't as simple as that. There are two other important things to be considered.

- High pressures are expensive. This is because high pressures need special pumps. The higher the pressure, the more expensive the pump – and the more likely it is to break down.

- All chemical reactions go faster at higher temperatures – and slower at lower temperatures. If you have the temperature too low, the **reaction rate** is too slow. You might get a good yield of ammonia, but you have to wait too long for it.

Why is nitrogen so unreactive?

Nitrogen gas contains diatomic molecules, N_2. Before nitrogen can react, these molecules have to be split up into separate atoms, N. The nitrogen atoms in N_2 are bonded together by a **triple bond**, which holds them together very strongly. It needs a lot of energy to split the atoms apart, so nitrogen does not react readily unless it is heated to high temperatures, or provided with a catalyst.
Compare the quantities of energy needed to split apart N_2 and H_2 molecules.

$$N{\equiv}N \quad 945 \text{ kJ per mole}$$
$$H{-}H \quad 435 \text{ kJ per mole}$$

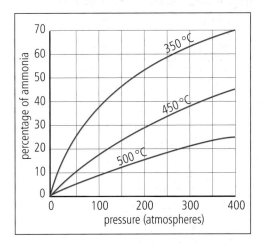

Picture 5 The percentage yield of ammonia under different conditions of temperature and pressure. For example, a percentage yield of 50% means that half of the nitrogen and hydrogen is turned to ammonia. The other half is unchanged.

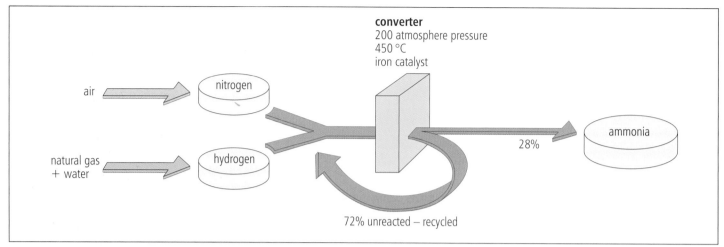

Picture 6 The Haber Process, used to manufacture ammonia.

So we have several factors to weigh up in deciding the best conditions for making ammonia. A very high pressure would give a good percentage yield of ammonia – and a good rate too. But it would cost too much because of the pump problem. A low temperature would give a good percentage yield of ammonia, but the rate would be too slow.

The conditions that are actually used are a compromise – a balance between these opposing factors. A medium pressure of 200 atmospheres and a medium temperature of 450 °C are usually chosen. This gives a yield of 28% ammonia. Not too bad in the circumstances.

■ The Haber Process in use today

Picture 6 summarises the Haber Process as it is used today in Britain. The actual process is more complicated than this, and involves several stages that are not shown. But the most important stage is the one shown here, in which nitrogen and hydrogen are converted to ammonia.

Notice that 72% of the nitrogen and hydrogen are unreacted and have to be recycled. That means you have to separate the ammonia from the unreacted gases. Table 1 compares some properties of ammonia, nitrogen and hydrogen. You should be able to think of a way of separating the ammonia (question 4).

Table 1 Some properties of ammonia, nitrogen and hydrogen.

Property	Ammonia	Nitrogen	Hydrogen
Appearance	Colourless gas	Colourless gas	Colourless gas
Boiling point	−33 °C	−196 °C	−253 °C
Solubility in water at 20 °C (cm^3 of gas dissolved by 100 cm^3 water)	68 000	1.5	3.0

■ The economic costs of the Haber Process

The raw materials for the process are

- Air, which supplies the nitrogen.
- Natural gas (methane) and water, which supply the hydrogen and the energy needed to heat the reactants.
- Iron, which is the catalyst and does not get used up.

All these materials are plentiful, so ammonia can be produced cheaply. Picture 7 shows the main costs involved in making ammonia.

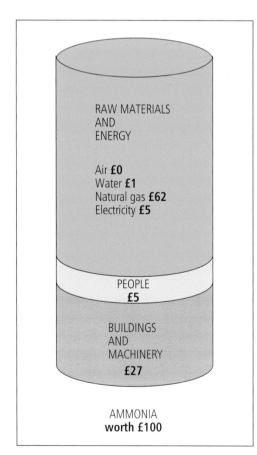

Picture 7 The main costs involved in making ammonia.

USING THE AMMONIA TO MAKE FERTILISERS

Ammonia can be used as a fertiliser on its own, but being a gas it is difficult to apply to the soil. Usually, the ammonia is converted to ammonium salts, which are solids and easier to apply. The most popular is ammonium nitrate, 'NITRAM'. To make ammonium nitrate you need to react ammonia with nitric acid.

There are many other kinds of fertiliser. Picture 8 summarises the most important ones. Notice 'NPK' fertiliser, which contains the three elements plants need most: nitrogen, phosphorus and potassium. You can get different NPK fertilisers with different proportions of the three elements, to suit the needs of your land.

■ What's the best place to put a fertiliser plant?

Ammonia has many uses, and picture 9 shows some of them. By far the biggest use is in making fertilisers.

To avoid transporting ammonia too far, all the chemical processes for making fertilisers are carried out on the same site. The biggest fertiliser plant in Britain is at Billingham-on-Tees (picture 10). This plant is well placed for all the necessary raw materials, as you can see from the map in picture 11. Question 5 looks more closely at this.

■ What are the environmental costs of the Haber Process?

The main environmental problems with ammonia manufacture are

● Accidental escape of toxic ammonia gas from the plant. However, such accidents are rare.
● Emission of nitrogen oxides and ammonia in the waste gases from the plant, causing air pollution. These emissions are normally tightly controlled.
● Effect on the landscape of a large industrial plant.

Against these environmental costs we must balance the value of ammonia and fertilisers to society. *For and against fertilisers* on page 109 looks at these issues in more detail.

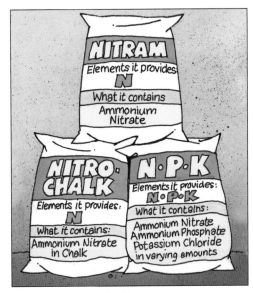

Picture 8 Types of fertiliser.

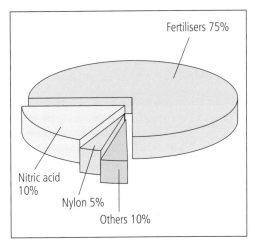

Picture 9 The major uses of ammonia.

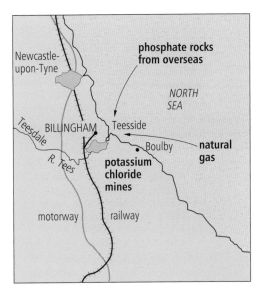

Picture 11 The location of the Billingham fertiliser plant.

Picture 10   The fertiliser manufacturing plant at Billingham.

■ Manufacturing nitric acid from ammonia

Nitric acid, HNO_3, is used to make ammonium nitrate fertiliser from ammonia. Nitric acid is also used in the manufacture of nylon and explosives.

The starting point for making nitric acid is ammonia (picture 12).

In the first stage, ammonia is mixed with air and compressed. The gases are then passed over a platinum/rhodium catalyst, heated to about 900 °C. This reaction takes place:

$$\text{ammonia} + \text{oxygen} \rightarrow \text{nitrogen dioxide} + \text{water}$$
$$4NH_3(g) + 5O_2(g) \rightarrow 4NO_2(g) + 6H_2O(g)$$

The NO_2 gas is then mixed with more air. The mixture of gases is passed up a tower where it meets a stream of water flowing downwards. This reaction takes place:

$$\text{nitrogen dioxide} + \text{oxygen} + \text{water} \rightarrow \text{nitric acid}$$
$$4NO_2(g) + O_2(g) + 2H_2O(g) \rightarrow 4HNO_3(aq)$$

A solution containing about 50% nitric acid flows out of the bottom of the tower.

Picture 13 The Kemira fertiliser plant in Cheshire. Ammonia, nitric acid and ammonium nitrate are all made on the same site.

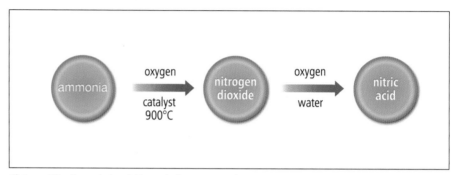

Picture 12 How nitric acid is made from ammonia.

Questions

1 a Write the formula of (i) the ammonia molecule and (ii) the ammonium ion.

b Give two ways to test for ammonia gas.

c Name the products that are formed when ammonia solution is added to: (i) hydrochloric acid; (ii) nitric acid; (iii) phosphoric acid.

2 Look at the graphs in picture 5 on page 105.

a What percentage yield of ammonia would you get using each of the following sets of conditions?
i) A temperature of 450 °C and a pressure of 400 atmospheres?
ii) A temperature of 450 °C and a pressure of 200 atmospheres?
iii) A temperature of 350 °C and a pressure of 400 atmospheres?

b Which set of conditions is actually used? Explain why these conditions are used rather than either of the others.

3 The Haber Process combines nitrogen and hydrogen to form ammonia.

a From what raw material is the hydrogen obtained?

b From what raw material is the nitrogen obtained?

c What other raw material does the process need?

d Which of these raw materials is/are non-renewable, and will eventually get used up?

e What might be used instead of any non-renewable raw materials once they are used up?

f What is the biggest single economic cost in the Haber Process?

g Why is the Haber Process so important to society?

4 In the Haber Process, ammonia has to be separated from unreacted nitrogen and hydrogen (picture 6 on page 106 explains this).

Use the data in table 1 on page 106 to suggest a method for separating the ammonia.

5 Look at the map in picture 11, showing the location of the fertiliser plant at Billingham. Explain why Billingham is a particularly good location for a fertiliser plant.

6 What do you think are the main environmental costs of manufacturing ammonia? List them under the four headings: people's health and safety; pollution of the environment; damage to the landscape; depletion of resources.

7 Calculate the percentage by mass of nitrogen in (i) ammonium nitrate, NH_4NO_3 and (ii) ammonium sulphate, $(NH_4)_2SO_4$ (N=14; H=1; S=32; O=16).

What do your answers suggest about these two compounds as nitrogenous fertilisers?

Activity

Finding out about a fertiliser

ICT **Urea** is a nitrogenous fertiliser which is popular in many tropical countries. Try to find out the following things about urea fertiliser. You will need to use advanced books or the Internet.

1 Its formula.
2 How it is manufactured.
3 The advantages of urea over other nitrogenous fertilisers.

For and against artificial fertilisers

Artificial fertilisers enable farmers to improve the fertility of the soil so they can grow more crops (picture 1). Artificial fertilisers include a range of chemicals which the plants need, but especially nitrates to provide plants with soluble nitrogen.

In 1950 the population of the world was 2500 million. In 2000 it was more than double that: at 6000 million. Without artificial fertilisers it would be impossible to feed everyone.

Yet there are disadvantages as well as advantages in using fertilisers.

For artificial fertilisers

Artificial fertilisers enable farmers to get more crops from the same area of land. This means that:

● the price of food is lower
● more people can be fed from the same area of land
● some land can be left unused by agriculture, for people and wildlife to enjoy.

Against fertilisers

Many people believe fertilisers damage the environment and people's health.

● Fertilisers can get washed out of the soil and into streams and rivers where they upset the balance of life (see topic B7).
● Nitrates from fertilisers can get into drinking water supplies. Nitrates can be harmful to health.
● The manufacture of fertilisers has an impact on the environment (see page 47).

Questions about fertilisers

Why do artificial fertilisers enable farmers to get more crops from the same area of land?

Explain how nitrates from fertilisers can get into drinking water supplies.

Suppose artificial fertilisers had never been invented. The world would be a very different place. Describe some of the differences.

Looking at organic food

Some people prefer to eat food that has been grown without fertilisers. Food that has been grown without fertilisers and pesticides is called 'organic' (picture 2). Go into your supermarket and have a look at the organic vegetables section. You could also look at some websites about organic food.

1 Obtain a leaflet about how organic vegetables are grown (you could contact the Soil Association). How is the soil kept fertile without artificial fertiliser?

2 Compare the difference in prices between organic and ordinary vegetables. Suggest reasons for any differences.

3 Organic vegetables are not available all the year round. Why not?

4 Does eating organic foods overcome the problems caused by artificial fertilisers? Explain your answer.

5 Apart form the matter of fertilisers, what other reasons are there for eating organic food?

Picture 1 Applying artificial fertiliser to winter wheat.

Picture 2 Organic food products.

D4

Sulphur and sulphuric acid

Sulphur is used to make sulphuric acid, the world's most popular chemical.

Picture 1 Sulphur around a volcanic vent.

People used to think that Hell was full of sulphur, or 'brimstone' as they used to call it. In fact, there *is* a lot of sulphur inside the Earth, and some of it reaches the surface in volcanic areas (picture 1). You can also smell sulphur dioxide near volcanoes, as the sulphur burns when it reaches the air. The pungent smell adds to the hellish impression. 'Fire and brimstone' sermons warned the congregation of the fate that awaited them down below.

SOURCES OF SULPHUR

We need a plentiful supply of sulphur to make sulphuric acid. Fortunately, there is more than enough of it around. The main sources are:

1 **Underground sulphur deposits,** especially in the US, Mexico and Poland. Steam is pumped down into the underground deposits. This melts the sulphur, which is pumped to the surface.

2 **Oil and natural gas.** Crude oil and natural gas contain sulphur compounds. These have to be removed before the fuels are used, otherwise the sulphur compounds form polluting sulphur dioxide when the fuel burns. Desulphurisation of oil and natural gas is an important source of sulphur.

3 **Sulphur-containing ores.** Some metals occur naturally as sulphide ores. For example, zinc occurs as zinc sulphide, ZnS. In the process of extracting the metal, the ore is roasted in air, and this produces sulphur dioxide. The sulphur dioxide is used directly in the manufacture of sulphuric acid.

WHAT IS SULPHUR LIKE?

Sulphur is a non-metallic element. It is a yellow solid made of S_8 molecules (picture 2). These molecules can stack together in two different ways, so there are two different crystalline forms of sulphur, called **rhombic** and **monoclinic**. This is an example of allotropy: see page 89. Rhombic sulphur is the more stable form.

■ Sulphur and sulphur dioxide

Sulphur burns in air with a blue flame, forming sulphur dioxide.

$$S(s) + O_2(g) \rightarrow SO_2(g)$$

Sulphur dioxide is a pungent-smelling, acidic gas. It is poisonous to all organisms, especially bacteria. For this reason it is used as a food preservative—its code number on ingredients lists is E220. It is used particularly for preserving fruit juices.

Sulphur dioxide can also be used for fumigation. You can fumigate, or sterilise, a room by burning sulphur in it. The gas diffuses to all parts of the room, killing all the bacteria. This method was once used to sterilise rooms where there had been disease.

SULPHURIC ACID

In the laboratory you will meet sulphuric acid, H_2SO_4, in two forms.

Concentrated sulphuric acid is 98% H_2SO_4 and 2% water. It is a very dangerous chemical, because it is a powerful dehydrating agent (see below). It must be handled very carefully because it is very corrosive.

Dilute sulphuric acid is about 10% H_2SO_4 and 90% water. It is much safer to handle, but must still be treated with care.

Sulphuric acid has all the typical properties of an acid (see page 158). In addition, concentrated sulphuric acid is a powerful dehydrating agent. It has a strong liking for water: when water and concentrated sulphuric acid are mixed, they get very hot and the water may boil up and spit. Whenever you mix sulphuric acid with water, you must always add the acid to the water, rather than the other way round, to reduce the risk of spitting.

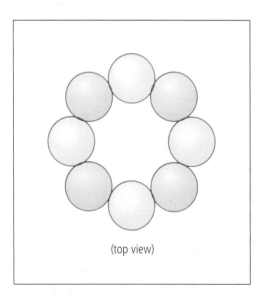

(top view)

Picture 2 The sulphur molecule S_8.

Concentrated sulphuric acid removes water from other substances. For example, if you add concentrated sulphuric acid to sugar, $C_{12}H_{22}O_{11}$, the sugar is dehydrated, leaving black carbon.

$$C_{12}H_{22}O_{11} \rightarrow 12C + 11H_2O$$
removed by sulphuric acid

Concentrated sulphuric acid has a similar dehydrating effect on most living material. That is why it is so corrosive and dangerous.

MAKING SULPHURIC ACID

Sulphuric acid is the most widely used of all industrial chemicals. It is used to manufacture a huge range of useful products (picture 3).

Such an important chemical has to be manufactured cheaply, and that means quickly. So reaction rates are very important in sulphuric acid manufacture.

■ How's it done?

Sulphur is the starting material for manufacturing sulphuric acid. There are three stages in the process, summarised in picture 4.

Stage 1
Sulphur, S, is burned in air, to give sulphur dioxide, SO_2.
   This reaction is fast.

Stage 2
The sulphur dioxide is cooled, then reacted with oxygen to convert it to sulphur trioxide, SO_3:

$$\text{sulphur dioxide} + \text{oxygen} \rightleftharpoons \text{sulphur trioxide}$$
$$2SO_2(g) + O_2(g) \rightleftharpoons 2SO_3(g)$$

This is the most difficult part of the process, because it is a slow and reversible reaction. To speed it up, it is carried out under these special conditions:

- With a catalyst. The catalyst is vanadium pentoxide, V_2O_5. At one time platinum was used, but V_2O_5 is cheaper.

- At a high temperature. However, there is a problem with the temperature, because the reaction is reversible (see I9). At high temperatures the position of equilibrium moves to the left, so you get less sulphur trioxide. So an *intermediate* temperature of 450 °C is used as a compromise.

Stage 3
Finally, the sulphur trioxide made in stage 2 is reacted with water to give sulphuric acid, H_2SO_4.

$$\text{sulphur trioxide} + \text{water} \rightarrow \text{sulphuric acid}$$
$$SO_3(g) + H_2O(l) \rightarrow H_2SO_4(aq)$$

This reaction is fast – too fast, in fact. The sulphur dioxide reacts with water so readily that a fine mist of sulphuric acid droplets is formed. To avoid this, the sulphur trioxide is first absorbed in 98% sulphuric acid. This gives 99.5% sulphuric acid, which is then watered down.

This process is called the **Contact Process**, and it is used all over the world to make sulphuric acid.

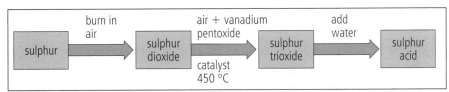

Picture 4   An outline of the Contact Process for making sulphuric acid.

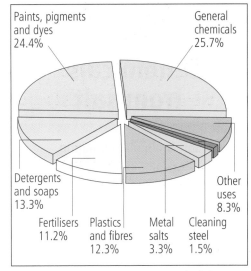

Picture 3   The major industrial uses of sulphuric acid.

Questions

1   The major manufacturer of zinc in Britain is also a major manufacturer of sulphuric acid. Explain why.

2   There are three raw materials for making sulphuric acid. What are they?

3   In the second stage of the Contact Process, a temperature of 450°C is used. Why is the temperature not: (a) higher, (b) lower than this?

4   What else, apart from a high temperature, is used to make the second stage of the Contact Process go quickly?

5   What mass of sulphuric acid could be manufactured from 32 tonnes of sulphur? (S=32, O=16, H=1)

Picture 5   This tanker is carrying sulphuric acid. The tank is lined with glass. Why?

D5

Chemicals from salt

Salt is not just for eating. It's an important raw material.

When you sprinkle salt on your food, you may think it comes from the sea. It's more likely to be from the salt mines of Cheshire (picture 1) – though these salt deposits come from seas of long ago.

The largest of the Cheshire mines produces 2 million tonnes of salt a year. Fortunately, few people have to work down these mines. Most of the salt is extracted by solution mining. Salt is soluble in water, but most of the other stuff in the mine is not. Water is pumped into the mine and the salt dissolves, leaving impurities behind. It is pumped back to the surface as a strong solution (brine), so there's no need for anyone to go down the mine. What a pity coal doesn't dissolve in water.

WHAT'S SALT USED FOR?

Some of the salt is made very pure and used for adding to food – but this isn't anything like the biggest use.

A lot of salt is used on the roads in winter to melt the ice: (picture 2).

But the most important use of salt is as a raw material for making other chemicals. Industry uses many sodium compounds. Most of them start life as salt, which chemists know as sodium chloride, NaCl.

Of all the manufacturing processes which use salt as a raw material, the biggest is the manufacture of chlorine and sodium hydroxide by electrolysis. This is called the **chlor-alkali** process. It produces many useful products, as you can see from picture 3.

Picture 1 The scene above the salt mines in Cheshire. The salt is brought out by solution mining, so there are no spoil heaps.

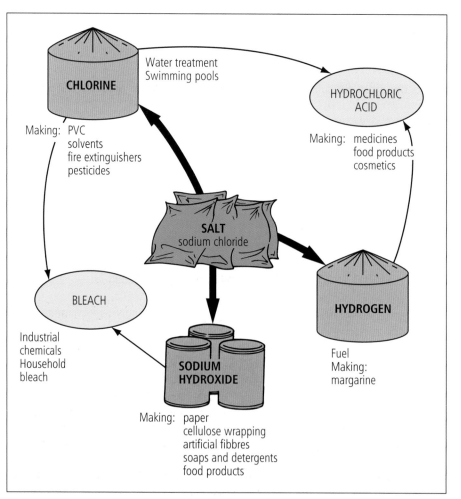

Picture 3 Uses of products of sodium chloride electrolysis.

CHLORINE

Water treatment
Swimming pools

Making: PVC
solvents
fire extinguishers
pesticides

HYDROCHLORIC ACID

Making: medicines
food products
cosmetics

SALT
sodium chloride

BLEACH

Industrial chemicals
Household bleach

SODIUM HYDROXIDE

Making: paper
cellulose wrapping
artificial fibbres
soaps and detergents
food products

HYDROGEN

Fuel
Making:
margarine

Picture 2 Salt is used to melt ice on roads in winter.

1000 kg	370 kg		607 kg	684 kg	17 kg
SALT	+ WATER	ELECTRICITY ⟹	CHLORINE +	SODIUM HYDROXIDE +	HYDROGEN
cost: £30	cost: very small	cost: £55	value: £90	value: £100	value: £10

Picture 4 Adding value in the chlor-alkali process.

THE ELECTROLYSIS OF BRINE

We look at the basic principles of electrolysis in topic J2.

When electricity is passed through a solution of sodium chloride in water, it decomposes to form sodium hydroxide, chlorine and hydrogen:

sodium chloride + water   → sodium hydroxide + chlorine + hydrogen
$$2\,NaCl(aq) \quad + 2H_2O(l) \rightarrow \quad 2NaOH(aq) \quad + \quad Cl_2(g) \; + \; H_2(g)$$

These three **co-products** are all very useful chemicals.

Chlorine gas comes off at the anode, and hydrogen gas at the cathode. The sodium hydroxide solution is formed around the cathode. There is more in topic J2 about the chemical reactions in this process.

The industrial process is carried out in a specially designed cell called a **membrane cell**. Details of this cell are on page 247.

■ Uses of the products

Picture 3 shows some of the many ways the products are used. Notice that the major products, sodium hydroxide, chlorine and hydrogen, all have major uses in their own right. But they can also be combined together, to make bleach or hydrochloric acid.

THE ECONOMICS OF THE CHLOR-ALKALI PROCESS

Picture 4 shows the economic costs involved in the process. You can see that the value of the products is much more than the value of the salt and water. The electricity used in the process costs much more than the salt. The process involves other costs as well, of course. Think about what they are (see question 3).

■ Supply and demand: a three-way problem

The three products of the chlor-alkali process are all useful. There are no useless waste products. That's good, because the costs of the process are shared out between the three products.

There is a problem though. Suppose you are in the chlor-alkali business. You sell your chlorine to a water treatment company and your sodium hydroxide to a paper-maker. What happens if the water treatment company goes out of business?

You have to go on making sodium hydroxide for the paper-maker. But the chemical equation tells us that you can't make sodium hydroxide on its own. *You have to make all three products.* You must go on making chlorine and store it – and look for another buyer quickly. You might decide to lower the price of chlorine to encourage customers to buy yours instead of someone else's.

All industries experience problems of **supply and demand.** When demand falls, you lower the price to encourage more buyers. For the chlor-alkali business, with its three linked co-products, the problems are particularly complex.

Picture 5 In some parts of the country there is a shortage of iodide ions in the drinking water. A small amount of sodium iodide is added to the sodium chloride to make 'iodised salt'. This makes sure you get the iodide you need in your diet.

Questions

1 a Give the names and formulas of the products made by the electrolysis of sodium chloride.

 b Give at least two major uses of each of these products.

2 a Salt is extracted from underground mines by solution mining.
  i) Explain how solution mining works.
  ii) What property of sodium chloride does this method use?

 b The salt that comes straight up from the mines isn't pure enough to use as table salt.
  i) What impurities do you think it contains?
  ii) What method would you use to purify it?

3 Look at picture 4, which summarises the costs involved in the chlor-alkali process. Apart from electricity what other costs will be involved in running this process?

4 a Write an equation for the reaction that occurs when sodium chloride solution is electrolysed.

 b Suppose 117 g of sodium chloride are electrolysed. Calculate the mass of (i) sodium hydroxide, (ii) chlorine, and (iii) hydrogen that will be formed. (Na=23; Cl=35.5; O=16; H=1)

Metals

Metals as materials

Without metals modern civilisation would literally collapse. In this topic we look at the properties of metals that make them so useful.

Picture 1 Metals are essential to many modern structures.

THE PROPERTIES OF METALS

There are 92 naturally occurring elements, and 78 of them are metals. The special properties of metals make them excellent construction materials.

Picture 2 shows the characteristic properties of metals. These are physical properties – we look at chemical reactions of metals in topic E2. Notice that the properties of metals are very different from the properties of non-metals like oxygen, chlorine or sulphur. The characteristic physical properties of metals are a result of their *metallic bonding* (see topic C7).

METALS ARE STRONG

There are different meanings of the word 'strength'. Most metals have high *tensile strength*, which means they can support a heavy load. Because of this they can be used to make large structures like buildings and bridges. Iron and steel are the metals normally used in such structures. 'Steel' is the name given to alloys of iron. There are many different types of steel (see page 128).

Picture 3 Most metals are hard. The blade of a hacksaw is specially hardened.

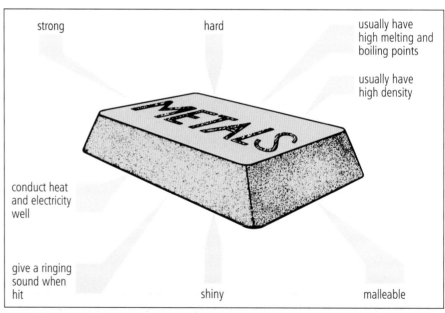

strong	hard	usually have high melting and boiling points
		usually have high density
conduct heat and electricity well		
give a ringing sound when hit	shiny	malleable

Picture 2 Typical properties of metals.

METALS ARE HARD

For thousands of years metals have been used to make weapons and tools which need to be hard. Knives and saws need to be hard so they don't get blunt. Drills need to be hard to cut through other materials. It's usually some form of steel that is used for tools like this.

METALS USUALLY HAVE HIGH MELTING AND BOILING POINTS

There are a few exceptions – for example, mercury is a liquid at room temperature. But metals generally have high melting points and this makes them useful wherever high temperatures are involved. That's why metals are used to make cooking utensils, car engines and tools which get hot, such as drills.

METALS ARE MALLEABLE

'Malleable' means they can be hammered, bent and changed into different shapes without breaking. This is very different from a non-metallic material like glass, which is brittle and shatters when you try to bend it.

Because metals are malleable, they can be made into all sorts of useful shapes. For example, the door of a car is made by pressing a flat sheet of steel into shape. Aluminium cooking foil is made by rolling sheets of the metal until they are very thin.

Metals become more malleable when they are hot. In a steel mill, the metal is shaped while it is red hot.

METALS ARE GOOD CONDUCTORS OF ELECTRICITY

Metals are the only materials which conduct electricity when they are solid. Copper is a particularly good conductor, and most electrical wires are made from copper.

METALS USUALLY HAVE HIGH DENSITY

High density is often a disadvantage, because it makes metal objects heavy. Aluminium's low density makes it very useful, for example for making aeroplanes and bicycles.

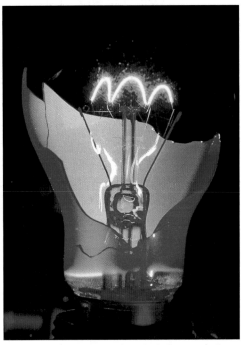

Picture 4 The filament of a light bulb is made from tungsten, which has a melting point of 3410 °C.

Picture 5 Aluminium is very malleable, so foil can be wrapped into any shape.

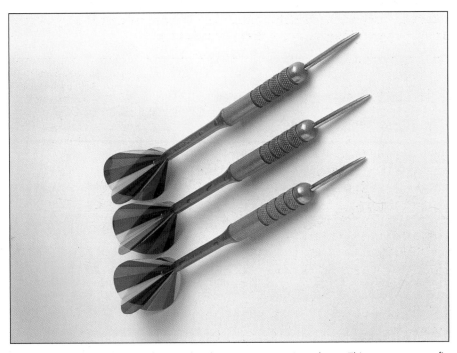

Picture 6 Tungsten darts can be very thin, because tungsten is so dense. This means you can fit more of them into the treble twenty!

■ Comparing metals

Picture 7 compares some of the properties of copper and aluminium. The different properties lead to different uses. Table 1 compares the properties of some commonly used metals. Use the table to answer questions 2 and 3 at the end of this topic.

In fact the metals in the table are often used, not on their own, but mixed together as alloys.

Table 1   Properties of some commonly used metals.   **** best, * worst.

Metal	Density/ (g/cm^3)	Melting point (°C)	Tensile strength (relative)	Electrical conductivity (relative)	Corrosion behaviour	Cost per tonne
Aluminium	2.7	659	**	***	Corrodes very slowly	£1000
Copper	9.0	1083	****	****	Corrodes very slowly	£1100
Iron	7.9	1540	****	**	Corrode (rusts) quickly	£120
Lead	11.3	328	*	*	Corrodes very slowly	£320
Silver	10.5	961	***	****	Corrodes slightly (tarnishes on surface)	£111 000
Tin	7.3	232	*	*	Does not corrode	£3300
Zinc	7.1	420	***	**	Corrodes very slowly	£660

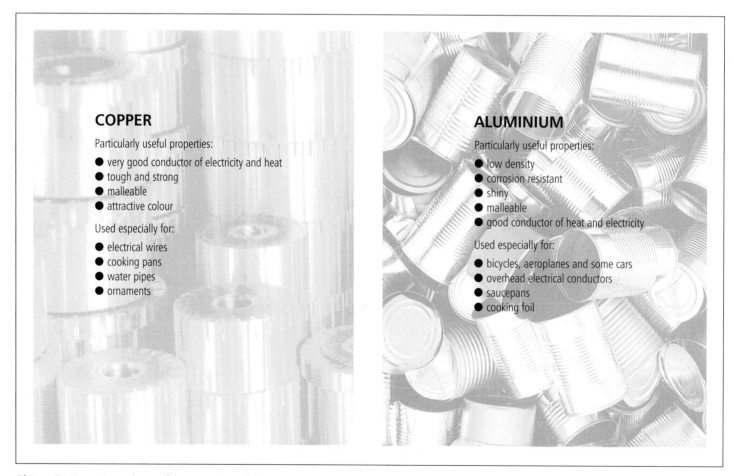

COPPER

Particularly useful properties:
- very good conductor of electricity and heat
- tough and strong
- malleable
- attractive colour

Used especially for:
- electrical wires
- cooking pans
- water pipes
- ornaments

ALUMINIUM

Particularly useful properties:
- low density
- corrosion resistant
- shiny
- malleable
- good conductor of heat and electricity

Used especially for:
- bicycles, aeroplanes and some cars
- overhead electrical conductors
- saucepans
- cooking foil

Picture 7   Properties and uses of copper and aluminium.

■ Alloys

An alloy is a mixture of two or more metals. Alloys are made by mixing molten metals and then allowing them to solidify. Alloys are used instead of pure metals because they have better properties. For example, brass is an alloy of copper and zinc. Brass is stronger than either of these metals. What is more, alloys can be designed and made with specific properties to match specific needs.

Table 2 gives some important alloys. There is more about steel alloys and their uses in topic E3. Note that the compositions given in the table are *typical* ones. In fact the compositions can be varied to give different properties for different needs. You can use the table to answer question 4 at the end of this topic.

The properties of metals can be explained in terms of the special way their atoms are arranged.

Picture 8 Coins are made from alloys. 'Silver' coins are 75% copper and 25% nickel. 'Copper' coins are 97% copper, 2.5% zinc, and 0.5% tin.

Table 2 Some important alloys. (See topic E3 for more about steel alloys.)

Name of alloy	Typical composition	Special properties
Brass	copper 70%, zinc 30%	Harder than pure copper
Bronze	copper 90%, tin 10%	Harder than pure copper
Duralmin	aluminium 96%, copper 4%	Stronger than pure aluminium
Solder	tin 50%, lead 50%	Low melting point (203°C)
Mild steel	iron 99.7%, carbon 0.3%	Stronger and harder than pure iron
Stainless steel	iron 70%, chromium 20%, nickel 10%	Harder than pure iron, doesn't rust
Manganese steel	iron 86%, manganese 13%, carbon 1%	Very hard
Cast iron	iron 97%, carbon 3%	Hard but brittle

Questions

1 In each of the following examples, which typical metal property is being used? Look at picture 2 on page 116 to remind yourself of typical metal properties. (Note: more than one property may be involved.)

   a saucepans are made from metal

   b bells are made from metal

   c the heating 'element' of an electric fire is made from metal

   d car engines are made from metal

ICT 2 Plot bar charts to compare (a) the densities and (b) the melting points of the metals in table 1 on page 118.

3 Use table 1 on page 118 to explain why:

   a the chain on a padlock is made from iron, not aluminium

   b tent poles are made from aluminium, not iron

   c the head of a hammer is made from iron, not lead or aluminium

   d deep-sea divers wear boots made of lead

   e 'silver' coins are not made from silver

   f metal dustbins are made from iron coated with zinc, but not from iron or zinc alone

   g 'tin' cans are not made of solid tin

   h overhead electrical cables are made from aluminium, not copper.

4 Use table 2 above to answer these questions about alloys.

   a Suggest reasons for the following.

      i)   aircraft are made from duralumin, not pure aluminium

      ii) electricians use solder to join wires together, not tin or lead

      iii) 'copper' coins are made from an alloy of copper, zinc and tin, not pure copper

      iv) bridges are made from mild steel, not pure iron

      v)   nails are made from iron, not cast iron

      vi) doorknockers are made from brass, not copper (give at least two reasons).

   b Which of the three kinds of steel given in the table would be best for making each of the following? Give the reason for your answer.

      i)   the body of a car

      ii) table cutlery

      iii) reinforcing wires in concrete

      iv) crossovers on railway lines

5 Look again at the typical properties of metals shown in picture 2 on page 116. Which, if any, of these typical properties are not shown by each of the following metals: (a) iron (b) sodium (c) lead (d) mercury?

Reactions of metals

In this topic we look at the typical reactions of metals, and how metals can be placed in order of their reactivity.

Picture 1 The first metals to be used by humans were the unreactive ones. This gold death mask has stayed untarnished for 3500 years.

In many ways it would be useful if all metals were unreactive. Then we would not have to worry about corrosion. But unfortunately many metals are reactive – and some are very reactive indeed.

Picture 2 summarises some of the typical chemical reactions of metals. Not all metals give all these reactions, because some metals are more reactive than others. Let's look at the different reactions in turn.

HOW DO METALS REACT WITH OXYGEN?

Oxygen is a reactive non-metal, and it is all around us in the air. Many metals react with the oxygen in the air to form oxides (topic B2). For example, with aluminium:

$$\text{aluminium} + \text{oxygen} \rightarrow \text{aluminium oxide}$$
$$4Al + 3O_2 \rightarrow 2Al_2O_3$$

You can investigate the reactivity of metals by heating them in air and seeing how vigorously they react.

Table 1 shows how some common metals react when they are heated in air. You can see that some metals react better than others. We can use results like these to place metals in order of reactivity. This order is called the **reactivity series**. Picture 4 shows the reactivity series for a number of metals.

Picture 3 Bright sparks from fireworks are often burning metal powders.

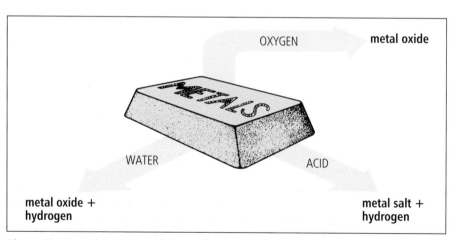

Picture 2 Some of the ways a metal may react.

Table 1 The results of heating some metals in the air.

Metal	How it reacts	Product
Aluminium	Burns slowly, forming a white surface layer	Aluminium oxide, Al_2O_3
Copper	Does not burn. Oxidises, turning black on surface	Copper oxide, CuO
Iron	Only burns when in powder or wool form	Iron oxide, Fe_3O_4
Magnesium	Burns readily with a brilliant white glow, forming white powder	Magnesium oxide, MgO
Sodium	Burns very readily, forming white powder	Sodium oxide Na_2O

Very reactive metals like sodium react with oxygen as soon as they are exposed to air. Less rreactive metals like zinc and iron react when they are heated in air. However, these less reactive metals do react with air very slowly, even at room temperature. This slow reaction with air is called corrosion, or rusting in the case of iron. The reaction is faster if water is present as well as air.

The very unreactive metals, like gold, don't react with oxygen at all. That's why gold is so popular for jewellery – it doesn't corrode in air, so it keeps its shine.

The reactivity series applies to other reactions of metals, not just their reaction with oxygen. Reactive metals, like sodium and magnesium, have a strong tendency to react with non-metals, like chlorine and oxygen. When they react, they form compounds like sodium chloride and magnesium oxide. Unreactive metals have little tendency to react with non-metals. We can sum up by saying

Reactive metals tend to combine and form compounds
Unreactive metals tend to stay uncombined.

One result of this is that a more reactive metal can take away oxygen from a less reactive metal. This is useful in the extraction of metals from their oxides (see topic E3).

HOW DO METALS REACT WITH WATER?

Water is a compound of hydrogen and oxygen, H_2O. As you might expect, reactive metals tend to take the oxygen from water, leaving the hydrogen (picture 6). When this happens, hydrogen gas is formed:

metal + water → metal oxide + hydrogen

For example, with magnesium:

magnesium + water → magnesium oxide + hydrogen
$$Mg \quad + \quad H_2O \rightarrow \quad MgO \quad + \quad H_2$$

More reactive metals like sodium form a hydroxide when they react with water:

sodium + water → sodium hydroxide + hydrogen
$$2Na \quad + \quad 2H_2O \rightarrow \quad 2NaOH \quad + \quad H_2$$

Table 2 summarises the reactions of metals with air, water and acids. The metals are listed in order of reactivity.

Notice that only the highest metals in the reactivity table react with water. These metals are reactive enough to take the oxygen in H_2O away from the hydrogen. However, metals that do not react in cold water will sometimes react at higher temperatures. Magnesium reacts quickly when it is heated in steam.

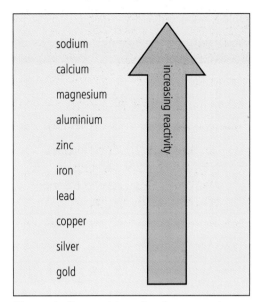

sodium
calcium
magnesium
aluminium
zinc
iron
lead
copper
silver
gold

increasing reactivity

Picture 4 The reactivity series of some metals.

Picture 5 Potassium is so reactive that it bursts into flame when it is put into water.

Picture 6

Table 2   Reactions of metals with air, water and acids.

Reactivity series of metals	Reaction with air	Reaction with water	Reaction with dilute acid
Sodium, Na	Burn less and less vigorously	React with cold water less and less vigorously, giving hydrogen	React with dilute acid less and less vigorously, giving hydrogen
Calcium, Ca			
Magnesium, Mg			
Aluminium, Al			
Zinc, Zn		React with steam, giving hydrogen	
Iron, Fe			
Lead, Pb	React slowly to form a layer of oxide	Do not react	
Copper, Cu			Do not react
Silver, Ag	Do not react		
Gold, Au			

Picture 7   These turbine blades are used in a power station. They are turned by high pressure steam at a high temperature. What metal might they be made from?

HOW DO METALS REACT WITH ACIDS?

Topic G1 describes the nature of acids. All acids contain two parts. One part is hydrogen. The other part is a non-metal or a group of non-metals. For example, hydrochloric acid contains hydrogen combined with chlorine: its formula is HCl. Reactive metals remove the chlorine from hydrochloric acid, releasing hydrogen:

metal + hydrochloric acid → metal chloride + hydrogen

Picture 8 illustrates this. Notice that the reaction is similar to the reaction of metals with water, but here the metal is competing for chlorine instead of oxygen. For example, with zinc:

zinc + hydrochloric acid → zinc chloride + hydrogen
$$Zn + 2HCl \rightarrow ZnCl_2 + H_2$$

You can see from table 2 the way different metals react with dilute hydrochloric acid.

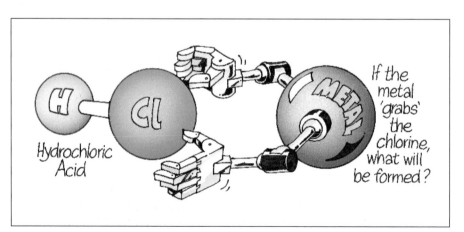

Picture 8

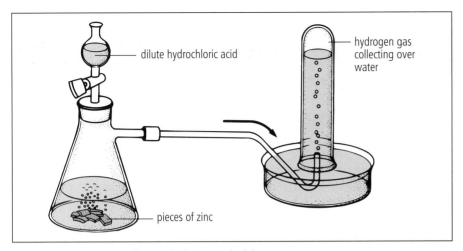

Picture 9 Making and collecting hydrogen in the laboratory.

Dilute sulphuric acid and dilute nitric acid react in a similar way. Whereas hydrochloric acid forms chlorides, sulphuric acid forms sulphates and nitric acid forms nitrates. These are all **salts** (topic G2). In general:

$$\text{metal} + \text{acid} \rightarrow \text{metal salt} + \text{hydrogen}$$

The reaction of a metal with an acid is a useful way of making hydrogen in the laboratory. Usually a moderately reactive metal is chosen, so that the hydrogen comes off neither too quickly nor too slowly. Zinc is often used. Picture 9 shows apparatus that can be used to collect test tubes of hydrogen in the laboratory.

The reactivity of metals with acids can cause corrosion problems when there are acidic gases in the air. Sulphur dioxide is an acidic gas which pollutes the air in industrial areas, causing acid rain. This acidity can make metal objects like bridges, cars and statues corrode faster than they would do in unpolluted air.

DISPLACEMENT REACTIONS OF METALS

If you dip a piece of zinc into a solution of a copper compound such as copper sulphate, the zinc displaces the copper. The blue copper sulphate loses its colour, and the zinc gets coated in red-brown copper metal (picture 10).

$$\text{zinc} + \text{copper sulphate} \rightarrow \text{zinc sulphate} + \text{copper}$$
$$\text{Zn(s)} + \text{CuSO}_4\text{(aq)} \rightarrow \text{ZnSO}_4\text{(aq)} + \text{Cu(s)}$$

This is an example of a displacement reaction: **a more reactive metal displaces a less reactive metal from its compounds**. You can think of it as the more reactive metal taking away the non-metal from the less reactive metal. It's similar in this way to the reactions of metals with water and acids, illustrated in pictures 6 and 8.

If you dip a piece of *silver* into a solution of copper sulphate, nothing happens. This is because silver is less reactive than copper, and will not displace it. Displacement reactions are used to produce electricity in batteries (see picture 11). There is more about this in topic J3.

HOW DO THE USES OF METALS DEPEND ON THEIR REACTIVITY?

The reactivity of metals limits their usefulness. Very reactive metals like sodium would be no use at all for constructing bridges and cars. Imagine what would happen when it rained! Magnesium is less reactive than sodium, and its lightness makes it useful in construction. Magnesium was once used to build racing cars, but not any more because of the safety hazards (see question 6).

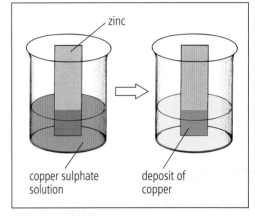

Picture 10 The displacement reaction between zinc and copper sulphate solution.

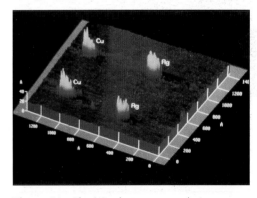

Picture 11 The tiniest battery ever made. It measures just 70 nanometres or 7×10^{-8} metres across – one-hundreth the size of a red blood cell. The battery operates because copper (Cu) is more reactive than silver (Ag).

Picture 12 Rhubarb is rather acidic. What kind of saucepan should you cook it in?

On the other hand, very *unreactive* metals like silver and gold are excellent for constructing things. The trouble is, the very unreactive metals are rare, and therefore expensive. For construction purposes, metals must be cheap. The most common construction metals are the abundant, moderately reactive ones – like aluminium, iron and copper.

MAKING PREDICTIONS USING THE REACTIVITY SERIES

If you know the position of a metal in the reactivity series, you can predict how it will react. For example, chromium comes below zinc but above iron in the reactivity series. Using table 2, we might predict these things about chromium:

● it will react with acids to give hydrogen;

● it will not react with cold water, but it will react with steam;

● it will burn with difficulty in air, forming chromium oxide.

Try making these kinds of predictions in questions 4 and 5.

COMPARING METALS WITH NON-METALS

Metals have very different properties from non-metallic elements like oxygen, chlorine and sulphur. The differences between metals and non-metals are covered in a number of different topics in this book. Table 3 summarises the most important differences.

Some elements show both metal and non-metal properties – particularly elements near the middle of the Periodic Table. For example, carbon (graphite) conducts electricity even though in other ways it behaves as a non-metal.

Table 3   A comparison of metals and non-metals.

Property	Metals	Non-metals
Physical properties		
State at room temperature	Usually solids (occasionally liquids)	Solids, liquids or gases
Melting and boiling point	Usually high	Often low
Electrical conductivity	Conduct when solid	Do not conduct
Strength	Strong and malleable	Often weak and brittle if solid
Density	Usually high	Often low
Chemical properties		
Reaction with air	Reactive metals form oxides	May react to form oxides
Nature of oxides	Usually solids. Give alkaline solutions when they dissolve in water	Solids, liquids or gases. Give acidic solutions when they dissolve in water
Reaction with water	Very reactive metals give hydrogen	Usually no reaction
Reaction with acids	Reactive metals give hydrogen	Usually no reaction
Type of ions formed	Positively charged	Negatively charged

Questions

Use table 2 on page 122 to help you answer questions 1 and 2.

1 What would you expect to happen in each of the following cases? Say what you would expect to see, and name all the products you would expect to be formed. If you would expect no reaction to occur, say so.

a calcium is added to water

b silver is added to dilute hydrochloric acid

c lead oxide is heated with magnesium

d calcium is heated in air

e aluminium is heated with lead

f zinc is heated in steam

2 For each of the reactions in question 1:

a write a word equation summarising the reaction

b write a balanced equation using formulas

3 Magnesium reacts with water, but only very slowly. Picture 13 shows an experiment used to investigate the

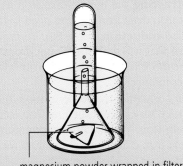

magnesium powder wrapped in filter paper and secured with paper clip

Picture 13 Testing the reaction of magnesium with water. After several hours, the tube has filled with gas.

reaction of magnesium with water. Look carefully at the picture, then answer these questions.

a Bubbles slowly rise from the magnesium powder. What are they bubbles of?

b Why is magnesium powder used, instead of bigger lumps?

c Suggest one change you could make to the experiment so the magnesium reacts faster.

4 Potassium comes above sodium in the reactivity series. Predict how you would expect potassium to react in each of the following cases. In each case name the products you would expect to be formed.

a potassium is heated in air

b potassium is added to water

c potassium is added to dilute hydrochloric acid

5 Vanadium is a metal you may not have heard of before. It is used to make special steels for tools such as spanners.

Vanadium comes below aluminium but above zinc in the reactivity series.

Predict how you would expect vanadium to react in each of the following cases. In each case name the products you would expect to be formed.

a vanadium is heated in air

b vanadium is added to cold water

c vanadium is heated in steam

d vanadium is added to dilute hydrochloric acid

e vanadium oxide is heated with aluminium

f magnesium oxide is heated with vanadium

g a piece of vanadium is dipped into a solution of copper sulphate

h a piece of copper is dipped into a solution of vanadium sulphate

6 Magnesium has been used for making cars because it is very light. But it is no longer used because of safety hazards. What would happen if a magnesium car caught fire, then firemen used water to fight the fire?

7 Zirconium is a silvery metal. Suppose you were given a piece of foil made from zirconium. Describe the tests you would do on it to find out where zirconium comes in the reactivity series. Describe how you would use the results of these tests to place zirconium correctly.

8 Below you will find information about 10 elements **A** to **J**.

a For each element, say whether you think

i) it is a metal

ii) it is a non-metal

iii) you cannot tell from the information given

b For each of elements **A**, **C**, **E** and **F**, give two further properties that you would expect the element to have.

Element **A** is a grey solid which does not conduct electricity.

Element **B** is a colourless gas.

Element **C** is a grey solid which gives off hydrogen when acid is added.

Element **D** is a solid which does not react with air, water or acid.

Element **E** is a yellow solid which shatters when hit with a hammer.

Element **F** is a shiny, dense solid.

Element **G** is a solid which burns in air.

Element **H** is a solid which burns in air to give an acidic gas.

Element **I** is a liquid which conducts electricity.

Element **J** is a solid which floats on water but does not react with it.

Extracting metals

All metals come from Earth. This topic is about the ways we get metals from their ores.

All metals come from the Earth. This topic is about the ways we get metals from their ores.

Most metals are too reactive to exist on their own in the ground. Instead, they exist combined with other elements as compounds, called ores. Table 1 shows the ores of some common metals. You can see that many ores are oxides. This is because oxygen is a reactive element and is very abundant on Earth.

A few metals are so unreactive that they occur in the earth in an uncombined state, as the pure metal. Gold is an example.

Gold has been used by humans for more than 5000 years. More reactive metals like iron were not used by humans until methods for extracting them had been developed (see table 2).

Table 1 The ores of some common metals. Most metals have more than one ore. The ores shown here are the especially important ones.

Metal	Name of the ore	What's in the ore
Aluminium	Bauxite	Aluminium oxide, Al_2O_3
Copper	Copper pyrites	Copper iron sulphide, $CuFeS_2$
Iron	Haematite	Iron oxide, Fe_2O_3
Sodium	Rock salt	Sodium chloride, $NaCl$
Tin	Cassiterite	Tin oxide, SnO_2
Zinc	Zinc blende	Zinc sulphide, ZnS

HOW DO YOU GET METALS FROM ORES?

Ores are the **raw materials** for making metals. One of the useful things about chemistry is that it gives us ways of turning raw materials into substances we need – like metals.

Getting a metal from its ore is called **extracting** the metal. Take iron as an example. Iron ore is iron oxide, Fe_2O_3. To get iron from iron ore you need to take away the oxygen. Taking away oxygen is called **reduction** (topic B2). To reduce iron oxide to iron you need a **reducing agent** that will grab the oxygen from the iron (picture 2). This 'oxygen grabber' must be more reactive than iron, otherwise the iron will hang on to the oxygen and stay combined.

What can we use to reduce iron ore? One possibility would be to look at the reactivity series of metals (topic E2). Any metal above iron in the reactivity series will 'grab' the oxygen from iron oxide, leaving iron. For example, aluminium is above iron in the reactivity series, so if we heat iron oxide with aluminium metal, aluminium will take the oxygen from the iron:

$$\text{aluminium} + \text{iron oxide} \rightarrow \text{aluminium oxide} + \text{iron}$$
$$2Al + Fe_2O_3 \rightarrow Al_2O_3 + 2Fe$$

In this reaction, aluminium is the reducing agent. It gets oxidised to aluminium oxide. Iron oxide gets reduced to iron.

Picture 2 To turn iron oxide into iron, you need a reducing agent that will 'grab' the oxygen from the iron.

Picture 1 Panning for gold in the Californian Gold Rush. Gold is one of the few metals which occur in the earth uncombined.

Table 2 Metals listed in order of reactivity, with the dates of their discovery.

Metal	When it was first discovered
Potassium	1807
Sodium	1807
Calcium	1808
Magnesium	1808
Aluminium	1827
Zinc	1746
Iron	around 1000 BC
Tin	around 2000 BC
Lead	before 3000 BC
Copper	before 3000 BC
Silver	before 3000 BC
Gold	before 3000 BC

But there is a problem with making iron this way. Aluminium actually costs more than iron! So this method would be too expensive for making iron on a large scale. A cheaper reducing agent than aluminium is needed, and the one that is used is carbon.

Carbon, in the form of coke, can be made cheaply from coal. At high temperatures, carbon has a strong tendency to react with oxygen, so it is a good reducing agent. The details of the extraction of iron using carbon are given on the next page.

Carbon is useful for extracting a number of other metals besides iron. For example, you can use carbon to get copper from copper oxide:

$$\text{copper oxide} + \text{carbon} \rightarrow \text{copper} + \text{carbon monoxide}$$
$$CuO \quad + \quad C \quad \rightarrow \quad Cu \quad + \quad CO$$

But some metals are too reactive to be extracted this way. They hang on to the oxygen so strongly that the carbon can't take it away. These are the metals towards the top of the reactivity series, like sodium, magnesium and aluminium. To extract these metals, you have to use **electrolysis**. This is described in more detail in topic J1.

Table 3 summarises the methods used to extract different metals. The metals are listed in order of reactivity, and you can see that the method used depends on the metal's position in the reactivity series.

Table 3   A summary of methods used for extracting metals.

Metal	Method
Potassium Sodium Calcium Magnesium Aluminium	Electrolysis of molten ores
Zinc Iron Tin Lead	Reduction of ores using carbon
Copper	Heating copper sulphide in air
Silver Gold	Metals occur uncombined

FROM ORE TO METAL

Extracting the metal from its ore is just one stage (a very important one) of making things from metal. Picture 3 shows all the stages.

Over millions of years, natural processes in the Earth have formed rich deposits of ores in certain parts of the Earth's crust. But even the richest deposits do not contain pure ore. The ore is mixed with lots of useless dirt and rock, which have to be separated off as much as possible. This is called **concentrating** the ore.

Some ores are already fairly concentrated when they are dug up – iron ore is often over 85% pure Fe_2O_3. But other ores are much less concentrated – copper ore usually contains less than 1% of the pure copper compound.

After concentration, the ore is reduced to the metal using one of the ways you have read about. The metal made in this way is usually quite impure, so it must then be purified.

Now at last the pure metal can be made into whatever products are needed – wires, cars, saucepans, bikes and so on. But it doesn't even end there. When the product is worn out and finished with, the metal can be reclaimed as scrap. This is recycling, and there is more about it on page 130.

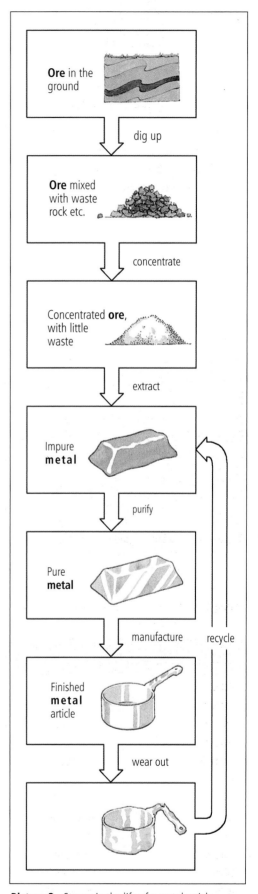

Picture 3   Stages in the life of a metal article.

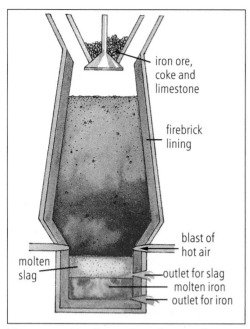

Picture 4 A blast furnace for making iron from iron ore.

AN IMPORTANT EXAMPLE: THE EXTRACTION OF IRON

Iron is the cheapest and most important metal available to us, and it is produced in huge amounts in **blast furnaces** (picture 4).

The best quality iron ore comes from places such as Scandinavia, the USA and Australia. It is concentrated enough to use straight away. Iron ore and coke (carbon) are fed in at the top of the furnace. Limestone is added as well, to remove impurities. A blast of hot air is sent in at the bottom of the furnace (this is how the furnace gets its name). The carbon burns in the air blast and the inside of the furnace gets very hot. There are a number of reactions in the furnace that produce iron. Here are the most important:

● Carbon burns in the air blast to form carbon monoxide:

$$\text{carbon} + \text{oxygen} \rightarrow \text{carbon monoxide}$$
$$2C + O_2 \rightarrow 2CO$$

● Carbon monoxide takes oxygen from iron oxide, reducing it to iron:

$$\text{iron oxide} + \text{carbon monoxide} \rightarrow \text{iron} + \text{carbon dioxide}$$
$$Fe_2O_3 + 3CO \rightarrow 2Fe + 3CO_2$$

● The carbon in the coke also reduces some of the iron oxide directly:

$$\text{iron oxide} + \text{carbon} \rightarrow \text{iron} + \text{carbon monoxide}$$
$$Fe_2O_3 + 3C \rightarrow 2Fe + 3CO$$

At the high temperature of the furnace, the iron is molten. It runs out at the bottom of the furnace. Some of the impurities in the iron ore combine with the limestone to form a molten slag. This floats on the molten iron at the bottom of the furnace and runs out separately. It is used for making roads.

■ From iron to steel

The iron that comes out of the blast furnace is impure, because it contains about 4% carbon and smaller amounts of other elements. These impurities make it brittle. Before use, the iron is purified. The carbon content is reduced to about 0.15%, which helps make the metal tough and hard. It is then called **steel**. Other metals may be added to improve the quality of the steel.

One way of making steel on a large scale is shown in Picture 5. The furnace contains a mixture of scrap steel and molten iron from the blast furnace. The water-cooled lance blasts oxygen through the furnace, starting a violent reaction that oxidises the impurities in the iron. Carbon, for example, changes into carbon monoxide and escapes from the furnace as a gas. Other impurities, such as phosphorus, form acidic oxides that are removed from the steel by adding lime. The lime is a base and reacts with any acidic impurities, making a slag that floats on the molten metal.

The steel made in this way is sent to factories which turn it into countless useful products (picture 6 on the next page). Notice in picture 6 how the percentage of carbon in the steel affects its properties. The more carbon, the harder the steel becomes, but high carbon steels can be brittle. Eventually all these products get worn out and rusty, and they go as scrap iron to be recycled. About a third of all iron and steel gets recycled.

Eventually iron rusts (topic B3). Rust is iron oxide – the same compound as iron ore. So iron starts and ends its life as iron oxide.

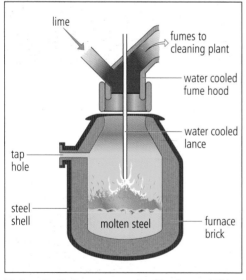

Picture 5 Basic oxygen steelmaking furnace. This type of furnace produces most of the steel that is manufactured in the UK.

Picture 6 Some uses of carbon steels.

MINING METALS – THE BENEFITS AND DRAWBACKS

Metals mean mining. If we want metals, there have to be mines where the ores are dug up.

Most of the metals we use in Britain are mined in other countries. There are benefits to be had from mining ores: it gives people jobs, and it helps create wealth for the community and the country.

But there are drawbacks too, because mining affects the environment. Mines are often **open cast**: that means they are on the surface, like quarries (picture 7). Open-cast mining makes huge holes which are an eyesore and which destroy the habitats of wildlife. Even underground mines can cause environmental problems: sometimes they cause **subsidence**, when the land above sinks into the mine below (picture 8).

Mines produce enormous amounts of waste. The dug up ore is mixed with useless rock and dirt, and this has to be separated when the ore is concentrated. This is done at the mine itself, because the cost of transporting the ore together with the waste would be far too high. The waste that is separated off has to be dumped somewhere, and often this leads to huge, ugly spoil heaps near to the mine.

Eventually, the ore gets used up and the mines become exhausted. Then the mine has to close, and this can bring serious unemployment to the local community. Sometimes the mine has to close before it is exhausted. If demand for the metal falls, its price falls too. It may no longer be worth keeping the mine open. This is what happened with many of the tin mines in Cornwall (picture 9).

So mining metals has its problems. The fact that these problems are often in another country doesn't make them any less serious. But remember how much we use metals: if we want these metals, we have to face the problems that come from getting them out of the ground. And it is often possible to reduce these problems. For example, open-cast workings and spoil heaps can be reclaimed and landscaped so that wildlife can return to them.

WHAT DETERMINES THE PRICE OF A METAL?

Metals vary enormously in price (picture 10). Why? Obviously it has something to do with abundance – if a metal is plentiful, it is likely to be cheap. Look how cheap iron is compared with gold. Iron makes up 5% of the Earth's crust, whereas gold is only 0.000 000 4%.

But it isn't only abundance that matters. Aluminium is even more abundant than iron, yet it is more expensive. This is because aluminium is fairly reactive, so it is more difficult than iron to get from its ore.

Picture 7 An open cast copper mine in Bulgaria.

Picture 8 Mining subsidence.

Picture 9 A disused tin mine in Cornwall.

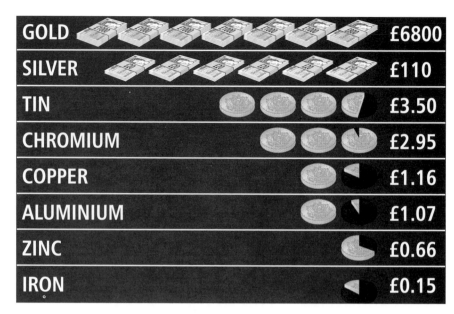

GOLD		£6800
SILVER		£110
TIN		£3.50
CHROMIUM		£2.95
COPPER		£1.16
ALUMINIUM		£1.07
ZINC		£0.66
IRON		£0.15

Picture 10 The relative prices of a kilogram of different metals.

There are three major factors affecting the price of any metal.

1 *Its abundance in the Earth's crust.*
2 *The concentration of the ore.* If the deposits of ore are concentrated, the metal is cheaper to produce because the ore does not need so much purifying.
3 *The cost of reduction.* To get the metal, the ore must be reduced. The less reactive the metal, the easier the ore is to reduce. So the cost of reduction of unreactive metals like copper is less than for reactive ones like aluminium.

You can try explaining the relative costs of metals in *The prices of metals* on page 133.

HOW LONG WILL METALS LAST?

Our supplies of metal ores will not last forever. Picture 12 shows how long the known reserves of certain metals will last. 'Known reserves' are the amounts of ore which we know it is worth mining at present prices.

Notice that the reserves of some metals will last much longer than others. Some metals, such as copper, are in very short supply. What should we do as reserves of these metals run out?

● *Try to find new reserves.* As old ore deposits run out, it is very likely that new ones will be discovered. But this cannot go on for ever!

● *Try to find other materials to replace the metals.* For example, copper pipes are being replaced by plastic ones.

● *Use the metals more carefully, and avoid waste.* We can save a lot of metal by recycling scrap material and using it again.

RECYCLING METALS

Have you recycled any metal lately? You might have put drink cans in a recycling 'bank'. Maybe you recently sold an old car for scrap. This kind of scrap metal can be melted down and used again – in other words, recycled.

All metals can be recycled. Recycling makes sense because

● it saves money;
● it means we need to dig up less metal ore, so reserves last longer;
● it solves the problem of waste disposal. Recycling metals stops them causing a litter problem and spoiling the environment.

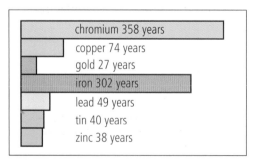

Picture 11 Dealers on the London Metal Exchange. The price varies constantly according to supply and demand.

| chromium 358 years |
| copper 74 years |
| gold 27 years |
| iron 302 years |
| lead 49 years |
| tin 40 years |
| zinc 38 years |

Picture 12 How long reserves of different metals will last.

Unfortunately, recycling isn't always easy. The scrap metal has to be collected and transported to the place where it will be processed. Each metal has to be separated from other materials – it's no use trying to recycle aluminium if it is mixed with iron. All this separating and transporting costs money, and if the cost is too high, recycling isn't worthwhile.

Ordinary people like you and me can do a lot to help by separating and transporting the metal ourselves. It's worth saving aluminium drink cans: even if you don't earn anything from them yourself, you have the satisfaction of knowing you are saving resources and preventing a litter problem!

Of course, recycling metals is more worthwhile when the metal is an expensive one. Even millionaires don't throw away gold jewellery when they are tired of it. They have it melted down instead. Practically all the gold we use gets recycled; compare this with aluminium, of which only 40% is recycled.

Metals are not the only materials that can be recycled. Glass, paper, cloth and plastics can all be recycled too. Old glass bottles returned to Bottle Banks can be melted down to make new bottles. Once again, this saves resources and solves a litter problem.

Picture 13 Aluminium cans, crushed into blocks for recycling.

Activities

A How much do metals cost?

ICT Get a copy of a newspaper or look on a website which has a lot of financial and business news. You should be able to find a section giving the prices of metals.

Try to work out the current prices of as many different metals as possible.

You will notice that there are often several different prices for the same metal. Try to work out what the various prices refer to, and why they are different.

B A recycling survey

Do a survey in your class to find out how much the families of people in the class recycle metals. You could try and find out who recycles aluminium foil, bottle tops and cans. You could ask whether any family has recently sold metal for scrap – for example an old car, or copper piping, or lead from the roof.

C Metal mining in Britain

ICT Britain used to be a major source of metal ores. Today most of the mines are closed because the ores have run out.

Try to find an example of metal mining in Britain, preferably near to your home.

It might be an old mine that is now closed, or it might even still be open. Use libraries, newspapers, websites or just ask around to find out about the mine. In particular try to find out:

- What metal ore was mined there?
- When was the mine opened? When did it close?
- Where was the ore processed into metal? Near the mine, or somewhere else?
- What impact has the mine had on the environment? Are there any spoil heaps or quarrying scars? Is there any subsidence?

Questions

1 Explain the meaning of the words that are underlined in the following passage.

Most metals occur in the Earth as ores. First the ore is dug up and then it has to be <u>concentrated</u>. Then the metal is <u>extracted</u> from the ore using a <u>reducing agent</u>.

2 Give an example of a metal that occurs in the Earth: (a) as an oxide; (b) as a chloride; (c) as a sulphide; (d) uncombined, as the metal itself.

3 Chromium metal is manufactured by heating chromium oxide, Cr_2O_3, with aluminium. The products are chromium and aluminium oxide.

  a What substance is oxidised in this reaction, and what is reduced?

  b Write a balanced equation for the reaction.

  c Does chromium come above or below aluminium in the reactivity series? Explain your answer.

  d Give two important uses of chromium metal.

4 a Iron is the cheapest of all metals. Give two reasons why.

  b Gold occurs uncombined and does not need extracting from an ore. Why, then, is it so expensive?

  c The Romans used iron, copper, lead, gold and other metals. Yet they never used aluminium, one of the most versatile of metals. Why not?

  d Give one important use of tin. What materials might replace tin for this use when reserves of the metal run out?

  e Less than half the iron we use gets recycled, yet practically all gold is recycled. Explain the difference.

5 Zinc is made by reducing zinc oxide, ZnO, in a blast furnace similar to the one used to make iron (picture 4, page 128).

  a What is the reducing agent in this process?

  b Write two equations to show the reactions that occur in the furnace to reduce zinc oxide to zinc.

6 What methods would you expect to be used to extract each of the following metals from their ores?

  a magnesium

  b lead

  c nickel (nickel comes between iron and lead in the reactivity series)

  d vanadium (vanadium comes between aluminium and zinc in the reactivity series).

Atmospheric corrosion of zinc

The map in picture 1 is about the corrosion of the metal zinc. It shows how fast zinc corrodes in different parts of England and Wales. Use the map to answer these questions.

1 The rates of corrosion are given in 'g per m² of zinc per year'. What do you think this means?

2 Suppose you had the job of producing a map like this one.

What experiments would you do?

3 What general rule can you make about the parts of the country where zinc corrodes particularly fast?

4 What general rule can you make about the parts of the country where zinc corrodes particularly slowly?

5 The rate of corrosion of zinc is affected by air pollution.

i) What type of air pollutants would tend to make zinc corrode faster?

ii) Give one example of this type of air pollutant.

6 Would you expect a similar pattern for the corrosion of iron? Explain your answer.

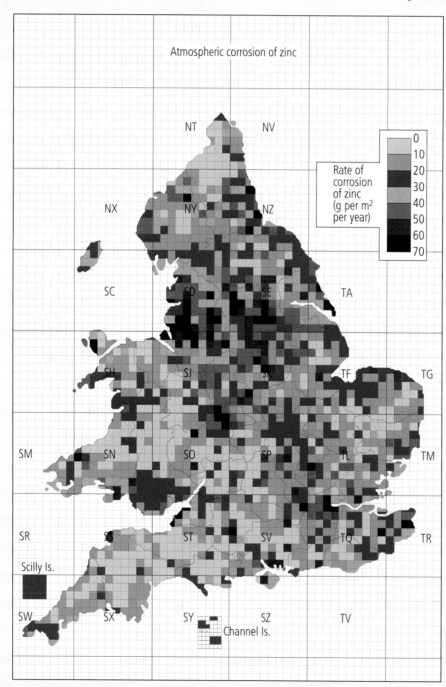

Picture 1 The atmospheric corrosion of zinc.

The prices of metals

Table 1 gives the average abundance of a number of metals in the Earth's crust.

Table 1 The average percentage abundance of some metals in the Earth's crust.

Metal	Average percentage abundance
Aluminium	8
Chromium	0.01
Copper	0.0055
Gold	0.000 0004
Iron	5
Silver	0.000 007
Tin	0.0002
Zinc	0.007

1 Make a list of the metals in order of abundance. Put the most abundant first.

2 Use picture 10 on page 130 to list the metals in order of price, cheapest first.

3 How well do the two lists match up? If the price of a metal depends on its abundance, you would expect the order to be the same in both your lists. Do you notice any exceptions?

4 The order of reactivity of these metals (most reactive first) is

aluminium, zinc, chromium, iron, tin, copper, silver, gold

Use this order of reactivity to try and explain any exceptions you noticed in (3).

5 Table 2 gives the lowest concentration of ore deposits from which four different metals can be economically extracted. For example, the table shows that it is not worth extracting iron from ore deposits that are less than 25% pure iron ore.

Try to give explanations for the relative sizes of the figures for the four metals. For example, why is it worth using copper ore deposits that are only 0.06% pure, but not worth using iron ore unless it is at least 25% pure?

Table 2 The lowest concentrations of ore deposits from which metals can be economically extracted (in the case of gold the figure is for the pure metal, not the ore).

Metal	Concentration (% of deposit)
Aluminium	32
Iron	25
Copper	0.06
Gold	0.0014

Mining copper in Papua New Guinea

One of the biggest copper mines in the world is on Bougainville Island in Papua New Guinea, north of Australia. It is an enormous open-cast pit.

Every day, about 100 000 tonnes of ore and rock are mined. From this, just 400 tonnes of pure copper are extracted. The copper ore contains small amounts of silver and gold, and these help pay the cost of extracting the metal.

Picture 1 shows what happens to each tonne of ore and rock after it is dug up.

Purification of the ore produces enormous amounts of powdered waste rock. This waste is dumped in the river, and a lot of it ends up in a huge delta at the mouth of the river.

1 What percentage of the ore and rock is pure copper?

2 What percentage of the ore and rock is waste?

3 The percentage of copper in the ore is so low that it is not worth extracting the copper alone.

However, there is a special factor about this mine that makes it pay. What is this special factor?

4 This mine produces enormous quantities of waste rock. Explain why.

5 What advantages do you think this mine brings to the island of Bougainville?

6 What disadvantages do you think this mine brings to the island?

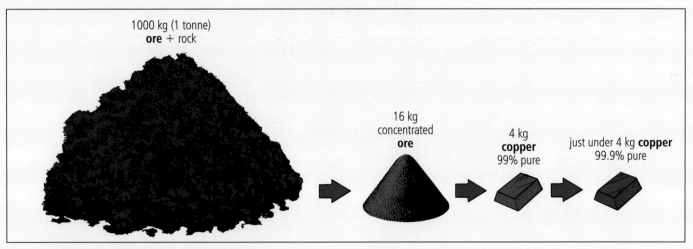

1000 kg (1 tonne) **ore** + rock

16 kg concentrated **ore**

4 kg **copper** 99% pure

just under 4 kg **copper** 99.9% pure

Picture 1 What you get from each tonne of ore and rock.

Families of elements

A guided tour of the Periodic Table

The Periodic Table is our classification system for the elements.

Picture 1 In a supermarket, similar foods are classified together to make it easier to find your way around.

If you visit a supermarket regularly, you will know that it uses a classification system. The food products are not all mixed up on the shelves – if they were, it would take ages to find what you want. Instead, similar food products are grouped together (picture 1). If you are an experienced shopper, you know which part of the supermarket to go to for what you want.

There are 92 naturally occurring elements. This is less than the number of products in your average supermarket, but it is still useful to have a way of classifying elements so that similar ones are grouped together. We have already seen that elements can be classified as metals and non-metals (topic E1), but these are two rather large groups. The Periodic Table provides us with a more precise classification system. The system was developed by a Russian chemist, Dmitri Mendeléev, in 1869.

Like the supermarket, the Periodic Table groups similar elements together. Like an experienced shopper, a scientist knows what type of elements to expect in different parts of the table. Picture 2 shows the usual form of the Periodic Table. There may be a similar one on the wall of your science laboratory. There is an expanded version of this table in the Data section.

Picture 2 The Periodic Table. The elements after 92 are all artificially made.

	group 1	group 2											group 3	group 4	group 5	group 6	group 7	group 0
period 1						hydrogen H 1												helium He 2
period 2	lithium Li 3	beryllium Be 4											boron B 5	carbon C 6	nitrogen N 7	oxygen O 8	fluorine F 9	neon Ne 10
period 3	sodium Na 11	magnesium Mg 12											aluminium Al 13	silicon Si 14	phosphorus P 15	sulphur S 16	chlorine Cl 17	argon Ar 18
period 4	potassium K 19	calcium Ca 20	Sc 21	Ti 22	V 23	chromium Cr 24	manganese Mn 25	iron Fe 26	cobalt Co 27	nickel Ni 28	copper Cu 29	zinc Zn 30	Ga 31	germanium Ge 32	arsenic As 33	selenium Se 34	bromine Br 35	Kr 36
period 5	Rb 37	Sr 38	Y 39	Zr 40	Nb 41	Mo 42	Tc 43	Ru 44	Rh 45	Pd 46	silver Ag 47	cadmium Cd 48	In 49	tin Sn 50	Sb 51	Te 52	iodine I 53	Xe 54
period 6	Cs 55	Ba 56	Lanthanides see below	Hf 72	Ta 73	W 74	Re 75	Os 76	Ir 77	platinum Pt 78	gold Au 79	mercury Hg 80	Tl 81	lead Pb 82	Bi 83	Po 84	astatine At 85	Rn 86
period 7	Fr 87	Ra 88	Actinides see below	Rf 104	Db 105	Sg 106	Bh 107	Hs 108	Mt 109									

Lanthanides	La 57	Ce 58	Pr 59	Nd 60	Pm 61	Sm 62	Eu 63	Gd 64	Tb 65	Dy 66	Ho 67	Er 68	Tm 69	Yb 70	Lu 71
Actinides	Ac 89	Th 90	Pa 91	U 92	Np 93	Pu 94	Am 95	Cm 96	Bk 97	Cf 98	Es 99	Fm 100	Md 101	No 102	Lr 103

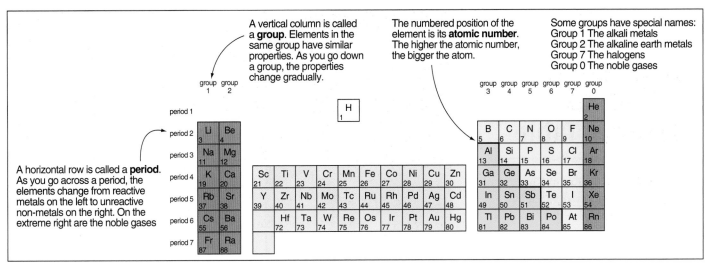

Picture 3 Names used in the Periodic Table.

THE PARTS OF THE PERIODIC TABLE

Picture 3 shows the names we use to describe the different features of the Periodic Table. You find particular types of elements in particular areas, or **blocks**, of the table, as shown in picture 4.

■ Why does the Periodic Table classify elements so well?

The arrangement of elements in the Periodic Table is linked to the arrangement of electrons in their atoms. There is more about this in topic J5.

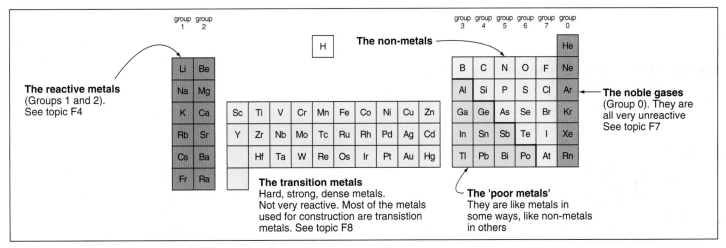

Picture 4 The blocks within the Periodic Table.

Questions

1 How do the properties of elements change as you go (a) down a group (b) across a period?

2 To which block of the Periodic Table does each of the following elements belong?

   a chromium, Cr
   b argon, Ar
   c calcium, Ca
   d germanium, Ge
   e sulphur, S

3 Which of the following elements will be most like selenium, Se?

   Bromine, Br; arsenic, As; iodine, I; sulphur, S; aluminium, Al.

4 a Why is argon, Ar, used to fill light bulbs?
   b Would you expect bromine, Br, to conduct electricity?
   c Sodium, Na, and aluminium, Al, are in the same horizontal row (period). Which is more reactive? Explain your answer.

5 Whereabouts in the Periodic Table would you expect to find
   a the most reactive metal
   b the most reactive non-metal?

F2

Dmitri Mendeléev and the Periodic Table

The Periodic Table was invented by Dmitri Mendeléev in 1869.

Picture 1 Dmitri Mendeléev was born in Siberia in 1834, the youngest of 15 children. His father went blind when Dmitri was young, and his mother worked hard to bring up the family. She managed to run a glass factory at the same time, and saved up to send Dmitri to be educated. She died, exhausted, shortly after he started his university studies at St Petersburg.

After studying, Mendeléev became a professor at St Petersburg University. He wrote a famous textbook and was a brilliant teacher. Everyone wanted to come to his lectures. At that time, women were not allowed in university classes, so Mendeléev gave extra classes for women in his spare time. He was very down-to-earth – he always travelled third class in trains, along with the peasants. He cut his hair once a year, in spring when the warm weather set in.

By 1869, over 60 elements had been discovered, and scientists were wondering what to do with them all. The time was right to look for a way to classify elements. By this time, a very important piece of information was known about most elements—their atomic weights. (Nowadays we call 'atomic weight' *relative atomic mass*.)

DMITRI CLASSIFIES THE ELEMENTS

Dmitri Mendeléev was a chemistry professor in St Petersburg in Russia. He looked for a way to classify the elements, and he started by collecting as much information as he could about all of them. Mendeléev enjoyed playing cards, and one day he tried writing out a card for each element. On each card, he wrote the name of the element, and also its atomic weight (picture 3). The atomic weights were important because they meant he could put the cards in order (picture 4).

Next, Mendeléev tried arranging the cards in sets—and he noticed an amazing thing (picture 5). *Cards with similar elements* came together. For example, sodium and potassium, both very reactive metals, came together. Fluorine and chlorine, both reactive non-metals, also came together.

From this discovery, Mendeléev made the first Periodic Table. Picture 6 shows part of it. You will see that it is different in some ways from the modern version shown on the previous page. But the basic idea of vertical groups containing similar elements is the same.

MAKING PREDICTIONS

Mendeléev still had to convince other scientists that his ideas were right. Many of them didn't believe in his classification. The best way to test a scientific idea is to use it to make *predictions*. If the predictions turn out to be right, people are more likely to believe your theory. You haven't *proved* the theory, because your next prediction might turn out to be wrong. But the more correct predictions you make, the more people will believe the theory.

Picture 2 A Periodic Table on a wall in St Petersburg, Russia, where Dimitri Mendeléev worked.

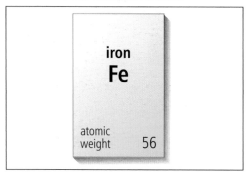

Picture 3 An 'element' card.

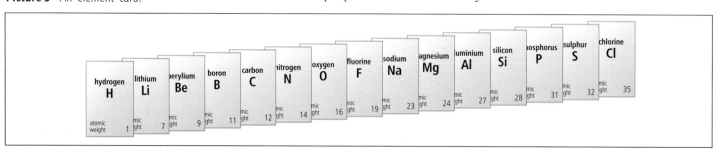

Picture 4 The cards arranged in order of atomic weight.

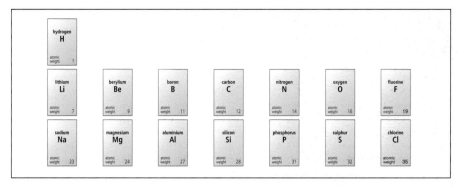

Picture 5 The cards arranged in sets.

When Mendeléev drew up his Periodic Table, he found that there were gaps in it (marked ? in picture 6). He decided that these must correspond to missing elements that had not yet been discovered. He realised he could use his Periodic Table to make predictions about these missing elements.

For example, you can see there is a missing element between silicon, Si, and tin, Sn in picture 6. Mendeléev knew the properties of silicon and tin, and he knew that properties change steadily as you move down a group. So he was able to predict the properties of the missing element, which he called 'eka-silicon'. For example, he predicted that the relative atomic mass of 'eka-silicon' would be the average of silicon (28.1) and tin (118.7), which comes to 73.4. He also predicted the colour (grey), density and melting point of 'eka-silicon'.

Well, in 1886 'eka-silicon' was discovered in Germany and named germanium. Sure enough, its properties were almost exactly what Mendeléev predicted. Its relative atomic mass, for instance, was 73.6, compared with the prediction of 73.4! Mendeléev's prediction about other missing elements—gallium and scandium— also turned out to be very accurate. Now everyone had to admit that he was right. There is more about Mendeléev's predictions in *The gaps in Mendeléev's table* on page 151.

Today, you will find a modified version of Dmitri Mendeléev's Periodic Table on the walls of chemistry laboratories the world over. One of the most recently discovered elements, mendelevium, number 101, is named after him (picture 7). But remember: it was only by making successful predictions that Mendeléev convinced the world he was right.

Picture 7 Mendeléev working in his office in 1903.

Questions

You may need to re-read the topic to answer some of the following questions.

1. a Why was the time right in 1869 for Mendeléev to look for a way of classifying elements?

   b Mendeléev made his breakthrough by writing the names of elements on cards. Why did this help?

   c Many scientists did not believe Mendeléev's ideas at first. How did he convince them?

2. Describe in your own words how Mendeléev predicted the properties of elements that had not yet been discovered.

3. Mendeléev listed the elements in order of their atomic weight.

   a What name do we use for 'atomic weight' nowadays?

   b The modern Periodic Table lists the elements in order of their atomic *number*.

   i Explain what is meant by the atomic number of an element.

   ii Why did Mendeléev not list elements in order of atomic number as we do today?

					GROUP								
		1	2	3	4	5	6	7	8				
Period 1		H											
Period 2		Li		Be	B	C	N	O	F				
Period 3		Na		Mg	Al	Si	P	S	Cl				
Period 4	K	Cu	Ca	Zn	?	?	Ti	?	V	As	Cr	Se	Mn	Br	Fe Co Ni
Period 5	Rb	Ag	Sr	Cd	Y	Ir	Zr	Sn	Nb	Sb	Mo	Te	?	I	Ru Rh Pd

Picture 6 Part of Mendeléev's Periodic Table. Missing elements are marked' ?'

F3

Across a period

The properties of elements vary widely across a period – from reactive metal to unreactive gas.

Picture 1   This painting by Joseph Wright of Derby portrays the discovery of phosphorus by Hennig Brandt in 1669. Brandt called his discovery 'cold fire' because phosphorus glows in the dark.

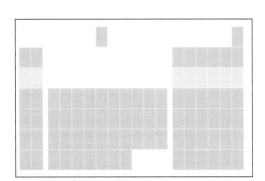

Picture 2   Period 3 of the Periodic Table.

Each horizontal row of elements in the Periodic Table is called a period. It starts with a reactive metal and finishes with a very unreactive gas. Between these two extremes there is a gradual shift of properties as the atomic number increases. Let's look in more detail at a typical period—period 3, which begins with sodium and ends with argon (pictures 2 and 3).

PHYSICAL PROPERTIES

	Na	Mg	Al	Si	P	S	Cl	Ar
Structure	← giant metallic →			giant covalent	← simple molecular →			
Electrical conductivity	← good →			semi-conductor	← very poor →			

Table 1   Structure and electrical conductivity of the elements, Na to Ar.

Table 1 gives the structure and electrical conductivity of the elements in period 3. Sodium, magnesium and aluminium, the first three elements in this period, are all metals. You can learn more about sodium in topic F4, *Sodium and family*. The next element, silicon, is called a semi-conductor because its electrical conductivity is between that of a metal and a non-metal.

 The next two elements, phosphorus and sulphur, are non-metallic solids and the last two, chlorine and argon, are gases.

CHEMICAL PROPERTIES

■ Reactivity and ion formation

Sodium, magnesium and aluminium are reactive metals. They readily lose electrons and produce positive ions, so they form ionic compounds (see topic J6). The charge on the metal ion is linked to the group number of the metal (table 2).

Table 2   The charge on a metal ion is linked to its group number

Element	Group	Ion formed
sodium	1	Na^+
magnesium	2	Mg^{2+}
aluminium	3	Al^{3+}

sodium	magnesium	aluminium	silicon	phosphorus	sulphur	chlorine	argon
Na	Mg	Al	Si	P	S	Cl	Ar
11	12	13	14	15	16	17	18

Picture 3   Period 3—sodium to argon.

The non-metals in the period are much less predictable. Phosphorus and chlorine are very reactive elements but argon, the last element in the period, is a member of the noble gas group and has no compounds at all. The bonds in non-metal compounds can be either ionic or covalent.

Let's look more closely at some compounds of the elements in this period.

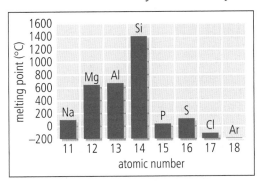

Picture 4 Melting points of the elements Na to Ar.

Oxides

Formula	Na₂O	MgO	Al₂O₃	SiO₂	P₂O₅	SO₃
Type of bond	ionic	ionic	ionic	covalent	covalent	covalent
Acid or base?	base	base	ampho-teric	weak acid	acid	acid
Structure	giant ionic	giant ionic	giant ionic	giant covalent	simple molecular	simple molecular

Formula row (LaTeX): Na_2O, MgO, Al_2O_3, SiO_2, P_2O_5, SO_3

Table 3 Some oxides of the elements from sodium to sulphur.

Oxides of the *metals* in this period have giant ionic structures while the oxides of *non-metals* tend to have simple molecular structures (table 3). Notice that the oxide of silicon (quartz) is giant covalent, a different type of structure from that of the other oxides. (See picture 7, on page 85.)

The oxides of the metals tend to be bases, while those of the non-metals are acids (table 3). The behaviour of aluminium oxide is different. It is amphoteric—it reacts with both acids and bases (picture 5).

Aluminium shows some properties that are typical of a metal, and some that are typical of a non-metal. For this reason, it is sometimes called a 'poor metal'. The general trend in chemical properties across period 3 is

metal → poor metal → non metal

We find the same pattern in other periods.

Picture 5 The protective coating of aluminium oxide on these saucepans is amphoteric. It will be attacked by the strongly alkaline detergent used in this dishwasher.

Questions

1 a Look at the graph in Picture 4. Describe how the melting points of elements in this period vary with atomic number.

  b How does the structure of these elements (see table 1) help to explain the variation in their melting points?

2 Here are the densities of the elements in the period Na–Ar:

	Na	Mg	Al	Si	P	S	Cl	Ar
density (g/cm³)	0.97	1.74	2.70	2.33	1.82	1.96	0.0029	0.0027

  a Plot a graph to show how the densities of the elements vary with increasing atomic number.

  b Do you notice a pattern in your graph? Use the data in Table 1 to try to explain the variation in the densities of these elements.

3 a In Table 1, what link do you notice between the electrical conductivities of the elements and their structures?

  b In Table 3, what pattern can you see in the formulas of the oxides?

4 Aluminium is one of a group of elements in the Periodic Table which are described as 'poor metals' (see page 137, topic F1).

  a In what ways does the oxide of aluminium seem to be different from the oxides of other metals?

  b Why is aluminium called a 'poor metal'?

5 Elements X, Y and Z are in the second period of the Periodic Table (Li–Ne). Use the patterns you have read about in this topic to identify each element from their descriptions below. Give the name and atomic symbol for X, Y and Z.

  a Element X is a gas which does not form any compounds.

  b Element Y has two crystalline forms. One of the oxides of Y is a weakly acidic gas whose formula is YO_2.

  c Element Z is a soft metal whose density is 0.54 g/cm³. Its oxide, Z_2O, dissolves in water to give a solution of very high pH.

F4

Sodium and family

The alkali metals are a group of reactive metals in the Periodic Table.

lithium	
Li	
3	
sodium	
Na	
11	
potassium	
K	
19	
rubidium	
Rb	
37	
caesium	
Cs	
55	
francium	
Fr	
87	

Picture 1 Group 1 – the alkali metals.

Picture 2 'Low sodium' salt is one-third sodium chloride, NaCl, and two-thirds potassium chloride, KCl. Both compounds taste salty. Replacing sodium with potassium makes the salt healthier for people suffering from high blood pressure.

Picture 1 shows Group 1 of the Periodic Table. We will be looking mainly at the first three elements, lithium, sodium and potassium. Rubidium and caesium are rare and extremely reactive, and you never meet them in school laboratories. Francium is radioactive and does not occur naturally.

ALKALI METALS ARE SIMILAR

The alkali metals in Group 1:

- are all reactive metals. They have to be stored under oil to stop them reacting with the air
- all form ions carrying a single plus charge (e.g. Li^+, Na^+, K^+)
- form compounds with similar formulas (e.g. lithium chloride LiCl, sodium chloride NaCl, potassium chloride KCl). This is handy – if you know the formula of a sodium compound, say, you can quickly work out the formula of a similar potassium compound
- all react with non-metals to form salts. These salts are all white, crystalline and soluble in water
- are soft and can be cut with a knife
- all have low density – lithium, sodium and potassium will float on water.

Notice that where physical properties like strength and density are concerned, the alkali metals are pretty feeble compared with transition metals like iron and copper. But when it comes to chemical reactivity, they're much more impressive.

◼ Alkali metal compounds

The compounds of alkali metals all have similar properties.

- Alkali metal compounds all have giant ionic structures (topic C7).
- Alkali metal compounds are normally white solids.
- Alkali metal compounds are always soluble in water.

ALKALI METALS ARE DIFFERENT

The alkali metals are all very reactive, but they get more reactive as you go down the group. Let's look at an example.

◼ The reaction of alkali metals with water

All the alkali metals react with water, forming hydrogen and the metal hydroxide. For example, with sodium:

$$\text{sodium} + \text{water} \rightarrow \text{sodium hydroxide} + \text{hydrogen}$$
$$Na(s) + 2H_2O(l) \rightarrow 2NaOH(aq) + H_2(g)$$

The sodium hydroxide makes the water become alkaline. That is why these are called the alkali metals. The reaction is highly exothermic – it gives out a lot of heat.

When sodium is put into water, the sodium melts and skids around the surface as hydrogen is given off. Sometimes the hydrogen catches fire – the reaction gives out enough heat to ignite it.

If you move down the group, to potassium, the reaction with water is even more vigorous (see picture 5 on page 121, topic E2). Once again hydrogen is given off, but this time it catches fire immediately, and the potassium may explode dangerously. Rubidium and caesium explode as soon as they are put into water.

Table 1 summarises the reactions of lithium, sodium and potassium with water. Notice that lithium, following the trend, reacts relatively quietly. Table 1 also shows the reaction of these three metals with air. Once again, you can see there is a gradual increase in reactivity as you go down the group.

Table 1 Reactions of lithium, sodium and potassium with water and air.

Element	Reaction with water	Reaction with air
Lithium	reacts steadily $2Li(s) + 2H_2O(l) \rightarrow 2LiOH(aq) + H_2(g)$	tarnishes slowly to give a layer of oxide
Sodium	reacts vigorously $2Na(s) + 2H_2O(l) \rightarrow 2NaOH(aq) + H_2(g)$	tarnishes quickly to give a layer of oxide
Potassium	reacts violently $2K(s) + 2H_2O(l) \rightarrow 2KOH(aq) + H_2(g)$	tarnishes very quickly to give a layer of oxide

FLAME COLOURS

Some metal compounds give a characteristic colour to a Bunsen burner flame. Lithium compounds give a brilliant red flame colour; sodium compounds give yellow–orange, and potassium compounds lilac. There is more about flame tests in topic F5.

Changes in physical properties

The melting points of the alkali metals decrease gradually as you go down the group. Lithium at the top of the group melts at 180°C, caesium at the bottom melts at 29°C. There is a similar trend in the hardness of the metals. Lithium is the hardest, but it can still be cut with a knife. Sodium is easier to cut – a bit like butter from the fridge. Potassium is easier still – like butter at room temperature.

EXPLAINING THE REACTIVITY OF GROUP 1 METALS

Group 1 elements have a single electron on their outer shell (picture 3). (Topic J5 explains electron structure.) When a Group 1 metal, M, reacts, it loses this electron, forming a positive ion M^+. This gives the metal a stable electron structure, with a full outer shell. All the metals in Group 1 behave this way, so their chemical reactions are similar.

Picture 3 shows that potassium has one more electron shell than sodium. This means the outer shell electron in potassium is further from the positive nucleus, so it is not attracted so strongly. It is therefore lost more easily than the outer shell electron in sodium. Because potassium loses its electron more easily than sodium, it is more reactive. This idea explains why, in general, the metals become more reactive as you go down the group.

WHAT ARE THE ALKALI METALS USED FOR?

One familiar use of sodium is in sodium vapour lamps, the yellow street lamps you often see in cities. In general, though, the alkali metals are so reactive that as *elements* they have few uses. But they have many important *compounds*, and these have lots of uses.

Sodium compounds are particularly important: your home probably contains sodium chloride (salt), sodium hydrogencarbonate (bicarbonate) and sodium hydroxide (oven cleaner), to name just three. You will come across compounds of the alkali metals in several other topics in this book.

Questions

1 List the alkali metals in order of reactivity, with the most reactive first.

2 How do each of the following properties of alkali metals change as you move down the group?
   a relative atomic mass
   b melting point
   c hardness
   d density
   e chemical reactivity

3 Rubidium comes just below potassium in Group 1. Predict the following properties of rubidium.
   a what happens when it is exposed to air
   b the equation for the reaction of rubidium with water
   c how readily rubidium can be cut with a knife

4 Look at the label from 'LoSalt' shown in picture 2. Here is part of the information section of the label:

> It is suggested that people receiving medication for diabetes, heart or kidney disorders should consult their family doctor who will advise on how to use this salt alternative.
>
> 1 g of LoSalt contains approximately 131 mg of sodium and 346 mg of potassium.

   a What is the mass in grams of (i) sodium (ii) potassium in 1 g of 'LoSalt'?
   b Add together the masses of sodium and potassium which you worked out in (a). Why don't they add up to 1 g?
   c Name one other compound, other than potassium chloride, that could be used to replace sodium chloride in salt. Why do you think it is *potassium* chloride that is actually used?

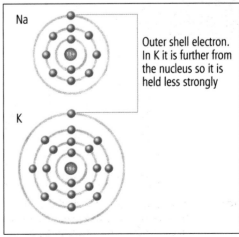

Outer shell electron. In K it is further from the nucleus so it is held less strongly

Picture 3 The electron structures of sodium, Na, and potassium, K. Both have one electron in the outer shell.

Magnesium and family

Group 2 is another family of reactive metals in the Periodic Table.

| beryllium Be 4 |
| magnesium Mg 12 |
| calcium Ca 20 |
| strontium Sr 38 |
| barium Ba 56 |
| radium Ra 88 |

Picture 1 Group 2 – the alkaline earth metals.

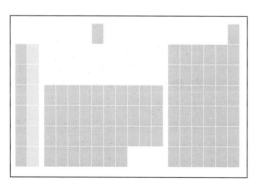

Picture 2 Group 2 in the Periodic Table.

Group 2 is called the **alkaline earth metals**. They are not quite as reactive as the metals in Group 1. Picture 2 shows their position in the Periodic Table.

GROUP 2 METALS ARE SIMILAR

Apart from beryllium, which often behaves differently, the metals in group 2:

- are reactive and tarnish quickly when exposed to the air
- form ions with two positive charges (e.g. Mg^{2+}, Ca^{2+}, Ba^{2+})
- form compounds with similar formulas (e.g. magnesium chloride, $MgCl_2$, calcium chloride, $CaCl_2$, barium chloride, $BaCl_2$)
- react with non-metals to form salts which are white
- have low density but will not float on water.

The metals in this group are not as reactive as the alkali metals of Group 1. None of the Group 2 metals have to be stored under oil, although they corrode in air far more rapidly than transition metals like iron and copper.

GROUP 2 METALS ARE DIFFERENT

■ Changes in chemical properties

The trend in chemical behaviour in Group 2 is similar to that in Group 1. *The metals become more reactive as you go down the group.* We can see this pattern in the reactions of the Group 2 metals with water.

When placed in *hot* water, magnesium reacts only slowly to give hydrogen gas and magnesium oxide:

$$\text{magnesium} + \text{water} \rightarrow \text{magnesium oxide} + \text{hydrogen}$$
$$Mg(s) + H_2O(l) \rightarrow MgO(s) + H_2(g)$$

Magnesium oxide is slightly soluble in water and weakly alkaline. This is why it is used as a cure for stomach acidity in mixtures such as *Milk of Magnesia.*

Calcium, which is immediately below magnesium in Group 2, reacts briskly with *cold* water, giving off a rapid stream of hydrogen. The following reaction is taking place:

$$\text{calcium} + \text{water} \rightarrow \text{calcium hydroxide} + \text{hydrogen}$$
$$Ca(s) + 2H_2O(l) \rightarrow Ca(OH)_2(aq) + H_2(g)$$

The alkali which is formed, calcium hydroxide, is more soluble in water and a stronger alkali than magnesium oxide. It is also known as slaked lime and has many industrial uses (see topic D2).

Try to predict what will happen when strontium and barium are added to water.

EXPLAINING THE REACTIVITY OF THE GROUP 2 METALS

We can explain the reactivity of Group 2 metals in the same way as for Group 1 metals (page 143). All Group 2 metals have two electrons in the outer shell. They lose their electrons readily, forming M^{2+} ions. As you go down the group, the outer shell electrons get further from the nucleus. The outer shell electrons are therefore lost more easily, making the metals more reactive.

PHYSICAL PROPERTIES OF GROUP 2 METALS

Group 2 metals have higher melting points than those in Group 1, and are much harder. The densities of Group 2 metals are also greater than those of Group 1 metals—but they are still very low. For example, a car part which weighs 32 kg if made of steel or 11 kg if made of aluminium would weigh only 7 kg if made of magnesium.

Unfortunately, the Group 2 metals are not particularly strong, even though they are light. They are often combined with other metals to produce alloys with more useful properties. Magnesium alloys combine lightness with strength. They are used in making parts for aircraft, spacecraft, cars and portable tools.

Picture 3   We use compounds of Group 2 metals to add colour to firework displays.

THE BIOLOGICAL IMPORTANCE OF MAGNESIUM AND CALCIUM

Plants need magnesium for healthy growth. In soils where magnesium compounds are deficient, green plants fail to develop and their leaves turn yellow. This is because magnesium is one of the elements needed to make chlorophyll, the green pigment which brings about photosynthesis (see topic I3).

In its ionic form, Ca^{2+}, calcium is an essential part of the diet of animals (picture 4). A deficiency of calcium prevents bones and teeth from developing properly. This leads to rickets, a condition in which bones soften and deform.

There is an abundance of rocks and minerals in the Earth's crust containing calcium. Many of these are derived from the remains of skeletons and shells of ancient sea creatures.

Picture 4   Bones are largely made from calcium phosphate, $Ca_3(PO_4)_3$. This is unreactive and does not deteriorate like the rest of the body.

GROUP 2 FIREWORKS

Group 2 metals produce the kind of colourful combustion you can see in picture 3. Compounds of Group 2 metals produce characteristic flame colours. Barium compounds turn a flame pale green, strontium gives crimson and calcium brick red. Which Group 2 metals might have produced the colours in picture 3?

Magnesium does not have a characteristic flame colour. However, magnesium is useful because it burns with a brilliant white light. It is used in distress flares and in fireworks that give a white light.

■ Flame tests

Flame colours are useful way to identify metals in compounds. In a flame test, a sample of a compound is held on a wire in a Bunsen burner flame (picture 5). The compound vaporises in the flame, and gives the flame a characteristic colour. Table 7 in the Data Section summarises the flame colours produced by different metals.

Flame tests can be used to find out *how much* of a metal is present in a sample. An **atomic emission spectrometer** is a sophisticated instrument which measures the intensity of a flame colour. The more of the metal there is, the more intense the colour. This method is used in steelworks, to find out the composition of a sample of steel.

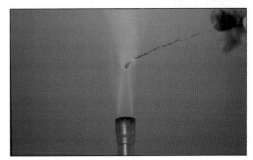

Picture 5   Carrying out a flame test. Which metal might give this colour?

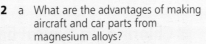

Questions

1   a   Which of the Group 2 metals is most reactive?

   b   Describe what you would expect to see when this metal reacts with water.

   c   Write both word and symbol equations to represent the reaction of this metal with water.

2   a   What are the advantages of making aircraft and car parts from magnesium alloys?

   b   What are the disadvantages of using magnesium for this purpose?

3   Explain why strontium is more reactive than calcium but less reactive than barium.

4   A Group 2 metal, P, burns fiercely in air, producing a white ash, Q. When water is added to Q, it does not dissolve but the mixture of Q and water is weakly alkaline. Q dissolves readily in dilute hydrochloric acid and a white solid, R, can be crystallised from this solution. When sodium hydroxide solution is added to a solution of R in water, a white precipitate, S, is produced.

Identify the substances P, Q, R and S by writing the name and formula of each one.

Chlorine and family

The halogens are a typical group of non-metals in the Periodic Table.

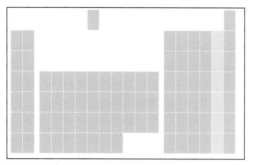

Picture 2   Group 7 in the Periodic Table.

fluorine
F
9
chlorine
Cl
17
bromine
Br
35
iodine
I
53
astatine
At
85

Picture 3   Group 7 – the halogens

Testing for chlorine

We use the bleaching action of chlorine to test for the gas. Hold a piece of damp indicator paper in a tube of gas. If the indicator is bleached, the gas is chlorine.

Picture 1

FANCY A SWIM?

Everyone knows the smell of chlorine – it's the smell you get in swimming pools. It gets in your hair and your swimming costume, and your skin smells of it even when you are dry. What's more, the chlorine in the swimming pool water can really make your eyes sting.

Why do they put this stuff in swimming pools? The trouble is, you can easily get infected with diseases from swimming pool water. It's full of people, some of them with sore throats, ear infections or worse. And it's usually warm, which encourages the germs to breed.

The chlorine is put in the water to kill the germs. Chlorine is a reactive element, and it combines with many substances. Chlorine reacts with substances in the cells of living things, killing the cells. In fact, chlorine has been used as a poison gas.

Fortunately, there isn't enough chlorine in swimming pools to do much damage to you – apart from affecting some of the cells on the surface of your eyes. But the people who look after swimming pools do have to be careful about the amount of chlorine they use.

Household bleach also smells of chlorine. Bleach contains chlorine and chlorine compounds. These reactive substances combine with dyes in cloth, and turn them into colourless compounds. Bleach also kills bacteria, so it's good for pouring down toilets and other places where germs may lurk.

■ Chlorine – a typical halogen

Chlorine has many of the typical properties of its family, the halogen family. They form Group 7 of the Periodic Table (pictures 2 and 3).

The elements in a group of the Periodic Table are *similar* to each other – but they also *change* gradually as you go down the group. Group 7 shows this very well. In this topic we will concentrate mainly on the first three halogens: chlorine, bromine and iodine (picture 4). The first halogen, fluorine, is so reactive that it is very difficult to handle. The last halogen, astatine, is radioactive and does not occur naturally.

HALOGENS ARE SIMILAR

The three halogens in picture 4 don't *look* very similar. But a closer look at their properties shows they have a lot in common.

The halogens:

- are all poisonous and smelly
- are all non-metals
- all form diatomic molecules (e.g. Cl_2, Br_2, I_2)
- often form compounds with similar formulas (e.g. sodium chloride, NaCl; sodium bromide, NaBr; sodium iodide, NaI)
- all react with metals to form salts
- all form ions carrying a single negative charge (e.g. Cl^-, Br^-, I^-).

The best known salt is common salt, sodium chloride, NaCl. It contains chlorine in the form of chloride ions, Cl^-. The other halogens form similar salts: sodium bromide and sodium iodide are white solids, very similar to common salt. They contain halide ions: Br^- and I^-.

HALOGENS ARE DIFFERENT

Picture 4 shows some of the differences between the halogens. Notice the gradual change in properties, from gas to liquid to solid as you go down the group. The bar chart in picture 6 compares the boiling points of the halogens. There is also a gradual change in the intensity of colour, from pale to dark.

These gradual changes are typical of the variation of properties in a group of non-metals. Following the trend, it will not surprise you to learn that fluorine, at the top of the group, is a pale yellow gas.

Notice that the trend within a group of *non-metals* is the opposite of that in a group of *metals*. With non-metals, the most reactive element is at the *top* of the group. With metals, the most reactive element is at the *bottom* of the group.

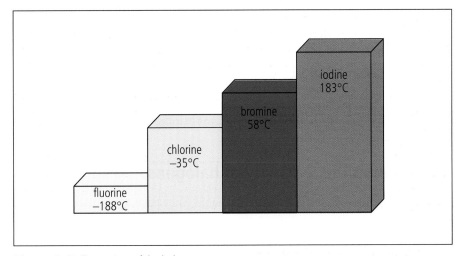

Picture 6 Boiling points of the halogens.

CHEMICAL REACTIVITY OF THE HALOGENS

The halogens are pretty reactive – in fact, fluorine is the most reactive of all the non-metals (picture 7). But once again, *there is a gradual change as you go down the group: the halogens become steadily less reactive.* Table 1 shows some examples of this. Notice the reaction with iron, for example. Chlorine reacts vigorously, but iodine hardly reacts at all.

- Dense pale green gas
- Smelly and poisonous
- Occurs as chlorides, especially sodium chloride in the sea
- Relative atomic mass 35.5

- Deep red liquid with red-brown vapour
- Smelly and poisonous Occurs as bromides, especially magnesium bromide in the sea
- Relative atomic mass 79.9

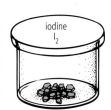

- Grey solid with purple vapour
- Smelly and poisonous
- Occurs as iodides and iodates in some rocks and in seaweed
- Relative atomic mass 126.9

Picture 4 Chlorine, bromine and iodine.

Picture 5 Iron wool burning in chlorine. Notice the brown iron chloride that is formed.

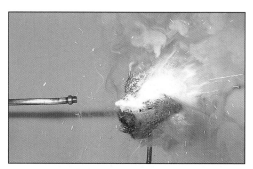

Picture 7 When a stream of fluorine is directed onto iron wool, the iron reacts violently and forms iron fluoride.

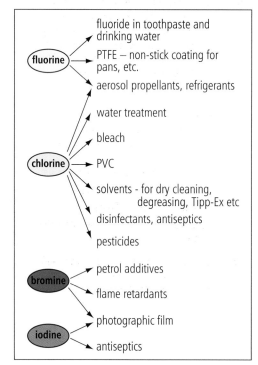

Picture 8 Some of the important uses of the halogens.

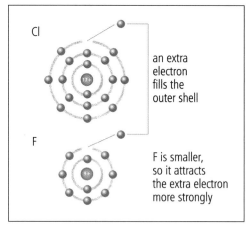

Picture 9 The electron structures of flourine, F, and chlorine, Cl. Both have 7 electrons in the outer shell.

Table 1 Some reactions of halogens.

Reaction	Chlorine	Bromine	Iodine
With coloured dyes	bleaches quickly	bleaches slowly	bleaches very slowly
With iron	iron wool reacts vigorously with chlorine after heating to start it off. Iron chloride is formed. $2Fe + 3Cl_2 \rightarrow 2FeCl_3$	iron wool reacts steadily with bromine, but needs heating all the time. Iron bromide is formed. $2Fe + 3Br_2 \rightarrow 2FeBr_3$	iron wool reacts very slowly with iodine, even when heated. Iron iodide is formed $2Fe + 3I_2 \rightarrow 2FeI_3$
With hydrogen	chlorine and hydrogen explode explode in sunlight $H_2 + Cl_2 \rightarrow 2HCl$	bromine and hydrogen only react when heated $H_2 + Br_2 \rightarrow 2HBr$	iodine and hydrogen react slowly even when heated $H_2 + I_2 \rightleftharpoons 2HI$
With chlorides	no reaction	no reaction	no reaction
With bromides	displaces bromine e.g. $Cl_2 + 2NaBr \rightarrow Br_2 + 2NaCl$	no reaction	no reaction
With iodides	displaces iodine e.g. $Cl_2 + 2NaI \rightarrow I_2 + 2NaCl$	displaces iodine e.g. $Br_2 + 2NaI \rightarrow I_2 + 2NaBr$	no reaction

Displacement reactions of halogens

Table 1 shows how halogens react with compounds of other halogens. Look at the reactions of the three halogens with bromides, for example. If you add chlorine to a solution of sodium bromide, the chlorine **displaces** bromine. Chlorine is more reactive than bromine, so chlorine replaces bromine and forms sodium chloride.

chlorine + sodium bromide → bromine + sodium chloride
$$Cl_2(aq) + 2NaBr(aq) \rightarrow Br_2(aq) + 2NaCl(aq)$$

The results in table 1 show the general rule that **a more reactive halogen will displace a less reactive one from its compounds**.

Explaining the reactivity of halogens

The halogens form Group 7 of the Periodic Table. They have seven electrons in the outer shell of their atoms (picture 9). When a halogen, such as chlorine, reacts, it gains an electron from another atom. It forms a negative ion, Cl^-. This gives the halogen a stable electron structure with a full outer shell. All the halogens behave in this way, so their chemical reactions are similar and they all form ions with a single negative charge.

Picture 9 shows that chlorine has one more electron shell than fluorine. This means that the chlorine atom is bigger, so the outer shell is further away from the positive nucleus. This means that chlorine attracts electrons less strongly than fluorine does. Because chlorine attracts electrons less strongly, it is less reactive than fluorine. This explains why, in general, the halogens become less reactive as you go down the group. Compare this with the behaviour of the alkali metals (page 143).

USING HALOGENS

Because halogens are so reactive, they form lots of compounds. Many of these compounds are useful for making all sorts of things we need. Picture 8 shows some of them.

Chlorine is the most useful of all the halogens, and is manufactured in large amounts by the electrolysis of salt solution. There is more about this in topic D5.

HYDROGEN HALIDES

All the halogens form compounds with hydrogen, for example hydrogen chloride, HCl; hydrogen bromide, HBr; hydrogen iodide, HI.

All the hydrogen halides are gases. They are all very soluble in water, forming strongly acidic solutions. For example, hydrogen chloride, HCl(g), dissolves in water to form hydrochloric acid, HCl(aq). There is more about hydrochloric acid in topics G1, G2 and G3.

Picture 10 Photographic film uses silver halides, such as silver iodide, which darken when exposed to light. The energy of sunlight causes silver iodide, AgI, to split up into silver and iodine. The silver gives a dark colour.

Questions

1 List the halogens in order of reactivity, with the most reactive first.

2 How do each of the following properties of the halogens change as you go down the group?
   a boiling point
   b melting point
   c intensity of colour
   d relative atomic mass

3 Fluorine (F_2), at the top of group 7, is the most reactive halogen. Make predictions about the following reactions involving fluorine. In each case, say what will happen, and write equations for the reactions in (b) and (c).
   a a red dye is exposed to fluorine
   b iron wool is put in a jar of fluorine
   c fluorine is added to a solution of potassium chloride

4 Astatine, At, is the last element in Group 7. Very little is known about its properties, because it is radioactive and unstable. Predict the following properties of astatine, using the information about other halogens given in this topic.
   a the formula of astatine molecules
   b the appearance of astatine
   c the boiling point of astatine
   d the reaction, if any, of astatine with iron

5 The name 'halogen' comes from Greek words meaning 'salt maker'. Why do you think this name was chosen?

Chemicals from the sea

The sea is salty. This isn't just because of sodium chloride—which is what we normally think of as salt. Many different ionic salts are dissolved in the sea. The ions from these salts are separated and spread out through the water, so sea water is a mixture of different ions (picture 1).

It happens that sodium ions and chloride ions are the commonest in sea water. When you evaporate away all the water, you are left with a mixture of solid salts, of which sodium chloride is the most abundant (picture 2). You can buy 'sea salt' to put on your food—though you might not notice that the taste was any different from pure sodium chloride.

The sea is an important source of chemicals, and not just sodium chloride.

Two elements that are extracted from sea water are bromine and magnesium. You can see from picture

1 that neither of these elements is the most abundant in sea water. But it is possible to make the sea water more concentrated by evaporating away some of the water. When you do this, sodium chloride starts to form crystals before any other compounds crystallise out. After NaCl has crystallised, the solution that is left behind is more concentrated in bromide, magnesium and other ions than it was before.

Bromine can be obtained from the concentrated solution of Br^- ions by bubbling chlorine through it (see question 2 below.)

Magnesium can be extracted from sea water as solid magnesium chloride. Magnesium can then be obtained by electrolysing the molten magnesium chloride.

1   Look at picture 1. List the elements in sea water according to their group in the Periodic Table (leave out sulphate and drogencarbonate, which each contain more than one element).

2   1 litre of sea water contains about 1.9 g of Br^-. How many litres of sea water contain 1 kg of bromine?

3   Bromine is extracted from concentrated sea water by bubbling chlorine, $Cl_2(g)$, through it.

$$Cl_2(g) + 2Br^-(aq) \rightarrow 2Cl^-(aq) + Br_2(aq)$$

Explain why this reaction happens. Would it be possible to obtain bromine by adding *iodine* instead of chlorine? (You may need to look back at page 148.)

4   There are many other elements in sea water apart from the ones mentioned here. The oceans even contain an estimated eight million tonnes of gold compounds. Explain why it is not economic to get gold from the sea.

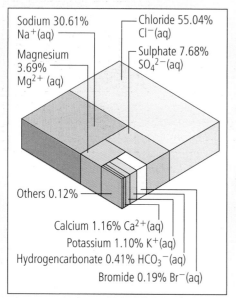

Sodium 30.61% $Na^+(aq)$
Magnesium 3.69% $Mg^{2+}(aq)$
Chloride 55.04% $Cl^-(aq)$
Sulphate 7.68% $SO_4^{2-}(aq)$
Others 0.12%
Calcium 1.16% $Ca^{2+}(aq)$
Potassium 1.10% $K^+(aq)$
Hydrogencarbonate 0.41% $HCO_3^-(aq)$
Bromide 0.19% $Br^-(aq)$

Picture 1   The percentages by mass of different ions in sea water.

Picture 2   Commercial production of sea salt.

The gaps in Mendeléev's table

4

A table with gaps in

Topic F2 (page 138) explains how Mendeléev drew up his famous Periodic Table, in 1869. Picture 1 shows part of his table. You can see that it is a bit different from the modern Periodic Table. For one thing, Mendeléev put the transition metals like Cu in the same groups as some non-transition elements like K. For another thing, he left gaps where he believed there should be elements that had not yet been discovered. This was his big breakthrough. Scientists working before him had tried drawing up tables like this, but they didn't think to leave gaps for missing elements. This spoiled the pattern of properties, so no one took their work very seriously.

Picture 2 shows the Periodic Table in its modern form, with gaps for the elements that were missing when Mendeléev drew up his table in 1869. The missing elements are highlighted in pink.

Mendeléev's great triumph was to make predictions about the missing elements. Topic F2 describes how he predicted the properties of the element between silicon and tin – and amazed everyone by getting them right.

Use picture 2 to help you answer these questions.

1 Look at the gap between aluminium, Al, and indium, In, in group 3. Mendeléev called this missing element 'eka-aluminium'. Use the information in table 1 to predict the following properties of 'eka-aluminium' – which we now call gallium, Ga. Explain how you work out your predictions.
   a Its relative atomic mass (Mendeléev called it 'atomic weight').
   b Its density.
   c Its boiling point.
   d The formula of its oxide.

2 When you have done this, look at the answers, which are printed upside down at the bottom of the page. How good were your predictions?

3 Compare the Periodic Table in picture 2 with the full modern Periodic Table shown in the Data Section.

	GROUP							
	1	2	3	4	5	6	7	8
Period 1	H							
Period 2	Li	Be	B	C	N	O	F	
Period 3	Na	Mg	Al	Si	P	S	Cl	
Period 4	K Cu	Ca Zn		Ti	V As	Cr Se	Mn Br	Fe Co Ni
Period 5	Rb Ag	Sr Cd	Y Ir	Zr Sn	Nb Sb	Mo Te	I	Ru Rh Pd

Picture 1 Mendeléev's Periodic Table of 1869. The missing elements are shown in pink.

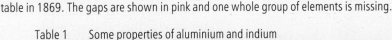

Picture 2 The Periodic Table in its modern form, with gaps for the elements that were missing from Mendeléev's table in 1869. The gaps are shown in pink and one whole group of elements is missing.

Table 1   Some properties of aluminium and indium

Element	Symbol	Date discovered	'Atomic weight'	Density (g/cm³)	Boiling point (°C)	Formula of oxide
Aluminium	Al	1827	27	2.70	2447	Al_2O_3
Indium	In	1863	115	7.30	2080	In_2O_3

a Give the symbols of the six elements that are missing from the table in picture 2.

b Write down the dates of discovery of the elements you listed in (a). Use the table in the Data Section to help you. Which of these elements would Mendeléev have heard about in his lifetime? (He died in 1907.)

c A complete group of elements is missing from picture 2. Which group is this?

d Why was this group of elements undiscovered for so long?

Answers to Question 2

Properties of gallium, Ga. Relative atomic mass 70; density 5.90 g/cm³; boiling point 2237 °C; formula of oxide Ga_2O_3.

The noble gases

The noble gases – Group 0 of the Periodic Table – are very unreactive.

helium He 2	
neon Ne 10	
argon Ar 18	
krypton Kr 36	
xenon Xe 54	
radon Rn 86	**Picture 2** Group 0 – the noble gases.

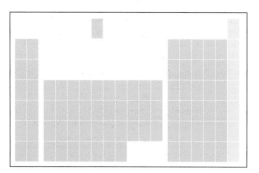

Picture 3   Group 0 in the Periodic Table

Table 1   Some properties of the noble gases.

Picture 1   The brown bottle on this diver's back contains 'heliox', a mixture of helium and oxygen

WHY DEEP-SEA DIVERS HAVE SQUEAKY VOICES

Deep under the sea the pressure is very high, and this means that divers need to breathe high-pressure air. The trouble is that under high pressure the nitrogen in the air dissolves in the diver's blood. This is not a problem until the diver rises to the surface. Then the nitrogen comes out of solution and forms bubbles in the blood. This causes a painful condition called 'the bends', which can even be fatal.

To avoid the 'bends', modern divers do not breathe air at all, but a mixture of helium and oxygen (picture 1). Helium is a very unreactive gas, and very insoluble, so it hardly dissolves in the blood. This means the diver does not get the 'bends'. The only problem is that helium has very low density, so when it vibrates in the diver's voice-box, it produces a higher note than air, making the diver's voice squeaky like Mickey Mouse.

WHAT ARE THE NOBLE GASES LIKE?

Helium is the first member of the family of noble gases, Group 0 in the Periodic Table (pictures 2 and 3). Like all the other members of the group, helium is very unreactive. There are small amounts of noble gases present in the air (see table 1).

The noble gases are unreactive because of the arrangement of electrons in their atoms. They all have a filled outer shell of electrons, and this means they cannot form bonds to other atoms. There is more about this in topic J5.

The noble gases are so unreactive that even the highly reactive elements like fluorine and potassium have no effect on them. Hence the name 'noble'; it is as if they keep themselves apart from the ordinary, reactive elements.

Most gases are diatomic: their molecules consist of two atoms joined together. But the noble gases are **monatomic**, because they are unable to form bonds to other atoms, even to themselves.

Name	Symbol	Density compared with air	Percentage in dry air	Chemical reactivity	Date of discovery
helium	He	less dense	0.0005	extremely unreactive	1868/1895
neon	Ne	slightly less dense	0.0018	extremely unreactive	1898
argon	Ar	more dense	0.93	extremely unreactive	1894
krypton	Kr	more dense	0.0001	extremely unreactive	1898
xenon	Xe	more dense	0.00001	extremely unreactive	1898
radon	Rn	more dense	usually too little to detect	extremely unreactive (but radioactive)	1900

Uses of the noble gases

The lack of reactivity of noble gases makes them very useful, especially helium, neon and argon, which are the commonest. Table 2 lists some of the important uses.

Table 2   Some uses of noble gases.

Gas	Use	Reasons for use
Helium	Breathing gas for divers Airships and balloons Supercooling for high-performance magnets	Unreactive and insoluble Low density and non-flammable Boiling point of liquid helium is $-269\,°C$
Neon	In red display lights for advertising	Neon glows red when electricity flows through it
Argon	For filling light bulbs To provide a 'gas blanket' for welding	Unreactive, so it prevents the white-hot filament burning The unreactive argon surrounds the hot welding metal and prevents it getting oxidised

Picture 4   Noble gases are useful in lighting. Argon is used to fill ordinary light bulbs, and neon is used in red display signs.

HOW THE NOBLE GASES WERE DISCOVERED

The noble gases are invisible and unreactive, and this makes them very difficult to spot when they are mixed with other gases in air. In 1894, there was no reason to suspect they existed at all.

In that year, Sir William Ramsay did an interesting experiment. He wanted to see what happened when you remove all the gases from air. He did this by passing air over heated copper and heated magnesium. He *expected* to have nothing left at the end. He reasoned that everything in the air would react, either with the hot copper, or with the hot magnesium. In fact, he found that from every 100 cm³ of air, about 1 cm³ always remained behind.

William Ramsay was such a good experimenter that he knew he hadn't made an error. No matter how often he repeated the experiment, he always had the same proportion of gas left behind. He did lots of experiments on the left-over gas to try and make it react with something. He tried the most reactive substances he knew, including fluorine, phosphorus and potassium, but it never did anything. So he called this rather boring new gas argon, from a Greek word meaning lazy or inactive.

A whole new family

Discovering argon was a problem as far as the Periodic Table was concerned. There was no gap for it to fit into. William Ramsay made a bold prediction. He said there could be only one explanation – argon must be just one member of a *whole new family*. He predicted that other, similar elements must exist, and he started doing experiments to try and find the missing members of the family. This was similar to the way Dmitri Mendeléev made predictions about missing elements when he first discovered the Periodic Table (see topic F2).

He soon found the first one. In 1868 astronomers had seen a certain frequency of light from the Sun which didn't correspond to any known element. They suggested there must be a new element in the Sun, and they called it *helium* after the Greek word for the Sun. In 1895 William Ramsay showed that helium also exists on Earth, and that it is a very unreactive gas – like argon.

He examined liquid air in his hunt for other members of the family, and eventually discovered neon, krypton and xenon. Apart from the radioactive gas radon, this completed the family, which we now call the noble gases.

Questions

Table 1 may help you with some of these questions.

1 Explain the following.
  a All the noble gases are unreactive, so any of them could be used to fill light bulbs. Why is argon used instead of any other?
  b Why is helium the only noble gas that can be used in airships?

2 Read the section on 'How the noble gases were discovered' before you answer (a) to (f) below.
  a Why were the noble gases a particularly difficult group of elements to discover?
  b Why was argon easier to find than the other noble gases?
  c Why was it important that William Ramsey's experiments were very accurate?
  d William Ramsey named the first noble gas that he discovered argon. Was it actually pure argon?
  e What made William Ramsey look for other noble gases as soon as he had discovered the first one?
  f Why are two dates given for the discovery of helium?

3 Although the noble gases are very unreactive, some of them have in fact been made to combine with other elements. Use advanced books or websites to find out about some of the compounds of the noble gases.

Transition metals

The transition metals form the central block of the Periodic Table.

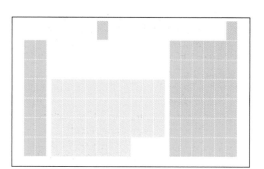

Picture 1 The transition metals in the Periodic table

EVERYDAY METALS

We use transition metals in millions of ways every day because they have so many useful properties. Their physical properties are typical of metals (topic E1). They generally have greater:

- hardness
- tensile strength
- malleability
- density
- ductility
- electrical and thermal conductivity
- melting points and boiling points.

than other groups of elements in the Periodic Table. Transition metals are much less reactive than the metals in Groups 1 and 2. They usually have excellent corrosion resistance.

Let's look at some more properties which the transition metals have in common.

titanium	vanadium	chromium	manganese	iron	cobalt	nickel	copper
Ti	V	Cr	Mn	Fe	Co	Ni	Cu
22	23	20	25	26	27	28	29

Picture 2 Some important transition metals.

COLOURED COMPOUNDS

Crystalline copper salts and their solutions are blue. You may have seen the green corrosion product on statues made from bronze, an alloy of copper (picture 3). Compounds of transition metals produce the vivid colours we see in oil paintings and precious stones (picture 4). *Compounds of these metals are usually coloured.*

Picture 3 The weathering of a bronze statue produces a green copper compound.

There are some exceptions. You can make blue copper sulphate crystals, $CuSO_4.5H_2O$, turn white by heating them. This happens because the crystals lose water and produce a white powder called anhydrous copper sulphate, $CuSO_4$. The colour change can be reversed by adding water. This can be used as a chemical test for the presence of water.

CATALYTIC PROPERTIES

Catalysts speed up the rate of a chemical reaction without getting used up themselves. You can learn more about them in topic I6. Many catalysts are either transition metals or their compounds.

Picture 4 Artists give colour to their paintings with pigments which often contain transition metal compounds.

Catalytic converters are used in car exhaust systems to reduce the emission of polluting gases (see page 227). The catalyst surface is usually covered in finely divided platinum or rhodium. These are expensive transition metals – but remember catalyst are not used up. They can, however, be inactivated or *poisoned* by lead compounds. This is why cars which are fitted with catalytic converters must be run on unleaded petrol.

Transition metals or their compounds are also used as catalysts in the manufacture of ammonia (page 105), and in the production of margarine (page 189) and plastics (page 206).

VARIABLE IONIC CHARGE

Metals in Group 1 of the Periodic Table always produce ions with a *single* positive charge, M^+. Metals in Group 2 always produce ions with two positive charges, M^{2+}. The charges on transition metal ions, on the other hand, are variable.

Iron atoms can lose two electrons to give Fe^{2+} or lose three electrons to give Fe^{3+}. When iron combines with oxygen, for example, we can get either iron(II) oxide, FeO, or iron(III) oxide, Fe_2O_3. Compounds which contain Fe^{2+} ions are called iron(II) compounds, and are usually green. Compounds which contain Fe^{3+} ions are iron(III) compounds, and are usually brown.

In the same way, copper atoms may form Cu^+ ions or, more often, Cu^{2+} ions. This again gives rise to two types of compound – copper(I) compounds containing Cu^+ ions and copper(II) compounds containing Cu^{2+}.

It is often easy to convert one kind of ion into the other. For example, iron(II) compounds are easily converted to iron(III):

$$Fe^{2+} \rightarrow Fe^{3+}$$

Iron is *oxidised* in this reaction, because electrons are removed from Fe^{2+}. (See topic J3, *Redox and electron transfer.*)

USING TRANSITION METALS

Transition metals have many useful properties. But, for many engineering applications, they must be made stronger. The most important way of doing this is by alloying the metal with at least one other element.

Steels are the most frequently used alloys. They contain iron mixed with small proportions of carbon and other elements. There is more about steel alloys in topic E3.

As the percentage of carbon increases, the hardness and strength of the metal at first increases. As a result, mild steel is both malleable and, to some extent, strong. But when the carbon content increases above about 1%, the strength of the metal begins to decrease. This is why cast iron is very hard but brittle.

When one or more of the transition metals are specially added to a steel, we get **alloy steels**. There are some examples in Table 2 in topic E1.

Picture 6 Iron(II) chloride, $FeCl_2$, (left) and iron(III) chloride, $FeCl_3$. Iron(II) compounds contain the green Fe^{2+} ion. Iron(III) compounds contain the brown Fe^{3+} ion.

Questions

1 Titanium alloys are used in supersonic aircraft like Concorde. They are strong, light, resistant to corrosion and can withstand high temperatures.

   a In what part(s) of Concorde would these alloys be most useful? Explain why.

   b Describe another use for which you think titanium alloys might be suitable. Explain why they could be used in this way.

2 Find out which transition metal or transition metal compound is used as a catalyst in the manufacture of each of the following products:
   a ammonia
   b nitric acid
   c margarine.

3 a Write down the formula of each of the following transition metal compounds. You may need to refer to Table 4 in the Data Section for the formulas of some ions.
      i   iron(II) hydroxide
      ii   iron(III) hydroxide
      iii iron(II) sulphate
      iv   iron(III) sulphate
      v   copper(I) oxide
      vi   copper(II) oxide

   b Copper(II) oxide can be converted to copper(I) oxide. Use the formulas in your answers to part (a) of the question to explain why this change involves reduction.

4 Platinite is an alloy which contains 46% nickel and 54% iron. When heated, it expands at exactly the same rate as glass. It is used in light bulbs. Make a labelled sketch of a light bulb and explain which part(s) could be made from platinite.

G

Acids and ions

G1

Looking at acids

Acids can be nasty, but they are also very useful. In this topic, we see what acids are like.

Picture 1 An ant biting a termite. The ant makes a wound with its jaws, and then sprays on methanoic acid.

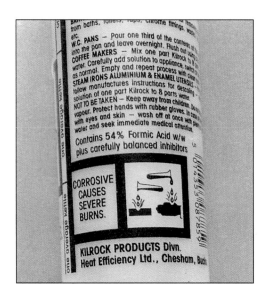

Picture 2 This kettle descaler contains methanoic acid (formic acid). The acid is strong enough to react with calcium carbonate, but not strong enough to damage the metal.

Table 1 Typical properties of acids.

Acids taste sour
Acids kill cells
Acids react with metals, giving off hydrogen
Acids are neutralised by bases, forming salts
Acids react with carbonates, giving carbon dioxide
Acids change the colour of indicators
Acids have pH less than 7

Picture 1 shows an ant biting its victim. As it bites, it sprays acid onto the open wound. No wonder it stings. The acid is sometimes called called formic acid, after the Latin word *formica*, meaning an ant. Its modern name is methanoic acid. Not long ago, people used to make methanoic acid by boiling up a saucepanful of ants. Picture 2 shows a more agreeable use of methanoic acid – to descale kettles. Like all acids, it reacts with carbonates – and kettle scale is calcium carbonate.

Living things are very sensitive to acids, and too much acid can kill (see later). Fortunately, your body is able to use bases (topic G2) to neutralise acid.

WHAT DO ACIDS DO?

Table 1 summarises some of the most important properties of acids. Let's look at some of them.

■ Acids kill cells, or stop them working properly

This makes acids dangerous to handle. Your most vulnerable part is your eyes, because they have living cells on the surface. **You should never let acids get on your skin, and you should always wear eye protection when you are handling acids**.

But this property can be useful too, because acids kill undesirable things like bacteria in food. Pickling food in vinegar (acetic acid) is an ancient way of preserving it. It makes the food taste sharp, but many people like the taste, so we go on pickling food even though we have other ways of preserving it.

■ Acids react with metals, giving off hydrogen

Metals that are above copper in the reactivity series react with acids, and hydrogen is given off. The metal forms a salt and dissolves. This is why acids are so corrosive to metals (picture 3). For example, magnesium reacts with sulphuric acid:

magnesium + sulphuric acid → magnesium sulphate + hydrogen

$$Mg(s) + H_2SO_4(aq) \rightarrow MgSO_4(aq) + H_2(g)$$

There is more about the reaction of metals with acids in topic E2.

◼ Acids are neutralised by bases

There is more about neutralisation and bases in topic G2. **Alkalis** are a special type of base. In many ways, alkalis are the opposite of acids.

◼ Acids react with carbonates, giving off carbon dioxide

All carbonates fizz in acid, giving off carbon dioxide. The carbonate forms a salt and usually dissolves. This is why acid rain attacks buildings made of limestone, which is calcium carbonate.

For example, when copper carbonate reacts with hydrochloric acid:

copper carbonate + hydrochloric acid → copper chloride + carbon dioxide + water

$$CuCO_3(s) \quad + \quad 2HCl(aq) \quad \rightarrow \quad CuCl_2(aq) \quad + \quad CO_2(g) \quad + H_2O(l)$$

There is more about this kind of reaction in topic G0.

Picture 3 Bluebells are pink when they grow on ant heaps. Why?

WHAT'S GOING ON?

There are many different acids. Table 2 shows some of them. Clearly they must have something in common, because they have similar properties.

Look at the formulas of the acids in table 2. You will see that they all contain the element hydrogen, H. But there are plenty of substances that contain hydrogen that are *not* acids – water, to name just one.

> **To be an acid, a substance must contain hydrogen in the form of hydrogen ions, H^+(aq).**

There is more about this idea in topic G3 and in *Ideas about acids* (page 161).

When a metal reacts with an acid, the hydrogen in the acid is replaced by the metal. The hydrogen is given off as a gas. So in the reaction of magnesium with sulphuric acid, H_2SO_4, hydrogen gets replaced by magnesium, giving magnesium sulphate, $MgSO_4$.

When a base neutralises an acid, it reacts with the hydrogen ions and turns them into neutral water. More about this in topics G2 and G3.

Table 2 Some common acids.

Name	Formula	Strong or weak?	Where it's found
hydrochloric acid	HCl	strong	• in the stomach • many important uses
sulphuric acid	H_2SO_4	strong	• in acid rain • many important uses
nitric acid	HNO_3	strong	• in acid rain • many important uses
ethanoic acid (also called acetic acid)	CH_3COOH	weak	• in vinegar
methanoic acid (formic acid)	HCOOH	weak	• ants, nettles
citric acid	$C_6H_8O_7$	weak	• in lemons, oranges, other citrus fruits

Picture 4 The limestone (calcium carbonate) in this gravestone has slowly reacted with acid in the rain over many years.

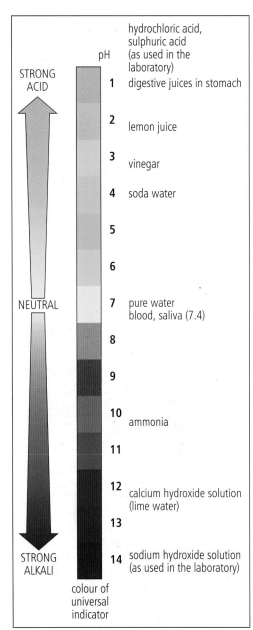

Picture 5 The pH scale. This shows the pH of some common substances. The colours shown are a rough guide only, because they vary according to the brand of indicator used.

The pH scale (left side labels):
- STRONG ACID
- pH
- hydrochloric acid, sulphuric acid (as used in the laboratory)
- 1 — digestive juices in stomach
- 2 — lemon juice
- 3 — vinegar
- 4 — soda water
- 5
- 6
- NEUTRAL
- 7 — pure water, blood, saliva (7.4)
- 8
- 9
- 10 — ammonia
- 11
- 12 — calcium hydroxide solution (lime water)
- 13
- STRONG ALKALI
- 14 — sodium hydroxide solution (as used in the laboratory)
- colour of universal indicator

INDICATORS – THE ACID DETECTORS

Indicators are substances that change colour depending on whether they are in acidic or alkaline solution. Litmus is a common indicator. It is red in acid and blue in alkali. Many natural plant colours are indicators—there's an example in picture 3. Some flowers actually change colour because of changes in acidity.

Universal indicator is a mixture of indicators. It can have several different colours, depending on the pH (picture 5).

■ The pH scale

The pH scale is a measure of acidity. On the pH scale:

Acids have pH less than 7
Neutral substances, like water, have a pH of 7
Alkalis have a pH greater than 7.

The stronger an acid, the lower its pH. Picture 7 shows the pH of some common substances.

Living things can only survive within a narrow range of pH values. Human blood normally has a pH of 7.4, and your body only works within the pH range 7.0 to 7.8. One of the problems with acid rain is that it makes the pH of lakes and rivers too low for many organisms to survive (see *Bringing Trout Back to Loch Fleet* on page 167). The pH of soil is important in deciding how well plants can grow in it.

STRONG AND WEAK ACIDS

Picture 5 shows that the hydrochloric acid you use in the laboratory has a lower pH than vinegar. This means the hydrochloric acid is more acidic. There are two reasons for this.

Vinegar contains an acid called ethanoic acid, its older name is acetic acid. Like most of the acids made by living things, ethanoic acid is a **carboxylic acid** (see topic H4). Carboxylic acids are fairly weak. Hydrochloric acid is a much stronger acid. (There is more about strong and weak acids in topic G3.)

Also, the solution of hydrochloric acid you use in the laboratory is more concentrated than the acetic acid solution in vinegar. Both hydrochloric acid and vinegar are solutions in water, but in vinegar the acid is more dilute (watered down) than in hydrochloric acid. If you added water to the hydrochloric acid, you could dilute it enough to have the same pH as the vinegar.

Often a weak acid is preferable to a strong one. Hydrochloric acid is too strong to put on food, so we use weak acids like ethanoic acid (vinegar) and citric acid (lemon juice). For de-furring a kettle, a weak acid like methanoic acid is less likely to corrode the metal than a strong acid like sulphuric acid.

Surprisingly, we all have a strong acid in our stomachs. It is hydrochloric acid, and it helps to digest food. Fortunately, it is a fairly dilute solution, and the stomach has a special lining to stop it doing much harm. But sometimes your stomach produces too much hydrochloric acid, and then you may suffer from acid indigestion.

Activities

A What do people think acids are?

Everyone has heard of acids, but their ideas are not always very scientific! Try asking people (family, neighbours, friends) what they think acids are. You could ask some of these questions.

1 What do acids do?
2 What different kinds of acids are there?

3 Why do acids behave the way they do? (A tricky one, this!)

B Hunt the acid

Many food and drinks have acids added to them. Look at the ingredients lists of some food and drink items. Find at least 10 that contain acids. Make a list of your results, showing the food or drink item and the acid it contains.

After you have done your survey, answer these questions.

1 How many different acids did you find?
2 Why do you think manufacturers put acids in foods and drinks?
3 Are the acids that are used generally strong or weak?
4 Only certain acids are permitted by the government for use in food and drinks. Why are some acids permitted, but not others?

1 How do acids react with each of the following?
   a reactive metals
   b bases
   c carbonates

2 What acid would you find in each of the following places?
   a a car battery
   b a grapefruit

   c your stomach
   d vinegar

3 For each of the following, say whether you think it would have a pH of

   A below 5   B about 7   C above 9

   a vinegar
   b rain water
   c sulphuric acid used in the laboratory
   d sodium hydroxide solution used in the laboratory
   e sea water
   f sodium hydrogencarbonate solution.

4 Hydrochloric acid and sulphuric acid are both acids.
   a Give three properties that you would expect both these acids to have.
   b Give one difference between these two acids.

5 Some people like lemon in tea instead of milk. When you put a piece of lemon into tea, the colour of the tea changes slightly. Why do you think this happens?

Ideas about acids

People have known for centuries what acids do. But it has taken longer to build up ideas about why acids behave that way. Ideas have changed gradually, and new ideas have built on older ones.

Of course, theories of acids cannot start until you have detailed information about the properties of acids. Nearly a thousand years ago, Arabic chemists were making acids. Jabir and Al-Razi wrote instructions for making sulphuric, nitric and hydrochloric acids. They also investigated alkalis: the word itself comes from Arabic 'al-qali', meaning potassium carbonate. But it was a long time before these early investigations led to a theory of acids.

Boyle 1675: acids contain special particles   Robert Boyle was an Irish nobleman. He tried to explain why acids are corrosive and attack metals and other solids. He suggested that acids contain special kinds of particles, which squeeze into spaces in the solid like tiny wedges and break it apart.

Picture 1   Jabir, the great Muslim chemist

Lavoisier 1777: all acids contain oxygen

The Frenchman Antoine Lavoisier did many experiments on burning. He found that when you burn non-metal elements like sulphur and phosphorus, you get acidic gases. He knew that burning always involves oxygen, so he decided that oxygen must be the thing that all acids have in common. It was Lavoisier who invented the name 'oxygen', from Greek words meaning 'acid-maker' (oxy means 'sour' in Greek, and the gen bit means 'producer').

In fact, Lavoisier's theory was proved wrong by the Englishman Humphry Davy in 1810. Davy showed that most acids contain oxygen, but not all of them.

Laurent 1854: all acids contain hydrogen

The Frenchman Auguste Laurent knew that acids react with metals to give hydrogen. He decided that the hydrogen must be coming from the acid – so all acids must contain hydrogen. He was right, but there are many substances that contain hydrogen and are not acids. Laurent's theory needed to go further.

Arrhenius 1887: all acids produce hydrogen ions in solution   The Swedish chemist Svante Arrhenius modified Laurent's theory. Acids conduct electricity, which suggests they contain ions. Arrhenius proposed that it must be hydrogen ions, $H^+(aq)$, that give acids their special properties.

Picture 2   Svente Arrhenius

Arrhenius' theory has been improved a bit, but it is still basically this theory that we use today. It is a good theory because it explains most of the things we know about acids.

1 Look at the acids in table 2 on page 159. Which of them does not fit Lavoisier's theory?

2 Give the formula of two substances that contain hydrogen but are not acids.

3 In what way did Arrhenius' theory build on Laurent's?

4 Arabic chemists worked on acids nearly a thousand years ago. Why do you think it took so long before their work was built on?

5 Try to work out what the name 'hydrogen' comes from. (Like 'oxygen', it comes from Greek words.)

6 'If Lavoisier hadn't got the theory of acids wrong, *hydrogen* would be called *oxygen*'. Explain.

Picture 1 This tooth is being dissolved by a strong acid. In your mouth the acid is not so strong, but it still attacks your teeth.

Picture 2 This flue-gas desulphurisation plant removes acid sulphur dioxide from the exhaust gases made by burning coal. The plant uses calcium carbonate as a base to neutralise sulphur dioxide, producing calcium sulphate, a salt.

Acids corrode many things, including teeth (picture 1). Acid forms in your mouth after you have eaten sugary food. Decay starts when the pH gets below 5.5. (Remember: the stronger the acid, the lower the pH.) Picture 3 shows how the pH in your mouth changes as a result of eating a sweet.

Tooth enamel is the hardest material in your body. It is made from a form of calcium phosphate. This substance is insoluble in water, but it does dissolve in acid. When the pH in your mouth gets lower than 5.5, tooth enamel starts to dissolve – and then you're in trouble.

The best way to avoid tooth decay is to avoid eating sugary food. Cleaning your teeth helps too: for one thing, it clears away at least some of the bacteria which make the acid. Many toothpastes also help to take away the acidity. This is because they contain a substance which will **neutralise** acids – a **base**.

People often need to neutralise acids. Picture 4 shows the pH conditions preferred by different vegetables. You can see that many vegetables dislike acid soil. A gardener uses a base such as lime (calcium hydroxide) or limestone (calcium carbonate) to neutralise acid in the soil.

People use bases – also called **anti-acids** – to neutralise stomach acid when they have indigestion. Magnesium hydroxide ('Milk of Magnesia') is often used. We use bases like sodium hydrogencarbonate to treat acid insect bites and stings.

WHAT KIND OF SUBSTANCES ARE BASES?

Bases are usually oxides, hydroxides or carbonates of metals. Table 1 lists some examples. (By the way, ammonia is a rather unusual base, because it doesn't contain a metal. There is more about ammonia as a base in topic D3.)

You may not have come across the word base in a chemical sense before – in everyday language it has quite a different meaning. But you may well have heard the word **alkali**. An alkali is a special kind of base – a base that dissolves in water (picture 5). Most of the bases in table 1 are also alkalis, because they dissolve in water. When they dissolve, they give a solution whose pH is greater than 7. The stronger the alkali, the higher the pH.

Like acids, strong alkalis are corrosive and dangerous. Sodium hydroxide is often called 'caustic soda' – caustic means burning. In fact, alkalis can do even more damage to your skin and eyes than acids. **Never let alkalis get on your skin, and always wear eye protection when you are using them**.

There are strong and weak alkalis, just as there are strong and weak acids. Sodium hydroxide is a strong alkali, but magnesium hydroxide is weak – which is why it is safe to use it as an anti-acid to treat indigestion.

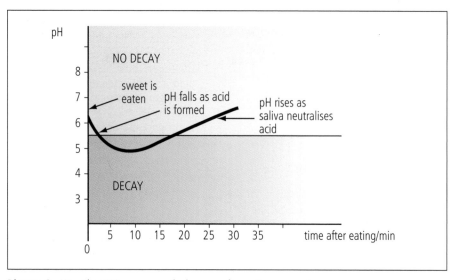

Picture 3 How the pH in your mouth changes after eating a sweet.

Table 1 Some important bases. Those marked * are also alkalis.

Name	Formula	Where it is used
*sodium hydroxide (caustic soda)	NaOH	in the home, for removing grease; many uses in industry
*calcium hydroxide	Ca(OH)$_2$	in farms and gardens, to neutralise soil acidity
magnesium oxide	MgO	in the home, as an 'anti-acid' medicine
calcium carbonate	CaCO$_3$	in farms and gardens; to neutralise acidified lakes
*sodium hydrogencarbonate (bicarbonate of soda)	NaHCO$_3$	in the home, as an 'anti-acid' medicine; in baking powder
*ammonia	NH$_3$	in the home, as a cleaning liquid

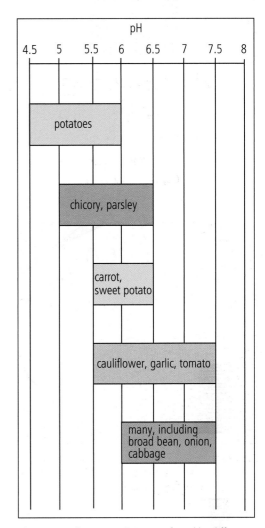

Picture 4 The pH conditions preferred by different vegetables.

The pH of *saliva* is just over 7. This means saliva is very slightly alkaline, so it can neutralise acid in your mouth. Chewing-gum manufacturers claim that chewing can help reduce tooth decay, because it makes the saliva flow. (But chewing-gum usually contains sugar....)

WHAT HAPPENS WHEN A BASE NEUTRALISES AN ACID?

Acids contain hydrogen ions, H^+(aq). The (aq) means the hydrogen ions are dissolved in water. When a base neutralises an acid, it joins with the H^+ and turns it into neutral water (more about this in topic G3). At the same time, the metal in the base takes the place of the hydrogen in the acid, and forms a metal compound called a **salt**.

For example, when hydrochloric acid is neutralised by sodium hydroxide:

$$\text{hydrochloric acid} + \text{sodium hydroxide} \rightarrow \text{sodium chloride} + \text{water}$$
$$\text{HCl(aq)} + \text{NaOH(aq)} \rightarrow \text{NaCl(aq)} + \text{H}_2\text{O(l)}$$

Notice that the sodium, Na, has taken the place of hydrogen, H, in the acid, forming sodium chloride, NaCl. Sodium chloride is a salt – the common salt we put on our food. But scientists use the word 'salt' to describe any compound formed by the reaction between a base and an acid. All salts contain two parts: a metal part which comes from the base, and a non-metal part which comes from the acid. So there are lots of salts, of which sodium chloride is just one.

MAKING SALTS

The same general reaction happens whenever an acid is neutralised by a base. We can summarise it as

acid + base → salt + water

If the base happens to be a carbonate, then carbon dioxide is formed as well.

Table 2 shows some more examples of making salts. Notice that each acid has its own family of salts – for example, sulphuric acid forms sulphates, and hydrochloric acid forms chlorides. Each base also forms a family of salts – sodium hydroxide forms sodium salts, calcium hydroxide forms calcium salts.

In the laboratory, the method that we use to make a salt depends on whether the salt is soluble or insoluble in water.

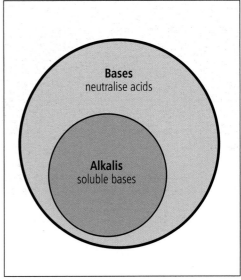

Picture 5 Bases and alkalis.

Table 2 Some examples of making salts.

BASES \ ACIDS	sulphuric acid forms sulphates containing SO_4^{2-}	nitric acid forms nitrates containing NO_3^-	hydrochloric acid forms chlorides containing Cl^-
Sodium hydroxide forms *sodium salts* containing Na^+	sodium sulphate Na_2SO_4	sodium nitrate $NaNO_3$	sodium chloride $NaCl$
Calcium hydroxide forms *calcium salts* containing Ca^{2+}	calcium sulphate $CaSO_4$	calcium nitrate $Ca(NO_3)_2$	calcium chloride $CaCl_2$
Magnesium oxide forms *magnesium salts* containing Mg^{2+}	magnesium sulphate $MgSO_4$	magnesium nitrate $Mg(NO_3)_2$	magnesium chloride $MgCl_2$

■ Insoluble salts

To make an insoluble salt, such as barium sulphate, we use a method known as **precipitation** (Topic G4, page 000). Mixing a solution containing barium ions with another solution containing sulphate ions gives a precipitate of barium sulphate, $BaSO_4$.

$$Ba^{2+}(aq) + SO_4^{2-}(aq) \rightarrow BaSO_4(s)$$

■ Soluble salts

If the salt is soluble in water, we can make it by either of two methods, depending on whether the base dissolves in water.

(a) Using an insoluble base or carbonate

A salt such as copper(II) sulphate is made by neutralising sulphuric acid with copper(II) oxide or copper(II) carbonate. For example,

sulphuric acid + copper(II) oxide → copper sulphate + water

$$H_2SO_4(aq) \quad + \quad CuO(s) \quad \rightarrow \quad CuSO_4(aq) \quad + H_2O(l)$$

We can make pure copper(II) sulphate by adding small amounts of copper(II) oxide to warm sulphuric acid until the pH of the mixture is about 7 (picture 6). When this happens, the acid has been neutralised and no more copper(II) oxide dissolves. Filtering removes the undissolved solid. Blue crystals of copper(II) sulphate appear when the filtrate evaporates.

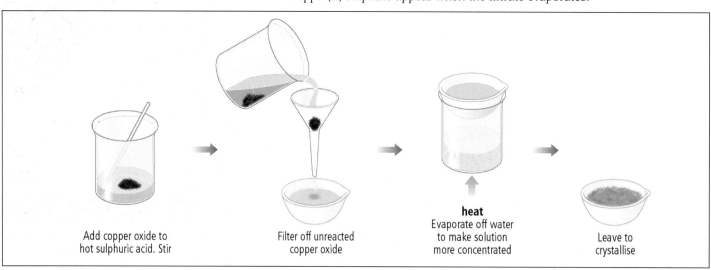

Add copper oxide to hot sulphuric acid. Stir

Filter off unreacted copper oxide

heat Evaporate off water to make solution more concentrated

Leave to crystallise

Picture 6 Making copper(II) sulphate.

(b) Using an alkali (a soluble base)

When an *alkali* reacts with an acid, both reactants are soluble in water. They usually mix without any visible sign of a reaction. We have to use an indicator to find out when the acid has been neutralised. For example, to make sodium sulphate, we add an alkali, sodium hydroxide, to sulphuric acid containing a few drops of indicator:

sulphuric acid + sodium hydroxide → sodium sulphate + water

$$H_2SO_4(aq) \ + \ 2NaOH(aq) \ \rightarrow \ Na_2SO_4(aq) \ + 2H_2O(l)$$

The indicator changes colour when the acid has been neutralised. The volume of alkali that neutralises the acid can be found with the help of a **burette** and this method of making a salt is called a **titration.** (You will find more about titrations in topic C5).

To make *pure* sodium sulphate crystals, the titration is repeated *without* the indicator (picture 7). When enough alkali has been added to neutralise the acid, the mixture in the flask is left to crystallise to obtain pure sodium sulphate.

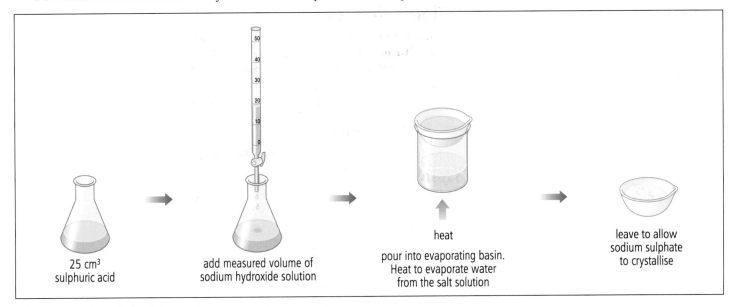

25 cm³ sulphuric acid

add measured volume of sodium hydroxide solution

pour into evaporating basin. Heat to evaporate water from the salt solution

heat

leave to allow sodium sulphate to crystallise

Picture 7 Making sodium sulphate.

A traditional way of cleaning tarnished copper is by rubbing it with a piece of lemon. Can you see how this works? The tarnish on the metal is a layer of oxide. Metal oxides are bases, and lemons contain citric acid. So when you rub the copper with the lemon, a salt is formed (copper citrate), and this makes the tarnish dissolve away.

Salts can also be made by reacting a metal with an acid (topic E2, page 122).

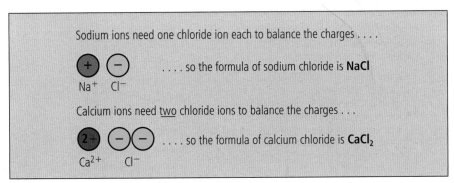

Sodium ions need one chloride ion each to balance the charges . . . .

. . . . so the formula of sodium chloride is **NaCl**

Na^+ Cl^-

Calcium ions need two chloride ions to balance the charges . . .

. . . . so the formula of calcium chloride is **CaCl₂**

Ca^{2+} Cl^-

Picture 9 The formulas of sodium chloride and calcium chloride.

Picture 8 Crystals of fluorite, calcium fluoride. Like many minerals, fluorite is a salt.

Table 4 Some ions commonly found in salts.

Metal ions	Non-metal ions
sodium Na^+	chloride Cl^-
potassium K^+	bromide Br^-
calcium Ca^{2+}	iodide I^-
magnesium Mg^{2+}	sulphate SO_4^{2-}
aluminium Al^{3+}	nitrate NO_3^-
iron(II) Fe^{2+}	phosphate PO_4^{3-}
iron(III) Fe^{3+}	
copper(II) Cu^{2+}	
zinc Zn^{2+}	
ammonium NH_4^+	

Some salts containing these ions:
potassium iodide K^+I^- or KI
iron(II) sulphate $Fe^{2+}SO_4^{2-}$ or $FeSO_4$
zinc chloride $Zn^{2+}(Cl^-)_2$ or $ZnCl_2$
sodium phosphate $(Na^+)_3PO_4^{3-}$ or Na_3PO_4

MORE ABOUT SALTS

All salts are ionic compounds – the base provides the positive metal ion and the acid provides the negative non-metal ion (there is more about ionic bonding in topic J6). Like other ionic compounds, salts are crystalline, have high melting points, and often dissolve in water.

Many salts occur in the earth as minerals. Calcium sulphate (gypsum) and calcium fluoride (fluorite) are examples (picture 8). If the salt is soluble in water, it is likely to get washed out of the earth by rain and end up in the sea. That's why the sea is so salty.

■ Working out the formula of a salt

Salts are ionic, and ions have electrical charges. Yet you don't get an electric shock when you handle a salt. This is because the ionic charges cancel out. There are equal numbers of + and – charges.

Sodium chloride, $NaCl$, is a simple example. It contains Na^+ and Cl^- in equal numbers, so there are as many + charges as – charges. Overall there is no electrical charge. But suppose we swap the sodium for calcium. Calcium ions are Ca^{2+}, so we need *two* Cl^- ions to balance them. So calcium chloride is $Ca^{2+}(Cl^-)_2$, or $CaCl_2$ (picture 9).

Now think about aluminium nitrate. Aluminium ions have three charges, Al^{3+}. Nitrate ions have one charge, NO_3^-. So Al^{3+} needs three NO_3^- ions to balance its charge, and the formula is $Al^{3+}(NO_3^-)_3$, or $Al(NO_3)_3$. The brackets show that the NO_3 is a single unit, and all of the NO_3 group is multiplied by 3.

Table 4 gives the charges on some ions that are often found in salts. Use the table to answer question 5.

Questions

1 What is the difference between a base and an alkali?

2 Classify each of the following as an acid, a base or a salt.

a CaO b HCl

c KCl d H_2SO_4

e $MgCO_3$ f $FeSO_4$

g $Zn(OH)_2$ h $Al(NO_3)_3$

3 a A certain rust remover contains hydrochloric acid. Rust is iron oxide. Name the salt that will be formed when the rust remover reacts with rust.

b Why is sodium hydroxide not used as a cure for acid indigestion, even though it neutralises acids?

c Most oven cleaners contain sodium hydroxide. You have to be careful when you use these cleaners not to let them get in contact with your eyes or skin. Suppose someone in your family has spilt oven cleaner on their skin. What common household substance could you use to treat the spill?

4 a Write word equations to show what would be formed in each of the following reactions. The first one has been done for you.

i) nitric acid + sodium hydroxide → sodium nitrate + water

ii) nitric acid + potassium hydroxide →

iii) sulphuric acid + calcium oxide →

iv) hydrochloric acid + magnesium →

v) nitric acid + calcium carbonate →

vi) sulphuric acid + copper carbonate →

b Now try to write balanced equations, using formulas, for as many of these as you can. Table 5 in Data Section will help you with the formulas.

5 Use table 4 to work out the formulas of the following salts.

a potassium bromide

b zinc iodide

c iron(III) chloride

d copper(II) sulphate

e ammonium chloride

f ammonium sulphate

g magnesium nitrate

h calcium phosphate

Bringing trout back to Loch Fleet

Loch Fleet is a small lake in Galloway, southern Scotland. It was once renowned among anglers for its brown trout, but since 1950 the numbers of trout in the loch have dropped disastrously (picture 1). By the mid-1970s they had disappeared completely.

What happened to the trout? Consider these facts.

- Brown trout are killed by acid. They cannot survive in water whose pH is below 5, and they are only healthy if the pH is above 6.5.
- At the beginning of 1986 the pH of the water in Loch Fleet was about 4.4.
- Brown trout are poisoned by aluminium compounds. They cannot stand a concentration of aluminium ions higher than 40 micrograms per litre.
- At the beginning of 1986 the concentration of aluminium ions in Loch Fleet was about 80 micrograms per litre.
- Loch Fleet is fed by streams draining off the surrounding hills. Water flows out of the loch into a river.
- All soil contains aluminium compounds, but they normally stay in the soil. Acid dissolves these aluminium compounds so they are washed out of the soil by the rain.
- Brown trout need calcium ions in their diet.

Scientists believed that the brown trout were being killed by two things in the water: acid and aluminium ions. They decided that the best way to tackle the problem was to neutralise the acidity with a base.

Neutralising the acid

They decided to use limestone (calcium carbonate) as the base. The simplest thing would be to add limestone to the loch itself. However, it would have to be re-treated every six months or so because new water keeps flowing in. So they decided to put the limestone on the surrounding land instead.

This was done in 1986 and 1987. Between 5 and 30 tonnes of limestone were added to each hectare (a hectare is about the same area as two football pitches). The graphs in picture 2 show the results.

Putting back the fish

In 1987, 300 brown trout were put into the loch. They didn't just survive – they started breeding. More fish were added in 1988. By 1989, brown trout in excellent condition were once again being caught in the loch.

You will need to use the information above to answer some of these questions.

1 Two things probably killed the brown trout: acid and aluminium.
   a Suggest a reason why the loch became acidic.
   b How did the aluminium get into the loch?

2 Look at the graphs in picture 3. What happened to each of the following after limestone was added to the land around the loch?
   a The pH of water in the loch
   b The concentration of calcium ions in the loch
   c The concentration of aluminium ions in the loch.

3 Using limestone helped the trout in three ways. What are they?

4 Why was it better to add limestone to the surrounding land, rather than adding it to the water in the loch itself?

5 Give three reasons why limestone (calcium carbonate) is a particularly good base to use in this situation.

6 Look at graph **A** in picture 2. What is the earliest date when the acidity would have been low enough to put trout back in the loch?

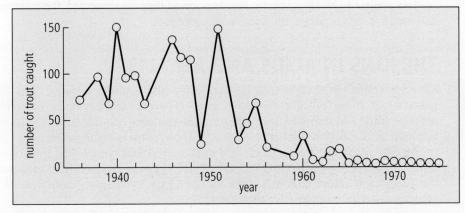

Picture 1   Numbers of brown trout caught in Loch Fleet since 1936.

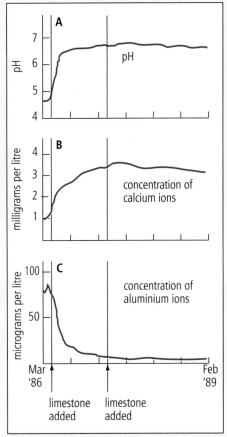

Picture 2   Changes in Loch Fleet from 1986 to 1989.

What happens when acids are neutralised?

Neutralisation means getting rid of hydrogen ions.

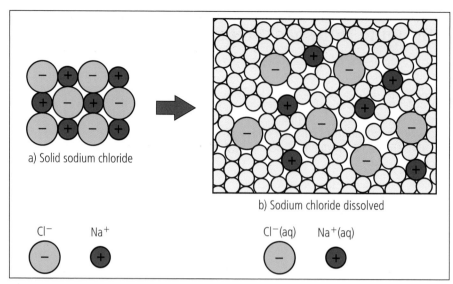

a) Solid sodium chloride

b) Sodium chloride dissolved

Cl⁻   Na⁺   Cl⁻(aq)   Na⁺(aq)

Picture 2 What happens when an ionic substance dissolves. (Remember, there are in fact millions of millions of molecules and ions.)

Emergency workers use alkali to neutralise an acid spill (picture 1). But how does the neutralisation take away the acidity?

There are many different acids, and they all have one thing in common: they contain hydrogen ions, H^+(aq). The (aq) means the hydrogen ions are dissolved in water. Before we go any further, we need to look at the way ions behave when they are in water.

WHAT HAPPENS WHEN AN IONIC SUBSTANCE DISSOLVES?

Let's use sodium chloride as an example. (It isn't an acid, of course, but it's a good example of an ionic substance.)

Solid sodium chloride has a giant ionic structure (see topic C7). It contains Na^+ and Cl^- ions arranged closely together in a regular lattice (picture 2a). There are equal numbers of Na^+ and Cl^- ions, so that the electric charges balance.

When you put sodium chloride into water, it dissolves. The Na^+ and Cl^- ions spread out into the water (picture 2b). We describe them as Na^+(aq) and Cl^-(aq). Now the ions are no longer regularly arranged – in fact, they are scattered through the water at random. What's more, now the Na^+ and Cl^- ions are separated they behave independently of each other. It's as if each has forgotten the other exists.

This applies to all ionic substances. As soon as they are dissolved, the positive and negative ions separate and behave independently.

Picture 1 In this simulated road accident, emergency workers practise clearing up an acid spill.

THE IONS IN ACIDS AND ALKALIS

All acids contain hydrogen ions, H^+(aq). They also contain negative ions to balance out these positive hydrogen ions. Different acids contain different negative ions. For example, hydrochloric acid contains chloride ions, Cl^-, and sulphuric acid contains sulphate ions, SO_4^{2-}. Table 1 shows some others.

Strong acids like hydrochloric acid split up into ions completely. But some acids do not split up into ions completely. There is dynamic equilibrium between the ionised and unionised forms of the acid (see topic I9 for more about dynamic equilibrium). For example, with ethanoic acid

$$CH_3COOH(aq) \rightleftharpoons CH_3COO^-(aq) + H^+(aq)$$
unionised form   ionised form

Table 1 The ions formed by different acids.

Acid	Formula	Ions it forms
hydrochloric acid	HCl	H^+ and Cl^-
sulphuric acid	H_2SO_4	$2H^+$ and SO_4^{2-}
nitric acid	HNO_3	H^+ and NO_3^-
ethanoic acid	CH_3COOH	H^+ and CH_3COO^-
methanoic acid	HCOOH	H^+ and $HCOO^-$
citric acid	$C_6H_8O_7$	H^+ and $C_6H_7O_7^-$

The equilibrium is normally well over to the left, so there is only a little $H^+(aq)$ present. This is why ethanoic acid is a **weak acid** (topic H4).

What about alkalis? Sodium hydroxide, NaOH, is a typical alkali. It contains sodium ions, Na^+, and hydroxide ions, OH^-. When sodium hydroxide dissolves in water, these ions separate as $Na^+(aq)$ and $OH^-(aq)$. **It is the $OH^-(aq)$ that gives alkali properties.** Indeed, all alkalis contain $OH^-(aq)$ ions, in the same way that all acids contain H^+ ions.

■ So what happens when an acid is neutralised by an alkali?

Let's take a simple example. When you add hydrochloric acid to sodium hydroxide solution, the acid is neutralised and you get a salt – common salt, sodium chloride.

hydrochloric acid + sodium hydroxide → sodium chloride + water

$$HCl(aq) \quad + \quad NaOH(aq) \quad \rightarrow \quad NaCl(aq) \quad + \quad H_2O(l)$$

Now, hydrochloric acid contains separate $H^+(aq)$ and $Cl^-(aq)$ ions, and a solution of sodium hydroxide contains separate $Na^+(aq)$ and $OH^-(aq)$ ions. What is more, sodium chloride contains separate $Na^+(aq)$ and $Cl^-(aq)$ ions (picture 3). So we can show all these ions separately:

$$H^-(aq) + Cl^-(aq) + Na^-(aq) + OH^-(aq) \rightarrow Na^-(aq) + Cl^-(aq) + H_2O(l)$$

If you look closely at this equation, you will see that $Na^+(aq)$ and $Cl^-(aq)$ are on both sides. They are not changed in this reaction – it is as if they are on the sidelines, watching the action going on between $H^+(aq)$ and $OH^-(aq)$, (picture 3). They are called **spectator ions**.

$Na^+(aq)$ and $Cl^-(aq)$ are there at the beginning of the reaction, and they are there at the end. At the end of the reaction, though, they are the only ions present, because $H^+(aq)$ and $OH^-(aq)$ have got together to make H_2O. Between them, $Na^+(aq)$ and $Cl^-(aq)$ make a solution of sodium chloride – salt. If we leave them out, the ionic equation becomes just

$$H^+(aq) + OH^-(aq) \rightarrow H_2O(l)$$

This is an example of an **ionic equation** (see box). This equation describes how *any* acid reacts with *any* alkali. It means that, whenever an acid reacts with an alkali, the same simple reaction happens: hydrogen ions react with hydroxide ions to form water. The other ions – negative ions from the acid and positive ions from the alkali – form a salt. That's why all neutralisation reactions amount to

acid + base → salt + water

This general rule applies to all bases, whether or not they are alkalis. (Remember, alkalis are a special type of base that dissolve in water.) Alkalis contain hydroxide ions; other bases may contain oxide or carbonate ions. But whatever the base, it always contains something that will join up with $H^+(aq)$ ions from acid and neutralise them.

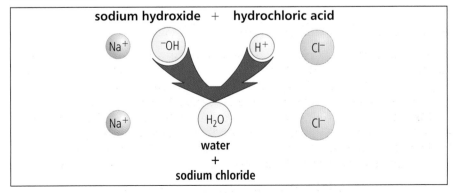

sodium hydroxide + hydrochloric acid

water
+
sodium chloride

Picture 3 What happens when an alkali neutralises an acid.

Ionic equations

Ionic equations are a special kind of balanced equation. They show the ions that are involved in a reaction. The equation

$$H^+(aq) + OH^-(aq) \rightarrow H_2O(l)$$

is a simple ionic equation.

Ionic equations are different from ordinary balanced equations.

● They only show the ions that actually react. The ions that are not involved in the reaction (the spectator ions) are left out.

● The equation is balanced for electric charge. In the equation above, the total charge on the left-hand side is $+1 + -1 = 0$, which is the same as the charge on the right-hand side.

Questions

1 What ion do all acids contain?

2 What ion do all alkalis contain?

3 Here is the equation for the reaction of nitric acid with potassium hydroxide.

nitric acid + potassium hydroxide →
potassium nitrate + water

$$HNO_3(aq) + KOH(aq) \rightarrow$$
$$KNO_3(aq) + H_2O(l)$$

a What ions does nitric acid contain?

b What ions does potassium hydroxide solution contain?

c Rewrite the equation showing all the ions separately (like the equation for the reaction of hydrochloric acid with sodium hydroxide).

d Which ions in the equation in (c) are spectator ions?

e Rewrite the equation, leaving out the spectator ions.

4 Repeat question 3, but this time for the reaction of sulphuric acid with sodium hydroxide.

sulphuric acid + sodium hydroxide →
sodium sulphate + water

$$H_2SO_4(aq) + 2NaOH(aq) \rightarrow$$
$$Na_2SO_4(aq) + H_2O(l)$$

Solids from solutions

You mix two clear solutions and suddenly a cloudy precipitate forms. How does it happen?

Picture 1 This shell is mainly made from calcium carbonate.

The shell in picture 1 is made of calcium carbonate. The mollusc that lives in it made the shell by bringing together calcium ions and carbonate ions from the sea water. Calcium carbonate is insoluble in water, so the shell doesn't dissolve, which is just as well for the mollusc.

The stalactites and stalagmites in picture 2 are also made of calcium carbonate. Like the shell they were formed from calcium ions and carbonate ions.

Forming stalactites and stalagmites can take centuries, and even a mollusc takes several months to build its shell. *You* can form a precipitate much more quickly by mixing solutions of calcium chloride and sodium carbonate in a test tube. The clear solutions will turn cloudy as a **precipitate** of insoluble calcium carbonate is formed.

WHAT'S GOING ON?

Let's look more closely at what happens when calcium chloride and sodium carbonate are mixed. Both these substances are soluble in water. The solution of calcium chloride contains dissolved calcium ions, $Ca^{2+}(aq)$, and chloride ions, $Cl^-(aq)$. The solution of sodium carbonate contains dissolved sodium ions, $Na^+(aq)$, and carbonate ions, $CO_3^{2-}(aq)$. (Look at topic G3 if you are unsure about ions in solutions.)

When you mix the two solutions, all four of these ions—$Ca^{2+}(aq)$, $Cl^-(aq)$, $Na^+(aq)$, $CO_3^{2-}(aq)$—are together in the same tube (picture 3). But calcium carbonate is insoluble, so $Ca^{2+}(aq)$ and $CO_3^{2-}(aq)$ ions cannot stay in solution together. Billions of these ions join together in a solid lattice which becomes a speck of solid. Between them, these specks make up the powdery precipitate that you see in the test-tube.

While this action is going on between the $Ca^{2+}(aq)$ and $CO_3^{2-}(aq)$ ions, what are the $Na^+(aq)$ and $Cl^-(aq)$ ions doing? *Nothing* —they are not involved in the reaction at all. They are **spectator ions**.

If you filter off the precipitate, you are left with a clear solution containing $Na^+(aq)$ and $Cl^-(aq)$ ions. It's a solution of sodium chloride. So, overall the reaction amounts to:

calcium chloride + sodium carbonate → calcium carbonate + sodium chloride

$$CaCl_2(aq) \quad + \quad Na_2CO_3(aq) \quad \rightarrow \quad CaCO_3(s) \quad + \quad 2NaCl(aq)$$

But the bit that really matters is the $Ca^{2+}(aq)$ and $CO_3^{2-}(aq)$ ions joining together. If we leave out the spectator ions, this amounts to just

$$Ca^{2+}(aq) + CO_3^{2-}(aq) \rightarrow CaCO_3(s)$$

When a mollusc builds its shell, and when stalactites and stalagmites grow, it's this reaction that is going on.

The equation given above is an ionic equation (see topic G3).

Picture 2 Stalactites and stalagmites.

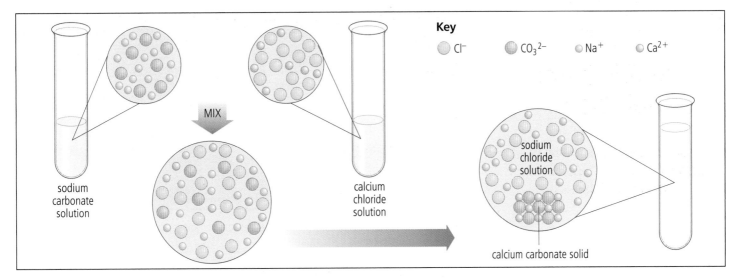

Picture 3 Making a precipitate of calcium carbonate.

Making salts by precipitation

Precipitation is a useful way to prepare insoluble salts. For example, barium sulphate is an insoluble salt. You can make it by mixing a solution containing barium ions with a solution containing sulphate ions. A white precipitate of barium sulphate is formed.

$$barium\ ions + sulphate\ ions \rightarrow barium\ sulphate$$
$$Ba^{2+}(aq) \quad + \quad SO_4^{2-}(aq) \quad \rightarrow \quad BaSO_4(s)$$

The solid barium sulphate can be filtered off, washed and dried.

There is more about making salts in topic G2.

More precipitation

The parking lines painted on roads get their yellow colour from lead chromate, $PbCrO_4$ (picture 4). Lead chromate is insoluble (if it weren't, the yellow lines would disappear when it rains). You make it by a precipitation reaction—all you have to do is mix solutions containing lead ions and chromate ions, and you get a yellow precipitate of lead chromate.

HOW CAN YOU TELL WHETHER A PRECIPITATE WILL FORM?

You get a precipitate when an insoluble substance is formed in a reaction. To predict whether a precipitate will form when two solutions are mixed, you need to know whether the products are soluble or insoluble. Fortunately, there are some simple rules that help you decide this.

Solubility rules

1 All compounds of sodium, potassium and ammonium are **soluble**, so they never form precipitates.
2 All nitrates are **soluble**.
3 Most chlorides are **soluble**, except silver and lead chlorides.
4 Most sulphates are **soluble**, except lead, barium and calcium sulphates.
5 Most carbonates and hydroxides are **insoluble**, except those of sodium, potassium and ammonium.

Picture 4 Lead chromate gives these parking lines their yellow colour.

Table 1 Using sodium hydroxide solution to identify metal ions.

1	Put 2 cm³ of the metal ion solution in a test-tube. Add 2 drops of NaOH(aq). Look for a precipitate and note its colour.
2	Add more NaOH(aq)—about 5 cm³ altogether—so it is in excess. Does the original precipitate dissolve?
3	Carry out any other tests that are necessary to identify the ion.

EYE PROTECTION MUST BE WORN

CORROSIVE Sodium hydroxide solution

Some metal ions are hazardous

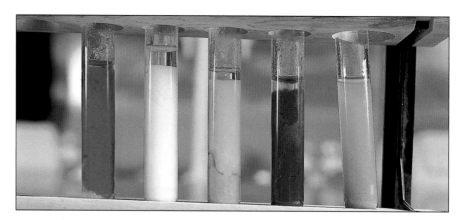

Picture 5 Precipitates of copper hydroxide, calcium hydroxide, nickel hydroxide, iron(III) hydroxide and cobalt hydroxide.

TESTING FOR IONS IN SOLUTIONS

Suppose someone gives you a solution of a metal compound and says 'Identify that'. What would you do?

Precipitation reactions often give us useful tests for finding out what ions are present in a solution. We'll look separately at metal ions (positively charged *cations*) and non-metal ions (negatively charged *anions*).

■ Testing for metal ions

An important test for metal ions in solution involves adding a solution of sodium hydroxide. Many metals have insoluble hydroxides, so they form a precipitate with sodium hydroxide solution, NaOH(aq). The colour of the precipitate is often a clue to the metal involved (picture 5). For example, copper ions, Cu^{2+}(aq), give a blue precipitate of copper hydroxide with sodium hydroxide solution.

copper ions + hydroxide ions → copper hydroxide
$$Cu^{2+}(aq) + 2OH^-(aq) → Cu(OH)_2(s)$$

We can use the test with sodium hydroxide solution, together with a few other tests, to build up a scheme for identifying metal ions. Some of the hydroxide precipitates dissolve again when you add extra NaOH(aq), and this gives us another clue about their identity.

The steps for identifying metal ions in this way are summarised in table 1.

Table 2 gives all the information that you need to build an identification scheme for metal ions (see question 8).

Table 2 Reactions of solutions of metal ions with sodium hydroxide solution (for details of flame tests, see topic F4).

Metal ion	What happens when you add a little NaOH(aq)?	What happens when you add excess NaOH(aq)?	Other tests to tell them apart
Sodium, Na^+(aq)	No precipitate	No precipitate	Flame test: yellow – orange
Potassium, K^+(aq)	No precipitate	No precipitate	Flame test: lilac
Ammonium NH_4^+(aq)	No precipitate	No precipitate	Boil the solution (C A R E) after adding NaOH(aq). Pungent smell of ammonia.
Calcium, Ca^{2+}(aq)	White precipitate of $Ca(OH)_2$(s)	White precipitate remains	None needed
Copper, Cu^{2+}(aq)	Blue precipitate of $Cu(OH)_2$(s)	Blue precipitate remains	None needed
Iron(II), Fe^{2+}(aq)	Green precipitate of $Fe(OH)_2$(s)	Green precipitate remains	None needed
Iron(III), Fe^{3+}(aq)	Brown precipitate of $Fe(OH)_3$(s)	Brown precipitate remains	None needed
Zinc, Zn^{2+}(aq)	White precipitate of $Zn(OH)_2$(s)	White precipitate dissolves	Filter off the precipitate and heat it. It turns yellow
Aluminium, Al^{3+}(aq)	White precipitate of $Al(OH)_3$(s)	White precipitate dissolves	Filter off the precipitate and heat it. It stays white

Tests for non-metal ions

Table 3 summarises the tests we can use to identify non-metal ions in solution. Several of these tests depend on precipitation reactions. For example, the test for chloride ions relies on the fact that silver chloride is insoluble. If you add a solution containing chloride ions to a solution containing silver ions, you get a white precipitate of silver chloride (picture 6).

$$\text{silver ions} + \text{chloride ions} \rightarrow \text{silver chloride}$$
$$Ag^+(aq) + Cl^-(aq) \rightarrow AgCl(s)$$

Bromide ions and iodide ions give pale yellow precipitates respectively.

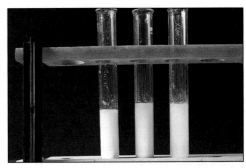

Picture 6 Precipitates of silver chloride, silver bromide and silver iodide. Note the different colours.

Table 3 Testing for non-metal ions in solution.

Non-metal ion	Test	What happens?
Chloride, Cl^-(aq)	Add a little dilute nitric acid to the solution in a test-tube. Then add a little silver nitrate solution	White precipitate of silver chloride, $AgCl$(s), which turns purple–grey when exposed to light
Bromide, Br^-(aq)	As for chloride	Pale yellow precipitate of silver bromide, $AgBr$(s)
Iodide, I^-(aq)	As for chloride	Yellow precipitate of silver iodide, AgI(s)
Sulphate, SO_4^{2-}(aq)	Add a little dilute nitric acid to the solution in a test-tube. Then add a little barium chloride solution	White precipitate of barium sulphate, $BaSO_4$(s)
Hydroxide, OH^-(aq)	Add a little of a solution containing Cu^{2+}(aq) (see table 2)	Blue precipitate of $Cu(OH)_2$(s)
Carbonate, CO_3^{2-}(aq)	Add dilute hydrochloric acid	Carbon dioxide evolved (turns lime water milky)

IRRITANT
Dilute hydrochloric acid

EYE PROTECTION
MUST BE WORN

CORROSIVE
Dilute nitric acid

Questions

1. What is a precipitate?

2. Look at this list of solutions.

   A calcium nitrate **B** sodium carbonate
   C potassium bromide
   D barium chloride **E** sodium sulphate
   F magnesium chloride
   G silver nitrate **H** zinc nitrate

   Which pair of solutions would you mix to get a precipitate of each of the following substances?

   (a) magnesium carbonate, (b) barium sulphate, (c) calcium sulphate, (d) silver bromide, (e) zinc carbonate.

3. Write ionic equations to represent the precipitation reactions between each of the following ions and NaOH(aq). You can find the answer to the first one on the previous page.

   a Cu^{2+}(aq)   b Fe^{2+}(aq)

   c Fe^{3+}(aq)   d Al^{3+}(aq)

4. Your teacher gives you a solution of iron chloride. It might contain Fe^{2+}(aq) or Fe^{3+}(aq). What test could you do to decide which of these two forms of iron it contains?

5. Your teacher gives you a colourless solution of a metal compound labelled X, and says, 'Identify that'. You carry out the following tests.

   A You add 2 drops of NaOH(aq). A white precipitate is formed. When you add excess NaOH(aq), the precipitate dissolves.

   B You add dilute nitric acid followed by barium chloride solution. A white precipitate forms.

   a Name two compounds that X could be.

   b What other test could you carry out to decide which of these two compounds it actually is?

   c What safety precautions would be needed in carrying out each of tests A and B?

6. The following are ionic equations for precipitation reactions, but they are not balanced. Rewrite each as a balanced ionic equation.

   a Ca^{2+}(aq) + OH^-(aq) → $Ca(OH)_2$(s)

   b Al^{3+}(aq) + OH^-(aq) → $Al(OH)_3$(s)

   c Pb^{2+}(aq) + Cl^-(aq) → $PbCl_2$(s)

7. Complete the following ionic equations by filling in the blanks.

   a Cu^{2+}(aq) + CO_3^{2-}(aq) → ………

   b Ag^+(aq) + Cl^-(aq) → ………

   c Fe^{2+}(aq) + $2OH^-$(aq) → ………

8. Identifying metal ions

   ICT Use table 2 to devise a flow diagram which another student could use to identify any of the metal ions in the table.

G5

Hard and soft water

Water is a good solvent. This means our tap water often contains dissolved solids.

Picture 1 The scum in this sink came from a precipitation reaction between soap and calcium ions in the hard water.

HARD WATER AND PRECIPITATION

Do you live in a hard water area? If so, you'll know that hard water makes soap difficult to lather. The soap forms a solid precipitate or 'scum' (picture 1). Hard water also leaves a solid deposit called 'fur' in kettles, pipes and shower-heads.

Water hardness is caused by dissolved substances, usually compounds of calcium. These calcium compounds get into the water from the rocks, especially in limestone districts. The calcium compounds contain calcium ions, $Ca^{2+}(aq)$, and these stay dissolved in the water right through the purification process at the waterworks.

■ Hard water and soap

Soaps are compounds of sodium or potassium. A common soap is sodium stearate, which we can call Na^+St^- for short. Sodium stearate dissolves in water, as you will know if you have ever left the soap in the bath water for too long. However, *calcium* stearate is insoluble. So when you add sodium stearate (soap) to hard water containing calcium ions, a precipitate of calcium stearate forms. This is the whiteish scum you see around the bath.

$$\begin{array}{ccc} \text{calcium ions} & + \text{ stearate ions} \rightarrow \text{calcium stearate} \\ \text{(from hard water)} & \text{(from soap)} & \text{(scum)} \\ Ca^{2+}(aq) & + \quad 2St^-(aq) \quad \rightarrow & CaSt_2(s) \end{array}$$

The soap will not form a lather until all the $Ca^{2+}(aq)$ ions have been removed. Picture 2 shows an experiment you can do to measure the hardness of a sample of water.

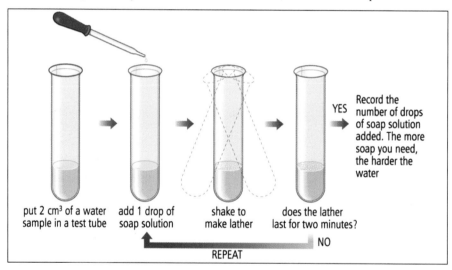

Picture 2 Testing water for hardness

GETTING RID OF HARDNESS

Hard water can be a nuisance in homes and a major problem in industry. To **soften** water you need to remove the calcium ions which cause the problem.

■ Purifying by precipitation

You can use precipitation to remove calcium ions from hard water. One way is to add sodium carbonate to the water. This removes the $Ca^{2+}(aq)$ ions as a precipitate of calcium carbonate.

$$\begin{array}{ccc} \text{calcium ions} & + & \text{carbonate ions} & \rightarrow \text{ calcium carbonate} \\ \text{(from hard water)} & & \text{(from sodium carbonate)} \\ Ca^{2+}(aq) & + & CO_3^{2-}(aq) & \rightarrow \quad CaCO_3(s) \end{array}$$

Another name for sodium carbonate is 'washing soda', and it was often used in the days when all the washing was done using soap.

Nowadays, many washing powders have a softener added to them. Phosphates are often used. Calcium phosphate, $Ca_3(PO_4)_2$, is insoluble—it's the main substance in teeth and bones. When the phosphate in the washing powder mixes with the $Ca^{2+}(aq)$ ions in the water, a precipitate of calcium phosphate forms. This takes the $Ca^{2+}(aq)$ ions out of the water.

Unfortunately, phosphates can cause a pollution problem if they get into rivers and streams. They cause the same kind of pollution as fertilisers (see topic B7). Many washing powder makers are now trying to find ways of softening water without using phosphates (picture 3).

■ Other ways of softening water

DISTILLATION

Your school science department probably has a **still** which makes distilled water. Distillation removes *all* impurities, but it is expensive because it uses a lot of energy. Distilled water is used where purity is particularly important—for cleaning contact lenses, say, or for science experiments.

ION EXCHANGE

The most convenient way to soften water is to use an ion exchange column. Many homes in hard water areas have them. The water is run through a column containing a special **ion exchange resin** (picture 4). The resin has sodium ions in it. When the hard water runs through the resin, calcium ions in the water are exchanged for sodium ions in the column. This removes calcium ions from the water and replaces them with sodium ions, which do not make the water hard.

Every so often, sodium ions have to be put back in the column. This is done by pouring a strong solution of salt through it.

Picture 3 Phosphates are added to washing powder to soften water, but they cause a pollution problem, so manufacturers are replacing them with different softeners.

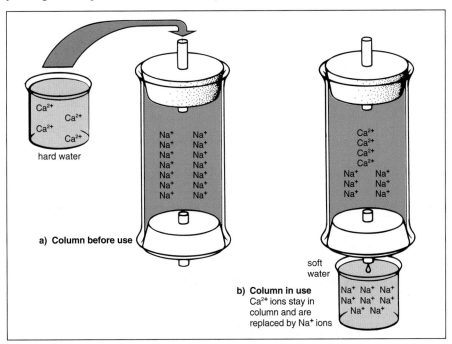

Picture 4 How an ion exchange column works.

DIFFERENT KINDS OF WATER HARDNESS

■ Temporary hard water

The kind of water you get from your tap depends on where it has come from. Hard water often comes from limestone areas. Limestone is rich in calcium carbonate, $CaCO_3$, a mineral which reacts with rain water to form calcium

Picture 5 The water which has collected in this loch is soft because Scottish granites and slates do not react with rain water.

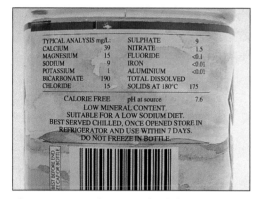

Picture 6 Mineral water is a kind of hard water which is believed to be good for your health. What kind of hardness does the label show? Bicarbonate is an old name for hydrogencarbonate.

hydrogencarbonate, $Ca(HCO_3)_2$ (see topic D2). This is soluble in water, so it allows calcium ions to enter the water supply. The reaction of rain water with calcium carbonate is a frequent cause of water hardness in Britain, where limestone is very common.

When a solution of calcium hydrogencarbonate is boiled, the dissolved solid decomposes:

calcium hydrogencarbonate → calcium carbonate + carbon dioxide + water

$$Ca(HCO_3)_2(aq) \rightarrow CaCO_3(s) + CO_2(g) + H_2O(l)$$

This reaction makes the water soft, because calcium ions come out of solution in the precipitate of calcium carbonate. Because the water can be softened by boiling, this kind of hardness is called **temporary hardness**.

Precipitation of calcium carbonate from temporarily hard water produces a *fur* in kettles. The precipitate can be a hazard in hot water pipes if it coats the inner surface of the pipes and cuts down the water flow. It can also be an advantage, though, because it seals the pipework and protects it from corrosion. This reduces the risk of poisonous compounds of copper and lead entering the water supply.

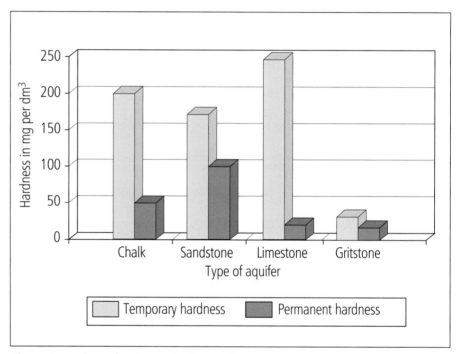

Picture 7 Hardness of water samples from aquifers.

■ Permanent hard water

Calcium hydrogencarbonate is not the only compound which causes water hardness. Soluble minerals such as calcium sulphate (gypsum) and magnesium sulphate (Epsom salts) occur naturally in some areas of Britain. When these sulphates dissolve in the water supply, we get **permanent hardness**. This type of water hardness *cannot* be removed by boiling, because the sulphates do not decompose when heated.

ESTIMATING THE HARDNESS OF WATER

The water supply is often affected by *both* temporary and permanent hardness. The total concentration of all dissolved solids in our tap water that cause either kind of hardness gives the **total hardness**. Table 1 gives some information about the hardness grades of different types of tap water. The maximum total hardness that is permitted is 300 mg per dm³.

The hardness of the water in your home will depend on where it comes from. Picture 7 gives some information about the dissolved solids in water supplied from different types of **aquifer**. An aquifer is an underground bed of rock which provides a supply of water. London is built over a chalk aquifer and receives some of its water from wells which are sunk into it.

HARD WATER AND HEALTH

Hard water is not all bad news. For one thing, it generally tastes more interesting than soft water. What is more, calcium ions are an important part of the diet, needed for making teeth and bones. You get calcium in some of your food, but hard water provides an added supply. Doctors also believe that the calcium ions in hard water may help prevent heart disease.

Table 1   The hardness grades of water. Hardness is measured in milligrams of dissolved solids per dm³.

Hardness grade of water	Hardness (mg/dm³)
Soft	0–50
Fairly soft	50–100
Neither hard nor soft	100–150
Hard	150–200
Very hard	200–300

Activity

Is your water hard?

Try and find the answers to these questions. You can get help with questions 1 and 2 by contacting your water company. Their address will be on the water bill, or in the telephone book.

1   Is your local water reckoned to be: **A** hard, **B** moderately hard, **C** soft?

2   Where does your local water supply come from? Does that explain your answer to (1)?

3   Do local people use any kind of water softening in their homes? You could try a survey in your class.

4   Try getting in touch with friends or relatives who live in other parts of the country. How hard is their water?

Questions

1   a   What is meant by 'hard water'?

   b   Why does the normal water purification treatment in a waterworks not remove hardness from water? (It may help you to look at topic D3.)

2   Look at the bar chart in picture 7.

   a   Which rock gives the softest water?

   b   Which rock gives the water with the most temporary hardness?

   c   Which rock gives the water with the most permanent hardness?

   d   Estimate the total hardness in water from the sandstone. What grade of water hardness would this give?

3   The amount of hardness in water varies from place to place across the country. The table gives estimates of the total water hardness in some major British cities.

	Total hardness (mg/dm³)
Bath	200–300
Birmingham	20
Cardiff	30
Leeds	60–200
London	250–300
Nottingham	140
Southampton	250–300

   a   Birmingham's water is piped from reservoirs in Mid-Wales. What does the data in the table tell you about the area in which this water is collected?

   b   What do the figures tell you about the sources from which London takes its water?

   c   There is a good deal of variation of levels in water hardness within many large cities. Suggest a reason why this variation should occur within a city.

   d   The city of Bath is also known as Bath Spa. What is a spa? How might Bath's development as a spa be linked to the level of water hardness there?

4   The River Severn rises in Mid-Wales and passes through the English towns of Shrewsbury, Bridgnorth, Worcester and Gloucester, in that order, before it reaches the sea. All these towns use the river for their water supply. Near the source of the river, the total water hardness is about 30 mg/dm³ but at its estuary it is about 210 mg/dm³.

   a   Suggest a reason for the variation in the total hardness of the river water.

   b   At which of the towns mentioned would you expect people to have to use most soap?

   c   From which part of the river would a textile manufacturing business want to take its water supply? Explain why.

5   a   i)   What is 'washing soda'?
      ii)   How does washing soda remove hardness from water?
      iii)   Why is washing soda only rarely used nowadays?

   b   How does an ion exchange column remove hardness from water?

Chemicals from oil

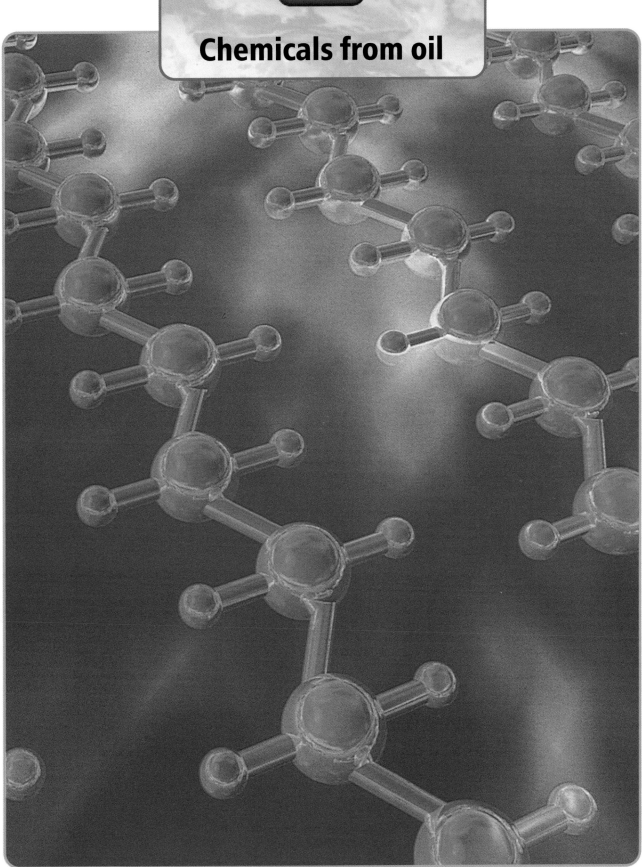

H1

Making oil useful

Many of the things we use every day are manufactured from crude oil. Most of the compounds in crude oil belong to a family called alkanes.

OIL CUTS COSTS

The guttering in picture 1 is made from a plastic called PVC. It cost £5 per metre, and the householders put it up themselves.

The guttering in picture 2 is made from cast iron. It cost £25 a metre, and it was put up by a builder because it is very heavy.

Apart from price, the plastic guttering has other advantages. It does not rust, so you don't need to paint it, and it does not hurt much if it falls on your head. Aluminium guttering has these advantages too, but it costs £30 a metre.

Like most plastics, PVC is made from crude oil. It is just one of thousands of oil products that we use every day. Many oil products are fuels like petrol and fuel oil. But crude oil can be used to make so many useful things that in a sense it is too precious to burn. Section I of this book looks at fuels: in this section we are mainly looking at the way that useful things like plastics can be made from crude oil.

■ Counting the environmental cost

One of the advantages of oil products like pvc is that they often cost less than traditional materials. But the *economic cost* of a product is not the only thing we need to consider. Whenever anything is manufactured, there is also an *environmental cost* to take into account (page 00). Some of the environmental costs of a plastic gutter go right back to when the crude oil was first brought out of the ground.

Have you ever got stained with oil on the beach? The chances are the oil came from a tanker carrying crude oil (picture 3). Sometimes tankers have collisions that cause crude oil to leak into the sea. More often, the oil gets there when the tanks are washed out. After the cargo of crude oil has been unloaded, the oil tanks have to be washed out with sea water, and if this is done carelessly, oil can get into the sea. Whichever way it gets there, the spilt oil is a menace to bathers and is often deadly to wildlife.

This kind of pollution is probably the biggest environmental cost associated with crude oil itself. There are also environmental costs when crude oil is turned into products at refineries and factories – though major accidents are fortunately very rare.

And don't forget, there are environmental costs when oil products are *used*. For example, plastics like PVC are not biodegradable, so they can cause a litter problem. And when fuels like petrol are burned, they can cause air pollution.

Picture 1   Plastic guttering costs £5 per metre.

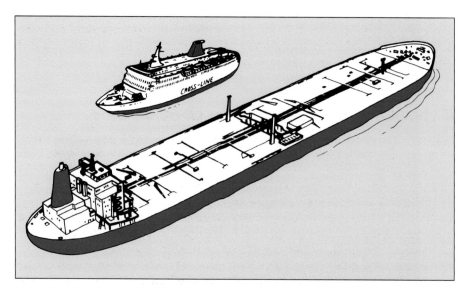

Picture 3   This tanker carries 350 000 cubic metres of crude oil, worth over £43 000 000.

Picture 2   Cast-iron guttering costs £25 per metre.

MAKING CRUDE OIL USEFUL

Until it has been processed, crude oil is not much use. This is because it is a mixture of many thousands of different compounds with different properties. They are called **hydrocarbons**, because they contain the elements hydrogen and carbon only.

To make crude oil useful, these compounds need to be sorted into batches with similar properties. These batches are called **fractions** and they are separated by **fractional distillation**. The idea behind this technique is that some of the compounds in crude oil are easily vaporised. They are **volatile**, with low boiling points. Others are less volatile and have higher boiling points.

In fractional distillation, the crude oil is heated to make it vaporise. The most volatile compounds vaporise first. The vapour is then cooled and condenses to form a liquid. Different liquid fractions of the oil are collected at different temperatures. The main fractions are summarised in table 1.

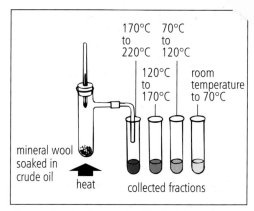

Picture 4   Distilling crude oil in the laboratory.

Table 1   Fractions from the distillation of crude oil.

Fraction	Colour	Boiling point range (°C)	Uses
refinery gas	colourless	below room temperature	gaseous fuel (e.g. bottled gas), making chemicals
gasoline (petrol)	colourless or pale yellow	30–160	motor car fuel, making chemicals
kerosine (paraffin)	colourless or yellow	160–250	heating fuel, jet fuel
diesel oil	brown	220–350	diesel fuel for lorries, trains etc., heating fuel
residue	dark brown	above 350	fuel for power stations, ships etc. Some is distilled further to give lubricating oil, waxes etc.

You can carry out a simple version of fractional distillation of crude oil in the laboratory, using the method summarised in picture 4. On an industrial scale the distillation is carried out in a huge tower. The most volatile fraction comes out at the top and the least volatile at the bottom (picture 5).

■ Looking at the fractions from crude oil

Table 1 shows the steady change in properties shown by the fractions from crude oil distillation. These different properties lead to different uses, which are also shown in table 1.

The composition of crude oil varies according to where it comes from. Picture 6 on the next page shows what you get from North Sea crude.

Fractional distillation is only the first stage in making useful products from crude oil. All the fractions go through further processes before they are used. For example, the gasoline fraction cannot be used for fuel on its own. It must be blended with other compounds to improve its performance. Some of the petrol fraction is not used for fuel at all: it is **cracked** to make chemicals (see topic H2).

Picture 5   At an oil refinery, fractional distillation is carried out in huge columns like this one. You can see pipes coming off at different levels on the tower: the pipes nearest the top carry the most volatile fractions.

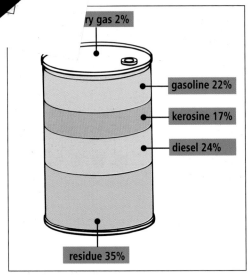

Picture 6 Percentages of different fractions obtained from a barrel of crude oil from the North Sea.

Name	Methane	Ethane
Molecular formula	CH_4	C_2H_6
Structural formula	H—C—H (with H above and below)	H—C—C—H (with H atoms above and below each C)
Molecular model		

Picture 8 The two simplest alkanes, methane and ethane. Both are gases. The molecular formula gives the number of each type of atom present. The structural formula shows how these atoms are joined together.

WHAT'S IN CRUDE OIL?

Crude oil was formed by the decay of living organisms (see page 220). Organisms contain many thousands of different compounds, and these turn into the thousands of different hydrocarbons you get in crude oil. But all hydrocarbons contain just the same two elements: carbon and hydrogen. How can there be so many of them?

Carbon is an unusual element. Carbon atoms can form four bonds to *other* atoms. What is more, carbon can also form strong bonds to other carbon atoms. This allows it to make **chains** of carbon atoms, with other atoms, particularly hydrogen, attached to the side (picture 7). This gives a huge range of different compounds, all based on the carbon chain. They are called **organic** compounds. Living things are made from organic compounds based on chains of carbon atoms.

THE ALKANES: A FAMILY OF HYDROCARBONS

The simplest type of organic compounds is those that have chains of carbon atoms with only hydrogen atoms in the side positions. Compounds whose molecules contain these simple hydrocarbon chains are called **alkanes**. Most of the hydrocarbons in crude oil are alkanes. Picture 8 shows methane and ethane, the two simplest alkanes, and table 2 gives more examples.

The alkanes are a *family* of compounds. Each member of the family has the same general type of molecule: a chain of carbon atoms, with hydrogen atoms attached to the side positions. What makes the members of the family different from one another is the size of the chain. Since carbon can form chains of any length, from very long to very short, you can see that there are many possibilities – so the alkanes are a very big family. Each member has a different name, but the names all end in **-ane**.

A family of organic compounds is called a **homologous series**. You can see from table 2 that the molecular formulas of the alkanes follow a pattern. There are always twice as many hydrogen atoms as carbon atoms, plus an extra two. We say that the **general formula** of alkanes is $\mathbf{C_nH_{2n+2}}$. For example, in ethane there are 2 carbon atoms, so $n=2$. Therefore $2n+2 = 6$, and there are 6 hydrogen atoms, so ethane is C_2H_6.

■ What are alkanes like?

ALKANES ARE SIMILAR

As a family, the alkanes have a lot of similarities. Alkanes are generally unreactiver: they do not react with acids or alkalis, or reactive metals, for example. However, all burn in air, forming carbon dioxide and water – which is why they are so useful for fuels (section I). They can all be **cracked** by heating so that their molecules break into smaller fragments. More about this in topic H2.

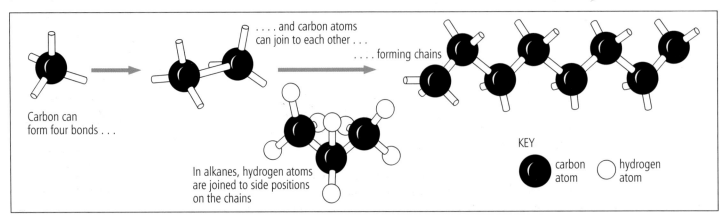

.... and carbon atoms can join to each other ...

.... forming chains

Carbon can form four bonds ...

In alkanes, hydrogen atoms are joined to side positions on the chains

KEY
● carbon atom
○ hydrogen atom

Picture 7 How carbon forms chains.

Table 2 Some alkanes.

Name	Molecular formula	Structural formula
methane	CH_4	(structure of methane)
ethane	C_2H_6	(structure of ethane)
propane	C_3H_8	(structure of propane)
butane	C_4H_{10}	(structure of butane)
hexane	C_6H_{14}	(structure of hexane)
octane	C_8H_{18}	(structure of octane)

Picture 9 Fuels such as gasoline contain liquid alkanes which are volatile. They form dense, flammable vapours which stay close to the ground and cause a fire risk.

Picture 10 Shell's gas separation plant at Mossmorran in Scotland. Gases are separated off from North Sea oil and sent here to be further separated into different alkanes. The big dome-shaped vessels you can see are storage tanks for propane (C_3H_8) and butane (C_4H_{10}). These gases are sold in cylinders as heating fuels.

ALKANES ARE DIFFERENT

Some of the properties of alkanes change as the carbon chain gets longer. For example, as the chain length increases the boiling point increases – the compounds become less volatile. The smallest alkanes – methane, ethane, propane and butane – are gases. Alkanes with 5 to 20 carbon atoms are liquids. Fuels like petrol and diesel are a mixture of liquid alkanes. Those with large chains containing more than 20 carbon atoms are solids. Candle wax is made of solid alkanes.

Alkanes also become more sticky, or **viscous**, as the chains become longer. This is because long chains get tangled up together, which makes it more difficult for the liquid to flow.

Table 3 in the Data Section gives more information about alkanes.

ISOMERISM: ARRANGING MOLECULES IN DIFFERENT WAYS

Butane, C_4H_{10}, has 4 carbon atoms and 10 hydrogen atoms. In butane, the carbon atoms are arranged in a line, as shown in picture 11a.

But there is another way that you can join together 4 carbon atoms and 10 hydrogen atoms. You can see this in picture 11b. The molecular formula of this second molecule is still C_4H_{10}, but its structural formula is different from that of butane – in fact it is a different compound (its name is 2-methylpropane). It will help you to understand how the two compounds compare if you build models of their molecules (Question 6).

Compounds, like the ones in picture 11, which have the same molecular formula but different structural formulas, are called **isomers**. Isomerism is very common in organic chemistry, because there are so many ways you can join carbon atoms to other atoms.

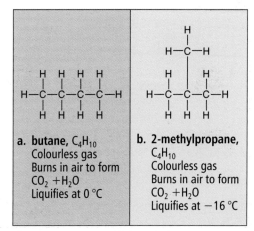

a. butane, C_4H_{10}
Colourless gas
Burns in air to form $CO_2 + H_2O$
Liquifies at $0\,°C$

b. 2-methylpropane, C_4H_{10}
Colourless gas
Burns in air to form $CO_2 + H_2O$
Liquifies at $-16\,°C$

Picture 11 Isomers with formula C_4H_{10}.

Isomers often have similar properties. Picture 11 gives some of the properties of the two isomers with formula C_4H_{10}.

The larger the molecule, the more isomers are possible. The first three alkanes (CH_4, C_2H_6 and C_3H_8) have only one isomer – can you see why? There are three isomers with molecular formula C_5H_{12} – try to draw their structures (see question 5 at the end). There are over four thousand million isomers with the molecular formula $C_{30}H_{62}$!

BACK TO CRUDE OIL

We use the differences in properties of the alkanes when we separate crude oil into fractions. The most volatile fractions contain the alkanes with the smallest molecules. Table 3 shows the approximate numbers of carbon atoms in the molecules in the different fractions. This explains why the fractions become more viscous as they get less volatile: the lowest volatility fractions contain alkanes with large molecules, so they are thick and sticky.

When you come across oil on the beach it is usually thick and sticky – even though crude oil comes out of the ground as a runny black liquid. When crude oil spills into the sea, the more volatile, less viscous hydrocarbons soon evaporate into the air. The thicker, less volatile compounds are left behind as a nasty mess that gets on your skin and clothes and clogs seabirds' feathers.

One thing that all hydrocarbons have in common is that they don't mix with water. What's more, they are less dense than water, so they float on it. Spills of crude oil wouldn't matter so much if the oil just sank to the bottom, or mixed with the water. One way of dealing with oil spills is to use detergents to make the oil mix with the water and disperse.

Table 3 The numbers of carbon atoms in the hydrocarbon chain in different fractions of crude oil.

Fraction	Number of carbon atoms in molecules
refinery gas	1 to 4
gasoline	5 to 9
kerosine	10 to 14
diesel oil	14 to 20
residue	over 20

Questions

1 a Place the following fractions in order of volatility, with the most volatile first.

Diesel oil, kerosine, refinery gas, residue, gasoline.

b Of the fractions in (a), which:
   i) is the most viscous
   ii) contains ethane
   iii) is used to make jet fuel
   iv) is used to make lubricating oil
   v) is darkest in colour?

2 Look at table 3 in the Data Section showing the properties of alkanes. Which alkane or alkanes:

a contains 10 carbon atoms

b is a gas at room temperature (25 °C)

c is a solid at room temperature

d burns to form carbon dioxide and water?

3 This question is about an alkane called heptane. To answer it you will need to use the Data Section and tables 1 and 3 in this topic.

a What is the formula of heptane?

b Is heptane a solid, liquid or gas?

c In what fraction of crude oil would you expect to find heptane?

d What colour is heptane?

e What would you expect to be formed when heptane burns in air?

f Write a balanced equation for the reaction when heptane burns.

4 The environmental costs of a manufacturing process can be considered under the headings:
   i) people's health and safety
   ii) pollution of the environment
   iii) damage to the landscape
   iv) depletion of resources.

a Choose an oil product as an example.

b For your chosen product, list the advantages that it brings to society.

c For your chosen product, give an example of the environmental cost under each of the four headings. (For example, under (ii) you might give the example of spillage of crude oil from tankers.)

5 a There are three isomers with molecular formula C_5H_{12}. Draw the structural formulas of the three isomers.

b Explain why there is only one isomer with molecular formula C_3H_8.

6 Making models of alkanes

a Use a model building kit to make molecular models of each of the following alkanes:
   i) methane, CH_4
   ii) ethane, C_2H_6
   iii) butane, C_4H_{10}.

b Build a molecule that has the same numbers and types of atoms as butane, but joined together in a different way.

c Find as many different ways as you can of joining together 6 carbon atoms and 14 hydrogen atoms.

The petrol blenders

When you buy clothes, food or a radio you shop around to get the right quality and the right price. Most people don't bother to shop around for petrol – except to find the cheapest. They assume that the quality will always be right, whatever the brand.

Yet getting the right quality isn't easy. At the oil refinery the people who blend petrol work hard to make sure it does the right things. In particular, the petrol needs to

● Avoid 'knocking' when the engine is running. 'Knocking' is a rattling sound caused by the petrol igniting too soon in the hot engine.

● Ignite easily when cold, so that the car will start even on a cold morning.

Picture 1 Does he realise all the trouble that goes into getting the petrol blend right?

To avoid 'knocking', the petrol blenders put special additives in the petrol. Lead compounds were used for a long time, but they are poisonous and cause pollution when they get into the air. Leaded petrol is gradually being replaced by 'unleaded', which uses different additives to prevent knocking.

Petrol for all seasons

A car engine burns a mixture of petrol vapour and air. The petrol is vaporised in the carburettor. Even in Britain, the petrol has to work at many different temperatures. On a cold winter's morning the temperature might be below freezing, but on a hot summer's day it could be 25 °C. In Russia or Canada the temperature range could be much greater.

Petrol is a blend of different hydrocarbons with different boiling points. This gives the petrol a boiling range, which might be from 25 °C to 200 °C. To suit the changing weather conditions, the petrol blenders change the blend several times a year. In November, for example, they change to a winter blend. With cold weather coming on, the petrol needs to vaporise more readily for colder starting. This means adding more volatile hydrocarbons, with lower boiling points, to the blend.

In April they change to a spring blend. In the warmer weather the volatile hydrocarbons evaporate from the petrol tank, which is wasteful and polluting. So the spring blend contains less volatile hydrocarbons.

1 Why does the blend of petrol in the pumps change several times a year?

2 Find table 3 in the Data Section, which gives information about different alkanes. (Remember: most of the hydrocarbons in petrol belong to the alkane family.)

   A particular blend of petrol has a boiling range from 25 °C to 220 °C.

   a Which alkanes in the table might be present in this blend?

   b Name one alkane from the table which might be added to the blend to make it suitable for warmer weather.

3 Petrol blends differ between countries. How do you think the petrol blend in India differs from that in Britain, for a particular time of year?

4 If you spill some petrol on your hands, it evaporates away very quickly. Yet your hands go on smelling of petrol for a long time. Can you suggest a reason why?

Making ethene: profit or loss?

Ethene, C_2H_4, is one of the most important industrial chemicals. It is used to make plastics like polythene, solvents like ethanol and much more besides.

Table 1 Costs involved in making one tonne of ethene.

Cost of raw materials (naphtha)	£600
Energy cost	£110
Cost of people, buildings, machinery	£200
Selling price of ethene	£400
Selling price of by-products	£550

Ethene is manufactured by cracking larger hydrocarbon molecules (see the next page for details of cracking). A mixture of hydrocarbons called naphtha is used. The process is carried out in huge plants like the one on page 187.

There are three main costs involved in making ethene:

● The cost of the raw material (naphtha).

● The cost of the energy to run the process. Cracking is done at high temperatures, so it uses a lot of energy.

● The cost of the people, buildings and machinery.

Against these costs you can set the money that you get when you sell the ethene. What is more, the process also has useful by-products which can be sold for fuel or as raw materials for other chemical processes.

The details of the costs involved in making one tonne of ethene are shown in table 1.

1 What are the total costs involved in making 1 tonne of ethene?

2 What is the total income from 1 tonne of ethene and by-products?

3 What is the profit from making 1 tonne of ethene?

4 What would happen to your profit in each of the following cases? Explain your answers.

   a The price of crude oil rises

   b The price of ethene rises.

5 It is cheaper to make ethene in very big plants than in small ones. Suggest why.

H2

Cracking molecules

Cracking is used to break big alkane molecules into smaller ones.

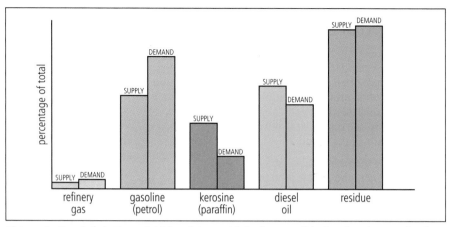

Picture 1 Supply (what's available) and demand (what's wanted) for fractions from crude oil.

A PROBLEM OF SUPPLY AND DEMAND

Look at the chart in picture 1. It shows the **supply** and **demand** for the different fractions of crude oil. 'Supply' means how much is available from distilling the oil; 'demand' means what we actually want.

For the more volatile fractions like petrol, demand is greater than supply. Because so many people drive cars, more petrol is needed than we can actually get from distilling oil. On the other hand, for the less volatile fractions like kerosine and diesel, supply is greater than demand. There is more than enough.

Wouldn't it be convenient if you could turn the low-demand fractions into the high-demand ones? Well, you can. The less volatile, less popular fractions like kerosine have larger molecules. By breaking the larger molecules into smaller ones, you can balance supply and demand. This breaking up of molecules is called **cracking**.

■ Breaking up molecules

Cracking is a chemical reaction, involving breaking bonds and making new ones. It is basically done by heating. When you heat a substance, its molecules move faster. The molecules collide with one another with greater energy as the temperature becomes higher. Eventually the molecules have so much energy that they begin to break up. Picture 2 illustrates this for decane, $C_{10}H_{22}$, which is an alkane found in the kerosine fraction.

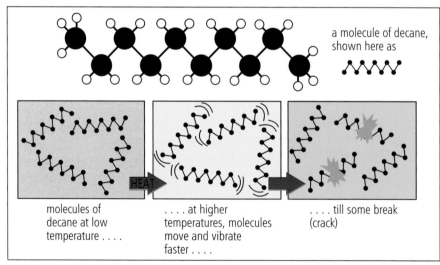

Picture 2 How cracking occurs in a molecule of decane.

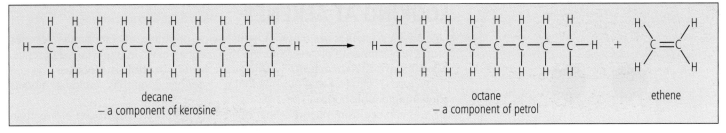

Picture 3 One result of cracking decane.

You can try doing this with a model of decane in Question 7. One thing you will notice is that, after the molecule has been broken in two, *there isn't enough hydrogen to go around*. There are not enough hydrogen atoms to make two smaller alkane molecules. Because of this, one of the new molecules does not become an alkane at all. Instead, it forms a **double bond** between two carbon atoms, and becomes an **alkene**. More about this below.

One result of cracking decane is shown in picture 3. There are other possible results because the decane molecule can crack apart in several different places. Notice that, like all cracking reactions, it gives two types of product:

- an alkane with a shorter chain than the original,
- a molecule containing a double bond – an alkene.

Both of these products are useful. The shorter chain alkanes can be blended with petrol to increase the supply. In effect, low-demand kerosine is being turned into high-demand petrol. What's more, petrol made by cracking is actually higher quality than the petrol you get by straight distillation.

Alkenes are very useful 'building block' substances for making all sorts of useful chemicals, as you will see below.

■ Cracking in practice

Picture 3 shows a single alkane being cracked. In practice a fraction containing a *mixture* of different alkanes is used. This gives a mixture of smaller alkanes and alkenes.

Heating is essential for cracking molecules. But the reaction can be helped by using a catalyst, which reduces the heating required. The alkane is vaporised and the vapour passes over the heated catalyst. Picture 4 shows the method that is used in the laboratory.

On an industrial scale, catalytic cracking is done in big 'cat cracker' plants (pictures 5 and 6). After cracking, the mixture of products is separated by distillation.

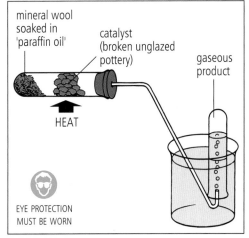

Picture 4 Cracking in the laboratory. In this experiment a purified form of lubricating oil is being cracked.

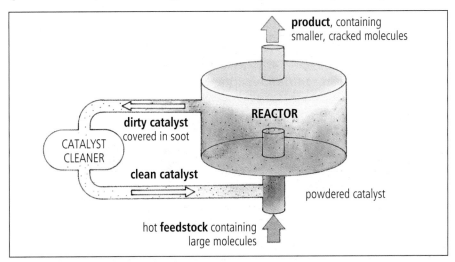

Picture 5 How a 'cat cracker' plant works.

Picture 6 A 'cat cracker' plant.

Cracking molecules

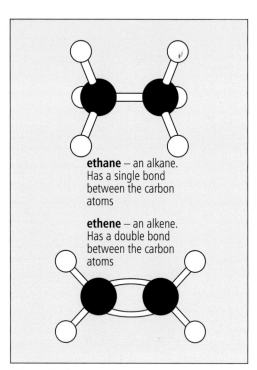

ethane – an alkane. Has a single bond between the carbon atoms

ethene – an alkene. Has a double bond between the carbon atoms

Picture 7 Ethane and ethene.

LOOKING AT ALKENES

Like alkanes, alkenes are a homologous series, or family, of compounds. Alkenes *sound* very similar to alkanes, but the two families have an important difference. **Alkenes are hydrocarbons with double bonds in their molecules.**

Picture 7 shows what we mean by a double bond. Try building models containing double bonds.

You can see from picture 7 that alkenes contain fewer hydrogen atoms than alkanes do. This is because the carbon atoms have fewer bonds available to join to hydrogens, having already used two to bond to each other. We say that alkenes are **unsaturated** because they have less than the maximum amount of hydrogen possible. Compounds like alkanes, with the maximum possible amount of hydrogen, are **saturated**.

■ Alkenes: the family

Members of the alkene family all have double bonds in their molecules, but different members have different numbers of carbon atoms. Table 1 gives a few examples of alkenes. You can see from the molecular formulas that there are always twice as many hydrogen atoms as carbon atoms. The general formula of alkenes is C_nH_{2n}.

All the alkenes have names ending in **-ene**. The first part of the name is the same as for the corresponding alkane.

Table 1 The three simplest alkenes

Name	Molecular formula	Structural formula
ethene	C_2H_4	
propene	C_3H_6	
butene	C_4H_8	

ALKENES AS BUILDING BLOCKS

■ Addition reactions

The double bond in alkenes makes them much more reactive than alkanes. Let's look at an example. If you shake up an alkene such as ethene with a solution of bromine in water, the bromine loses its colour. It has reacted with the ethene. The double bond in ethene breaks open and forms new bonds to bromine atoms (picture 8). This type of reaction, in which a double bond breaks and adds on two new atoms, is called an **addition reaction**.

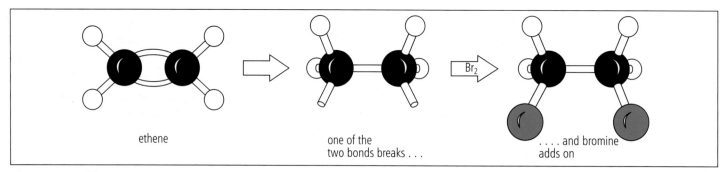

ethene

one of the two bonds breaks . . .

. . . . and bromine adds on

Picture 8 An addition reaction between bromine and ethene.

Alkenes do addition reactions with many other substances. This makes alkenes – especially ethene – very useful building blocks for making other organic chemicals. They are particularly useful for making addition polymers (page 206).

An important addition reaction of alkenes is with hydrogen. Alkenes react with hydrogen to form alkanes: the alkene becomes saturated. In the case of ethene, the reaction is:

$$\text{ethene} + \text{hydrogen} \xrightarrow[\text{nickel catalyst}]{\text{heat}} \text{ethane}$$

To make the reaction go quickly, a catalyst made of nickel and a temperature of 150°C are used. This reaction is called **hydrogenation**. Hydrogenation reactions are used to manufacture margarine.

■ Testing for alkenes

The addition reaction with bromine provides a useful test for alkenes. You shake an organic compound with bromine water. If the bromine water is decolorised, it shows the compound contains an alkene double bond (picture 9). A similar test is to shake the compound with an acidified solution of potassium manganate(VII). The potassium manganate(VII) loses its purple colour if an alkene double bond is present.

Alkanes do not decolorise bromine water or potassium manganate(VII).

FATS, OILS AND MARGARINE

Fats and oils are organic compounds with similar chemical structures. Here we are talking about edible oils like olive oil and corn oil. They should not be confused with inedible oils like lubricating oil. The molecules of oils and fats are built from substances called **fatty acids**. The main parts of fatty acids are long hydrocarbon chains. In oils, these hydrocarbon chains usually contain one or more double bonds: they are unsaturated. Solid fats, on the other hand, are usually saturated (picture 10). Animal fats tend to be more saturated than vegetable oils and fats.

We can use hydrogenation to change liquid oils to solid fats. This is how margarine is made. An unsaturated oil is reacted with hydrogen using a nickel catalyst. Hydrogen adds across the double bonds and the oil becomes saturated. The more hydrogen you use, the more saturated – and the more solid – the fat becomes. If you want a hard margarine, you use a lot of hydrogen. But if you want a soft, spread-from-the-fridge margarine you use less hydrogen.

There is now quite a lot of evidence linking saturated fats with heart disease. So the trend is towards eating more unsaturated vegetable fats and less saturated animal fats. Softer, 'polyunsaturated' margarines are reckoned to be healthier than harder margarines or butter.

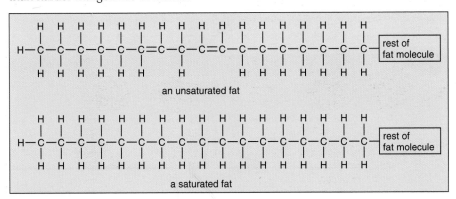

Picture 11

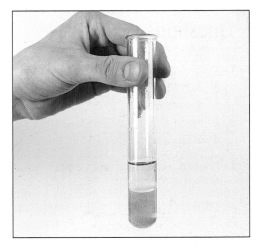

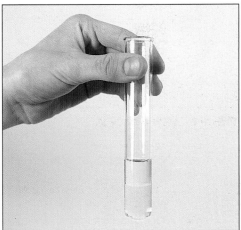

Picture 9 Hexene has been added to bromine water (top). When the tube is shaken the bromine water loses its red colour (bottom), showing that hexene is an alkene.

Picture 10 Butter and corn oil: saturated and unsaturated fats.

Questions

1 Explain what is meant by each of these words:
   a cracking
   b double bond
   c alkene
   d unsaturated

2 Cracking reactions are very important in oil refineries. Give *two* reasons why.

3 Dodecane is an alkane found in the kerosine fraction of crude oil. Its structure is:

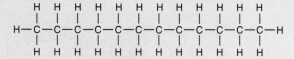

Write equations (similar to the one in picture 3 on page 187) to show two different sets of products that could be formed by cracking dodecane.

4 Table 2 at the top of the next column shows the demand for different fractions of North Sea oil in summer and in winter. Use the table to answer questions (a) to (c). You may also need to refer to table 1 on page 181 to remind yourself of the uses of the different fractions.
   a Why is the demand for diesel oil and residue greater in winter than in summer?
   b Why is the demand for petrol fairly constant in summer and winter?
   c What could an oil company do to cope with the changing demand between summer and winter?

Table 2 Demand for North Sea oil fractions in summer and winter.

Fraction	Percentage of total demand	
	Summer	Winter
refinery gas	3.6	3
gasoline (petrol)	32	29
kerosine (paraffin)	12	6
diesel oil	17	23
residue	35.4	39

5 Look at table 1 on page 188.
   a What do the names of all the alkenes have in common?
   b The simplest alkane is methane, CH_4. Why is the simplest alkene not methene?
   c Write an equation to show the reaction that would occur when propene reacts with bromine.

6 The alkene with molecular formula C_4H_8 has three isomers. One of these isomers is shown in table 1. Draw the structural formulas of the other two isomers.

7 Cracking with models
   You will need a molecular modelling kit of the 'ball and stick' type. Use it to build a model of a molecule of decane. Its structure is shown in picture 3 on page 187. Make sure every hole has a stick in it.

   Now pull apart one – any one – of the carbon–carbon bonds in the model, so you get two fragments. This represents breaking a bond during cracking.

   Rearrange the atoms in the two fragments so that once again every hole has a stick in it.

   Try to identify the two molecules that you have formed.

Sticky stuff

Without adhesives our world would fall apart – literally. This book certainly would, and so would your shoes and probably the chair you're sitting on.

All glues start off runny and sticky, then turn solid. The solid holds the two surfaces together. How is this done? There are two main kinds of glue: solvent glues and polymerising glues.

Solvent glues

Solvent glues have a solid dissolved in a solvent that is volatile (easily vaporised). When the solvent evaporates away, the solid is left behind (picture 1). When you stick a stamp on a letter you are using a solvent glue – and you provide the solvent yourself. On the back of the stamp there is a solid gum, similar to starch. When you lick the stamp, the solid gum dissolves in water. When the stamp is stuck on to the letter, the water quickly evaporates and gets absorbed by the paper, leaving the solid to hold letter and stamp together.

Polystyrene cement, used in model-making, has polystyrene plastic dissolved in a volatile organic solvent. The solvent quickly evaporates away as the glue sets.

One problem with solvent glues is that the solvent vapour may be toxic.

Polymerising glues

The trouble with solvent glues is that tiny gaps are left where the solvent

Picture 2 The glue used to mend punctures on bicycle tyres contains rubber dissolved in a volatile solvent.

evaporates. This weakens the join. A polymerising glue has no solvent. It consists of a monomer which polymerises when the glue sets. (See topic H5 for more about polymerisation.) The polymer holds the surfaces together. The problem is, how do you stop it polymerising in the tube?

One way is to have a separate 'hardener' which you mix with the monomer when you're ready to use it. The 'hardener' contains a catalyst which starts the polymerisation reaction. Epoxy adhesives like 'Araldite' work in this way.

Another way is to use a catalyst that is naturally present in the air. For example, 'Super Glue' has a monomer which polymerises when it meets water (picture 3). When you spread the glue on the surface to be joined, it is

exposed to water vapour in the air. This starts the polymerisation reaction, which is very quick – as you will know if you've ever got this kind of glue on your skin by accident. In fact, 'Super Glue' is so good at sticking to skin that doctors use it in skin grafts.

1   Explain why polymerising glues are usually stronger than solvent glues.

2   The instructions on a tube of glue usually say something like: 'Surfaces to be joined must be clean, dry and free from grease'. Why is this important?

3   Wood and paper are easily glued together. Glass and metal are more difficult. Can you suggest why?

4   Why does polystyrene cement not set while it is in the tube?

5   All glues set more quickly at higher temperatures. Why?

6   Picture 3 shows the structural formula of the monomer that is in 'Super Glue'. It polymerises by addition polymerisation (page 206).

    Make a copy of the structural formula. Draw a ring around the double carbon–carbon bond that is responsible for addition polymerisation.

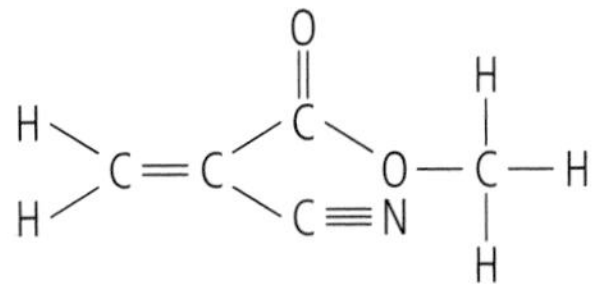

methyl 2-cyanoacrylate

Picture 3 The monomer in 'Super Glue'

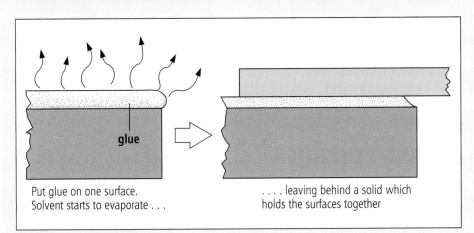

Put glue on one surface. Solvent starts to evaporate . . .

. . . . leaving behind a solid which holds the surfaces together

Picture 1 How a solvent glue works.

H3

Ethanol

Ethanol is one of the best known organic chemicals in our lives.

H H
| |
H–C–C–O–H
| |
H H

the –O–H group: all alcohols have this

Picture 1 The formula of ethanol.

Picture 2 Ethanol is used as a solvent for sweet-smelling oils in perfumes. The ethanol quickly evaporates from your warm skin, leaving behind the fragrant oils.

If you use the world 'alcohol' in ordinary conversation, most people think of drinks. But to a chemist, 'alcohol' means a whole family of organic chemicals. Ethanol is the most important member of this group. Ethanol is the alcohol in drinks, and it has many important uses.

THE ALCOHOL FAMILY

Like alkanes and alkenes, the alcohols are a family of related compounds—a homologous series. Each member of the series has the —O—H group in its molecule (picture 1). The —O—H group is called a **functional group** because it is responsible for the characteristic properties (or functions) of the alcohol family of compounds. The general formula of the alcohols is $C_nH_{2n+1}OH$, where n is the number of carbon atoms. The first five members of this series are shown in Table 1.

Table 1 The first five members of the alcohol family.

Name	Structural formula	Shortened structural formula	Melting point (°C)	Boiling point (°C)
methanol	H–C–O–H (with H above and below)	CH_3OH	−94	65
ethanol	H–C–C–O–H	C_2H_5OH	−117	78
propan-1-ol	H–C–C–C–O–H	C_3H_7OH	−126	97
butan-1-ol	H–C–C–C–C–O–H	C_4H_9OH	−90	117
pentan-1-ol	H–C–C–C–C–C–O–H	$C_5H_{11}OH$	−79	137

There is a general increase in melting points and boiling points as the number of carbon atoms in the alcohol increases. This is one of the ways in which alcohols are *physically* different from one another. However, alcohols have similar *chemical* reactions.

USING ETHANOL

Ethanol is a fuel, an excellent solvent and an important raw material for making other chemicals.

Many covalently bonded solutes which do not dissolve in water are soluble in ethanol. Quick drying lacquers for example, often contain ethanol as a solvent. Ethanol is volatile, so it evaporates quickly, leaving the dry lacquer. Ethanol is also used as a solvent in perfumes (picture 2).

Pure ethanol is a toxic liquid. Methanol, which is even more toxic, is sometimes added to it to put off anyone wanting to drink it. A dye is sometimes also added. This mixture of ethanol and methanol is known as methylated spirits or sometimes 'meths'. It is often used as a fuel, for example in camping stoves (picture 4), as well as being used as a solvent.

Ethanol is a raw material for making **esters**. These organic compounds are sweet-smelling liquids used as solvents, food flavourings and in the manufacture of cosmetics. There is more about esters in topic H4.

Vinegar, a weak solution of ethanoic acid, is produced from ethanol by a biochemical process. It involves oxidation caused by bacteria called **acetobacter**:

$$\text{ethanol} + \text{air} \xrightarrow{\text{acetobacter}} \text{ethanoic acid}$$

Because of this reaction, wine becomes 'vinegary' if it is left exposed to the air.

MAKING ETHANOL

Ethanol can be made naturally, by fermentation (see below). It can also be made synthetically from ethene, which is made by cracking oil fractions (see topic H2).

Ethene is converted into ethanol by an addition reaction:

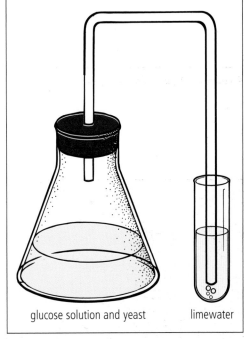

Picture 3   Fermenting glucose in the laboratory. What do you think the limewater is for?

In the chemical industry, the reaction is carried out at a temperature of 500 K in the presence of a catalyst. Because the reaction involves the addition of water, it is called **hydration**. In countries that have plenty of crude oil, this is an economic way of making ethanol since ethene is a crude oil product.

■ Fermentation

In countries where crude oil is a scarce and expensive raw material, it is often cheaper to produce ethanol by fermentation. Humans have been using this reaction for thousands of years to make alcoholic drinks.

During fermentation, sugars are broken down into ethanol and carbon dioxide by the action of enzymes in yeast.

$$\text{sugar} \xrightarrow{\text{yeast}} \text{ethanol} + \text{carbon dioxide} + \text{energy}$$

$$C_6H_{12}O_6(aq) \xrightarrow{\text{yeast}} 2C_2H_5OH(aq) + 2CO_2(g) + \text{energy}$$

Picture 3 shows apparatus that we can use to carry out fermentation in the laboratory. Ethanol can be separated from the fermented mixture by fractional distillation. The laboratory apparatus that we use for this type of distillation is shown on page 20.

REACTIONS OF ALCOHOLS

The —OH group in alcohol molecules makes them quite reactive. Alcohols are also flammable because of the ease of oxidising the hydrocarbon chain that is linked to the —OH group.

Here are some of the more important reactions of alcohols.

Picture 4 Ethanol (methylated spirits) makes an excellent fuel for campers because it is easily carried around and burns cleanly. However, it is flammable so it must be used carefully.

■ Combustion

Alcohols are good fuels because they burn easily and cleanly in air. For example,

$$\text{ethanol} + \text{oxygen} \rightarrow \text{carbon dioxide} + \text{water} + \text{energy}$$
$$C_2H_5OH + 3O_2 \rightarrow 2CO_2 + 3H_2O$$

We get the same combustion products by burning alkanes in air (topic I2).

Ethanol is highly flammable and burns with a blue flame that is difficult to see. It can easily cause dangerous fires if it is used carelessly.

■ Reaction with sodium

Alcohols react with sodium metal. The reaction is similar to that between sodium and water, although alcohols react less vigorously. Sodium displaces hydrogen from the –OH group in the alcohol, giving hydrogen gas. For example,

$$\text{sodium} + \text{ethanol} \rightarrow \text{sodium ethoxide} + \text{hydrogen}$$
$$2Na + 2C_2H_5OH \rightarrow 2C_2H_5O^-Na^+ + H_2$$

Compare this with the reactions of alkali metals with water in topic F4. Sodium ethoxide is a strong alkali, like sodium hydroxide.

■ Ester formation

Alcohols react slowly with carboxylic acids to produce another family of carbon compounds known as **esters**.

There is more about this reaction in Topic H4.

ETHANOL: AN ALTERNATIVE MOTOR FUEL

In the early 1970s there were worldwide shortages of crude oil because of conflict in the Middle East. Faced with a fuel crisis, the Brazilian government decided to use ethanol to replace some crude oil. Brazil is one of the world's largest producers of sugar cane and in the 1970s it began increasing its capacity to produce ethanol by fermenting cane sugar. This trend continued into the 1980s and by 1987 the Brazilians were producing 25 million tonnes of sugar cane a year. Of this, 7 million tonnes was used for food and the rest was fermented to give 12 000 million litres of ethanol!

Picture 5 Ethanol is a popular alternative to petrol in countries such as Brazil.

Picture 6 Smog is a cause of air pollution in densely populated areas such as Mexico City. Using ethanol as a motor fuel is one way of avoiding this problem.

Ethanol does not release quite as much energy as petrol when it burns but the difference is not great. In the mid 1990s, there were about a million cars in Brazil running on pure ethanol and another million running on an ethanol/petrol mix called 'gasohol'. The growth in Brazil of car engines burning ethanol slowed towards the end of the 1980s as the price of crude oil fell. Nevertheless, it has been estimated that during the 1980s the use of ethanol from homegrown sugar cane saved the Brazilian economy over $2000 million!

Another benefit of using ethanol as a motor fuel has been to reduce air pollution. In the city of São Paulo, where 15 million people live, cars burn only ethanol. This has reduced the kind of *smogs* that are sometimes seen in some very large cities (Picture 6). These smogs develop when bright sunlight decomposes hydrocarbons and other exhaust gases from cars. Ethanol burns more cleanly than hydrocarbons, reducing the smog problem.

Questions

1 a Write down the molecular formula of the alcohol which has six carbon atoms. Draw a diagram to show the arrangement of atoms in this molecule.

ICT b Plot a graph to show how the boiling points of the alcohols in Table 1 vary with the number of carbon atoms they contain. Use your graph to estimate the boiling point of the alcohol with six carbon atoms.

2 Carbon dioxide, one of the products of fermentation, is a gas. Why is this important in breadmaking?

3 Ethanol is a good *solvent* for covalently bonded *solutes*.

a Explain the meaning of the words in italics.

b Name three solutes which you would expect to be soluble in ethanol.

c Most perfumes contain ethanol. The ethanol is a solvent for the fragrant oils which give the perfume its smell (picture 2). Why is ethanol used, rather than water?

4 Ethanol and water behave in similar ways in some of their chemical reactions. Explain these similarities by comparing the arrangement of atoms in molecules of water and ethanol.

5 Read again the section on *Ethanol: an alternative motor fuel*, then answer the following questions.

a Ethanol has become a major alternative to petrol in Brazil, but it is unlikely to do so in Britain. Explain why.

b The use of ethanol as a fuel in Brazil is influenced by the price of crude oil. Explain why.

c Give one environmental advantage of using ethanol as an alternative to petrol.

d Can you suggest one environmental disadvantage of Brazil's policy of using ethanol as a replacement for petrol?

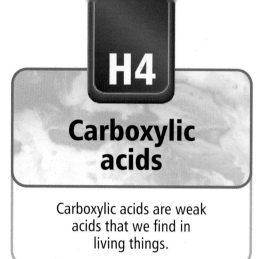

H4

Carboxylic acids

Carboxylic acids are weak acids that we find in living things.

Picture 1

Most of the fruit in picture 1 contains edible, weak acids that give the fruit a sharp taste. Oranges and lemons, for example, contain citric acid. Apples and gooseberries contain malic acid. Both these acids belong to a family of weak acids called the **carboxylic acids**.

A FAMILY OF ACIDS

Like alkanes and alcohols, carboxylic acids are grouped together in an *homologous series*. One of the simplest carboxylic acids is ethanoic acid (picture 2). A molecule of ethanoic acid has a hydrocarbon end with just one carbon atom joined to a *carboxyl* group, —COOH. Other members of this homologous series have similar structures but different hydrocarbon chains. The general formula for these simple carboxylic acids is $C_nH_{2n+1}COOH$.

The first three members of the homologous series are shown in Table 1.

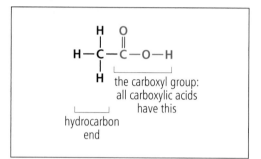

Picture 2 The molecular structure of ethanoic acid.

Table 1 The first three members of the carboxylic acid family.

Name	Structural formula	Shortened structural formula	Melting point (°C)	Boiling point (°C)
methanoic acid	H—C—O—H (with O double bonded)	HCOOH	9	101
ethanoic acid	H—C—C—O—H (with H's and O)	CH_3COOH	17	118
propanoic acid	H—C—C—C—O—H (with H's and O)	CH_3CH_2COOH	−21	141

Notice the arrangement of atoms in the carboxyl group. It is often shortened to –COOH when we write the structural formula of the acid. For example, we usually write the formula of ethanoic acid as CH_3COOH. The chemical properties of a carboxylic acid are decided by the *functional group, –COOH*.

Using the carboxylic acids

Ethanoic acid is the acid in vinegar. It is used as a flavouring and a preservative in foods that are pickled (picture 3). On the ingredients lists of these foods, you will often see *acetic acid*, the common name for ethanoic acid.

In the chemical industry, ethanoic acid is an important raw material. It is converted into a polymer called polyvinyl acetate (PVA), which is used to make water-based glues and emulsion paints. Ethanoic acid also reacts with cellulose from wood pulp to make a semi-synthetic polymer called cellulose acetate. This reaction is an example of ester formation (see the next page). We can use cellulose acetate as a plastic or a fibre. In the form of *rayon* fibres, it is used to make soft furnishings and fabrics that look silky (see picture 9, page 202).

There are many other uses of carboxylic acids. Aspirin is a carboxylic acid that is used not only to relieve pain and feverishness but also to reduce the swelling caused by arthritis and soft tissue injuries. Sometimes doctors prescribe aspirin to lower the risk of abnormal blood clotting in patients who have suffered a heart attack. However, regular use of aspirin can be dangerous. It is a weak acid and can easily damage the lining of the stomach if the dose is not carefully controlled.

Picture 3 Ethanoic acid is used to pickle cucumbers and other food. The dilute acid is safe to eat and makes them taste tangy. The acidity stops the growth of bacteria that would spoil the food.

Picture 4 Ancient people knew that chewing the bark of the willow tree relieved pain. The bark contains salicyclic acid, a carboxylic acid that gives aspirin its affect.

Reactions of carboxylic acids

ACIDIC BEHAVIOUR

Carboxylic acids have chemical properties that are typical of acids (see topic G1). However, they are **weak** acids and react much more slowly with metals, bases and carbonates than **strong** acids such as sulphuric acid and hydrochloric acid.

A salt of ethanoic acid is called an **ethanoate**. We can make ethanoates in the same way as we make salts of strong acids.

Metal + acid

A reactive metal, such as magnesium, dissolves in ethanoic acid to give the salt and hydrogen:

magnesium + ethanoic acid → magnesium ethanoate + hydrogen

$$Mg + 2CH_3COOH \rightarrow (CH_3COO)_2Mg + H_2$$

Alkali + acid

An alkali, such as sodium hydroxide, reacts with ethanoic acid to give the salt and water:

sodium hydroxide + ethanoic acid → sodium ethanoate + water

$$NaOH + CH_3COOH \rightarrow CH_3COONa + H_2O$$

Carbonate + acid

A carbonate, such as sodium carbonate, reacts with ethanoic acid to give the salt, carbon dioxide and water (picture 5).

$$\text{sodium carbonate} + \text{ethanoic acid} \rightarrow \text{sodium ethanoate} + \text{carbon dioxide} + \text{water}$$
$$Na_2CO_3 + 2CH_3COOH \rightarrow 2CH_3COONa + CO_2 + H_2O$$

Picture 5 Sherbet contains both citric acid and a carbonate. Can you explain what goes on when you mix sherbet with water?

FORMATION OF ESTERS

Carboxylic acids react with alcohols to form compounds called **esters**.

$$\text{carboxylic acid} + \text{alcohol} \rightleftharpoons \text{ester} + \text{water}$$

This reaction is reversible. To get more ester, you add concentrated sulphuric acid which removes the water as it is formed and shifts the equilibrium towards the products (see topic I9). The acid also speeds up the reaction by acting as a catalyst. (see topic I6).

Picture 6 Sports players often use oil of wintergreen to ease muscular pain and stiffness. This strongly smelling oil is an ester made from methanol and salicylic acid.

Esters are named after the acid and the alcohol from which they are made. When ethanoic acid reacts with ethanol, we get an ester called ethyl ethanoate. Picture 7 shows how this ester is formed.

Picture 7 Formation of ethyl ethanoate. The ester is produced when a molecule of water is removed from between the ethanol and ethanoic acid molecules. Notice how the name of the ester is related to its structure.

Table 2 shows the relationship between some more esters and the reactants that we use to make them.

Table 2   Naming esters.

Alcohol		Carboxylic acid		Ester	
Name	**Formula**	**Name**	**Formula**	**Name**	**Formula**
methanol	CH_3OH	methanoic acid	$HCOOH$	methyl methanoate	CH_3OOCH
ethanol	C_2H_5OH	propanoic acid	C_2H_5COOH	ethyl propanoate	$CH_3CH_2OOCCH_2CH_3$
methanol	CH_3OH	ethanoic acid	CH_3COOH	methyl ethanoate	CH_3OOCCH_3

Many esters are sweet-smelling and are often found in perfumes and food flavourings. They occur naturally in the smells of flowers and fruits. Volatile esters are used in solvents and in solvent glues.

Questions

1 Which one of the following formulas shows a carboxylic acid?

$CH_3CH_2CH_3$
$CH_2{=}CHCH_2CH_3$
$CH_3CH_2CH_2CH_2COOH$
C_2H_5OH

Explain how you made your choice.

2 Table 1 may help you answer this question.

a The fourth member of the homologous series of carboxylic acids is butanoic acid. Draw the full structural formula of this acid and write its shortened structural formula.

b Palmitic acid is a carboxylic acid that can be made from soap. It contains 16 carbon atoms. Write down its shortened structural formula.

3 Aspirin does not dissolve well in water but it can be made more soluble by converting it into its calcium salt.

a Describe how you could make the calcium salt of aspirin.

b Suggest why taking soluble forms of aspirin may be less harmful to the lining of the stomach than taking aspirin itself.

4 Kettle descalers are used to remove the 'fur' of calcium carbonate, $CaCO_3$, that sometimes builds up inside a kettle. They often contain a weak acid such as methanoic acid, $HCOOH$.

a Why does methanoic acid get rid of the fur inside the kettle?

b Why do kettle descalers contain an acid such as methanoic acid but not hydrochloric or sulphuric acid?

c Write a symbol equation to show the reaction between methanoic acid and kettle fur.

5 Sherbet contains sodium hydrogencarbonate and citric acid. Predict the reaction you would expect to happen when sherbet is added to water. Use picture 5 to support your answer.

6 a Look back at picture 6 on page 198. What is the name of the ester in oil of wintergreen?

b Write down the structural formula of each of the following esters:
i ethyl methanoate
ii the methyl ester of hexanoic acid, $C_5H_{11}COOH$.

Polymers

Polymers have long, thin molecules made by joining together lots of shorter units. In this topic we look at some natural and synthetic polymers

Picture 1 Both these shirts are made from polymers – one is natural, one is synthetic. Can you tell which is which?

The pages of this book are made from a polymer – cellulose – and the ink contains a polymer to make it stick to the pages. The fingers you use to turn the pages are covered with skin made from a polymer – protein. The eyes you read it with, and the brain you understand it with, are mostly protein too.

All organisms are built from natural polymers like starch, cellulose and protein. We have used naturally occurring polymers like wood, cotton and wool for thousands of years.

Yet the first *synthetic* polymers – synthetic fibres and plastics – were made less than a hundred years ago. Today they are everywhere, but they were not used on a large scale until the 1950s. Your grandparents would have used hardly any synthetic polymers when they were your age – ask them and see.

Why has it taken so long for humans to take advantage of these useful materials? One reason is that most modern polymers are made from oil – and the oil industry only really got going in the 1950s. Another reason is that scientists did not understand what polymers were before 1922. Once they understood the kind of molecules that polymers contain, scientists quickly learned how to make polymers to order.

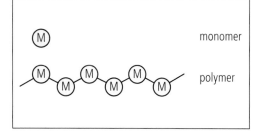

Picture 2 Monomer and polymer.

monomer

polymer

WHAT ARE POLYMERS?

In 1922, a German chemist called Hermann Staudinger suggested that rubber is made of molecular chains in which identical units are joined together. Many scientists didn't believe him – they thought it just contained clumps of small molecules.

Hermann Staudinger got it right. Like all **polymers**, rubber is made by joining together large numbers of small molecules called **monomers**. Picture 2 gives the general idea. The world 'polymer' comes from Greek words: the *poly* bit means many, and *mer* means part. The process of joining up monomers to form a polymer is called **polymerisation**.

Polymers are named after the monomer unit they contain. Polythene, for example, is made by joining together lots of ethene units – strictly speaking, its name should be poly(ethene). Picture 3 shows the idea another way. Most polymers have hundreds or thousands of monomers in a single chain.

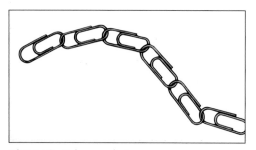

Picture 3 Polypaperclip!

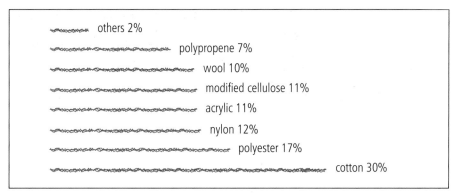

Picture 4 Popularity of clothing fibres in Western Europe. The percentages show the share of the total market in clothing fibres.

■ Classifying polymers

Natural polymers, such as rubber, silk and cotton are made by living things. Artificial or **synthetic polymers** include polythene, nylon and polyester.

Natural polymers come in many different forms (see below). Synthetic polymers are mainly either **plastics** or **fibres**. Plastics are flexible and easily moulded, whereas fibres form long, thin strands. We'll see the reason for the differences in their properties later in this topic.

Fibres are particularly useful for making clothes, because they can be spun into threads and woven into cloth. Picture 4 shows fibres that are commonly used in clothes. You can see we use both natural and synthetic polymers for clothing fibres.

Another way of classifying polymers is according to the way the monomers are joined together. There are **addition** and **condensation** polymers; there is more about addition polymers in topic H6.

■ Some natural polymers

CARBOHYDRATES: STARCH AND CELLULOSE

Starch and cellulose are polymers of glucose (picture 5). Starch molecules (picture 6) are just chains of glucose monomers joined together. This type of polymer is called a **polysaccharide** ('many sugars').

You can find out more about how the glucose units are joined together in the next topic. The important thing is that they can be easily joined up and easily separated again. This makes starch a convenient substance for storing glucose – and therefore storing energy. In a grain of wheat or a potato, the starch chains are coiled up so they pack closely together. This way a lot of energy is stored in a small space.

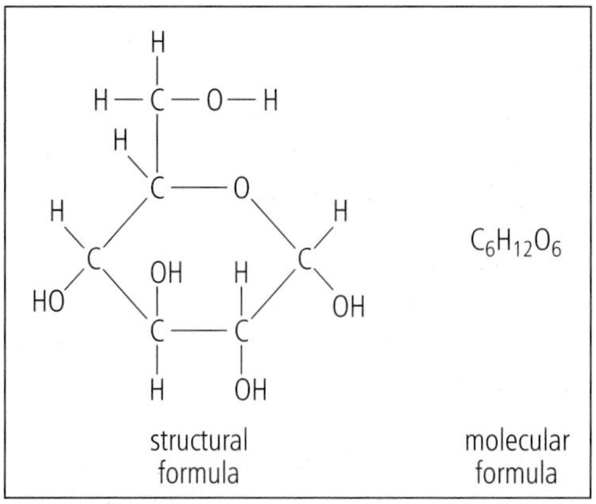

$C_6H_{12}O_6$

structural formula   molecular formula

Picture 5 Glucose: the monomer for starch and cellulose

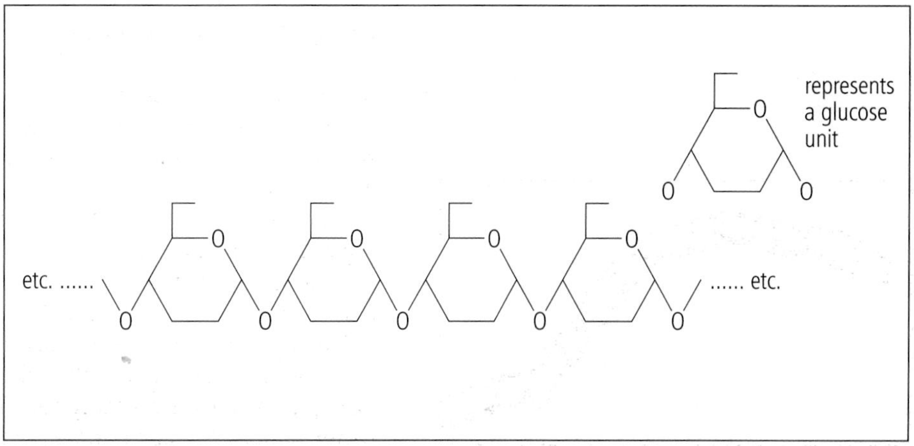

represents a glucose unit

etc. .... etc.

Picture 6 The structure of starch

Picture 7 Long-distance runners train their bodies to store lots of glycogen so they can keep going for a long time. When a marathon runner nears the end of the 26 mile race, he or she may run out of glycogen and suddenly feel extremely tired. This often happens after 20 miles and is called 'going through the wall'.

Picture 9 This shirt is made from a semi-synthetic fibre – a modified form of cellulose.

Animals store glucose in a polysaccharide that is very similar to starch, called **glycogen**. Glycogen can be quickly broken down to give a ready supply of glucose when energy is needed (picture 7).

Picture 8 shows the structure of cellulose. You can see that it's very similar to starch, but the glucose units are joined together in a different way. This makes cellulose tougher and more fibrous than starch. Cellulose is the structural material that plant cell walls are made of, and it gives plant cells their strength. Many of the materials we use, such as paper, cardboard, cotton and linen, contain mainly cellulose. Cellulose can be modified by treating it with chemicals to make semi-synthetic fibres such as rayon. Picture 9 shows an example.

Picture 8 The structure of cellulose.

PROTEINS

Many polymers have only one type of monomer unit. Starch, for example, contains only glucose units. Proteins, on the other hand, use several different monomer units. These units are called **amino acids**, and there are about 20 different ones found in naturally occurring proteins. Picture 10 on the next page shows the idea.

A typical protein molecule may contain thousands of amino acid units joined together. What is more, each amino acid may be one of around 20 different kinds. This means that many different proteins can be made – which is why protein materials are so varied. Hair, skin, muscle, egg white and silk are all made of types of proteins. In fact, there are enough different proteins for every human to have their own, unique set.

After you eat a protein food such as cheese, your digestive enzymes break the protein down into separate amino acids. Later, your cells polymerise the amino acids in a different order to form whatever protein they need. The instructions giving the right order are stored in another polymer, deoxyribonucleic acid (DNA). This is the substance from which our genes are made.

■ Synthetic polymers

PLASTICS

Plastics are very useful materials. They are easy to shape by moulding or melting, and they are usually cheap. Chemists can 'design' plastics with all sorts of properties to suit different uses.

The simplest and commonest plastic is polythene, which is made by polymerising ethene. You can see in the next topic how the ethene monomer units are joined together. Table 1 on the next page shows some common plastics and their uses.

FIBRES

Some polymers can be used as both plastics and fibres. For example, polypropene, which is the plastic used to make milk bottle crates, can be made into a fibre for ropes. Nylon is normally used as a fibre, but it can also be moulded as a plastic – it's used where a strong plastic is needed for things like gear wheels. You can read more about this below.

You can see some common synthetic fibres in table 1. Synthetic fibres have replaced natural fibres like cotton and wool for many uses. The synthetic fibres are

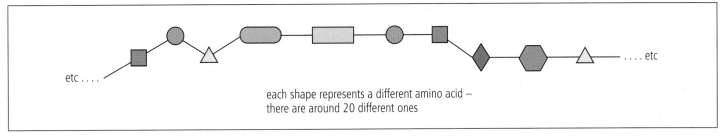

each shape represents a different amino acid –
there are around 20 different ones

Picture 10 The structure of protein.

Table 1 Some common synthetic polymers.

Polymer	Plastic or fibre	Monomer		Examples of uses
polythene	plastic	ethene	$H_2C{=}CH_2$	Plastic bags, squeezy bottles, washing-up bowls
polypropene	plastic, fibre	propene	$H_2C{=}CH(CH_3)$	Milk bottle crates, carpet, plastic rope
polystyrene	plastic	styrene	$H_2C{=}CH(C_6H_5)$	Plastic toys, expanded polystyrene for insulation
polyvinyl chloride (PVC)	plastic	vinyl chloride (chloroethene)	$H_2C{=}CH(Cl)$	Guttering and pipes, electrical insulation, floor covering
acrylic fibre	fibre	acrylonitrile (cyanoethene)	$H_2C{=}CH(CN)$	Fibre for clothing (substitute for wool)
nylon	fibre, plastic	1,6-diaminohexane and hexanedioic acid		Fibre for clothing, carpets, ropes. Plastic for engineering parts
polyester	fibre, plastic	ethanediol and benzenedioic acid		Fibre for clothing, boat sails. Plastic for videotape, photo film, drinks bottles

cheaper, and they are usually harder wearing. What is more, they are often easier to wash and iron: acrylic fibre does not shrink like wool, for example. Polyester does not need ironing as much as cotton.

Even so, many people prefer natural fibres to synthetic ones. Natural fibres feel less 'sweaty' to wear, and they often look more stylish – and expensive.

WHAT GIVES POLYMERS THEIR SPECIAL PROPERTIES?

As with all substances, the properties of polymers are decided by their structures. Polymer molecules are like long, thin chains, and we can think of polymers as one-dimensional giant structures.

A single polymer molecule is like a single piece of spaghetti – long, thin and flexible. Of course, a small piece of plastic or fibre would contain billions of these chains. In a plastic such as polythene, the chains are all tangled up together – rather like a bowlful of spaghetti (picture 11). Like spaghetti, the chains can slide over each other, which is why the plastic is flexible.

When you heat the plastic, the molecular chains move faster and slide over each other even more easily. The plastic softens and melts. One of the reasons plastics are so useful is that you can push around the chains and mould the plastic into any shape you want.

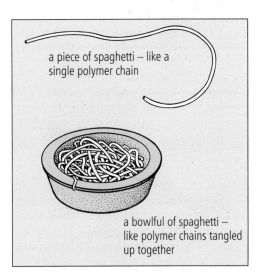

a piece of spaghetti – like a single polymer chain

a bowlful of spaghetti – like polymer chains tangled up together

Picture 11 Polymers are like spaghetti.

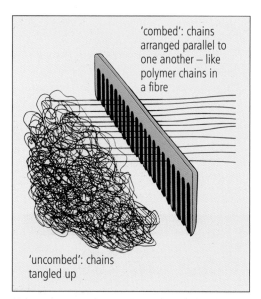

Picture 12 Combing.

Picture 13 Splitting a log is easy, because you are splitting separate strands of fibres. But cutting across the grain of the wood is more difficult because you have to break many polymer chains.

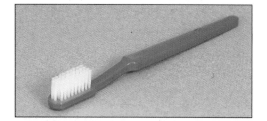

Picture 14 This is a nylon toothbrush. In the handle, the nylon is a plastic, but in the bristles, the nylon is in the form of a fibre.

■ What about fibres?

Imagine combing spaghetti with a large comb so that the spaghetti strands are brought parallel to one another (picture 12). This is the way the polymer chains are arranged in fibres. The strands that you see in a fibre like polyester or cotton contain bunches of parallel polymer chains.

The strands of fibre are difficult to break, because breaking one strand involves breaking many polymer chains all at once. But it is easy to pull the separate strands apart, because that doesn't involve breaking polymer chains. It's much easier to fray a rope than to break it. Picture 13 illustrates the same idea.

■ How can a plastic become a fibre?

The toothbrush in picture 14 is made of a single polymer – nylon. The handle is flexible and has been moulded: it is a plastic. The bristles are fibres. To make the nylon behave as a fibre, the polymer chains have to be made parallel, rather like combing the spaghetti in picture 12. This is done by drawing the fibres, as shown in picture 15.

Before a synthetic polymer like nylon or polyester can be used as a fibre, it has to be drawn by pulling it so the polymer chains line up. Nylon and polyester make good fibres because, once drawn, the chains stay in their parallel arrangement. Polythene doesn't make a good fibre because, after drawing, the chains tend to go back into the disorganised state of a plastic.

DESIGNING POLYMERS TO ORDER

Chemists can make polymers to suit most purposes. There is a plastic that doesn't stick to anything, which is useful for non-stick pans. It's called polytetrafluoroethene or PTFE. There is a fibre called kevlar that, weight for weight, is stronger than steel. It is used to make bullet-proof vests. There are even plastics that conduct electricity. One of the disadvantages of many plastics is their low melting point. But there are now plastic roasting bags that you can put in the oven, and there is even the possibility of a plastic car engine.

Suppose a manufacturer wants a polymer to do a particular job. Chemists first decide the type of polymer chain that is needed to give the required properties. Then they make the necessary monomers, usually by breaking down large molecules from crude oil. Finally, they join together the monomers to make the polymer. Polymer chemistry is a matter of breaking down big molecules, then building new ones.

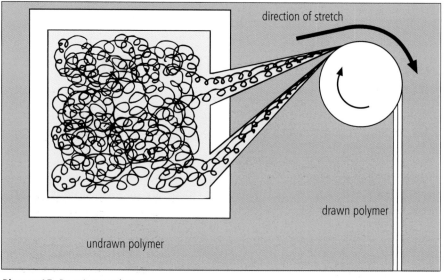

Picture 15 Drawing a polymer.

POLYMERS AND THE ENVIRONMENT

A big problem with synthetic polymers is getting rid of them when they're finished with. Natural polymers, like cellulose in paper and protein in wool, are not too bad. They rot fairly quickly as micro-organisms break them down and use them for food. They are **biodegradable.**

But micro-organisms can't break down synthetic polymers like polythene and nylon. In the 50 years or so that synthetic polymers have been around, micro-organisms have not had time to evolve the ability to use them for food. So plastics can be a serious litter problem. One way to dispose of plastics is to burn them, but this is a waste of useful material. Some plastics produce toxic gases when they burn: for example, PVC produces toxic hydrogen chloride.

One answer to the problem might be to **recycle** waste plastic. Unfortunately, this is not as easy as recycling, say, glass or steel. The trouble is that there are many different types of plastics in use, and it's often difficult to tell which is which. To recycle plastics effectively you would need to sort them out first, rather as you sort glass into different colours for a bottle bank. But although *you* may be able to tell the difference between polythene and polystyrene, many people cannot. Recycling of plastic is most effective where a single polymer is involved (picture 16). To make recycling easier, plastic containers are often marked with a code to show the type of polymer used (picture 17).

Picture 16 Wellington boots can be recycled because they are made from a single polymer, PVC.
(a) Before recycling.
(b) Shredding the boots to make PVC granules.

Picture 17 Recycling symbols help people to sort plastics into categories.

Activities

A Explaining polymers

A good way to test whether you understand an idea is to try to explain it to someone.

Find a person (a relative or neighbour, perhaps) who does not know much science. Use a simple model, such as 'polypaperclip' on page 200, to explain the following.

1 What a polymer is. (You may have to explain about molecules first.)

2 Why plastics are flexible.

3 Why fibres form strands.

B Investigating a plastic cup

You will need a plastic cup of the type you get from drink machines – but not the insulated type made from expanded polystyrene.

Try tearing the cup in two different directions. First, grasp the cup at the top and bottom and try tearing it apart so the top is separated from the bottom. Can you do it? Now try tearing again, but this time grasp each side of the cup and try tearing it so one side is separated from the other. What difference do you notice? Can you suggest an explanation? Think about the way the polymer chains are arranged in the cup. It may help you to look at picture 13.

Questions

1 Explain what the following words mean: (a) polymer, (b) monomer, (c) plastic, (d) fibre.

2 What is the monomer in each of the following polymers?
(a) polythene, (b) starch, (c) polypropene, (d) cellulose, (e) protein, (f) polyurethane

3 Each of the following materials contains polymers. For each material, say whether it is (i) natural or synthetic (ii) plastic or fibre.
(a) wood, (b) PVC, (c) linen, (d) polyester, (e) rubber, (f) leather, (g) raffia, (h) Perspex, (i) rayon

4 You often hear chemists say 'Crude oil is too valuable to burn.' Why do they say this? If it is true, what can be done about it?

5 a Why does plastic cause a particularly bad waste disposal problem?
b Some manufacturers are now making biodegradable plastics. One type, used for making shopping bags, consists of tiny grains of polythene stuck together with cellulose. Why does this make the plastic degradable? Will it degrade completely? Explain.

6 Explain the following.
a There are many types of protein, but very few types of starch.
b Starch and cellulose are both polymers of glucose. Starch is a good energy food, but good energy food, but cellulose has no value as an energy food.

From monomer to polymer

In this topic we look at how monomers can be joined to form polymers.

Picture 1 This paperweight is made from casting resin. A polymerisation reaction takes placewhen the resin sets hard.

The paperweight in picture 1 was made using casting resin. The clear plastic started off as a liquid monomer. When it was mixed with a special catalyst, the monomer polymerised and turned into a solid plastic.

Quick polymerisation is important for plastic or fibre manufacturers. But they do not want the polymer to break down again (**depolymerise**) quickly, or they might not sell much of their product.

Living things need to be able to join up monomers quickly and easily to form polymers such as starch and protein. They also need to be able to break them down quickly when necessary.

ADDITION POLYMERISATION

Most of the plastics we use every day are **addition polymers**. Let's look at polythene as an example. The monomer for polythene is ethene (picture 2). The double bond in ethene makes it rather reactive. It tends to break open, leaving free bonds which can join on to other atoms or molecules in an addition reaction (see page 188). If there's nothing else around, ethene molecules will join on to each other to make a long chain. This is **addition polymerisation**.

Ethene molecules do not polymerise on their own. To make the reaction happen, you need high pressure to squeeze the molecules close together, and a high temperature to give them enough energy to start breaking the double bonds. A catalyst is used to make the reaction go faster.

The commonest form of polythene is made using a temperature of about 200°C and a pressure of about 2000 atmospheres (20 MPa). It's impossible to get these conditions in the laboratory, so you won't be able to make polythene yourself.

The industrial process is carried out in large chemical plants. Apart from the cost of the ethene, the main cost of this process is the energy needed to produce the high temperature and pressure. Topic D1 looks at some of the costs involved in the whole process of turning crude oil into a polythene article such as a washing-up bowl.

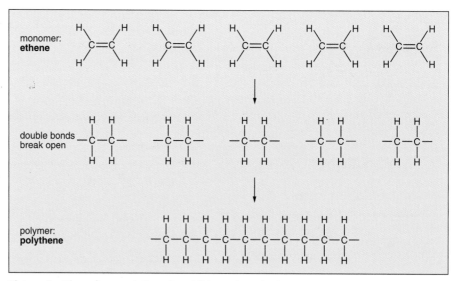

Picture 2 Ethene forms polythene by addition polymerisation.

■ Other addition polymers

Addition polymerisation needs a double bond in the molecule of the monomer. If you look at table 1 on page 203, you will see that most of the common plastics have this type of monomer. Polystyrene, PVC and polypropene are all addition polymers. Picture 3 shows the formation of PVC. Try working out some addition polymers in question 1.

Picture 3   PVC is formed by addition polymerisation. Note the Cl atoms.

THERMOPLASTICS AND THERMOSETS

All the plastic materials we have met so far can be softened and melted by heating, but they set again when cool. We call them **thermoplastics**. Thermoplastics are very useful because they can be moulded into any shape you want.

Some plastics behave rather differently. They do not soften at all when heated, but stay hard and rigid. If you heat them a lot, they just smoulder and char. This type of plastic is called **thermosetting**. You find thermosetting plastics in electrical fittings like plugs and sockets, where it is important that the plastic does not melt when it gets hot. The type shown in picture 4 is called urea–formaldehyde plastic. 'Bakelite', a similar plastic that is brown in colour, was the first synthetic plastic ever made.

Different structures, different properties

As always, we can explain the difference in properties if we look at the different structures. Picture 5 shows the polymer chains in thermoplastic and thermosetting polymers. In thermoplastics the polymer chains are free to slide past each other, so it's easy to change the shape.

In thermosetting polymers the chains are **cross-linked**. Instead of each chain being separate, neighbouring chains are linked together. This makes it difficult for polymer chains to move past each other, so the polymer is hard and rigid. Even when it is heated, the chains are still unable to move, so the polymer does not melt.

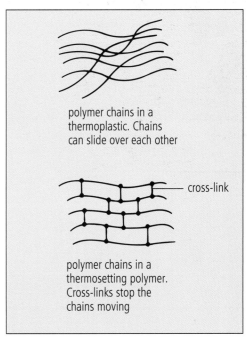

Picture 4   This electrical fitting is made from a thermosetting plastic which does not melt when it gets hot.

polymer chains in a thermoplastic. Chains can slide over each other

cross-link

polymer chains in a thermosetting polymer. Cross-links stop the chains moving

Picture 5   Polymer chains in a thermoplastic and in a thermoset.

Questions

1   If you know the structure of a monomer, you can work out the structure of the polymer it forms. For each of the following addition polymers, draw a section of the polymer chain containing at least three monomers. It may help you to look at picture 3. Use table 1 on page 203 to find the structures of the monomers.
   a   polypropene
   b   polystyrene
   c   acrylic fibre

2   The price of virtually all plastics depends on the price of crude oil. Explain why.
   If the cost of oil went up by 20%, would you expect the cost of polythene to go up by: (a) 20%, (b) less than 20%, (c) more than 20%? Explain your answer.

3   Explain the difference between a thermosetting polymer and a thermoplastic polymer. How can their differences be explained in terms of their molecular structures?

4   Gloss paint contains a polymer. When the paint is in the tin, the polymer chains are separate, without cross-links. When the paint has been applied, the polymer slowly reacts with oxygen from the air. Cross-links form between the chains, and the paint hardens.
   a   Draw pictures to represent paint polymer chains before and after the paint has hardened.
   b   Why do you think the paint does not harden while it is sealed in the tin?

Energy and chemistry

Energy and chemical reactions

We can use the kinetic theory to explain many of the things that happen around us.

Picture 1 The chemical reactions in fireworks transfer energy as heat, light and sound.

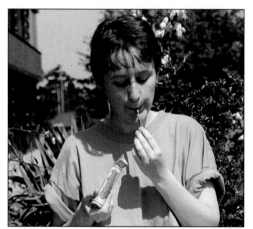

Picture 2 When sherbet mixes with water, an endothermic reaction takes place.

ENERGY OUT, ENERGY IN

Most chemical reactions give out heat. They are called **exothermic reactions**.

We rely on exothermic reactions for the energy we need to keep things going. Most of these exothermic reactions involve fuels.

Fuels are substances that react with oxygen to give out heat. Coal, natural gas, petrol and wood are all fuels. Fuels provide most of the energy needed by society for heating, cooking, transport, industry – and generally keeping everything going. Your own body is kept going by fuel, called food. You can find out more about fuels in topic I2.

Some reactions *take in* heat. We call them **endothermic reactions**. When an endothermic reaction happens you usually notice a fall in temperature. Have you ever noticed that sherbet feels cool in your mouth when you eat it? Sherbet is a mixture of citric acid and sodium hydrogencarbonate. When water is added they react together like this:

citric acid + sodium hydrogencarbonate
$$\rightarrow \text{sodium citrate + carbon dioxide + water}$$

The reaction is endothermic, so heat is taken in from your mouth, making it feel cool.

Many reactions in living things are endothermic. **Photosynthesis** is an important example. In photosynthesis, plants use energy from the sun to make sugars and starch.

Picture 3 illustrates the difference between exothermic and endothermic reactions.

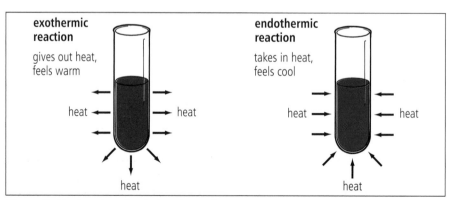

Picture 3 Exothermic and endothermic reactions.

Energy level diagrams

When changes happen, energy is transferred from one thing to another. A common way that energy can be transferred is by heating. When a fuel burns, energy is transferred from the fuel to something else – water in a saucepan for example. The more energy that's transferred to the water, the hotter the water gets.

We can represent the transfer of energy using an **energy level diagram**. Picture 4 shows an example. In this exothermic reaction, the chemicals are at a higher energy level at the beginning of the reaction than at the end. The difference between the two energy levels is the amount of energy that is transferred.

Picture 5 is an energy level diagram for an *endothermic* reaction. In this case, the chemicals are at a *lower* energy level at the beginning of the reaction. The energy taken in moves them to a higher energy level.

Do chemicals transfer energy in other ways?

It is very common for chemicals to transfer energy by heating. But they can transfer energy in other ways too, as you can see from picture 6.

Transferring energy from chemicals by means of electricity is very important in cells and batteries.

Often a chemical reaction transfers energy in more than one way. For example, a burning candle transfers energy by heating *and* as light.

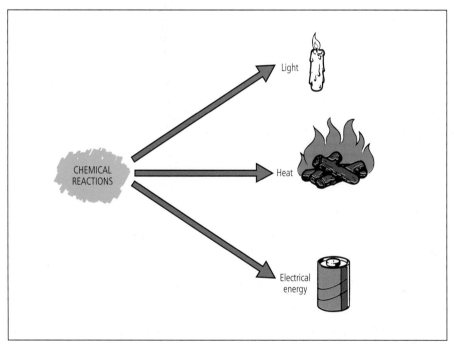

Picture 6   Energy transfers in chemical reactions.

GETTING CHEMICAL REACTIONS STARTED

Fuels do not start burning until they have been ignited. This is just as well. We do not want fuels bursting into flames until we are ready for them to do so. Burning is a chemical reaction, and like all reactions it goes faster at higher temperatures. At room temperature the reaction is so slow that it is effectively at a standstill. At the ignition temperature, the reaction is much faster. It gives out enough energy to keep itself going.

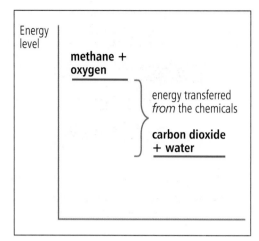

Picture 4   An energy level diagram for an exothermic reaction: the reaction of methane with oxygen.

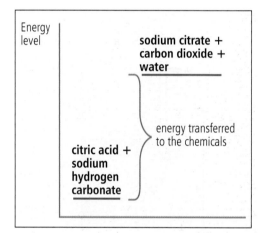

Picture 5   An energy level diagram for an endothermic reaction: the reaction of citric acid with sodium hydrogencarbonate.

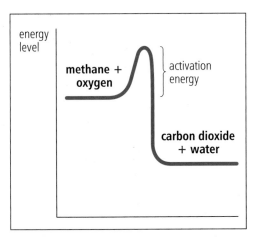

Picture 7 The activation energy represents the energy that must be put in to get a reaction started.

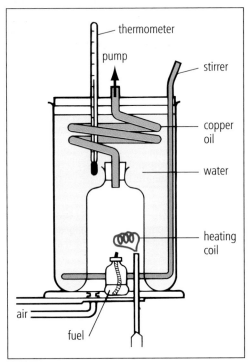

Picture 8 A fuel calorimeter.

All reactions need energy to get them started. But some need so little energy that they can start at room temperature without being heated. Rusting is an example of such a reaction, and so is the reaction of carbonates with acid.

The energy needed to get a chemical reaction started is called its **activation energy**. Picture 7 shows how activation energy can be represented on an energy level diagram. There is more about activation energy in topic I5.

HOW DO WE MEASURE THE ENERGY TRANSFERRED IN CHEMICAL REACTIONS?

The heat transferred in a chemical reaction can be measured using a calorimeter. Picture 8 shows the type of calorimeter that is often used to measure the heat transferred when a fuel burns. It is particularly useful for measuring the energy value of foods.

The idea is to burn the fuel so that heat is transferred to water. The experiment is done in two stages.

Stage 1. A measured mass of the fuel is burned in the calorimeter. The pump draws air through the central chamber in which the fuel is burned. The burning fuel produces hot gases. These heat the water as they pass through the copper coil. The temperature rise in the water is noted.

Stage 2. The electrical heater is switched on. It is allowed to heat the water until the temperature has risen to the same extent as it did with the fuel. The quantity of energy transferred electrically to the water is measured using a joulemeter.

Since the temperature rise is the same for each stage, the amount of energy transferred must be the same. So the amount of energy transferred by the burning fuel is found by simply reading the joulemeter.

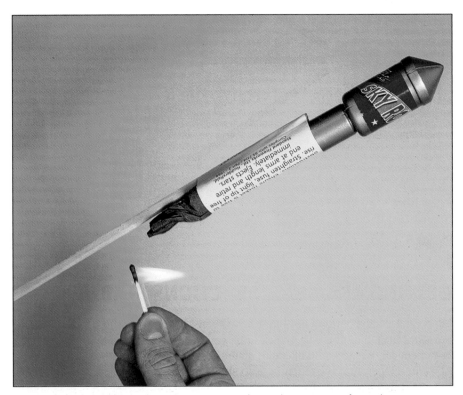

Picture 9 Providing the activation energy to start chemical reactions in a firework.

Table 1 shows the results obtained in an experiment using ethanol as a fuel.

Table 1   Results of an experiment to find the energy transferred by heating when ethanol burns.

Mass of ethanol used	= 2 g
Temperature rise	= 20 °C
Energy transferred electrically by heater to produce same temperature rise	= 60 kJ
So, energy transferred when 2 g of ethanol burns	= 60 kJ
So, energy transferred by 1 g of ethanol	= 30 kJ

This apparatus can be used to compare the energy values of different fuels. The energy values of foods are measured using similar apparatus. Picture 10 shows a simpler version of the apparatus that you may have used.

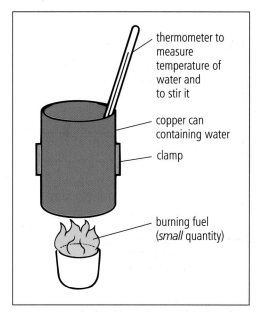

thermometer to measure temperature of water and to stir it

copper can containing water

clamp

burning fuel (*small* quantity)

Picture 10   A simple calorimeter for measuring the energy values of fuels. Compare it with the calorimeter in picture 8.

Questions

1 Look at the list of reactions below. For each reaction, say whether you think the reaction is exothermic or endothermic.

i) The burning of magnesium in air to form magnesium oxide.

ii) The decomposition of potassium chlorate by heat, forming potassium chloride and oxygen.

iii) The reaction of hydrogen with oxygen to form water.

iv) Respiration:
glucose + oxygen
→ carbon dioxide + water

2 Look at the experiment shown in picture 10.

a Why is this experiment a much less accurate way of comparing energy values than the method using the apparatus in picture 8?

b What changes could you make to the experiment to make it more accurate?

3 Some camping shops sell 'hand-warmers'. Each hand-warmer consists of a small packet made from porous fabric. The packet contains a dark grey powder. When you buy the hand-warmer, the packet is contained in an outer, airtight plastic bag. The directions for using the hand-warmer are given in picture 11.

a Try to decide how the hand-warmer works.

b What experiments could you do to check whether your explanation is correct?

DIRECTIONS

Open the outer plastic bag. Remove the inner packet. Shake it several times. Hold the packet in your hand. It will keep at a comfortable 60°C for several hours.

INGREDIENTS

Powdered iron, water (absorbed on cellulose), salt.

Picture 11

4 Draw energy level diagrams, like the ones in pictures 4 and 5, for each of the following reactions.

a The reaction in which hydrogen burns in oxygen to form water.

b Photosynthesis:
carbon dioxide + water
→ sugar + oxygen

c Respiration:
sugar + oxygen
→ carbon dioxide + water

5 Look at picture 7 and use it to answer the following questions.

a Why does the methane not burn until it is heated?

b Why does methane go on burning, without further heating, once it has started to burn?

Burning fuels

We get most of our energy from fuels. This topic is about different kinds of fuels and how they give us energy.

Picture 1

■ How much fuel have you used up today?

Probably more than you think. The food you ate is a fuel, and your home or school is probably heated by gas or oil, which are both fuels. If you used anything electrical, the electricity was generated in a power station probably fuelled by coal or gas. If you have travelled by bus, train or car today, you probably used up some petrol or diesel fuel.

Picture 2 shows Britain's primary energy sources. You can see that the large majority of Britain's energy comes from coal, oil and gas – the fossil fuels. More about fossil fuels in topic I4.

WHAT HAPPENS WHEN FUELS BURN?

Fuels are substances that react with oxygen to give out heat. The fuel is **oxidised**. This reaction is called burning, or **combustion**.

Picture 3 illustrates an experiment that can be used to investigate the substances formed when a fuel burns. When a fuel is tested in this apparatus, it is usually found that the anhydrous copper sulphate turns blue, and the lime water turns cloudy. This suggests that water and carbon dioxide have been formed.

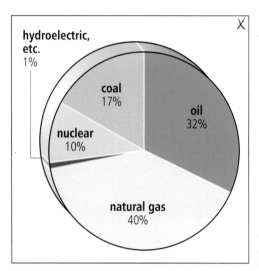

Picture 2 Britain's primary energy sources, 1999. A 'primary' energy source may be used directly, or may be used to generate electricity.

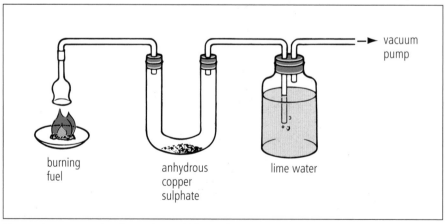

Picture 3 Investigating the products of burning fuels.

Most fuels contain carbon and hydrogen, and when the fuel combines with oxygen, the carbon forms carbon dioxide and the hydrogen forms water:

$$\text{fuel} + \text{oxygen} \rightarrow \text{carbon dioxide} + \text{water}$$

For example, natural gas is methane, CH_4.

$$\text{methane} + \text{oxygen} \rightarrow \text{carbon dioxide} + \text{water}$$
$$CH_4 + 2O_2 \rightarrow CO_2 + 2H_2O$$

These combustion products escape into the air as invisible gases. Burning fuels put about 20 thousand million tonnes of carbon dioxide into the Earth's atmosphere each year. This contributes to the 'greenhouse effect', and may change the world's climate (see B4).

What if there isn't enough oxygen?

If the air supply is limited when the fuel burns, there may not be enough oxygen available to convert the carbon to carbon dioxide (picture 5). The carbon may be converted to carbon *monoxide*, CO, instead. For example, with methane again:

$$\text{methane} + \text{oxygen} \rightarrow \text{carbon monoxide} + \text{water}$$
$$2CH_4 + 3O_2 \rightarrow 2CO + 4H_2O$$

Carbon monoxide is a very poisonous gas. It lowers the ability of the blood to carry oxygen. To make matters worse it is colourless and odourless, so you cannot tell when it is around. It is therefore very important that in fires and other places where fuel is burned there is a good air supply to make sure the fuel is completely oxidised to carbon dioxide.

If the air supply is *very* poor, there may not even be enough oxygen to oxidise the carbon to carbon monoxide. The carbon is simply given off as small particles which make a sooty smoke.

Most car engines burn petrol as a fuel. Petrol is a mixture of hydrocarbons, and if the engine is well maintained there is enough air to oxidise the petrol to carbon dioxide and water. However, if the engine is badly maintained, carbon monoxide is also formed. A certain amount of carbon monoxide is always present in vehicle exhaust gases, which is why they are poisonous.

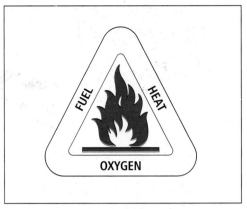

Picture 4 The 'fire triangle' shows the three ingredients needed to make a fire. Fire fighting involves removing at least one of the ingredients so the fire goes out.

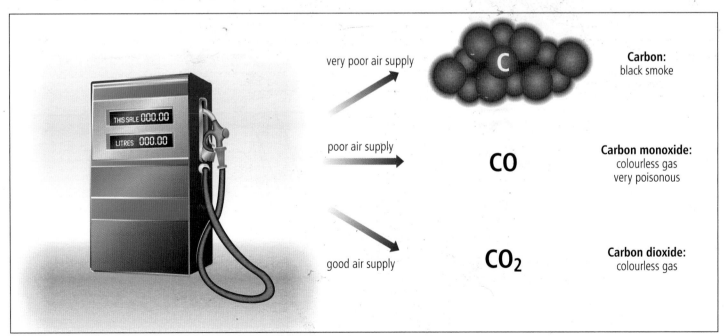

very poor air supply → Carbon: black smoke

poor air supply → CO Carbon monoxide: colourless gas very poisonous

good air supply → CO_2 Carbon dioxide: colourless gas

Picture 5 The products of burning fuel depend on the air supply.

Picture 6 Most power stations generate electricity by burning fuels like gas, oil or coal.

Carbon monoxide and sooty smoke are just two of the nasty products that may be formed when fuels burn. There are others – for example most solid fuels leave some kinds of ash. Many fuels contain sulphur, which is converted to sulphur dioxide when the fuel burns:

$$\text{sulphur} + \text{oxygen} \rightarrow \text{sulphur dioxide}$$
$$S + O_2 \rightarrow SO_2$$

Sulphur dioxide is a series air pollutant, and a major cause of acid rain. There is more about these and other air pollutants in topic B4.

WHAT MAKES A GOOD FUEL?

Different fuels have different properties. Picture 7 suggests some of the questions we might ask about the properties of a fuel.

No fuel is ideal. Coal is cheap and easy to store, but it is hard to light and it produces smoke and ash. Methylated spirit (ethanol) is easy to light and it produces hardly any smoke, ash or pollution – but it is expensive. When choosing a fuel, you have to balance up the advantages and disadvantages and then decide.

Activity

Fuels in the past

Find a person who is over 70 years old – perhaps a grandparent, or a neighbour. Ask them about the fuels that were used when they were your age. Try asking them about:

1 The fuels that were used for heating their home. Was every room heated? If not, which rooms were heated?

2 The fuels that were used for cooking their food.

3 The fuels that were used in the commonest forms of transport.

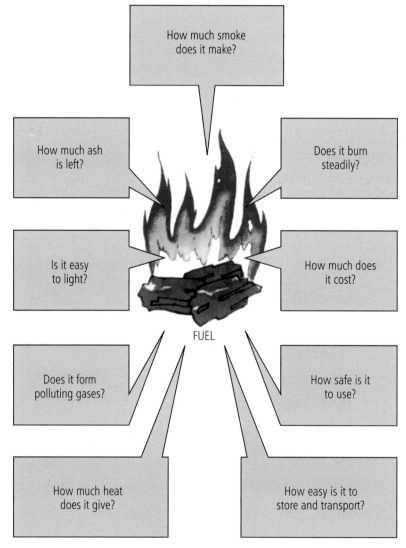

Picture 7 Important properties of a fuel.

Questions

1 **a** Name two substances that are always formed when a hydrocarbon fuel burns.

b Name two more substances that are sometimes formed when a hydrocarbon fuel burns.

c List seven properties that are important in a fuel that is to be used for cooking food.

2 You work for a firm which supplies household fuels. A person comes into your office one day and claims to have developed a new fuel. It is a grey solid.

a What would you want to know about the fuel before deciding whether to order supplies of it?

b You decide to take a sample of the fuel and send it to the laboratory for testing. What tests would you ask to have done on the sample?

3 Look again at picture 3.

a When charcoal is tested as a fuel in this apparatus, the lime water turns milky but the anhydrous copper sulphate stays white. Why?

b When hydrogen is tested as a fuel in this apparatus, the anhydrous copper sulphate turns blue but the lime water stays clear. Why?

c Suppose you wanted to test the fuel to see how much carbon was produced when the fuel burned. What changes would you make to the apparatus? Redraw the diagram to show your changes.

4 **a** Why is it dangerous to leave a car engine running when the car is in a closed garage?

b Car engines are fitted with a choke. When the choke is pulled out, the air supply to the carburettor is cut down. This makes the engine easier to start. When the engine is running with the choke pulled out, the exhaust is often black and smoky. Why?

c Cigarette smoke contains a considerable amount of carbon monoxide – this is one of the many reasons why smoking is so bad for your health. Why do you think carbon monoxide is in the smoke?

5 Look again at the fire triangle in picture 4. For each of the following fire fighting methods, use the fire triangle to explain why it puts out the fire.

a Carbon dioxide gas is directed at the fire from an extinguisher.

b A fire blanket is thrown over the fire.

c Water is thrown on the fire

Choosing the right fuel

Table 1 gives the properties of various fuels. Use the table to answer the questions

1 Barbecues are normally heated by charcoal. Suggest a reason why charcoal is used, rather than any other fuel in the table.

2 Ethanol is rarely used as a fuel, even though it is clean and convenient. Suggest a reason for this. Can you think of any examples of ethanol being used as a fuel?

3 Decide which fuel you would use for each of the following purposes. In each case, give a reason for your choice.

a Heating a house in a big town.

b Heating a cottage in an isolated part of Scotland.

c Heating the ovens in a large bakery.

4 Which of the fuels would be most suitable for fuelling an electric power station in

a Nottinghamshire, England?

b the Middle East?

Give reasons for your answers.

Table 1 The properties of various fuels.

Fuel	Relative cost per megajoule	Ease of lighting	Cleanliness when burning	Safety in use	Transport
Coal	0.6	Difficult	Dirty	Safe	By road or rail, in bulk
Fuel oil	0.7	Quite easy	Moderate	Fairly safe	By tanker or pipeline
Natural gas	0.4	Easy	Clean	Leaks can cause explosions	By pipeline direct to user
Ethanol (methylated spirit)	8.0	Easy	Very clean	Highly flammable—can cause accidental fires	By road, in bottles or drums
Charcoal	2.2	Difficult	Fairly clean	Safe	By road, in sacks

Carbon dioxide and the carbon cycle

The carbon cycle keeps the amount of carbon dioxide in the atmosphere in balance.

Picture 1 Burning the Brazilian forest. Deforestation puts extra CO_2 into the atmosphere when the trees are burned. Once the trees are gone, they can no longer remove CO_2 by photosynthesis.

Picture 2 The leaves of this nettle are spread out to expose as much chlorophyll as possible to sunlight.

THE CARBON CYCLE

What produces carbon dioxide?

Most fuels produce carbon dioxide when they burn (see topic I2). An even bigger source of carbon dioxide is **respiration**, the process by which all living things get energy from food. If we take glucose as the energy food, we can summarise respiration as:

$$\text{glucose} + \text{oxygen} \rightarrow \text{carbon dioxide} + \text{water}$$
$$C_6H_{12}O_6 + 6O_2 \rightarrow 6CO_2 + 6H_2O$$

All living things respire, plants as well as animals, so respiration produces a lot of carbon dioxide – picture 3 shows how much.

Although it looks like a fairly simple reaction, respiration actually occurs as a complicated series of reactions. The equation above gives the *overall* process. Overall, it is equivalent to the process of burning glucose – or other carbohydrates such as starch or cellulose (picture 1). Respiration is an exothermic change: it releases energy – which is why living things do it.

What removes carbon dioxide?

Carbon dioxide is removed from the atmosphere by **photosynthesis**. This is the process by which plants produce food. We can summarise photosynthesis as

$$\text{carbon dioxide} + \text{water} \rightarrow \text{glucose} + \text{oxygen}$$
$$6CO_2 + 6H_2O \rightarrow C_6H_{12}O_6 + 6O_2$$

The glucose produced in photosynthesis is then converted by the plant into starch and other materials (see topic H5). Like respiration, photosynthesis is actually a complicated series of reactions: the equation given above summarises the overall change.

Photosynthesis is an endothermic change: it takes in energy. The energy comes from sunlight. The key to photosynthesis is the pigment chlorophyll, a chemical which traps energy from sunlight and passes it on to other molecules. Chlorophyll is green and is found in the leaves of plants (picture 2).

How the cycle maintains balance

If you look at the equations for respiration and photosynthesis, you will notice that they are the reverse of one another. Respiration uses up glucose and oxygen, and produces carbon dioxide and water. Photosynthesis uses up carbon dioxide and water and produces glucose and oxygen. Both processes are part of the carbon cycle. As long as they balance one another, we need not worry about running out of food and oxygen, or getting suffocated by carbon dioxide.

Picture 3 illustrates the carbon cycle. You can see that the two processes do just about balance one another – but not quite (see question 3). The problem is that burning fossil fuels is effectively a one-way process. Fossil fuels are burned much faster than new supplies are formed. This not only means we are running out of fossil fuels: we are also increasing the proportion of carbon dioxide in the atmosphere. Scientists are concerned that this may lead to global warming.

Carbon dioxide and the oceans

Some of the carbon dioxide in the atmosphere is removed by the oceans. Carbon dioxide dissolves in water, and the oceans are so big that they can absorb very large amounts of CO_2. Some marine organisms convert dissolved carbon dioxide to calcium carbonate to build shells for themselves. Eventually, when they die, the calcium carbonate gets deposited as limestone rock (see topic D2).

So the oceans act as absorbers of carbon dioxide – but even the oceans are not big enough to absorb *all* the extra carbon dioxide that human activities are putting into the atmosphere.

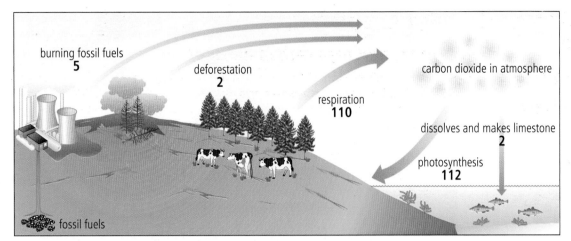

Picture 3 The carbon cycle. The numbers show the estimated total quantities of carbon involved in the processes per year for the whole world. They are in gigatonnes of carbon (1 gigatonne = 1000 000 000 tonnes).

CARBON DIOXIDE

Carbon dioxide is an important gas, not just because of its impact on the environment, but also because of its uses.

You should be familiar with carbon dioxide: you breathe out about 500 litres of it every day. You also swallow it every time you have a fizzy drink. Picture 4 summarises the most important properties of carbon dioxide.

■ Uses of carbon dioxide

Here are some of the major uses of carbon dioxide.

- **Fizzy drinks**. Drinks are made fizzy by pumping in carbon dioxide under pressure.
- **Fire extinguishers**. Because carbon dioxide is denser than air, it stays near to the ground. It can be used to 'blanket' a fire, preventing oxygen getting to it. CO_2 fire extinguishers contain the gas under pressure.
- **'Dry ice'**. If you compress and cool carbon dioxide gas, it forms solid carbon dioxide. This is called 'dry ice' because it does not melt, but turns straight back to carbon dioxide gas (sublimation). Dry ice sublimes at −78 °C, so it provides an excellent way of keeping things cold. It can also provide some spectacular effects as it sublimes.

CARBON DIOXIDE
- a colourless gas with no smell
- denser than air
- does not burn
- does not let things burn in it
- slightly soluble in water
- solution in water is weakly acidic
- turns lime water milky (see topic D3)

Picture 4 Properties of carbon dioxide.

Testing for carbon dioxide

You test for carbon dioxide by bubbling the gas through lime water. If the lime water turns milky, carbon dioxide is present.

Lime water is a solution of calcium hydroxide, $Ca(OH)_2$ (aq). Carbon dioxide reacts with it to form insoluble calcium carbonate, which is the milky precipitate.

$$Ca(OH)_2(aq) + CO_2(g) \rightarrow CaCO_3(s) + H_2O(l)$$

Questions

1 'All the food on Earth is produced by photosynthesis.' Is this true? If so, why?

2 The equation for respiration is the same as the equation for burning glucose. In what ways are respiration and burning similar? In what ways are they different?

3 Look at picture 3.
  a Calculate the total mass of carbon dioxide entering the atmosphere each year.

  b What is the total mass of carbon dioxide leaving the atmosphere each year?

  c Compare your answers to (a) and (b). Is the carbon cycle in balance?

  d What might be the consequences of the cycle being out of balance?

  e The figures in picture 3 are approximate estimates. Why does this make it difficult to draw conclusions about the balance of the carbon cycle?

4 a Write the equation for photosynthesis.

  b Use the equation in (a) to calculate the mass of glucose that could be produced from 1 kg of carbon dioxide.

  c What mass of carbon dioxide would be produced if you burned the glucose from (b)?

5 Three billion years ago when the Earth was quite young, the atmosphere contained very little oxygen, but lots of carbon dioxide. How did the oxygen that is now in the atmosphere get there?

6 Which properties of carbon dioxide make it particularly useful for extinguishing fires?

I4

Fossil fuels

Most of our fuels come from animals and plants that lived millions of years ago.

Picture 1 John Dalton collecting marsh gas. Marsh gas is mainly methane, formed from rotting vegetation. What is his young assistant doing?

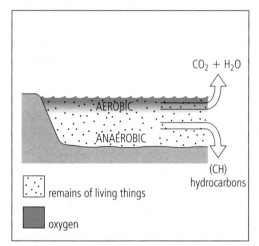

Picture 2 Aerobic and anaerobic decay in water. Near the surface, there is plenty of dissolved oxygen. Here, living things decay to give CO_2 and H_2O. Deeper in the water, there is very little oxygen, and they decay to give hydrocarbons.

Plants make their food by photosynthesis (see topic I3). They use the Sun's energy to turn carbon dioxide and water into carbohydrate foods such as glucose, $C_6H_{12}O_6$.

Normally, the plants then die and decay, or perhaps they get eaten by animals. Either way, the carbohydrate in the plant gets oxidised and converted back to carbon dioxide and water by respiration.

But sometimes, plants die and decay in conditions where the air can't get at them. These are called **anaerobic** conditions (picture 2). It might be because the plants are underwater. Without air the carbohydrate in the plants cannot be oxidised to carbon dioxide and water. Instead, slowly, over thousands of years, it gets turned into substances containing carbon and hydrogen, called **hydrocarbons** (topic H1). These substances make excellent fuels.

Fuels formed in this way – oil, gas and coal – are called **fossil fuels**. When fossil fuels are burned, they form carbon dioxide and water and release energy. They are releasing the energy of the Sun that was trapped by plants hundreds of millions of years ago.

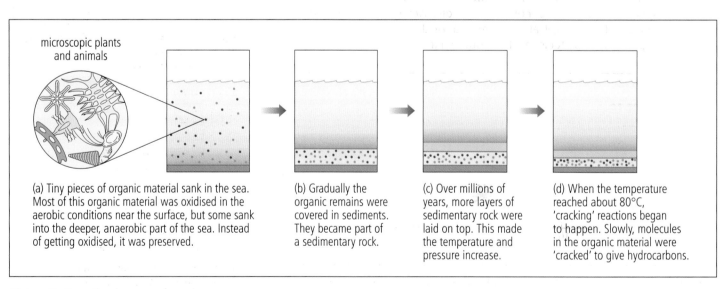

(a) Tiny pieces of organic material sank in the sea. Most of this organic material was oxidised in the aerobic conditions near the surface, but some sank into the deeper, anaerobic part of the sea. Instead of getting oxidised, it was preserved.

(b) Gradually the organic remains were covered in sediments. They became part of a sedimentary rock.

(c) Over millions of years, more layers of sedimentary rock were laid on top. This made the temperature and pressure increase.

(d) When the temperature reached about 80°C, 'cracking' reactions began to happen. Slowly, molecules in the organic material were 'cracked' to give hydrocarbons.

Picture 3 How oil and gas were formed.

HOW OIL AND GAS WERE FORMED

Think of the Earth millions of years ago. In the seas tiny algae grew, then died. On the land, plants grew, and as they died their remains were washed into the sea. Picture 3 explains how these remains were converted to hydrocarbons. (Look at topic K3 to find out more about sedimentary rocks, and at topic H2 to find out more about cracking reactions.)

The hydrocarbons formed in this way were a mixture of liquids and gases. They gradually leaked out of the sedimentary **source rocks** into porous rocks above. These **reservoir rocks** hold the liquid oil and natural gas. Picture 4 shows how oil and gas are extracted from the rocks.

Crude oil, or **petroleum** comes out of the ground as a black liquid. It is a mixture of many different hydrocarbons. It has to be purified and separated into different fractions. This is done at an oil refinery.

Crude oil gives us many important fuels and materials. More is given about them in topic H1.

Natural gas is mostly made of methane, CH_4. It burns with a clean flame and is very popular for heating homes and for cooking.

The North Sea isn't the only place where you find methane. Methane is often formed when organic material decomposes anaerobically. For example, it forms inside the gut of cows, where bacteria decompose grass in the absence of oxygen. In fact, an average cow produces about $500\,000\ cm^3$ of methane a day. Three cows could keep an average home supplied with all the gas it needs!

Biogas is a fuel made from waste material such as animal manure and dead plants. Like natural gas, it consists mainly of methane. The waste material is put in a **biogas digestor** where it decomposes anaerobically (picture 5). Biogas digestors are an important source of energy in some developing countries.

Coal is a solid fossil fuel, composed mainly of carbon. It was formed from the decayed remains of carboniferous forests, millions of years ago.

HOW LONG WILL FOSSIL FUELS LAST?

It took millions of years for fossil fuels to form, but it will not take long to use them up.

Picture 6 shows how long fossil fuels may last. Coal supplies are plentiful, but oil is likely to run out around the middle of this century. And at present we depend on oil more than any other fuel.

Of course, new supplies of fossil fuels are being discovered all the time, but this cannot go on forever. What's more, the new discoveries tend to be in places where the fuel is difficult to get at – like Alaska, or deep under the North Sea. Eventually, supplies of fossil fuels must run out. What will we do then?

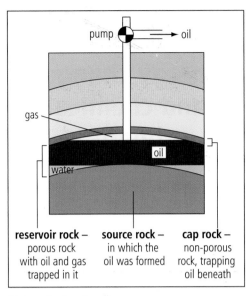

Picture 4 An oil well.

reservoir rock –	source rock –	cap rock –
porous rock with oil and gas trapped in it	in which the oil was formed	non-porous rock, trapping oil beneath

Picture 5 An underground biogas digestor. What do you think the various people in the picture are doing?

Questions

1. Coal, oil and gas are called fossil fuels. Why is the word 'fossil' used?

2. When you burn a fossil fuel like oil, you are releasing energy that originally came from the Sun. Explain why.

3. Crude oil and natural gas are usually found together. Explain why.

4. Oil and gas are always found in sedimentary rocks. Explain why.

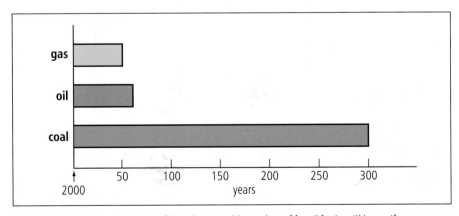

Picture 6 These are estimates of how long world supplies of fossil fuels will last – if we go on using them at the present rate.

Energy changes and chemical bonds

The energy changes in reactions come from making and breaking chemical bonds.

Picture 1 Burning methane in a gas cooker.

Substances are held together by chemical bonds. When a chemical reaction occurs, one substance changes to another. This means that chemical bonds must be broken, then re-made. It is this breaking and making of bonds that causes the energy changes in chemical reactions.

Chemical bonds hold atoms together. Breaking bonds involves pulling these atoms apart – and this needs energy. On the other hand, making new bonds gives out energy.

Breaking bonds takes in energy.
Making new bonds gives out energy.

AN EXAMPLE – THE REACTION OF METHANE WITH OXYGEN

Methane is the major component of natural gas. When methane burns, it reacts with oxygen, and energy is transferred by heating. The products are carbon dioxide and water. Picture 2 shows the molecules involved in the reaction.

In methane molecules, carbon atoms are bonded to hydrogen atoms. In oxygen molecules, oxygen atoms are bonded to one another. In the reaction between methane and oxygen, all these bonds have to be broken. This takes in energy. New bonds are then formed between carbon and oxygen in carbon dioxide, and between hydrogen and oxygen in water. This gives out energy. This is shown in the energy level diagram in picture 3 (on the next page).

Compare the energy given out with the energy taken in. More energy is given out than taken in. So overall, this reaction gives out energy – it is exothermic. This is just as well, considering how much we rely on the reaction for our household heating.

■ Putting numbers to the energy transfers

It is quite simple to show the sizes of the energy transfers involved in this bond breaking and bond making.

We can measure the amount of energy transferred by heating when 1 litre of methane burns. It is about 730 kJ. Remember 1 mole of methane has a volume of $24 \, dm^3$.

We can work out where this energy comes from if we know the amount of energy transferred when each bond is broken or made. Table 1 shows the **bond energies** of some bonds. Bond energy is the energy required to break 1 mole of the bonds.

We can use bond energies to work out the energy changes involved at each stage of burning methane. Table 2 shows the calculations. The overall energy given out is equal to the energy given out when bonds are made, minus the energy taken in when bonds are broken**.**

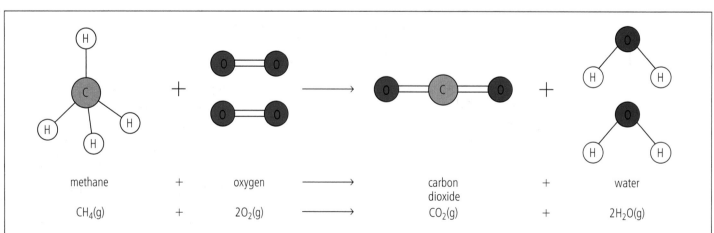

methane	+	oxygen	carbon dioxide	+	water
$CH_4(g)$	+	$2O_2(g)$	$CO_2(g)$	+	$2H_2O(g)$

Picture 2 The reaction of methane with oxygen.

Table 1   Bond energies

Bond	Bond energy/kJ per mole
C—H	435
O=O	498
O—H	464
C=O	805
H—H	436

Table 2   The energy changes when 1 mole of methane burns.

Breaking bonds

Break four C—H bonds in methane	**takes in**	4 × 435 kJ = 1740 kJ
Break two O=O bonds in oxygen	**takes in**	2 × 498 kJ = 996 kJ

Making bonds

Make two C=O bonds in carbon dioxide	**gives out**	2 × 805 kJ = 1610 kJ
Make four O—H bonds in water	**gives out**	4 × 464 kJ = 1856 kJ
Total energy given out	=	(1610+ 1856) − (1740 + 996) kJ = **730 kJ**

GETTING REACTIONS STARTED

Fuels need heating before they start burning. They must be supplied with the necessary **activation energy** to start off the reaction between the fuel and oxygen.

If you look again at picture 3 you can see *why* fuels like methane need heating to get them burning. Compare picture 3 with picture 7 on page 212.

Before the reaction can start, bonds have to be broken: C—H bonds in methane and O=O bonds in oxygen. This takes in energy – the activation energy needed to get the reaction started. At room temperature, this energy is not available, so the bonds do not break and the reaction does not start.

But if you heat the fuel with a match or spark, enough energy is transferred to break the necessary bonds, and the reaction starts. *All* reactions need activation energy to break bonds and get them started. For some reactions the bonds are quite easily broken so the activation energy is fairly low. Such reactions can start at room temperature, without heating. The reaction of sodium with water is an example of this type of reaction – as soon as you put the sodium in water, it reacts.

Other reactions need a lot of energy to break bonds and get them started. For example, charcoal (carbon) needs a lot of heating to get it burning. This is because the bonds holding the carbon atoms together are very strong.

Questions

1 Using the idea of breaking and making bonds, explain in your own words why fuels need heating before they start to burn.

2 Hydrogen burns in the presence of oxygen to form water. Burning 1 litre of hydrogen gives out about 5 kJ of energy.

hydrogen + oxygen → water
$$2H_2 + O_2 \rightarrow 2H_2O$$

a   Draw a diagram similar to picture 3 to show the breaking and making of bonds in this reaction.

b   Use the diagram to explain why hydrogen must be heated before it will start burning in oxygen.

c   Explain why the diagram shows that this reaction gives out energy rather than taking it in.

d   Use bond energies from table 1 to calculate the overall energy given out when 2 moles of hydrogen are burned. Set out your calculation in a similar way to table 2.

3 a   Set up table 2 as a spreadsheet on a computer.

b   What changes would you make to the spreadsheet if you wanted to calculate the energy given out when 1 mole of *ethane*, C_2H_6, burns?

4 'All the energy used by human beings comes from the breaking and making of chemical bonds.'

Is this true? Give some examples.

Can you suggest any exceptions?

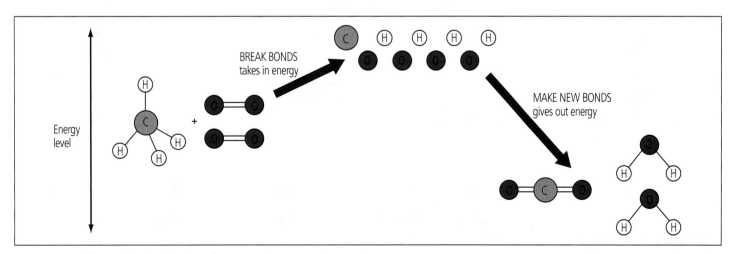

Picture 3   Breaking and making bonds in the reaction between methane and oxygen.

Controlling chemical changes

In industry and everyday life, it's important to be able to control how fast a chemical reaction goes.

Picture 1 This food was kept in the freezer so the reactions that make it go off happen slowly. To make cooking reactions happen quickly, it goes under a hot grill.

Most kitchens have a machine for speeding up chemical reactions and a machine for slowing them down. They are called a cooker and a fridge. Cooking food involves a lot of complicated chemical reactions, but like all reactions they are speeded up by higher temperatures. When food goes bad, that involves chemical reactions too, and they are slowed down by lower temperatures.

Chemical reactions can go at different speeds (rates). Some, like explosions, are incredibly fast. Some, like rusting, are much slower. By controlling the conditions, we can vary the rates of reactions to make them as fast or as slow as we want. This is useful, not just in cooking but in the chemical industry and in our own bodies.

WHAT AFFECTS THE RATE OF A REACTION?

Look at these examples:

- It takes less than 10 minutes to fry chips, but 20 minutes to boil potatoes.
- Potatoes cook faster if you cut them up small.
- Badly stained clothes can be cleaned by soaking them in a solution of biological detergent.
- Stained clothes become clean more quickly if you soak them in a more concentrated solution of detergent.

These examples show some of the factors that affect the rate of a chemical reaction. The factors that we will be looking at in this topic are:

- temperature
- surface area
- catalysts
- concentration
- gas pressure.

Temperature

All reactions go faster at a higher temperature. Temperature has a very noticeable effect. **The rate of many reactions is *doubled* by a temperature rise of just 10°C.** Temperature is one of the reasons why chips cook faster than boiled potatoes, The fat is much hotter than boiling water.

Lots of chemical reactions happen when food is cooked. An important one involves starch, the main component of foods like bread and potatoes.

Starch is a polymer containing many glucose molecules joined together. At high temperatures these chains break down into shorter chains called dextrins. Some of the dextrins combine with proteins in the food to form brown compounds. This is why many foods go brown on the outside (where the temperature is highest) when they are cooked (picture 2). The higher the temperature, the faster the reaction and the faster the food browns. However, just because the food is brown on the outside doesn't mean it's cooked right through. The slowest part of cooking is the conduction of heat from the outside to the middle.

Living things use **biochemical** reactions to keep going. They are catalysed by enzymes. The effect of temperature on enzyme-catalysed reactions is covered in topic I8.

Many industrial processes use high temperatures to make reactions go fast. The faster the reaction, the quicker you get products, which make the process more profitable. But there are limits. High temperatures are expensive, because they mean using a lot of energy. And sometimes a high temperature means you actually get a smaller yield of the product. This happens with the production of ammonia by the Haber Process (page 105). So in practice most industrial processes use moderately high temperatures – hundreds rather than thousands of degrees Celsius.

Surface area

Surface area is another reason why chips cook fast. The surface area of a solid means the amount of surface that is exposed to the outside. If you cut up a solid into pieces, the surface area gets larger (picture 3). Chips are cut up small, so more surface is exposed to the hot oil.

You use the surface area effect when you light a fire. Chopping up a big log into smaller pieces makes the burning reaction go much faster. Some modern coal-fired power stations use a **fluidised bed** (picture 4) to burn the coal quickly and efficiently. The coal is powdered into dust to give it a high surface area, and mixed

Picture 2 Chemical reactions involving starch and protein make food go brown on the outside when heated.

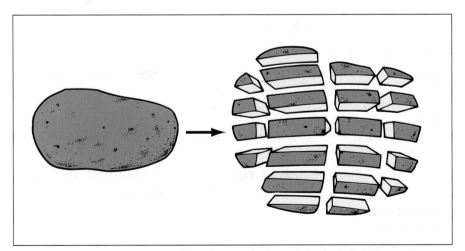

Picture 3 Cutting up a potato into chips. The more finely a solid is divided, the larger is its surface area.

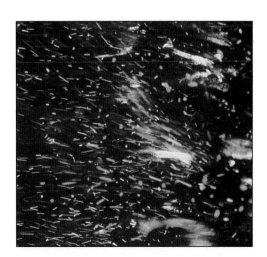

Picture 4 Burning powdered coal in a power station. The powdered coal has a high surface area, so it burns fast.

Picture 5 When the stonemason made this carving in 1670, the concentration of acid in the rain was much lower than it is today.

with an unreactive solid like sand. Air is blown through the bed from underneath, so a very high surface area of coal dust is exposed to oxygen. The coal burns very quickly, and there is less pollution than when you burn the coal in lumps.

Surface area effects are important in industry. Chemical engineers make sure that when a solid is involved in a reaction, it has a high surface area – like the catalytic converter in picture 9 on the next page.

Concentration

The stonemason who made the limestone statue in picture 5 expected it to last for centuries. It might have done, if the air had stayed as unpolluted as it was in 1670. Unfortunately, since the Industrial Revolution, more and more fossil fuels have been burned, making the rain more acidic (page 34). The concentration of acid in the rain has increased, so the rain has reacted faster with the limestone. The statue is now corroding much faster than it would have done in the seventeenth century.

In any reaction involving solutions, a concentrated solution always reacts faster than a dilute one. 'Concentrated' means the solution has a lot of solute dissolved in a particular volume. If you want to clean badly stained clothes, you soak them in a solution of detergent. If you use lots of detergent, the solution is concentrated and the stains are shifted quickly.

Gas pressure

We normally use the word 'concentration' for solutions. But gases can have their concentration changed too, by changing the pressure. A gas at high pressure is more concentrated than a gas at low pressure. The same amount of gas is squeezed into a smaller volume (picture 6). Gases react faster at higher pressure, and this is made use of in the petrol engine. The mixture of petrol vapour and air is compressed so that it reacts very quickly – explosively, in fact – when it is ignited by the sparking plug.

Picture 7 shows another example of the effect of increasing the concentration of a gas.

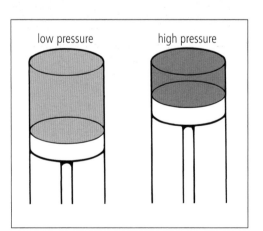

low pressure   high pressure

Picture 6 A gas at high pressure is more concentrated than a gas at low pressure.

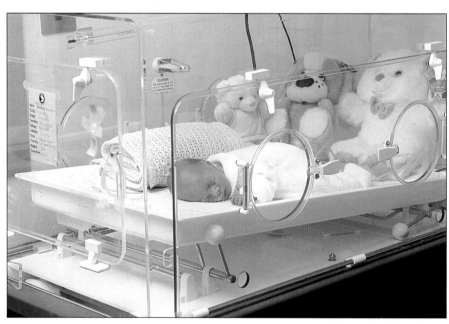

Picture 7 This premature baby is breathing air that is enriched with oxygen. The concentration of oxygen is greater than in normal air, so the baby does not have to breathe so hard to keep its body going at the necessary rate.

Catalysts

Picture 8 shows the effect of a catalyst on the decomposition of hydrogen peroxide, H_2O_2 (aq). Hydrogen peroxide decomposes very slowly to form water and oxygen:

$$2H_2O_2 \text{ (aq)} \rightarrow 2H_2O \text{ (l)} + O_2 \text{ (g)}$$

But if you add manganese dioxide powder, the hydrogen peroxide decomposes very rapidly. What is more, the manganese dioxide is not used up by the reaction: it is a catalyst.

Catalysts are substances that alter the rate of a chemical reaction without getting used up.

When the reaction has finished, the catalyst is still there. This makes catalysts particularly useful, because they can be used again and again.

Catalytic converters like the one in picture 9 are being fitted to many modern cars. Car exhaust contains polluting gases like carbon monoxide (CO) and nitrogen oxide (NO). These pollutants can react together to make less harmful gases. For example:

carbon monoxide + nitrogen oxide → carbon dioxide + nitrogen

$$CO(g) \quad + \quad NO(g) \quad \rightarrow \quad CO_2(g) \quad + \quad N_2(g)$$

Unfortunately, this reaction is very slow. But a catalyst made of platinum can speed it up so that 90% of the polluting gases are removed from the exhaust. Picture 10 summarises the process. The catalyst does not get used up, so it does not have to be replaced for years. The only problem is cost: the converter costs several hundred pounds. But many countries have now made catalytic converters compulsory on all new cars.

Catalysts are very important in industrial processes. Most industrial chemistry uses some kind of catalyst – the faster you can make your product, the better. Examples are the manufacture of ammonia (page 105), the cracking of oil (page 187) and the manufacture of plastics (page 206).

Different reactions need different catalysts. Transition metals and their compounds make particularly good catalysts.

Enzymes are biological catalysts. There is more about them in topic I8.

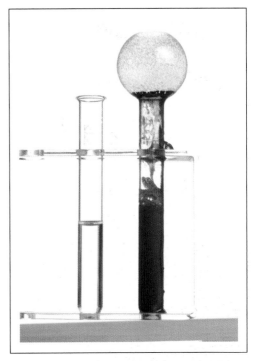

Picture 8 Both tubes contain hydrogen peroxide. Manganese dioxide has been added to the tube on the right, causing the hydrogen peroxide to decompose rapidly, blowing a bubble at the top of the tube.

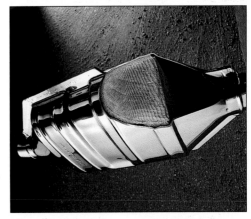

Picture 9 A catalytic converter in a car exhaust. Notice how the catalyst is arranged to give a high surface area.

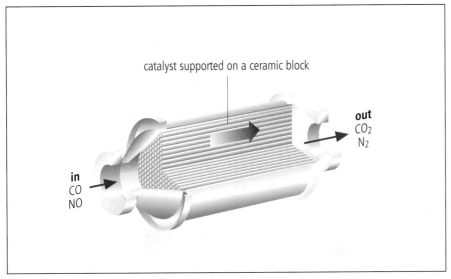

catalyst supported on a ceramic block

out
CO_2
N_2

in
CO
NO

Picture 10 A catalytic converter makes harmful pollutant gases react together, forming harmless products.

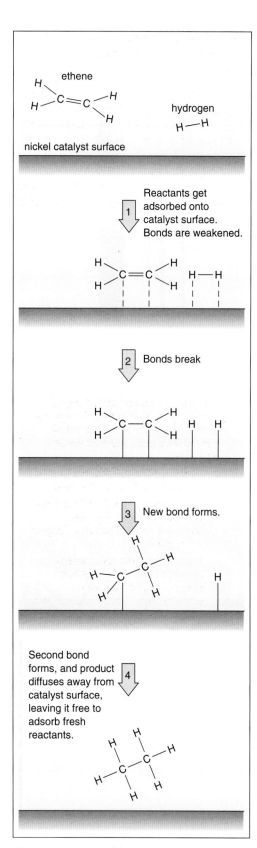

Picture 11 How a solid catalyst works. This example shows the addition reaction between ethene and hydrogen, using a nickel catalyst (see page 189).

HOW DO CATALYSTS WORK?

Different catalysts work in different ways. Most solid catalysts work by **adsorption**. The molecules of reacting substances get adsorbed onto the surface of the catalyst. This brings the molecules of reactants together. The bonds are weakened, so that they break more easily. The reactants can then form new bonds, to give the products. Picture 11 shows an example.

Because the reaction happens on its surface, the catalyst needs to have a large surface area to be most effective (picture 9).

EXPLAINING REACTION RATES

We can use the kinetic theory (topic C1) to try and explain the factors affecting the rates of reactions. This extension of the kinetic theory is called the **collision theory.** Picture 12 uses the collision theory to explain the effect of surface area, concentration and temperature on the reaction between zinc and hydrochloric acid.

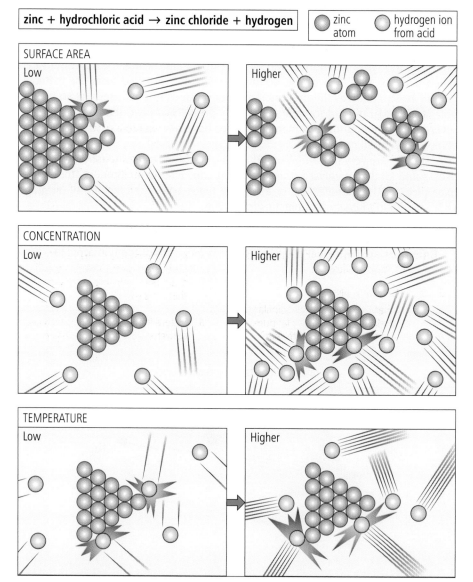

Picture 12 Using the collision theory to explain the factors affecting the rate of the reaction between zinc and hydrochloric acid.

Activities

A The apple browning problem

Apples go brown when they are cut up. This is a nuisance if you are making fruit salad – no-one likes brown apple. Plan an experiment to investigate different ways of slowing down apple browning, using the ideas in this topic. **Check your plan with your teacher before doing any experimental work**.

B The best temperature for biological washing powders

Plan an experiment to investigate the best temperature for a biological washing powder to work at. You will have to think carefully about how you will measure the effectiveness of the powder. **Check your plan with your teacher before doing any experimental work. Note: some people are allergic to biological washing powders.**

The collision theory says that:

Chemical reactions occur when particles of the reactants collide. They must collide with a certain minimum energy, called the activation energy.

For another example, take the reaction between methane (natural gas) and oxygen. Methane molecules have to collide with oxygen molecules before a reaction can happen. What's more, the molecules must collide with enough energy – the activation energy – otherwise they just bounce off each other harmlessly. The activation energy is needed to break the bonds in the molecules and get the reaction started (see page 222).

This is why methane and oxygen do not react at room temperature. To make them react, they need heating to provide the activation energy. In other words, they need to be ignited.

Questions

1 Give examples of chemical reactions that go:
- a very fast
- b very slowly
- c at a moderate rate

2 List the factors that affect the rate of a chemical reaction. For each factor give one example to illustrate it.

3 a What is a catalyst?
- b In what ways are enzymes similar to a non-living catalyst like platinum? In what ways are they different?

4 Explain the following.
- a Carrots cook more quickly if they are sliced.
- b When beer is being brewed the temperature in the fermentation tank must not be allowed to go above 21 °C or below 14 °C.
- c It is quicker to cook an egg by frying than by boiling.

5 Look at picture 5 on page 226. The protruding parts of the statue, like the nose, get worn away first. Why do you think this is?

6 Picture 9 on page 227 shows a catalytic converter in a car. The catalytic converter is arranged so that the car exhaust gases have to flow through the catalyst before they pass into the air. Look at the picture and read the text alongside it.
- a Why is it important that the catalyst has a large surface surface area?
- b Catalytic converters do not work well until the car engine has been running for several minutes. Suggest a reason why.
- c After several years' use, catalytic converters eventually have to be replaced. Suggest a reason why – remember that a catalyst does not get used up in a chemical reaction.

Measuring reaction rates

In this topic we look at ways of finding the speed of chemical reactions.

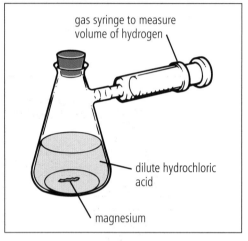

To investigate the rate of a reaction, we need to measure something that changes during the reaction. We choose some property that is easy to detect, such as the colour, or the volume of gas given off, and measure it at fixed times. It's like checking how far a runner has gone each minute. We can use these measurements to find how the amounts of the chemicals change with time. Then we can say:

$$\text{reaction rate} = \frac{\text{change in amount of substance}}{\text{time}}$$

Let's look at an example – the reaction of magnesium with hydrochloric acid. Picture 1 shows an experiment to measure the rate of this reaction.

We measure the volume of hydrogen given off at different times, and plot a graph like the one in picture 2.

If you look at the graph for Experiment X, you will see that in the first minute, 30 cm³ of hydrogen were given off. Now,

$$\text{reaction rate} = \frac{\text{change in amount of substance}}{\text{time}}$$

$$= \frac{30 \text{ cm}^3 \text{ hydrogen}}{1 \text{ min}}$$

$$= 30 \text{ cm}^3 \text{ hydrogen per minute}$$

This is the *average* rate of reaction over the first minute.

Fortunately, we don't have to do this kind of calculation all the time. We can tell how fast the reaction is going from the gradient of the graph. The steeper the graph, the faster the reaction.

■ Interpreting the graph

The graph in picture 2 shows the results of two experiments. In Experiment X the concentration of acid is 2 moles per dm³. In Experiment Y its concentration is 1 mole per dm³. Look carefully at the graph and notice these points.

- In both experiments the graph starts off steep. This is because the reaction starts off fast. The reaction then slows down and the graph becomes less steep. This is because the hydrochloric acid and magnesium are getting used up. In fact the magnesium runs out first, because there is more than enough hydrochloric acid in this experiment.
- The graph in Experiment X starts off twice as steep as the graph in Experiment Y. This means that the reaction in Experiment X starts off twice as fast. So doubling the concentration of the acid doubles the rate.
- Both graphs level off at the same volume. This is when the reaction stops. The reaction stops when all the magnesium is used up, and the same amount of magnesium (0.05 g) was used in both experiments. So both reactions produce the same *total* volume of hydrogen – though Experiment X produces it faster.

■ Another kind of graph

Another way of measuring the rate of a reaction is to time how long it takes for the reaction to reach a particular stage. It's like timing a runner over a fixed distance. The *faster* the runner, the *less* time it takes to cover the distance.

Picture 1 An experiment to investigate the rate of reaction between magnesium and hydrochloric acid. The volume of hydrogen given off is measured every minute using the gas syringe.

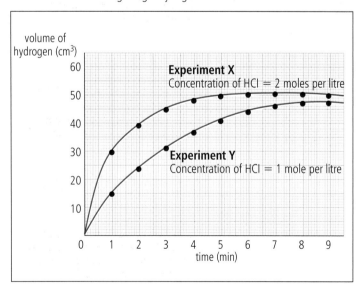

Picture 2 Results of an investigation into the effect of concentration on the rate of the reaction between magnesium and hydrochloric acid.

Let's look at an example of this second approach – the reaction between sodium thiosulphate and hydrochloric acid. When the two chemicals are mixed, a cloudy precipitate of sulphur slowly appears. You look down at the cross from above and see how long it takes to disappear (picture 3).

We time how long it takes for the reaction to produce enough sulphur to make the cross disappear. The reaction is repeated at different temperatures. It's the same cross each time, so we are timing how long it takes the reaction to reach a particular stage. The *faster* the reaction, the *less* time it takes for the cross to disappear. Picture 4 shows one student's results in this experiment. Look at the graph and notice these points.

- At *higher* temperatures, it takes *less* time for the cross to disappear. In other words, the rate is faster.
- For a 10 °C temperature rise (for example, from 30 °C to 40 °C), the time for the cross to disappear is roughly halved. In other words, the rate of the reaction is roughly doubled for a 10 °C rise.

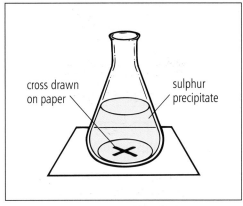

Picture 3 Following the reaction between sodium thiosulphate and dilute hydrochloric acid. When the two chemicals are mixed, a cloudy precipitate of sulphur slowly appears. You look down at the cross from above and see how long it takes to disappear.

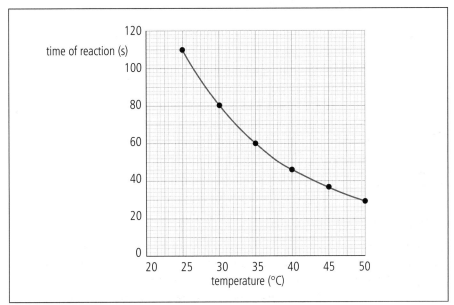

Picture 4 Results of an investigation into the effect of temperature on the rate of the reaction between sodium thiosulphate and hydrochloric acid.

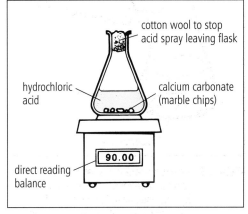

Picture 5 Investigating the rate of the reaction between calcium carbonate and hydrochloric acid.

Questions

1 Look at the graph for Experiment Y in picture 2. What is the average rate of the reaction, measured in cm³ of hydrogen per minute, over the first minute?

2 Make a sketch copy of the graph for Experiment X in picture 2. Now sketch the graph you would expect if the experiment was repeated with the temperature 10 °C higher. **ICT**

3 A student carried out an experiment to measure the rate of the reaction between calcium carbonate (marble chips) and hydrochloric acid. He used the apparatus shown in picture 5. He weighed the flask to find the mass of carbon dioxide given off at different times. His results are shown in table 1. **ICT**

Time (min)	Mass of CO₂ given off (g)
2.0	1.5
4.0	2.5
6.0	3.1
8.0	3.4
8.0	3.4
8.0	3.4
10.0	3.6
16.0	3.8

a Plot a graph of the results, with time on the horizontal axis.

b Compare the gradient of the graph at the start of the experiment and at the end. What does this tell you?

c On the same axes, sketch the graph you would expect if the experiment was done at a temperature of 30 °C instead of 20 °C.

d On the same axes, sketch the graph you would expect if the marble chips were ground into a powder before the start of the experiment.

Enzymes

Enzymes are biological catalysts that are very useful in industry.

Table 1 Important properties of enzymes.

Enzymes are

- proteins
- very specific – each enzyme controls one reaction
- inactivated by heating – most enzymes stop working above about 45 °C
- sensitive to pH – most enzymes work best in neutral conditions, around pH7.

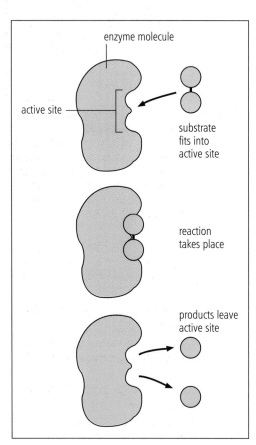

Picture 2 How an enzyme works. The substrate fits into the active site where the reaction takes place.

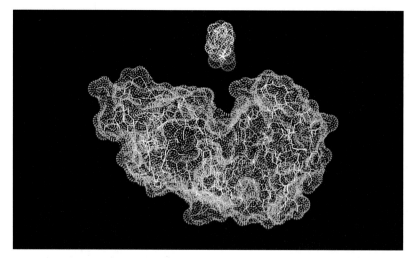

Picture 1 This computer-generated model shows an enzyme molecule (ribonuclease A) with its substrate next to its active site.

Without enzymes, all life would stop. Living things produce enzymes to catalyse the chemical reactions that go on inside them. Table 1 summarises the most important properties of enzymes.

HOW DO ENZYMES WORK?

An example of an enzyme is catalase. This enzyme is produced by organisms in order to break down hydrogen peroxide. Hydrogen peroxide is the **substrate** for catalase – the substance which the enzyme works on.

$$\text{hydrogen peroxide} \xrightarrow{\text{catalase}} \text{water} + \text{oxygen}$$
$$2H_2O_2(aq) \longrightarrow 2H_2O(l) + O_2(g)$$

Enzymes are very efficient catalysts. One molecule of catalase can break down six million molecules of hydrogen peroxide per minute!

Enzymes are made from proteins. The molecule of an enzyme has a special shape (picture 1). This shape includes an **active site**, which is where the reaction happens. The active site is exactly the right shape to fit a molecule of the substrate. Picture 2 represents what happens.

The precise shape of the active site means that enzymes are highly specific – they only work on the substrate that fits the site. What's more, the shape of the site is easily changed, particularly by heating or by changes in acidity. That's why enzymes only work in a narrow range of temperature and pH.

■ Enzymes and temperature

Most enzymes only work well between about 10 °C and 45 °C. Below about 10 °C, they only work very slowly. Above about 45 °C, they stop working altogether because their precise molecular shape is destroyed. Most enzymes work fastest at around 37 °C.

Our bodies have to be maintained at a precise temperature. You are a finely tuned biochemical machine, with thousands of enzyme-catalysed reactions running in harmony. If any of these reactions run too slow, or too fast, the whole machine gets out of control – as you will know if you've ever had a fever.

Food goes bad because of bacteria which grow in it. The bacteria use enzymes to break down the food. We can preserve food by making it very cold in a fridge or freezer, so the enzymes work very slowly. Alternatively, we can cook the food so that it gets hot enough to destroy the enzymes and kill the bacteria.

ENZYMES IN INDUSTRY

◼ Traditional uses of enzymes

Fermentation has been used in brewing and baking for thousands of years. During fermentation, sugars are broken down into ethanol and carbon dioxide by the action of enzymes in yeast.

$$\text{sugar} \xrightarrow{\text{yeast}} \text{ethanol} + \text{carbon dioxide} + \text{energy}$$

$$C_6H_{12}O_6(aq) \xrightarrow{\text{yeast}} 2C_2H_5OH(aq) + 2CO_2(g) + \text{energy}$$

Alcoholic drinks like wine and beer are made by adding yeast to a sugary solution. In the case of wine, the sugar comes from grape juice. In beer, it comes from malted barley. There is more about this in topic H3.

Fermentation is also used in baking. Yeast is one of the ingredients in bread dough. The bubbles of carbon dioxide formed in the fermenting dough make it rise.

Yoghurt and **cheese** also depend on enzymes for their manufacture. Special bacteria are added to milk. These bacteria contain enzymes which act on the sugars and proteins in milk. For example, the bacteria used to make yoghurt convert milk sugar (lactose) to lactic acid. This gives natural yoghurt a sharp taste.

◼ Modern uses of enzymes

Enzymes could transform the chemical industry of the future. Instead of using high temperatures and pressures to make reactions go quickly, scientists are finding that enzymes can do the job just as well, and at room temperature.

One of the first of the modern uses of enzymes was in washing powders. (picture 3).

Table 2 shows some of the types of enzymes with industrial uses. You can use it to answer Question 1 below.

Picture 3 'Biological' powders contain enzymes which can break down proteins and fats – the most important causes of stains on clothes.

Picture 4 Have you ever wondered how they make soft-centred chocolates? The sugary centre starts off hard, to make it easier to put the chocolate on the outside. But an enzyme is mixed with the sugar which slowly breaks down the sugar after the chocolate coating is on. As the sugar breaks down, it turns softer.

Table 2 Useful enzymes.

Type of enzyme	Substrate	What the enzyme does
Amylase	Starch	Breaks down long starch molecules into sugars
Cellulase	Cellulose	Breaks down long cellulose molecules into sugars
Protease	Protein	Breaks down proteins into amino acids
Lipase	Fat	Breaks down fat into smaller molecules

Questions

1 Use table 2 to decide what types of enzyme would be best for each of the following uses.

 a Putting in a washing powder to help it remove greasy stains.

 b Putting in a washing powder to help it remove bloodstains.

 c Breaking down starch to produce sugars (see picture 4).

 d Breaking down waste paper to produce sugars.

 e Breaking down tough fibres in meat to make it tender.

 f Removing hair from animal hides before they are used to make leather.

 g Removing the outer seed coating from cereal grains.

2 Some substances act as poisons and stop enzymes working properly. Look at picture 2 and suggest how enzymes get poisoned.

3 What are the major differences between enzymes and ordinary catalysts?

4 Consider the following information, then answer questions a and b below.

● Jellies are made from gelatin, which is made of protein. The protein chains form a network which traps water and sets into a gel.

● Pineapple contains an enzyme which breaks down proteins.

● If you try to make a fruit jelly with chunks of fresh pineapple in, the jelly will not set.

● If you use tinned pineapple chunks, the jelly does set

 a Explain why the jelly will not set when you use fresh pineapple.

 b Explain why it does set with tinned pineapple.

Some chemical reactions can go backwards as well as forwards. They settle down in a position of equilibrium.

WHAT IS A REVERSIBLE REACTION?

Fizzy drinks such as soda water contain dissolved carbon dioxide, $CO_2(aq)$. The drink is made by dissolving carbon dioxide in the water under pressure. To keep the carbon dioxide dissolved, you need to keep up the pressure – in other words, keep the top on the bottle.

As soon as you release the pressure, the carbon dioxide comes out of solution and you see a stream of bubbles of $CO_2(g)$ (picture 1). We say that this change is **reversible**: it can go in either direction.

$$CO_2(g) \underset{\text{decrease pressure}}{\overset{\text{increase pressure}}{\rightleftharpoons}} CO_2(aq)$$

The $\rightleftharpoons$ sign indicates a reversible change. Compare it with the arrow we normally use, which means a change that goes in one direction only.

▣ What's going on?

Once a fizzy drink has settled down with the top on, you can't see any changes happening. We say that it is in **equilibrium** – a balanced state.

But if you were able to see what was happening to the individual molecules in the bottle you would find that there was continual change going on (picture 2). Molecules of CO_2 are constantly coming out of the solution and moving into the gas phase. At the same time, CO_2 molecules are constantly going *back* into solution.

Now here's the important point. When the system is in equilibrium, *CO_2 molecules are coming out of solution as fast as they are going back, so the overall change is zero*. This is called **dynamic equilibrium**.

▣ Another example

If you heat calcium carbonate in a sealed container, it decomposes.

calcium carbonate $\rightleftharpoons$ calcium oxide + carbon dioxide
$$CaCO_3(s) \rightleftharpoons CaO(s) + CO_2(g)$$

But the calcium carbonate doesn't decompose completely. Some calcium carbonate is left unchanged. At the molecular level, CaO and CO_2 are reacting to form $CaCO_3$ as fast as the $CaCO_3$ is decomposing. It is at dynamic equilibrium.

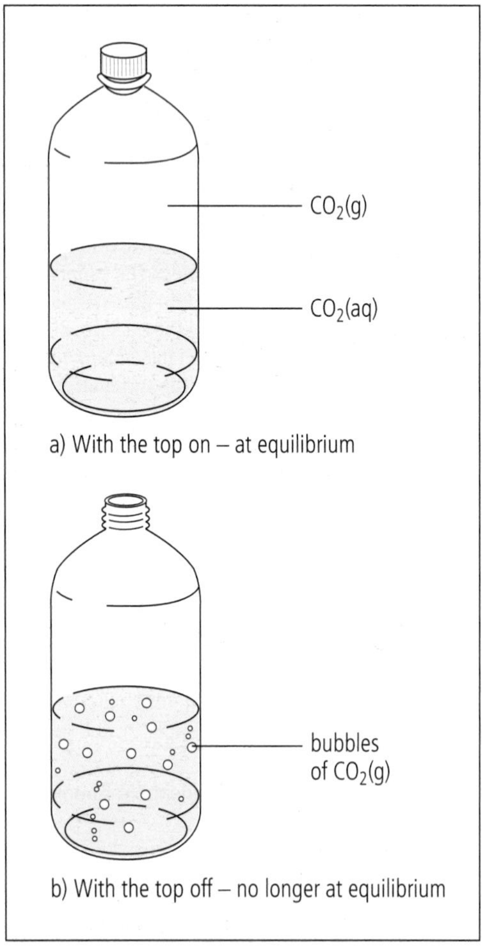

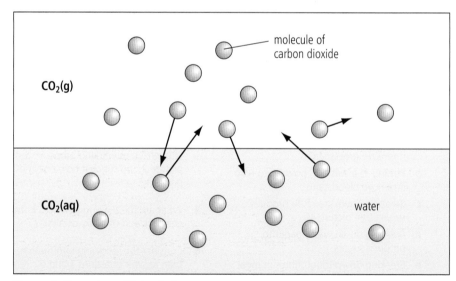

Picture 2 Dynamic equilibrium in fizzy water.

a) With the top on – at equilibrium

b) With the top off – no longer at equilibrium

$CO_2(g)$

$CO_2(aq)$

bubbles of $CO_2(g)$

Picture 1 Fizzy water: what you see.

WHAT DECIDES THE POSITION OF EQUILIBRIUM?

We can alter the balance point in equilibrium by altering the conditions around it. Let's go back to the carbon dioxide equilibrium in fizzy drinks. If you increase the pressure, more CO_2 dissolves in the water. The balance point of the equilibrium

$$CO_2(g) \rightleftharpoons CO_2(aq)$$

has moved to the *right*. On the other hand, if you increase the temperature, *less* CO_2 dissolves. You know how fizzy drinks go flat quickly when it's warm. So increasing the temperature moves the balance point to the *left*.

■ The general rule: Le Chatelier's Principle

There is a general rule about the effect of changing conditions on the position of equilibrium. It's called Le Chatelier's Principle, and it says

When you make a change to a system in dynamic equilibrium, the system moves so as to oppose the change.

For example, in the case of the CO_2 equilibrium, if you increase the pressure, the equilibrium moves so as to make more CO_2 dissolve. This reduces the pressure again.

Table 1 summarises the effect of different changes on the position of equilibrium.

■ Applying Le Chatelier's Principle

Let's look at an equilibrium reaction that is very important in industry: the reaction used in the Haber Process to make ammonia (see page 105). This is an exothermic reaction: it gives out heat.

$$\text{nitrogen} + \text{hydrogen} \rightleftharpoons \text{ammonia} + \text{heat}$$
$$N_2(g) + 3H_2(g) \rightleftharpoons 2NH_3(g)$$

To get as much ammonia as possible, we need to choose the conditions so that the position of equilibrium is well over to the right.

Let's look at temperature first. If we increase the temperature, Le Chatelier's Principle tells us that the position of equilibrium will move so as to reduce the temperature. This means it will move to the left, since this takes in heat. So increasing the temperature gives you *less* ammonia.

What about pressure? Le Chatelier's Principle says that if we increase the pressure the position of equilibrium will move so as to reduce the pressure again. This means it moves to the right, because there is less gas, and therefore less pressure, on the right-hand side. So increasing the pressure gives you *more* ammonia

So to get plenty of ammonia, you need a high pressure and a low temperature. However, in order to get the ammonia formed *quickly* enough, you need a high temperature. This means a compromise is necessary: You use an imtermediate temperature. More about this on page 106.

Table 1 The effect of different changes on the position of equilibrium.

Condition	Effect
Temperature	Increasing temperature makes the reaction move in the direction which takes in heat
Pressure	Increasing pressure makes the reaction move in the direction which produces less gas
Concentration	Increasing the concentration of one substance makes the equilibrium move in the direction that produces less of that substance
Catalyst	Using a catalyst does not affect the position of equilibrium, but means the reaction goes faster.

Picture 3 What conditions are best for drying wet clothes?

Questions

1 Explain what is meant by
   a a reversible reaction
   b dynamic equilibrium.

2 Sulphuric acid is manufactured by the Contact Process. The key reaction in the process is:

$$2SO_2(g) + O_2(g) \rightleftharpoons 2SO_3(g) + \text{heat}$$

   a Would high pressure or low pressure be needed to get a good yield of SO_3? Explain.
   b Would high temperature or low temperature be needed to get a good yield of SO_3? Explain.

3 Consider the decomposition of calcium carbonate

$$\text{heat} + CaCO_3(s) \rightleftharpoons CaO(s) + CO_2(g)$$

What conditions of temperature and pressure (high, medium or low) would you choose in order to get as much decomposition of $CaCO_3$ as possible?

4 The evaporation of water is a dynamic equilibrium

$$H_2O(l) \rightleftharpoons H_2O(g)$$

   a On which side of this equilibrium is heat needed?
   b Suppose you have some wet washing which you want to get dry. Use this dynamic equilibrium to explain the conditions you would choose for the best drying.

J

Electricity and chemistry

Using electrolysis

Electrolysis means using electricity to split up compounds.

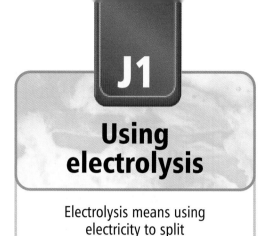

Picture 1 Humphry Davy (1778–1829), aged 23. He made many chemical discoveries, including 'laughing gas' (dinitrogen oxide) and six elements. He also invented a safety lamp which prevented explosions in mines.

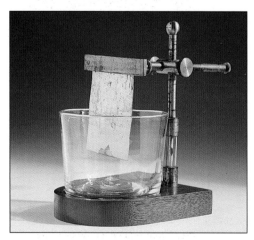

Picture 2 Electrolysis apparatus used by Humphrey Davy.

On October 6, 1807, Humphry Davy was beside himself with excitement. He had just melted some potassium hydroxide (he called it potash) and passed electricity through it. To his delight, tiny globules of a silvery molten metal floated to the surface and burst into lilac flames. He danced around the room in glee, and it was half an hour before he had calmed down enough to write his results in his notebook.

Humphry Davy had just discovered the element potassium, by using electrolysis to decompose potassium hydroxide. His experiment opened the way for the discovery of more new elements – he discovered sodium using a similar method just three days later. He had already investigated the electrolysis of water, and found that it gives two parts of hydrogen to one part of oxygen (picture 3). This confirmed that the formula of water is H_2O.

Humphry Davy's work with electrolysis led the way to many other things. Today, electrolysis is used to make aluminium, chlorine and many other useful chemicals, as well as for electroplating metals.

WHAT IS ELECTROLYSIS?

■ Some basic words

Humphry Davy's work on electrolysis made him world famous. His assistant in much of his work was a younger man called Michael Faraday. He continued Humphry Davy's work and made some even greater discoveries about electromagnetism.

Michael Faraday gave us the words we still use to describe electrolysis. Michael had a friend who was a Greek scholar, and he asked him to invent some new words to describe the basics of electrolysis. Table 1 gives some of the Greek words that were used.

Electrolysis means using electricity to split up (decompose) substances. The substance that is decomposed is called the **electrolyte**. Two **electrodes** are used to make electrical contact with the solution. They are usually made of an unreactive metal like carbon or platinum. The positive electrode is called the **anode** and the negative one is the **cathode**. Electricity is carried through the electrolyte by **ions** (picture 4).

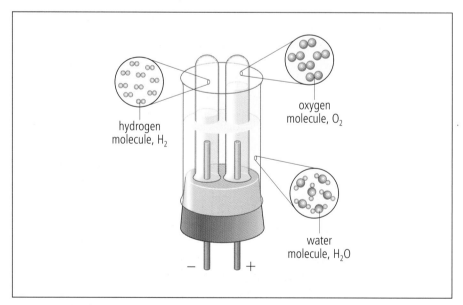

hydrogen molecule, H_2

oxygen molecule, O_2

water molecule, H_2O

Picture 3 The electrolysis of water. (The water has a little acid added, to make it conduct electricity better.)

Conductors and insulators

You can't electrolyse something unless it conducts electricity. But not *all* conductors are electrolytes. You can pass electricity through a metal for years and it doesn't decompose. This isn't surprising, because metals are usually elements, so you couldn't split them into anything simpler.

All electrolytes are ionic compounds. However, ionic compounds don't conduct electricity when they are solid. To conduct, they have to be in a liquid state, either molten or dissolved in water. This makes the ions free to move and carry electricity: more about this in topic J2. So electrolysis always involves ionic compounds, either molten or dissolved in water.

What is formed during electrolysis?

You can try some electrolysis experiments for yourself using the kind of apparatus shown in picture 3. You will find that you get one product at the cathode and one at the anode. Usually the products are elements. For example, when Humphry Davy electrolysed potassium hydroxide, he got potassium at the cathode and oxygen at the anode. The general rule is that:

At the cathode, a metal or hydrogen is formed.
At the anode, a non-metal is formed.

Electrolysis pulls the electrolyte apart, with one part going to each electrode. Just why this happens is explained in topic J2.

USING ELECTROLYSIS

In 1852, the price of aluminium was £250 a kilogram – 30 times the price of silver. Aluminium was an expensive oddity. The Emperor Napoleon III of France used aluminium plates when he really wanted to impress his guests.

By 1890, the price of aluminium had fallen to less than £1 a kilogram, a fraction of the price of silver. What had happened?

Aluminium is extracted from an ore called bauxite, which is mainly aluminium oxide. Aluminium is a reactive metal, which makes it difficult to extract from the ore. Before 1886, the only way to make it was by heating aluminium chloride with sodium. Sodium itself was expensive, which made aluminium cost even more. Then in 1886, a new process was developed. It used Humphry Davy's method of electrolysing a molten compound. The price of aluminium quickly fell, and the metal became widely available. The same basic method is still used. Today, aluminium is so cheap that if you eat a meal off an aluminium plate, it will probably be a disposable one that you throw away afterwards.

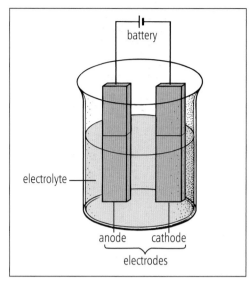

Picture 4 The basics of electrolysis.

Table 1 The words we use to describe electrolysis come from Greek. The word *electro* comes from the Greek word for amber because electricity was first made by rubbing amber. (Amber is a kind of naturally occurring plastic.)

Greek word	English spelling	English translation
ΕΛΕΚΤΡΟΝ	electro-	amber
ΚΑΤ	cat-	down
ΑΝ	an-	up
ΙΟΝ	ion	going
ΟΔΟΣ	-ode	way
ΛΥΣΙΣ	-lysis	splitting

Picture 5 The statue of Eros in Piccadilly Circus is made from aluminium. When it was made in 1884, aluminium was an expensive novelty.

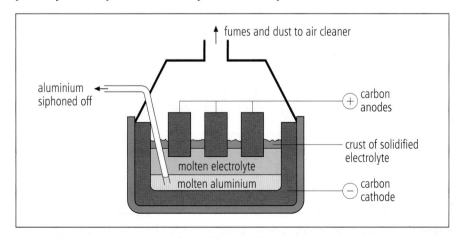

Picture 6 How aluminium is manufactured by electrolysis.

■ Extracting aluminium

Picture 6 shows the equipment that is used to manufacture aluminium today. The electrolyte is molten aluminium oxide, mixed with another aluminium compound called cryolite to make the melting point lower. The electrolysis cell is lined with carbon, and this lining becomes the negative electrode (the cathode). Molten aluminium collects at the bottom and is tapped off. The anodes are blocks of carbon. Oxygen is given off at the anodes and they slowly burn away, producing carbon dioxide gas. Replacing the anodes adds to the running costs of the process. The reactions that take place at the electrodes are described further in topic J2.

The voltage used is only 5 V, but a plant producing 100 tonnes of aluminium a day needs a current of about 30 million amps. The heating effect of the electric current keeps the electrolyte molten. The cost of electricity is a major part of the total cost of aluminium (picture 7). Because of this, aluminium plants are usually built near to sources of cheap electricity, such as hydro-electric plants.

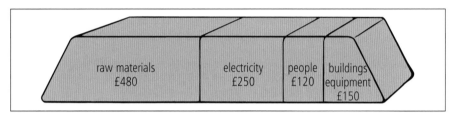

Picture 7 The main costs involved in making £1000 worth of aluminium.

■ Other metals are extracted by electrolysis

All the more reactive metals are extracted using electrolysis (see topic E3 for details of metal extraction in general). Usually the chloride of the metal is used, because these have lower melting points. There are more details in the next topic.

ELECTROPLATING

Have you ever used silver knives and forks? It might have been solid silver, but it's more likely to have been silver *plate*. Look for the letters EPNS: they stand for Electro-Plated Nickel Silver, which is nickel with a thin layer of silver plated on top.

Electroplating is one of the useful applications of electrolysis. It's used to plate a thin layer of a valuable metal on top of a less valuable one. This may be to make the metal look more attractive, or to protect it from corrosion. Steel is often protected in this way. Table 2 gives some examples of the uses of electroplating.

■ How it's done

Picture 8 shows the basic method. The object that has to be electroplated is connected to the negative terminal of the electrical supply, making it the cathode. The anode is a pure piece of the plating metal – silver in this example. The electrolyte

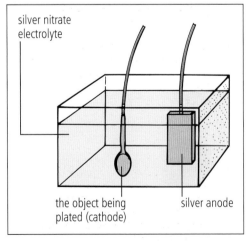

Picture 8 Electroplating with silver.

Table 2 Some ways that electroplating is used.

What's plated on top?	What's underneath?	Uses
silver	nickel	cutlery
chromium	steel	shiny metal trimmings for cars, bikes, kettles
zinc	steel	protecting steel from corrosion in dustbins, wheelbarrows
tin	steel	'tin' cans for food

is a solution of a compound of the plating metal – silver nitrate in this example. During electroplating, metal dissolves from the anode and gets plated onto the cathode as a thin layer. In effect, metal is transferred from the anode to the cathode.

The metal layer only forms on the cathode where it is facing the anode. So the cathode has to be rotated so that it gets plated evenly all over. This means the equipment needs to be rather more complicated than the simple version in picture 7. It's also important that the object being plated is very clean, otherwise the plating metal does not stick to it properly.

There is more about how electroplating works in topic J2.

PURIFYING COPPER BY ELECTROLYSIS

Copper that is used for making electrical equipment has to be very pure. Electrolysis is used to purify the copper. The impure copper is the anode in the electrolysis cell shown in picture 10. The cathode is a thin sheet of very pure copper, and the electrolyte is a solution of copper sulphate. When a current passes through the cell, copper moves from the anode to the cathode, as in electroplating. Most of the impurities fall to the bottom of the cell, and the copper plated on the cathode is 99.99% pure.

Picture 9 This teapot has been electroplated with silver.

Activity

Looking for electroplate

Look around in your home for articles that are electroplated. Look at things like teapots, kettles, forks, spoons, rubbish bins, bicycles and cars. Decide, as far as you can:

1 what metal is plated on top,

2 what metal is underneath,

3 what the purpose of the plating is.

Choose one of the items and look very closely at it. Are there any places where the plating is less good? Can you see any sign of where the electrical connection was made?

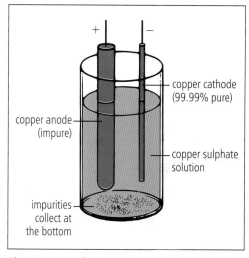

Picture 10 Purifying copper by electrolysis.

Questions

1 Give the words that fit in the blanks in the following.

Electrolysis means __(a)__ a substance using __(b)__. The substance being electrolysed is called an __(c)__. Two __(d)__ are used, one positive and called the __(e)__, one negative and called the __(f)__. Normally, a metal or hydrogen is formed at the __(g)__ and a non-metal is formed at the __(h)__.

2 Look at the electroplating bath in picture 8. What *two* changes would you have to make if you wanted to gold-plate the spoon instead of silver-plating it?

3 Look at the electrolysis cell for the manufacture of aluminium shown in picture 6.

a The electrolyte does not need heating to keep it molten. Why?

b What would happen if you reversed the connections of the cathode and anode?

c The graphite anodes gradually disappear during the electrolysis. What are they turning to? (Think about the product that is given off at the anode.)

4 You can buy plastic items that look metallic. They have been electroplated to coat them with a metal such as chromium.

a What is the difficulty with electroplating plastic?

b How do you think this difficulty is overcome?

5 In an electroplating bath, you have to rotate the cathode so that it gets plated all over. Suggest a design for a cell that would plate the cathode all over without rotating it. Use a sketch to illustrate your design.

6 Look at table 1. Use it to explain how the following words were derived. You may have to do some inspired guesswork!

a electrolysis

b cathode

c anode

d ion

7 Sir Humphry Davy discovered six new elements in two years using electrolysis. But he could not have made his discoveries without something else being discovered first. What was this earlier discovery?

Explaining electrolysis

We can use ideas about ions to explain what goes on in electrolysis – and to predict the products

Picture 1 Electrolysing sodium chloride solution on an industrial scale. These are membrane cells (page 247).

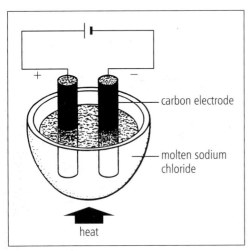

Picture 2 Electrolysing molten sodium chloride in the laboratory.

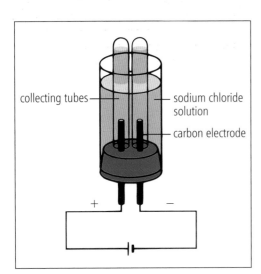

Picture 3 Electrolysing sodium chloride solution in the laboratory.

■ Useful things from salt

Salt—sodium chloride—is an excellent source of chemicals, and most of them are made by electrolysis.

Solid sodium chloride does not conduct electricity. To make it conduct, you can either melt it or dissolve it in water to give an aqueous solution. So there are two ways of doing electrolysis on sodium chloride: on the molten compound or on the aqueous solution. Pictures 2 and 3 show how these experiments could be done in the laboratory – in industry, of course, they use different equipment (picture 1).

Table 1 shows what you get when you electrolyse sodium chloride in the two different ways. We'll look at the two ways in turn.

Table 1 The products of electrolysing sodium chloride.

	At the anode (+)	At the cathode (−)	Left behind
molten sodium chloride, NaCl(l)	chlorine, Cl_2 (g)	sodium, Na (l)	nothing
sodium chloride in solution, NaCl(aq)	chlorine, Cl_2 (g)	hydrogen, H_2 (g)	sodium hydroxide NaOH(aq)

ELECTROLYSIS OF MOLTEN ELECTROLYTES

It's easy to predict the result of electrolysing a molten electrolyte. The compound just gets split into two parts, a metal and a non-metal. The metal is formed at the cathode and the non-metal at the anode.

■ What's going on?

To explain what happens in electrolysis, you need to remember that all electrolytes contain ions (charged particles). In sodium chloride, the ions are Na^+ and Cl^-. You'll need to remember too that an electric current in a metal is a flow of electrons, and that electrons are negatively charged.

When the sodium chloride is solid, the ions are held tightly in a regular lattice (page 92). They cannot move. But when the sodium chloride is melted, the ions are freed from their lattice and they can move.

Picture 4 shows what happens. Opposite charges attract, and the positive ions are attracted to the negative electrode, the cathode. Because of this, positive ions are sometimes called **cations**. In the same way, the negative ions are attracted to the anode. They are sometimes called **anions**.

This explains how the ions get separated, but what happens when they reach the electrodes? The second part of picture 4 shows it.

AT THE CATHODE

Let's look at the sodium ions first. Na^+ ions are positively charged because they are short of one electron. The cathode, on the other hand, has an *excess* of electrons—that's where it gets its negative charge from. The electrons are pushed onto the cathode by the battery in the circuit.

When the Na^+ ions arrive at the cathode, they attract electrons from it. The electron cancels out the positive charge on the Na^+, leaving it as a neutral Na atom. The Na^+ has been **discharged**, and it forms molten sodium metal.

We can represent the happenings at the cathode like this:

$$\text{sodium ion + electron} \rightarrow \text{sodium atom}$$
$$Na^+(l) \quad + \quad e^- \quad \rightarrow \quad Na(l)$$

AT THE ANODE

Now let's see what happens to the Cl^- ions when they arrive at the anode. It's the opposite to the situation at the cathode. This time the Cl^- ions have one electron too many. The anode, on the other hand, has a *shortage* of electrons—that's why it's positively charged. The electrons have been pulled off the anode by the battery. The battery is a kind of electron pump, pulling electrons off the anode and pumping them round to the cathode.

When the Cl^- ions arrive at the anode, the anode attracts their electrons. The Cl^- ions lose their extra electron, leaving them as neutral Cl atoms. Like all Cl atoms, they prefer to go around in pairs, so they join up and form Cl_2 molecules. The Cl^- has been **discharged**, and it becomes chlorine gas.

We can represent these events at the anode like this:

$$\text{chloride ion} - \text{electron} \rightarrow \text{chlorine atom}$$
$$Cl^-(l) \quad - \quad e^- \quad \rightarrow \quad Cl(g)$$

Then:

$$2Cl(g) \rightarrow Cl_2(g)$$

Overall it amounts to:

$$2Cl^-(l) - 2e^- \rightarrow Cl_2(g)$$

■ Another example

We can apply these ideas to the electrolysis of molten aluminium oxide. This is used in the manufacture of aluminium, described in topic J1. Aluminium is formed at the cathode and oxygen at the anode.

Aluminium oxide contains Al^{3+} and O^{2-} ions. At the cathode, molten aluminium is formed.

$$Al^{3+}(l) + 3e^- \rightarrow Al(l)$$

Notice that *three* electrons are involved for each aluminium ion. That is because there are *three* positive charges on each ion.

At the anode, oxygen is given off.

$$O^{2-}(l) - 2e^- \rightarrow O(g)$$

then:

$$2O(g) \rightarrow O_2(g)$$

This time *two* electrons are involved per oxygen ion, because of the *two* negative charges on the O^{2-} ion.

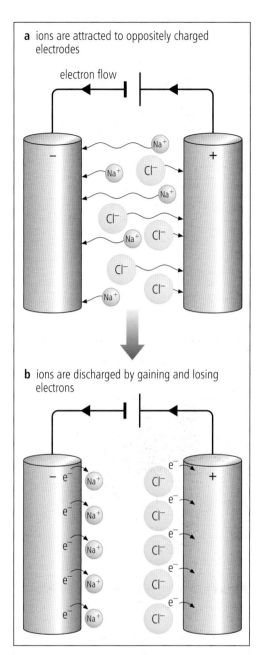

a ions are attracted to oppositely charged electrodes

electron flow

b ions are discharged by gaining and losing electrons

Picture 4 What happens when molten sodium chloride is electrolysed.

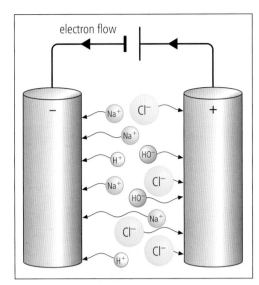

electron flow

Picture 5 What happens when aqueous sodium chloride is electrolysed. Now look at pictures 6 and 7.

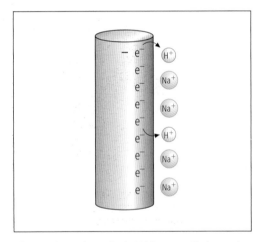

Picture 6 At the cathode H$^+$ ions are discharged and Na$^+$ ions stay in solution.

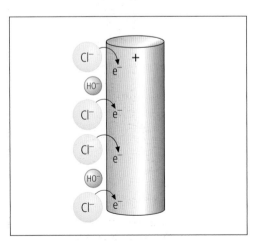

Picture 7 At the anode Cl$^-$ ions are discharged and OH$^-$ ions stay in solution.

ELECTROLYSIS OF AQUEOUS SOLUTIONS

You can try electrolysing some aqueous solutions using the apparatus shown in picture 3. You will find that at the cathode you always get either a metal or hydrogen. At the anode you always get a non-metal. For example, in the electrolysis of sodium chloride solution, *hydrogen* is formed at the cathode, and chlorine at the anode. Left behind is a solution of sodium hydroxide.

■ Behind the scenes

Aqueous electrolytes are more complicated than molten ones, because we have to think about the water as well as the electrolyte itself. But we can use the same basic idea of ions being attracted to the electrodes and then getting discharged.

First, a word or two about water. One of the odd things about water is that, although it's a molecular substance, it does contain a few ions. A few water molecules split up to give hydrogen ions and hydroxide ions:

$$water \rightarrow hydrogen\ ions + hydroxide\ ions$$
$$H_2O(l) \rightarrow \quad H^+(aq) \quad + \quad OH^-(aq)$$

Only about one water molecule in a billion does this, so there aren't enough ions to make water conduct electricity very well on its own. But we do have to bear these H$^+$ and OH$^-$ ions in mind when it comes to the products of electrolysis.

A solution of sodium chloride contains four different ions: Na$^+$ and Cl$^-$, and H$^+$ and OH$^-$ from the water. Picture 5 shows what happens. The positive ions, Na$^+$ and H$^+$, travel to the cathode, attracted by its negative charge. The Cl$^-$ and OH$^-$ ions travel to the anode. So we have two ions at each electrode. Pictures 6 and 7 show what happens next.

AT THE CATHODE (picture 6)
We have both Na$^+$ and H$^+$ ions at the cathode, but only one type of ion gets discharged. We know it's the hydrogen ion, because hydrogen is the product at the cathode. But why not the sodium? Well, sodium is a very reactive metal. Like all reactive metals it tends to stay in the combined form, as a compound, rather than become an element. Another way of saying this is that sodium 'prefers' to be an ion than an atom. So the less reactive hydrogen is discharged in preference to the sodium.

Hydrogen ions gain an electron from the cathode and become hydrogen atoms. The atoms pair up to form H$_2$ molecules. We can show all this as:

$$H^+(aq) + e^- \rightarrow H(g), \text{ then: } 2H(g) \rightarrow H_2(g).$$

The Na$^+$ ions are left behind in the solution.

AT THE ANODE (picture 7)
Two types of ion arrive at the anode: Cl$^-$ and OH$^-$ (picture 9). Only the Cl$^-$ gets discharged. Overall, it amounts to:

$$2Cl^-(l) - 2e^- \rightarrow Cl_2(g)$$

The OH$^-$ ions are left behind in solution.

So, to summarise, we have H$^+$ ions discharged as hydrogen gas at the cathode, and Cl$^-$ ions discharged as chlorine gas at the anode. Left behind in solution are Na$^+$ and OH$^-$ ions, in other words a solution of sodium hydroxide. All these products—hydrogen, chlorine and sodium hydroxide—are very useful, so this is a very important manufacturing process. There is more about this 'chlor-alkali' process in topic D5.

Picture 8 Silver plate.

■ The general rules

Here are some general rules that you can use to predict the products of electrolysis of *any* aqueous solution.

1 Decide what metal and non-metal ions are in the electrolyte. Remember that it will also contain H^+ and OH^- from the water.
2 For the cathode product, decide how reactive the metal is. (Look at the reactivity series in the Data Section if you are not sure.) If the metal is in roughly the upper half of the series, then hydrogen will be the product at the cathode. If the metal is in the lower half, then the metal itself will be the product.
3 For the anode product, you can assume it will be oxygen unless the compound contains a halogen (chlorine, bromine or iodine).
4 Decide what ions are left behind in solution after the others have been discharged. There will be a positive ion and a negative one, and between them they make the product that is left behind.

Try using these rules to predict electrolysis products in question 4.

■ Explaining electroplating

We can explain electroplating using the idea of ions.

Usually in electrolysis the electrodes are made of an unreactive substance like carbon or platinum. They don't play any part in the reactions. In electroplating, though, the anode actually takes part.

Look at the electroplating cell in picture 8 on page 240. When the cell is switched on, silver ions (Ag^+) are attracted to the cathode, which is the object being plated. They gain electrons from the cathode and are discharged. This forms silver, which plates the cathode (picture 9).

$$Ag^+(aq) + e^- \rightarrow Ag(s)$$

Exactly the opposite happens at the anode. Silver atoms in the anode turn to silver ions. These go into solution and replace the Ag^+ ions that are being discharged at the cathode.

$$Ag(s) \rightarrow Ag^+(aq) + e^-$$

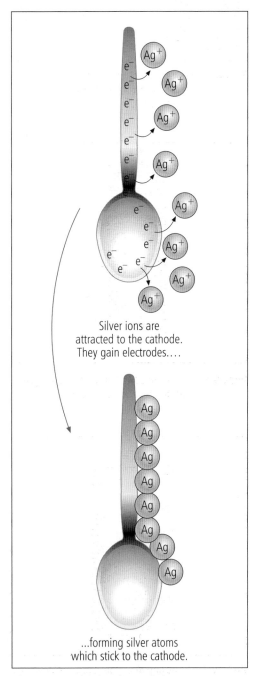

Silver ions are attracted to the cathode. They gain electrodes....

...forming silver atoms which stick to the cathode.

Picture 9 Explaining electroplating.

PURIFYING COPPER USING ELECTROLYSIS

On page 241 we explain how electrolysis is used to purify copper. Picture 10 shows the method in use. It works in the same way as electroplating. Copper ions are discharged at the pure copper cathode:

$$Cu^{2+}(aq) + 2e^- \rightarrow Cu(s)$$

At the impure copper anode, copper atoms turn into ions:

$$Cu(s) \rightarrow Cu^{2+}(aq) + 2e^-$$

These replace the copper ions that are discharged at the cathode.

Picture 10 Purifying copper by electrolysis. The large sheets are cathodes.

Questions

1 When molten sodium chloride is electrolysed, sodium is formed at the cathode. But when aqueous sodium chloride is used, the cathode product is hydrogen. Why the difference?

2 Predict what would be formed: (i) at the anode, and (ii) at the cathode when each of the following molten substances are electrolysed using carbon electrodes:

   a magnesium bromide, MgBr₂(l),

   b calcium chloride, CaCl₂(l),

   c lithium oxide, Li₂O(l),

   d sodium hydroxide, NaOH(l).

3 Write equations for the discharge reactions at each electrode for the reactions in question 2. You will need to use the Data Section to find the charges on the ions concerned.

4 Predict what would be formed (i) at the anode and (ii) at the cathode when each of the following aqueous solutions are electrolysed using carbon electrodes:

   a sodium bromide solution, NaBr(aq),

   b copper iodide solution, CuI₂(aq),

   c zinc chloride solution, ZnCl₂(aq),

   d silver nitrate solution, AgNO₃(aq),

   e dilute hydrochloric acid, HCl(aq).

5 Write equations for the discharge reactions at each electrode for the reactions in question 4. You will need to use the Data Section to find the charges on the ions concerned.

6 Look at the electroplating cell in picture 8 on page 240. What would happen if the anode was replaced by carbon instead of silver?

A better way to electrolyse salt

The electrolysis of salt is a major industry, producing chlorine, sodium hydroxide and hydrogen. It is called the chlor-alkali industry. The right design of electrolysis cell is crucial. Two things are especially important for a successful cell design.

1 It must give pure products. If you've done the electrolysis of sodium chloride yourself, you'll know that it is difficult to stop the chlorine at the anode mixing with the sodium hydroxide that's formed around the cathode.

2 There must be as little damage to the environment as possible.

The mercury cell
The first commercial cells solved the purity problem by using a flowing mercury cathode. Mercury cells make very pure products, and they are still used today. But there are environmental problems because mercury is very toxic.

Chemical engineers have now developed safer methods for electrolysing salt. The latest is the membrane cell.

The membrane cell
The basic design of the membrane cell is shown in picture 1. It works continuously, with sodium chloride solution flowing in one side and sodium hydroxide flowing out of the other. Hydrogen comes off

continuously from the cathode, and chlorine from the anode.

The key to the working of the cell is a cleverly designed membrane between the anode and cathode compartments. It is an 'ion-selective' membrane which only lets Na^+ ions and water through. This means that sodium hydroxide solution forms only in the cathode compartment, so the products can't mix.

1 The mercury cell and the membrane cell both make very pure sodium hydroxide. Why are membrane cells now preferred to mercury cells?

2 Look at picture 1.
a What ions are present in the anode compartment? (Remember there are ions from the water as well as from the sodium chloride.)
b What ions are present in the cathode compartment? (Remember the effect of the membrane.)
c Which ion is discharged at the cathode?
d Explain why the sodium hydroxide flowing out of the cathode compartment is pure and uncontaminated with chlorine.

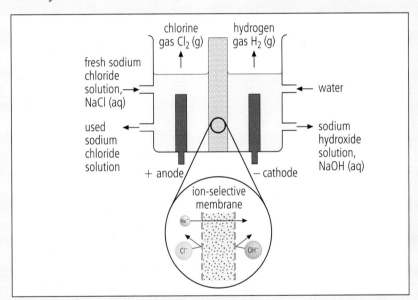

Picture 1 The basic design of a membrane cell.

Redox and electron transfer

There is always a transfer of electrons between the substances in a redox reaction.

Picture 2 The statue of Little Mermaid in Copenhagen is covered in copper. When it was new it was bright as a new copper coin. But it has slowly oxidised, and coppery Cu has turned to green Cu^{2+}.

OILRIG

Oxidisation

Is

Loss of electrons

Reduction

Is

Gain

Picture 3

Picture 1 Redox reactions occur on a huge scale in a blast furnace, where iron oxide is reduced to iron by carbon monoxide. This blast furnace is in Scunthorpe.

MAKING SENSE OF REDOX REACTIONS

Many reactions in chemistry, including some important industrial processes, are redox reactions. Topic B2 explains the basic ideas behind redox. In this topic we will take these ideas further.

■ Redox in the manufacture of aluminium

We use electrolysis to extract aluminium metal from its ore (topic J1). The following equations summarise the reactions which take place in the electrolysis cell:

$$\text{aluminium oxide} \rightarrow \text{aluminium} + \text{oxygen}$$
$$2Al_2O_3(s) \quad \rightarrow \quad 4Al(l) \quad + \quad 3O_2(g)$$

A redox reaction is taking place. Aluminium is reduced because it loses oxygen. But what is being oxidised? To understand this, we need broader definitions of oxidation and reduction than we have used so far.

There are many examples of redox reactions which do not involve oxygen at all. But in *all* of them *electron transfer* is taking place. Electrons are being transferred from one substance to another. We can understand redox reactions better if we give oxidation and reduction the following meanings:

Oxidation is loss of electrons
Reduction is gain of electrons

Picture 3 may help you to remember this.

REDOX WITHOUT OXYGEN

Here are some examples of how the idea of electron transfer helps us to understand redox reactions.

■ Metal extraction by electrolysis

Aluminium is produced at the cathode during the electrolysis of its ore (topic J2). Aluminium ions take electrons from the cathode:

$$\text{aluminium ions} \rightarrow \text{aluminium}$$
$$Al^{3+}(l) + 3e^- \quad \rightarrow \quad Al(l)$$

Aluminium is *reduced* in this reaction because it *gains* electrons. At the same time, oxygen gas is given off at the anode:

$$O^{2-}(l) - 2e^- \rightarrow O(g)$$

then

$$2O(g) \rightarrow O_2(g)$$

Because the oxide ion, O^{2-}, loses two electrons, it is *oxidised*.

In general, **reduction always occurs at the cathode and oxidation always occurs at the anode**.

■ Displacement reactions involving metals

A more reactive metal will displace a less reactive one from its salt (topic E2). For example,

zinc + copper sulphate solution → zinc sulphate solution + copper
$$Zn(s) + \quad CuSO_4(aq) \quad \rightarrow \quad ZnSO_4(aq) \quad + \quad Cu(s)$$

The sulphate ions in this reaction are **spectator** ions (page 169). We can leave them out and rewrite the equation as follows:

$$Zn(s) + Cu^{2+}(aq) \rightarrow Cu(s) + Zn^{2+}(aq)$$

Notice what happens to zinc:

$$Zn(s) \rightarrow Zn^{2+}(aq) + 2e^-$$

It is *oxidised* because it loses electrons. These are transferred to the copper ion:

$$Cu^{2+}(aq) + 2e^- \rightarrow Cu(s)$$

The copper ion is gaining electrons and so is being *reduced*. Picture 5 summarises this. We can use this kind of electron transfer to produce a current in an electric cell. Picture 6 shows one way it can be done.

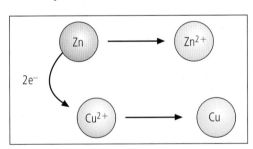

Picture 5   Electron transfer from zinc to copper ions.

Picture 4   Silver crystals can be grown in the laboratory by placing a more reactive metal than silver in a solution of silver nitrate. A redox reaction occurs, in which Ag^+ ions gain electrons and are reduced.

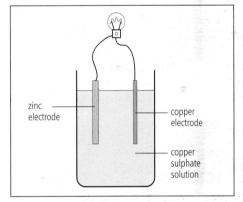

Picture 6   A simple electric cell. Electrons are transferred from zinc to copper ions down the wire, producing an electric current.

Questions

1   Each of the processes shown below involves either reduction or oxidation. Copy the equations and complete them by adding the correct number of electrons to the left or right hand side. State in each case whether reduction or oxidation takes place.

a $Na \rightarrow Na^+$ b $Pb^{2+} \rightarrow Pb$

c $Mg \rightarrow Mg^{2+}$ d $S^{2-} \rightarrow S$

e $2Br^- \rightarrow Br_2$ f $Ni \rightarrow Ni^{2+}$

g $I_2 \rightarrow 2I^-$ h $2O^{2-} \rightarrow O_2$

i $4OH^- \rightarrow O_2 + 2H_2O$ j $Fe^{3+} \rightarrow Fe^{2+}$

2   Here are some equations showing redox reactions:

a $Cu(s) + 2Ag^+(aq) \rightarrow Cu^{2+}(aq) + 2Ag(s)$

b $Mg(s) + Cu^{2+}(aq) \rightarrow Mg^{2+}(aq) + Cu(s)$

c $2Fe^{3+}(aq) + Sn^{2+}(aq)$
$\rightarrow 2Fe^{2+}(aq) + Sn^{4+}(aq)$

d $Zn(s) + 2H^+(aq) \rightarrow Zn^{2+}(aq) + H_2(g)$

e $Mg(s) + ZnSO_4(aq)$
$\rightarrow MgSO_4(aq) + Zn(s)$

f $Cu(s) + 2AgNO_3(aq)$
$\rightarrow Cu(NO_3)_2(aq) + 2Ag(s)$

Copy and complete the table opposite to show what redox changes take place in each of the reactions. The first one has been done for you:

3   Explain why. in electrolysis, reduction always occurs at the cathode, and oxidation always occurs at the anode.

4   Look closely at picture 4.

a   Identify the metal which has been placed into silver nitrate solution in the photo (look at the top of the picture).

b   Try to explain the faint blue colour of the solution in the tube. (Silver nitrate solution is colourless.)

	Reduction		Oxidation	
	from	to	from	to
a	$Ag^+(aq)$	$Ag(s)$	$Cu(s)$	$Cu^{2+}(aq)$
b				

Inside atoms

The word 'atom' means 'indivisible', but we know now that atoms can be split into smaller parts – a nucleus and electrons.

Picture 1 The Sun is too hot for atoms to exist as they do on Earth. On the Sun they are permanently split up.

Picture 2 Ernest Rutherford and J. J. Thomson, the men who started taking atoms apart.

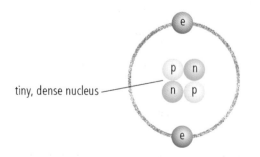

tiny, dense nucleus

■ 'Thou knowest no man can split the atom'

So said John Dalton, the man who gave us the Atomic Theory, about 200 years ago. He would have been surprised 100 years later, when scientists began to break up atoms. First they chipped off little bits, like the electrons discovered by J. J. Thomson in 1897. Then in 1919 Ernest Rutherford split nitrogen atoms by firing alpha particles at them, and after that no atom was safe.

In 1932 the neutron was discovered, and it made a very handy 'bullet' for shooting at atoms to make them split. In 1939, two Germans, Otto Hahn and Fritz Strassmann, published a paper saying they had split uranium atoms by firing neutrons at them. By the end of the year over 100 more papers had been published about this **atomic fission**, as it was called. Then suddenly all publications ceased. The Second World War had started, and governments realised that splitting the atom was more than a scientific curiosity.

Nuclear fission releases enormous amounts of energy, which is behind the destructive power of the atomic bomb. Controlled, it can be used to generate electricity in nuclear power stations.

WHAT'S IN AN ATOM?

Over 70 sub-atomic particles have now been discovered. Fortunately, only three of them are really important in deciding how materials behave. They are protons, neutrons and electrons. Picture 3 summarises the structure of the atom and the properties of protons, neutrons and electrons.

	particle	charge (relative to a proton)	mass (relative to a proton)	where found
p	proton	+1	1	in the nucleus
n	neutron	0	1	in the nucleus
e	electron	−1	1/1840	moving around outside the nucleus

Picture 3 The properties of protons, neutrons and electrons.

The nucleus at the centre is made of protons and neutrons. It is tiny, but very dense. The electrons move around outside the nucleus. They move in a random and chaotic way, but to make the picture simpler they are shown here as if they travel in 'orbits' around the nucleus.

Protons and electrons are electrically charged. Yet an atom like sodium, Na, does not have an overall electrical charge. This is because *the numbers of protons and electrons are equal*, so their charges cancel out (picture 5a). If we take away an electron, the atom becomes a positive ion, Na^+. If we add an electron, the atom has an overall negative charge: it becomes a negative ion, like Cl^- (picture 5b).

NUMBERING ATOMS

The numbers of protons, neutrons and electrons in an atom decide its properties. As far as chemists are concerned, the most important thing is the number of *electrons*. Because they are on the outside, the electrons decide how a particular atom behaves in a chemical reaction. In topics J5 and J6 we will look more closely at the way the electrons are arranged.

The number of electrons in an atom is equal to its number of protons, and this is called the **atomic number**, symbol Z. **The atomic number (symbol Z) is the number of protons in the atom**. Each element has its own unique atomic number. For example, the simplest atom, hydrogen, has just one proton and one electron, so $Z=1$. The largest naturally occurring atom, uranium, has $Z=92$: in other words, it has 92 protons and 92 electrons.

If you split an atom in two, you get two new atoms. They have different atomic numbers from the original atom, *so they are new elements*. For example, when a uranium atom splits, you get one fragment with 56 protons and another with 36. These are barium ($Z=56$) and krypton ($Z=36$).

If you look at a copy of the Periodic Table, you will see that the elements are arranged in order of increasing atomic number. You can read more about this in topic J5.

BUT WHAT ABOUT THE NEUTRONS?

■ Isotopes

Neutrons don't have any electrical charge, so they don't have to be balanced out by a particle with an opposite charge. This means you can add neutrons to an atom without altering its number of protons or electrons. So an element can have different 'versions' of its atoms. Each version has the same number of protons and electrons as all the other versions, but a different number of neutrons. These different versions, or **isotopes**, vary in mass, but they are all atoms of the same element.

Isotopes are atoms of a particular element with the same number of protons and electrons but different numbers of neutrons.

Let's look at an example – the simplest example of all, in fact. Picture 6 shows two isotopes of hydrogen. Both of them have one proton and one electron, so they both have the same chemical properties. But the second isotope has one neutron as well as the one proton in its nucleus. This makes the atom almost twice as heavy. In fact this isotope is sometimes called 'heavy hydrogen'. It is also known as deuterium.

Although it's heavier, deuterium has the same chemical properties as hydrogen. It reacts the same way, and it forms the same kind of compounds. For example, 'heavy water' contains deuterium in place of hydrogen. It has the same chemical properties as ordinary water, and you wouldn't notice the difference if

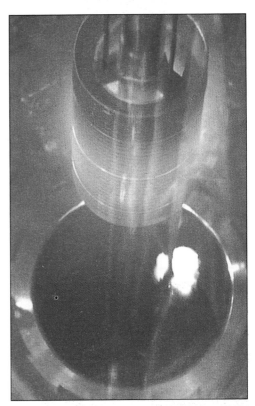

Picture 4 The blue glow from this underwater nuclear reactor is caused by the neutrons it is emitting. Neutrons make excellent 'bullets' for splitting the atom.

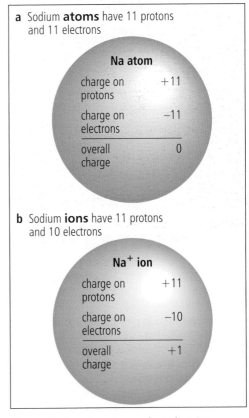

a Sodium **atoms** have 11 protons and 11 electrons

Na atom	
charge on protons	+11
charge on electrons	−11
overall charge	0

b Sodium **ions** have 11 protons and 10 electrons

Na^+ ion	
charge on protons	+11
charge on electrons	−10
overall charge	+1

Picture 5 A sodium atom and a sodium ion.

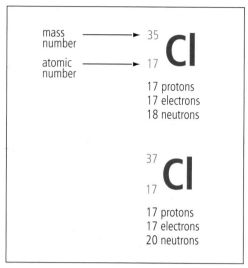

Picture 7 The atomic number and the mass number of chlorine isotopes.

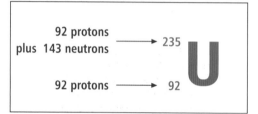

Picture 8 A uranium-235 atom.

Activity

Convincing John Dalton

Explaining an idea to another person is an excellent way of improving your own understanding, as well as theirs.

John Dalton, who produced the Atomic Theory, said 'Thou knowest no man can split the atom.' Imagine he were brought by time travel to the present. Could he be convinced he was wrong?

Work in pairs for this activity. One person will play John Dalton, the other will play themselves trying to persuade him. He would need some convincing, and would be likely to want some proof.

You will need to prepare your cases before you start. 'John Dalton' will find it useful to read Ideas about atoms on page 66. The other person will find it useful to re-read this topic.

After the activity, discuss how it went. Was 'John Dalton' convinced?

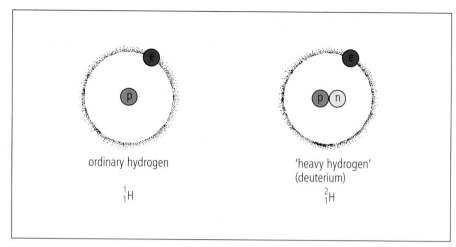

Picture 6 Two isotopes of hydrogen.

you drank it. It's just a little denser.

Isotopes of an element have the same chemical properties. They differ in a few physical properties such as density.

■ Mass number

To make it easy to tell isotopes apart, each atom is given a **mass number**, as well as its atomic number.

The mass number (symbol A) is the number of neutrons plus the number of protons.

The protons and neutrons give the atom most of its mass, because electrons weigh very little. So the mass number tells you the relative mass of the atom.

The mass number of ordinary hydrogen atoms is 1, and the mass number of 'heavy hydrogen' is 2. Picture 7 illustrates this idea for another element, chlorine. It also shows how the symbol of an element can be written with the atomic number and mass number included.

Table 1 sums up the difference between atomic number and mass number.

Table 1 Atomic number and mass number.

Atomic number, Z	Mass number, A

• Z = number of protons
    = number of electrons
	• A = number of protons
	    + number of neutrons

• Fixed for a particular element	• Varies depending on which isotope of the element it is

If we know the atomic number and mass number of an atom, we can work out the number of protons, neutrons and electrons it must contain. For example, uranium has several isotopes. The isotope that is used in nuclear reactors is uranium-235, or $^{235}_{92}$U. Like all uranium atoms, it has an atomic number of 92, so it must have 92 protons (and 92 electrons). It has a mass number of 235, which means its number of protons and neutrons together is 235. So its number of neutrons must be $(235-92) = 143$ (picture 8).

■ Isotopes everywhere

How do we know the mass number of atoms? They are much too small to weigh directly. Fortunately, a clever invention called the mass spectrometer makes it possible to find the mass of atoms indirectly.

The mass spectrometer shows that most elements have more than one isotope, and some have as many as 20. Not all of these isotopes are stable. Some are radioactive and decay into other isotopes by giving out ionising radiations. Much of the early work on radioactive isotopes was done by Marie Curie and her daughter Irene: see *Marie Curie's search for radium*, page 261 for more about this.

RELATIVE ATOMIC MASS

The relative atomic mass of an element is the mass of its atoms compared to atoms of other elements. Table 1 in the Data Section lists relative atomic masses.

But which atoms are we talking about? Most elements have more than one isotope, and different isotopes have different masses. Relative atomic mass is actually an *average* mass for all the different isotopes. It is adjusted (weighted) to take account of the proportions of the different isotopes. If a particular isotope is present in larger amounts, it makes a bigger contribution to the average.

For example, chlorine has two stable isotopes. In natural chlorine, 75% of the atoms have mass number 35, and 25% have mass number 37. The weighted average of these mass numbers is 35.5 (picture 9). This is the relative atomic mass of chlorine.

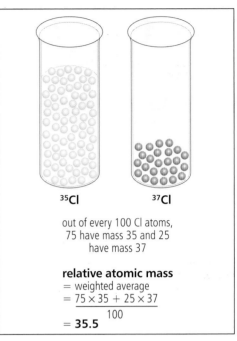

^{35}Cl ^{37}Cl

out of every 100 Cl atoms, 75 have mass 35 and 25 have mass 37

relative atomic mass
= weighted average
$$= \frac{75 \times 35 + 25 \times 37}{100}$$
$$= \mathbf{35.5}$$

Picture 9   The abundance of two isotopes of chlorine.

Questions

1 Give the words that fit in the blanks in the following. The missing words are:
negative, positive, nucleus, isotopes, equal, mass number, atomic number, electrons.

Atoms are made of three kinds of sub-atomic particles. Protons and neutrons are found in the small central part of the atom, called the __(a)__. Moving around outside are the __(b)__. Protons have one unit of __(c)__ charge, and electrons have an equal __(d)__ charge. In a neutral atom, the number of protons and electrons is __(e)__. This number is called the __(f)__. The number of protons added to the number of neutrons in an atom is called the __(g)__. Atoms with the same atomic number but different mass numbers are called __(h)__.

2 An atom of a particular element contains 13 protons, 14 neutrons and 13 electrons.
a   What is its atomic number?
b   What is its mass number?
c   Name the element (you will need to look in the Data Section) and write its symbol, including atomic number and mass number.

3 Make a copy of table 2 (right). Fill in all the blank spaces.

4 Which of the atoms in table 2 below are isotopes of the same element?

5 a   All atoms of a particular element have the same atomic number. Explain why.
b   Atoms of the same element can have different mass numbers. Explain why.

6 a   Bromine, Br, has two isotopes, with mass numbers 79 and 81. Naturally occurring bromine contains the two isotopes in equal amounts. What is the relative atomic mass of bromine?
b   Boron, B, has two stable isotopes, with mass numbers 10 and 11. Naturally occurring boron contains 20% boron-10 and 80% boron-11. What is the relative atomic mass of boron?

7 Picture 6 shows two isotopes of hydrogen. There is a third isotope, called tritium, which is unstable and radioactive. Tritium atoms contain two neutrons.
a   How many (i) protons, and (ii) electrons do tritium atoms contain?
b   What is (i) the atomic number, and (ii) the mass number of tritium?
c   What similarities and differences would you expect between tritium and ordinary hydrogen?

8 Convert table 2 into a spreadsheet. See **ICT** if you can programme your spreadsheet so that you only need to enter the number of protons and neutrons for each element. The spreadsheet should calculate everything else for you.

Table 2

Symbol	number of protons	number of neutrons	number of electrons	atomic number	mass number
$^{1}_{1}$H	1	0		1	
$^{2}_{1}$H		1		1	
$^{4}_{1}$He					
	6	6			12
$^{63}_{29}$Cu	29				
	29	36			
$^{56}_{26}$Fe					
		12	12		

Arranging electrons

The chemical properties of an atom are decided by the way electrons are arranged.

Picture 2 Filling electron shells is like filling a rack. You fill the lowest shells first.

Picture 1 Niels Bohr (right) in conversation with Albert Einstein. Perhaps Bohr is explaining the electronic structure of atoms. Einstein certainly looks pleased.

ELECTRONS IN ORBIT

Niels Bohr was a Danish scientist. He was interested in the way electrons are arranged in atoms. In 1913 he suggested a model for the electronic structure of atoms which we still use today.

Niels Bohr suggested that electrons move around the nucleus in orbits, rather like the orbits of planets around the Sun. We know now that the orbits aren't as precise and predictable as that (see picture 4), but the model is still a good one. It helps explain many of the properties of atoms.

FILLING UP THE SHELLS

The electron orbits are called **shells** – and they work a bit like a series of shelves in a rack (picture 2). Each shell can only hold a limited number of electrons. The first shell is nearest to the nucleus, and it is the first to get filled up with electrons. When it's full, the second shell starts filling. This shell is a little further away from the nucleus, and the electrons in it have more energy. When this second shell is full, the third shell starts filling, and so on. Each shell is further away from the nucleus than the previous one, and the electrons in it have more energy.

The first shell can hold just two electrons, and the second can hold eight. Let's see what happens with the three simplest elements, hydrogen (atomic number, $Z=1$), helium ($Z=2$) and lithium ($Z=3$). Hydrogen has just one electron, and that goes into the first shell. Helium has two electrons, and they both go into the first shell, which is now filled. Lithium has three electrons. Two of these fill the first shell, and the third electron goes into the second shell (picture 3).

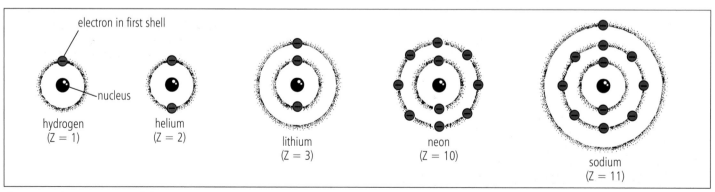

Picture 3 The arrangement of electrons in shells.

Table 1 The electronic structures of the first 20 elements.

Element	Atomic number, Z	First shell	Second shell	Third shell	Fourth shell	Summary of structure
hydrogen, H	1	•				1
helium, He	2	••				2
lithium, Li	3	••	•			2,1
beryllium, Be	4	••	••			2,2
boron, B	5	••	•••			2,3
carbon, C	6	••	••••			2,4
nitrogen, N	7	••	•••••			2,5
oxygen, O	8	••	••••••			2,6
fluorine, F	9	••	•••••••			2,7
neon, Ne	10	••	••••••••			2,8
sodium, Na	11	••	••••••••	•		2,8,1
magnesium, Mg	12	••	••••••••	••		2,8,2
aluminium, Al	13	••	••••••••	•••		2,8,3
silicon, Si	14	••	••••••••	••••		2,8,4
phosphorus, P	15	••	••••••••	•••••		2,8,5
sulphur, S	16	••	••••••••	••••••		2,8,6
chlorine, Cl	17	••	••••••••	•••••••		2,8,7
argon, Ar	18	••	••••••••	••••••••		2,8,8
potassium, K	19	••	••••••••	••••••••	•	2,8,8,1
calcium, Ca	20	••	••••••••	••••••••	••	2,8,8,2

And so it goes on. By the time you get to neon ($Z=10$), the second shell has also been filled up. After the second shell, the third shell starts filling, so sodium ($Z=11$) has one electron in the third shell. By the time we reach argon ($Z=18$) the third shell has eight electrons and is full, so after that the fourth shell begins.

Table 1 shows the electronic structures of the first 20 elements. Notice that there is a short way of summarising the electronic structure by showing the numbers of electrons in each shell. Thus sodium's structure is shown as 2,8,1. This means there are 2 in the first shell, 8 in the second and 1 in the third.

■ How do we know about electron shells?

Of course, we can't see directly how electrons are arranged. They are so small and so fast-moving that we can never say exactly where they are (picture 4). Niels Bohr had the idea of looking at the light that atoms give out, called **atomic spectra**. Picture 5 shows the atomic spectrum of hydrogen. You can see it has dark lines corresponding to some colours. Niels Bohr measured the frequencies of these lines, and used them to work out the energy levels of the electron shells.

Picture 4 Electrons move so quickly that we can never say exactly where they are — like the fast-moving blades of this fan.

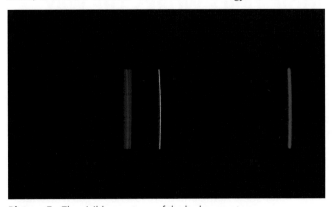

Picture 5 The visible spectrum of the hydrogen atom.

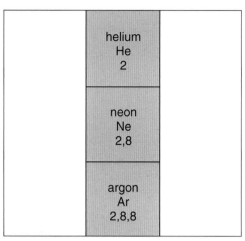

Picture 6 The first elements in group 0, showing their electronic structures.

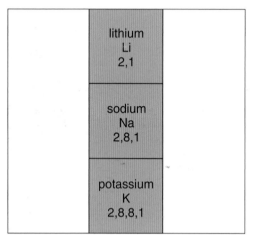

Picture 7 The first elements in group 1.

Picture 8 Caesium reacts explosively with water. Like sodium, caesium is in group 1. Caesium loses its one outer shell electron even more readily than sodium does.

ELECTRONIC STRUCTURE AND THE PERIODIC TABLE

If you look closely at the electronic structures in table 1, you will notice some interesting patterns. *Elements in the same group of the Periodic Table have the same number of electrons in their outer shell.* As far as chemical properties are concerned, the outer shell is the most important one. Chemical reactions involve changes to the numbers of outer shell electrons. Let's look at some examples.

■ Group 0: The noble gases

There are three noble gases in table 1: helium, neon and argon. We've shown them and their electronic structures in picture 6. *They all have filled outer shells of electrons.* The other members of group 0 have this structure too. Now, noble gases are very stable and unreactive – that's why they are called noble. Scientists believe that their stability comes from having a filled outer shell.

The electronic structure of a noble gas is very stable.

In fact, other atoms try to get this stable arrangement of electrons when they take part in chemical reactions. More about this later.

■ Group 1: The alkali metals

There are three alkali metals in table 1: lithium, sodium and potassium. We've shown them in picture 7. Notice the similarity: *they all have just one electron in their outer shell* – as do the other members of this group. This single electron is quite easily removed from the atom, because it is the furthest away from the nucleus.

Removing the outer electron leaves the atom with a filled outer shell. It has a stable electronic structure like the noble gas neon. Alkali metals all tend to lose an electron very easily, which makes them very reactive (picture 8). They give the electron to a non-metal such as a halogen (see below). Having lost the electron, the atom has become a positive ion. For example, sodium forms Na^+.

■ Group 7: The halogens

There are two halogens in table 1: fluorine and chlorine. Both have 7 electrons in their outer shell. This is the pattern for all members of group 7. They only need one more electron to get the stable electronic structure of a noble gas. So halogens all tend to gain an electron easily, which makes them reactive. They can gain the electron from a metal, such as an alkali metal – which tend to give them away rather easily. Having gained the extra electron, the halogen atom now has a negative charge: it has become an ion. For example, chlorine forms Cl^-.

WHY THE PERIODIC TABLE WORKS THE WAY IT DOES

When Dmitri Mendeléev made the first Periodic Table in 1869, he had no idea about electrons – they were not discovered until 1897. When he arranged the elements in groups, all he had to go on was relative atomic mass. The modern Periodic Table arranges elements in order of atomic number, but Mendeléev arranged them in order of mass. Fortunately this gives the right order, with one or two exceptions.

Now we know about the electronic structure of atoms, we can see how the Periodic Table works. *The pattern of the Periodic Table corresponds to the pattern of electron shells.* Each period corresponds to a particular electron shell. As you go across a period, the shell is being filled. At the start of each period there is an alkali metal with one electron in its outer shell. At the end there is a noble gas with a filled shell. Picture 9 illustrates the idea.

The elements in a particular group all have the same number of electrons in their outer shell. That's why they all have similar properties. They are not *identical*, though, because they have different numbers of electrons in their *inner* shells.

The number of the group tells you the number of outer shell electrons. For example, the elements in group 6 all have 6 electrons in their outer shell.

HOW DO THE ELEMENTS CHANGE AS YOU MOVE ACROSS A PERIOD?

The elements in groups 1, 2 and 3 at the beginning of the period have a small number of outer shell electrons. They tend to lose these to form positive ions (e.g. Na^+, Mg^{2+}, Al^{3+}).

The elements in groups 4 and 5 in the middle of the period have outer shells that are half full. They don't tend to form ions; instead they *share* electrons and form covalent bonds (topic J6).

The elements in groups 6 and 7 near the end of the period have outer shells that are nearly full. They tend to gain electrons and often form negative ions (e.g. S^{2-}, Cl^-).

The elements in group 0 at the end of the period have stable electronic structures. They do not gain or lose electrons, so they do not form compounds at all.

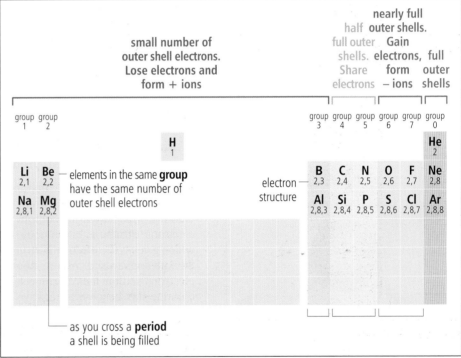

Picture 9 Electronic structure and the Periodic Table. Only the first three periods are shown.

Questions

1 Explain what the following statements mean.

a 'The electrons in an atom are arranged in shells.'

b 'The electronic structure of a sodium atom is 2,8,1.'

2 Look at table 1 on page 255.

a Find the elements beryllium, magnesium and calcium in the table. Write down the electronic structure of each.

b What do the electronic structures of all three elements have in common?

c What group of the Periodic Table are they in?

d What kind of ion would you expect them to form when they react?

3 Draw diagrams, similar to the ones in picture 3, to show the arrangement of electrons in the following atoms.

a carbon, C,   b oxygen, O,

c aluminium, Al,   d chlorine, Cl.

4 Look at the copy of the Periodic Table at the end of the Data section. How many electrons do each of the following elements have in their outer shell?

a germanium, Ge, b strontium, Sr,

c selenium, Se,   d iodine, I,

e caesium, Cs.

5 How many (i) protons and (ii) electrons are there in the following ions? Use table 1 on page 255 to help you.

a Na^+ b Cl^-

c Mg^{2+} d S^{2-}

e Al^{3+} f O^{2-}

6 a i) Write down the electronic structure of a magnesium atom, Mg.

ii) Explain why magnesium forms ions with formula Mg^{2+}, not Mg^+ or Mg^-.

b i) Write down the electronic structure of a chlorine atom, Cl.

ii) Explain why chlorine forms ions with formula Cl^-, not Cl^{2-} or Cl^+.

7 The noble gases form group 0 of the Periodic Table. What other number could this group be given? Why do you think 0 is used instead?

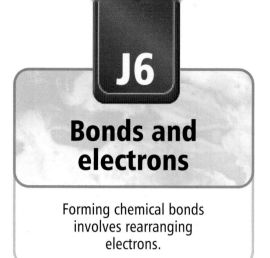

Bonds and electrons

Forming chemical bonds involves rearranging electrons.

In a molecular model like the one in picture 1, the bonds between atoms are represented by 'sticks'. But what makes the bonds in a real molecule?

For a long time chemists wondered about the answer to this question. Electrolysis provided the clue. If electricity can be used to pull atoms apart, it seems likely that electricity is holding them together in the first place.

ELECTRON SHELLS AND BONDING

Today, we believe that bonds are formed by rearranging the outer shell electrons of atoms. In this topic we will look at a simplified version of what may happen.

When atoms form bonds, they usually end up with the stable electronic structure of a noble gas.

In practice, this usually means getting eight electrons in the outer shell.

There are two types of bond. **Ionic bonds** (sometimes called electrovalent bonds) involve ions, and are formed between metals and non-metals. **Covalent bonds** involve molecules, and are formed between non-metals.

■ Ionic bonding

Ionic bonding involves transferring electrons from a metal atom to a non-metal, producing positive and negative ions.

Picture 2 shows how ionic bonding happens in sodium chloride. Sodium has one electron in its outer shell, and chlorine has seven. Sodium gives its electron to chlorine. This leaves the sodium with eight electrons in its outer shell, the same electronic structure as the noble gas neon. The chlorine has eight electrons too, which gives it the electronic structure of the noble gas argon.

So both sodium and chlorine now have stable electronic structures. Having lost an electron, sodium has become a positive ion, Na^+. Having gained an electron, chlorine has become a negative ion, Cl^-. These oppositely charged ions attract each other, and this electrical attraction is what makes an ionic bond. Many billions of ions together form a regular lattice. You can read more about ionic lattices in topic C7.

The lower part of picture 2 shows all this in a simplified way, with only the outer shells drawn. This is called a 'dot–cross' diagram, because we show the electrons from different atoms as dots and crosses. Of course, all the electrons are really identical.

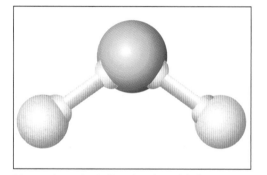

Picture 1 In this ball-and-stick model of a water molecule, the sticks represent bonds. But what are the bonds in a real molecule?

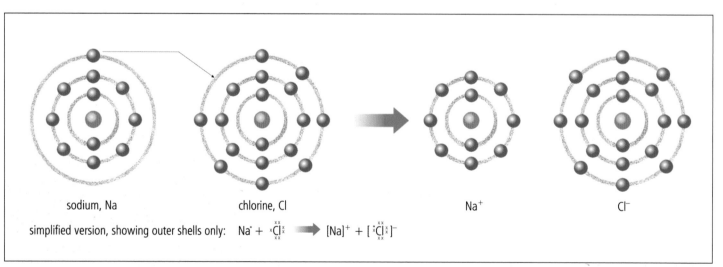

simplified version, showing outer shells only: $Na^• + {}^x_xCl^x_x \longrightarrow [Na]^+ + [{}^x_xCl^x_x]^-$

Picture 2 Forming an ionic bond between sodium and chlorine.

Calcium chloride:

$$Ca \underset{\bullet}{\bullet} + \underset{\times \times}{\overset{\times \times}{\times Cl \times}} + \underset{\times \times}{\overset{\times \times}{\times Cl \times}} \Longrightarrow [Ca]^{2+} + [\underset{\times \times}{\overset{\times \times}{\bullet Cl \times}}]^- + [\underset{\times \times}{\overset{\times \times}{\bullet Cl \times}}]^-$$

Magnesium oxide:

$$Mg \underset{\bullet}{\overset{\bullet}{\bullet}} + \underset{\times \times}{\overset{\times \times}{O \times}} \Longrightarrow [Mg]^{2+} + [\underset{\times \times}{\overset{\times \times}{\bullet O \bullet}}]^{2-}$$

Picture 3 Two examples of ionic bonding.

Picture 4 Crystals of sodium chloride. They are made up of Na^+ and Cl^- ions, held together by ionic bonding.

Picture 3 shows two more examples of ionic bonding. Notice these points.

- All the atoms form ions with eight electrons in the outer shell. This makes them stable like noble gases.
- The metals form positive ions, and the non-metals form negative ions.
- Calcium and magnesium have two electrons in their outer shell: two electrons to give away. In the case of calcium chloride, this means that two chlorines are needed. In magnesium oxide, only one oxygen is involved, because each oxygen needs two electrons to fill the outer shell. It gets both these electrons from the one magnesium atom.

■ Covalent bonding

Covalent bonding involves sharing pairs of electrons between non-metal atoms.

Non-metal atoms need only one or two electrons to get noble gas structures. When two non-metals form a bond, they can't transfer electrons from one to another, because *both* need to gain electrons. Instead, they share electrons.

Picture 5 shows how this works when chlorine atoms bond together to make a chlorine molecule, Cl_2. Each chlorine atom has seven electrons in its outer shell. Each shares one electron with the other atom. This way, both atoms get a stable outer shell of eight electrons.

The shared electrons attract the nuclei of both Cl atoms at the same time, and this is what bonds the atoms together. It's called a covalent bond. There are no ions: the atoms are bonded together as an uncharged molecule.

A covalent bond consists of a shared pair of electrons. Each of the atoms that are bonded together contributes one electron to the pair. When we show a 'stick' in a molecular model, it represents a covalent bond. When we draw a picture of a molecule, we use a line to show the bond.

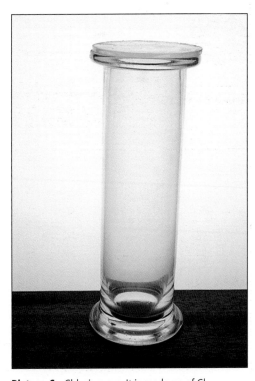

Picture 6 Chlorine gas. It is made up of Cl_2 molecules. The atoms in Cl_2 are joined together by covalent bonds.

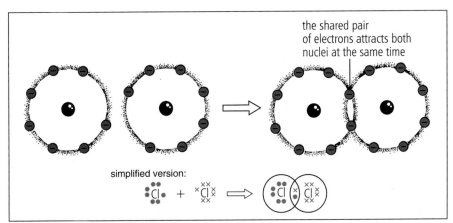

the shared pair of electrons attracts both nuclei at the same time

simplified version:

Picture 5 Forming a covalent bond between chlorine atoms (only outer shells are shown).

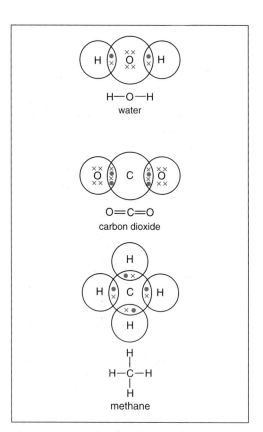

Picture 7 Examples of covalent bonding.

Substances with covalent bonding form simple molecular or giant covalent structures. You can read more about these structures in topic C6.

Picture 7 shows covalent bonding in some familiar molecules. Once again all the atoms have stable arrangements of outer-shell electrons. Notice that in carbon dioxide, the carbon shares *two* pairs of electrons with each oxygen. In other words, it is a double bond.

DRAWING DOT–CROSS DIAGRAMS

Here are the steps you need to follow when you draw a dot–cross diagram to show ionic or covalent bonds. You can practise using them in questions 4 and 5.

1 Decide how many electrons are in the outer shells of each of the atoms involved. The easiest way to tell this is from their group number in the Periodic Table.
2 Decide whether ionic or covalent bonding is involved. If the bond is between a metal and a non-metal, it will be ionic. Between two non-metals, it will be covalent.
3 If it's an ionic bond, transfer electrons from the metal to the non-metal so they both get noble gas arrangements. This usually means eight electrons in the outer shell. Draw a diagram as in picture 4.
4 If it's a covalent bond, share pairs of electrons between the non-metal atoms so they both get noble gas arrangements. Draw a diagram as in picture 7.

A word of warning. Dot–cross diagrams work for many compounds, but by no means all of them. If you take your study of chemistry further – and I hope you will – you'll discover many exceptions.

Questions

1 'Sodium chloride is held together by strong ionic bonds.' What are the bonds, and why are they strong?

2 Look at picture 1. The atoms in the model are held together by 'sticks'. What holds the atoms together in a real water molecule?

3 Humphry Davy, who did the first work on electrolysis, said 'Chemical and electrical attractions are produced by the same cause.' What did he mean? What name do we use today for 'chemical attractions'?

4 Look at the diagram for the bonding in a molecule of water in picture 7.
   a Why are two H atoms needed for each O atom?
   b What noble gas structure do (i) the H atoms, (ii) the O atoms have?

   c Atoms usually end up with eight outer shell electrons when they form bonds. Why does the H atom only end up with two?

5 Draw dot–cross diagrams to show the bonding in each of the following ionic compounds.
   a potassium fluoride, KF,
   b lithium oxide, Li_2O,
   c magnesium sulphide, MgS,
   d sodium sulphide, Na_2S,
   e aluminium fluoride, AlF_3.

6 Draw dot–cross diagrams to show the bonding in each of the following covalent substances.
   a hydrogen chloride, HCl,
   b ammonia, NH_3,
   c carbon tetrachloride, CCl_4,
   d phosphorous trifluoride, PF_3,
   e nitrogen, N_2.

Ernest Rutherford's big surprise

'It was quite the most incredible event that has ever happened to me in my life. It was almost as incredible as if you fired a 15-inch shell at a piece of tissue and it came back and hit you.'

So said Ernest Rutherford in 1909. He had just heard the results of an experiment done by two of his colleagues at Manchester University. They had fired alpha particles at a thin metal foil, using the apparatus shown in picture 1. Alpha particles are tiny, positively charged particles and they were using them as minute bullets.

They had expected all the alpha particles to go straight through the very thin foil. Picture 2 shows why they expected this. At that time, scientists believed that atoms consisted of tiny electrons stuck into a kind of blob of positive charge. The electrons are too tiny to deflect the alpha particles, which should shoot straight through the blob-like atom.

Ernest Rutherford's big surprise was that some of the alpha particles

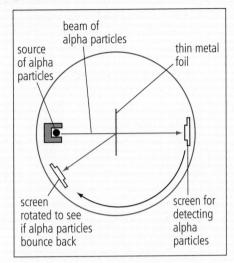

Picture 1 The alpha particle and foil experiment.

bounced back from the foil! Most of them went straight through, but about 1 in 10 000 bounced back. They must have collided with something inside the atoms. Rutherford, and all the other scientists, had to rethink their ideas about the structure of atoms.

1 Why did most of the alpha particles go straight through the foil, but some of them bounce back? You may need to look at picture 3 on page 250 to remind yourself of our modern idea of the structure of the atom.

2 Draw a picture, similar to picture 2 on this page, to explain what happened.

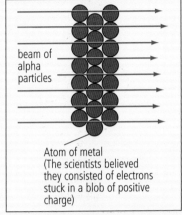

Picture 2 What the scientists expected to happen. They thought the alpha particles would pass straight through the atoms.

Marie Curie's search for radium

Marie Curie's interest was aroused when Henri Becquerel discovered radioactivity in uranium. She studied an ore of uranium called pitchblende, and she noticed something very interesting. *It was more radioactive than uranium itself.* She decided that there was only one explanation: there must be something in the pitchblende that was *more radioactive than uranium*.

So, with her husband Pierre, she set about looking for this highly radioactive substance. It was like searching for a needle in a haystack, and it took four years. They began work in 1898, when the Austrian government donated a tonne of pitchblende. They worked in a dilapidated shack with a leaking roof, patiently purifying the pitchblende to isolate the mystery substance. In 1902 the work was complete. All that was left of the tonne of pitchblende was a

fraction of a gram of a highly radioactive element which they named radium.

Marie Curie continued her work with radioactive elements, and was awarded two Nobel prizes. Her old shack was demolished, and a palatial laboratory, the Radium Institute, was built in Paris for her to work in. Her daughter Irene continued the work, and discovered many new radioactive isotopes. She too received the Nobel prize.

1 What made Marie Curie start searching for radium in pitchblende?

2 Why did it take so long to get pure radium from pitchblende?

3 Find radium, Ra, on the Periodic Table at the end of the Data Section. Which other element do you think it would be most similar to?

4 During the First World War, Marie Curie developed mobile

radiography units to help treat the wounded. What is radiography, and what has it to do with Marie Curie's scientific work?

Picture 1 Marie Curie and her daughter Irene in 1925.

Earth

The dynamic Earth

The Earth has its own energy source. Deep inside it is active and its crust is continually changing.

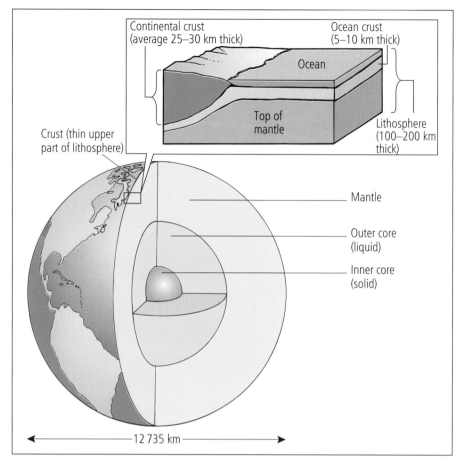

Picture 1 The layered structure of the Earth.

Picture 2 Cornish tin miners working underground.

PEELING BACK THE LAYERS

The Earth has a layered structure. We live on the topmost layer – the **crust** – which is made of solid rock. Compared with the Earth as a whole, the crust is thinner than the skin on an apple. At most it is 70 km thick beneath high mountains in the continental crust. Compare this with the diameter of the Earth which is about 12 735 km.

The crust is made from two layers, a lighter, thicker layer which makes up the continents and a heavier, thinner layer which goes underneath the continents and makes up the ocean floors. You can see these two layers in picture 1. The **oceanic crust** is made mainly of basalt and the upper **continental crust** has a high proportion of granite rocks. You can find out more about these in topic K3.

The temperature of the rocks increases with depth. Deep mines are often uncomfortably hot – picture 2 shows two miners working down a mine in Cornwall. They are 1.5 km beneath the surface where the temperature is around 36 °C. South African gold mines are even deeper and therefore hotter. They are up to 3 km deep and with temperatures approaching 50 °C. Beneath the crust lies the **mantle**, which is so hot (over 1000 °C) that the rocks soften in places and are probably the consistency of stiff Plasticine.

The core is white hot, about 4300 °C. The core is believed to be composed mainly of iron and nickel. At the surface of the Earth, both of these metals would boil at this temperature. Iron boils at 3000 °C, and nickel at 2900 °C, so why isn't the core a gas? The answer is *pressure*. The pressure due to the weight of the rocks around the core is so great that the centre of the core is forced to be a solid. The outer section of the core is at a lower pressure and is liquid.

Why is the inside of the Earth so hot?

One of the reasons that the deep interior of the Earth is so hot is that the Earth formed at a very high temperature. Because the inside is insulated by the outer layers some of this original thermal energy is still 'trapped' inside.

Also, some of the 92 elements of the Earth are unstable. They are the **radioactive** elements. The nuclei of such elements (mainly uranium, thorium and potassium) break up, giving out energy as they change into smaller nuclei. These elements are, in fact, quite rare, but the Earth is so large that it contains enough of them to produce huge quantities of energy. Some of these elements are found in crustal rocks.

This energy keeps the Earth hot inside, and every day 2.5 billion billion joules (or 2.5 exajoules) of energy escape from the Earth's surface and heat the air. This is about four times as much as the energy used by all the people on the Earth.

From heating energy to movement energy

Energy flows from the hottest part of the Earth, the core, outwards to the surface. This energy travels in two ways; by **conduction** and by **convection.**

When fluids are heated, they can move in warm currents that circulate through the fluid. These are called **convection currents.** The rocks in the mantle are only semi-solid, like Plasticine or very thick custard, so convection currents can circulate through it. These convection currents are very slow and sluggish, but their effect, nonetheless, is very dramatic. They shape the whole structure of the Earth's crust from the depths of the oceans to the high mountain ranges.

Look at picture 4. The convection currents rise through the mantle and reach the crust in the middle of the oceans. Here, hot **magma** (molten rock) bursts through the surface in underwater volcanoes. This magma solidifies to make new ocean crust – a line of towering underwater mountains running along the centre of the oceans. This is called a **mid-ocean ridge**.

The very top of the mantle and the crust form a firm rigid layer around the Earth called the **lithosphere**. The lithosphere is at least 100 km thick and 'floats' on top of the semi-solid mantle. So, as the convection currents move horizontally outwards from the mid-ocean ridge, the slabs of lithosphere move along too. New

Picture 3 The extinct volcanoes from which diamonds come are the deepest in the world. Molten rock was spewed up from a depth of 150 km. As well as diamonds, these volcanoes brought up chunks of the material from which the mantle is made.

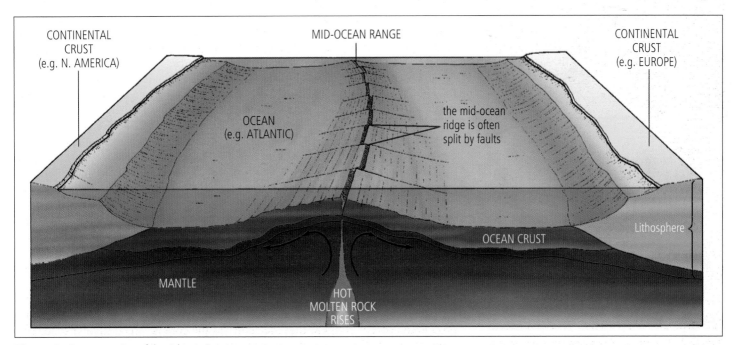

Picture 4 A cross-section of the Atlantic Ocean.

CONTINENTAL CRUST (e.g. N. AMERICA)

MID-OCEAN RANGE

CONTINENTAL CRUST (e.g. EUROPE)

OCEAN (e.g. ATLANTIC)

the mid-ocean ridge is often split by faults

MANTLE

HOT MOLTEN ROCK RISES

OCEAN CRUST

Lithosphere

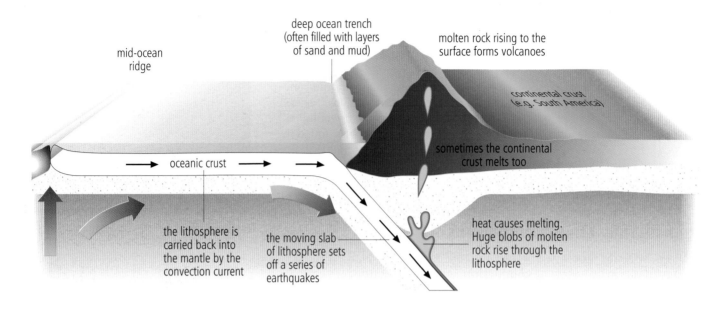

Labels on diagram:
- mid-ocean ridge
- deep ocean trench (often filled with layers of sand and mud)
- molten rock rising to the surface forms volcanoes
- continental crust (e.g. South America)
- oceanic crust
- sometimes the continental crust melts too
- the lithosphere is carried back into the mantle by the convection current
- the moving slab of lithosphere sets off a series of earthquakes
- heat causes melting. Huge blobs of molten rock rise through the lithosphere

Picture 5 The shrinking Pacific Ocean.

ocean crust is being made all the time from the mid-ocean ridges. Therefore, these slabs, or plates, are growing larger all the time. This causes the plates with the continents to move further apart. The effect is known as **sea-floor spreading**. It explains why the Atlantic Ocean is widening in this way by about four centimetres every year.

■ If the oceans are growing, why isn't the Earth getting bigger?

What goes up must come down. This saying applies to convection currents as well as to apples and rockets. At the edges of some oceans, the convection currents dive back down into the mantle. (This is because the material has cooled and is now denser.) Picture 5 shows a section across the Pacific Ocean. You can see that where the convection currents move downwards next to the continents, they are dragging some of the ocean crust down with them. This is called a **subduction zone**.

Old ocean crust is being re-cycled back into the mantle at the boundaries with the continents. So while the Atlantic Ocean is widening, the Pacific Ocean is very slowly shrinking. The Earth isn't getting any bigger or any smaller: it's in balance.

It is possible, after many millions of years for an ocean to close up altogether. Both continents in picture 6 have subduction zones dipping beneath them. The ocean in between gradually closes and the continents collide, forcing rocks to buckle and fold upwards into mountains. This is how the Himalayas were formed. India's continental crust is still moving northwards to create mountains like Everest.

PLATE TECTONICS

We have seen that the Earth's crust is divided into sections. These sections are called **plates**. Some plates have continents riding on top of them. They all fit together into a spherical jigsaw. Sometimes plates are destroyed; sometimes new plates are made. The plates move about the globe, driven by the convection currents within the mantle. All these processes happen very slowly, over many millions of years. The movements of these plates, and the things that go on at their boundaries, are called **plate tectonics**. Picture 7 shows the position of these plates today.

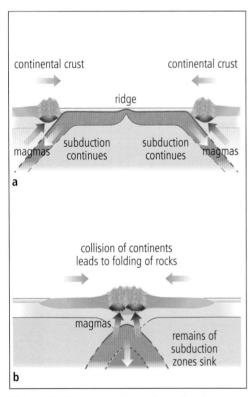

Labels on diagram a:
- continental crust
- continental crust
- ridge
- subduction continues
- subduction continues
- magmas
- magmas
- a

Labels on diagram b:
- collision of continents leads to folding of rocks
- magmas
- remains of subduction zones sink
- b

Picture 6 How mountains are formed during continental collision.

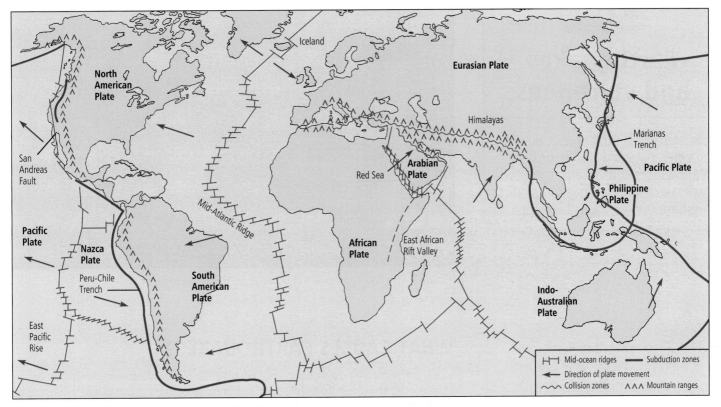

Picture 7 The Earth's plates, showing the position of the continents.

Questions

1 Write a couple of paragraphs to explain plate tectonics to your English teacher. Assume he/she has no scientific knowledge. Use a diagram to help.

2 Give the words that fit in the spaces labelled (a) to (r)

a The Earth has a __(a)__ structure. The centre of the core is hotter; the outer part of the core is __(b)__. The core is composed mainly of the elements __(c)__ and __(d)__. Between the core and the crust is the __(e)__ which is made of semi-solid rock. There are two kinds of crust, __(f)__ crust 'floats' on top of __(g)__ crust.

b The crust and the top rigid part of the mantle are called the __(h)__. The lithosphere is broken up into irregular segments called __(i)__. Thermal energy travels through the mantle in __(j)__ currents. These currents reach the crust in the middle of the __(k)__ at the __(l)__ ocean __(m)__. Here, hot molten rock rises to make new oceanic crust. The ocean crust and top rigid part of the mantle (the lithosphere) float on top of the __(n)__ and travel along the tops of the __(o)__ currents. At the edges of some oceans the ocean crust follows the __(p)__ current downwards, back into the __(q)__ This is called a __(r)__ zone.

Earthquakes and volcanoes

Scientists still can't predict exactly **when** natural disasters such as earthquakes and volcanic eruptions will take place. But they can predict **where** they are likely to happen.

Picture 1 The 1995 earthquake in Kobe, Japan, toppled large buildings.

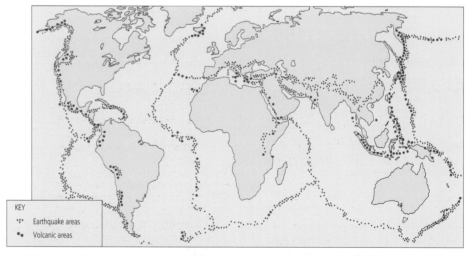

Epicentre – the point on the earth's crust directly above the focus

Focus – the point at which the earthquake actually happens

Picture 3 The focus and epicentre of an earthquake.

WHAT CAUSES EARTHQUAKES?

Look at picture 2. Compare the occurrence of earthquakes with the plate boundaries shown in picture 7, on the previous page. You can see clearly that earthquakes occur at the boundaries of the tectonic plates. Japan suffers from earthquakes because it is situated at the boundary between the Pacific Plate and the Eurasian Plate.

Earthquakes are caused by the movement of rocks in the lithosphere. As the plates of the Earth move about, rocks are put under immense pressure. Eventually the stress becomes so great that the rocks snap along a fault line. As the rocks break, energy is released as shock waves. These shock waves radiate outwards. They travel through and around the Earth and create the shaking effect that causes the damage.

The point at which the earthquake happens (where the rocks snap) inside the Earth is called the **focus** (picture 3). The point immediately above the focus, on the surface, is called the **epicentre**. It is at the epicentre that the damage is usually greatest.

KEY
Earthquake areas
Volcanic areas

Picture 2 This map shows where earthquakes and volcanoes occur worldwide.

VOLCANOES

Volcanoes are fascinating and breathtaking, but violent and dangerous. They may lie quiet for years and then suddenly erupt. They pour out molten rock (**lava**), ash or poisonous gases such as sulphur dioxide. All these products are formed because of melting in the mantle or in the crust. There are three locations where volcanoes are likely to occur on the Earth.

■ 1 At mid-ocean ridges

The rising convection current in the mantle causes the upper mantle rocks to melt. Molten rock is less dense than solid rock, so it rises. Iceland (picture 5) is on the Mid-Atlantic Ridge and is made entirely from solidified lava. The lava is basalt (see page 271) which is very runny, so it flows a long way and solidifies into wide, gently sloping sheets.

■ 2 At the 'ring of fire' – subduction zones

Volcanoes are common all around the edges of the Pacific Ocean. It has become known as the Ring of Fire. As the oceanic plate dives down into the mantle it starts to melt. Rocks in the lower part of the crust may start to melt too, and molten material rises towards the surface. These volcanoes tend to erupt much stickier, less fluid lava and clouds of ash and gases. The sticky lava makes it difficult for the gases to escape. Gas pressure builds up, causing explosive eruptions that cause more loss of life and damage to property.

■ 3 Hot spots

Some volcanoes, such as the island of Hawaii, occur in the middle of plates. They occur because they are above 'hot spots' in the mantle. Mushroom-shaped plumes of hot rock rise deep in the mantle and melt the rocks above – either in the upper part of the mantle or in the crust.

■ Ancient volcanoes

You may never have seen a 'live' volcano, but Britain has lots of 'dead' ones. Many landscape features are formed from ancient volcanoes (picture 6).

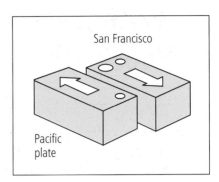

Picture 4 (a) The San Francisco earthquake, October 1989 (left).
(b) The cause of the San Francisco earthquake: the Pacific Plate sliding northwards and tearing against North America.

Picture 5 The eruption of an Icelandic volcano.

Picture 6 A volcanic 'neck' in France. The outer cone of this ancient volcano has worn away, leaving only the solidified lava in the central pipe.

Questions

1 Copy or trace picture 2 on page 268. Then, using picture 7 on page 267, which shows the different plates, label the volcanoes according to their type.

2 Explain each of the following terms: lava, epicentre, focus.

3 'All volcanoes are equally dangerous.' Do you think this is true? Explain your answer.

4 Why do earthquakes and volcanoes often occur in the same places?

5 a Suggest why there are no actual volcanoes, and very few earthquakes, in Great Britain.

  b Suggest a possible reason why there were large volcanoes in Britain many millions of years ago.

6 There are many earthquake monitoring sites on the Internet. **ICT** Use one of these sites to find out whether any earthquakes (big or small) have been going on anywhere recently.

Rocks and the rock cycle

Wherever you are you are unlikely to find yourself very far from rock – even if you don't know it.

Picture 1 Granite blocks in an ancient wall.

The wall in picture 1 contains granite blocks. You can see the crystals in the granite. The overall speckled effect shows that it's made of more than one **mineral**.

The statue in picture 2 is made from limestone. You can often see the remains of living creatures in it – fragments of sea shell that have become **fossilised**, that is, preserved in rock. It is just possible to see individual grains with the naked eye; they all appear to be made of the same mineral. Parts of the stone look worn or **weathered**.

Many houses are roofed with slate (picture 3). Slate has been popular for roofing since the middle of the nineteenth century. It can be split, or **cleaved** very easily into thin sheets. It is usually dark in colour – from purplish grey to green – and it is hard and smooth. You can't see individual grains or crystals in it.

■ Why are rocks so different?

The three rocks in pictures 1 to 3 were formed in three different ways.

Granite is a type of **igneous** rock. Igneous rocks have solidified from molten rock either in volcanoes, or inside the Earth's crust.

Limestone is a **sedimentary** rock. These rocks are usually laid down under water as a **sediment**. Sedimentary rocks are made from fragments worn away from older rocks, or from the remains of living organisms.

Slate is a type of **metamorphic** rock. The word 'metamorphic' comes from the Greek – *meta* meaning change, and *morphe* meaing shape. These rocks have been changed by heat or pressure, or by a combination of both. They could originally have been either igneous or sedimentary.

Picture 2 A limestone statue.

Picture 3 Slate roofs.

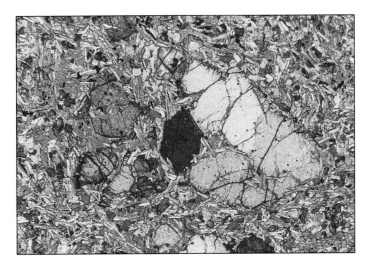

Picture 4 (a) Basalt. (b) Basalt seen through a microscope showing different minerals.

IGNEOUS ROCKS

Igneous rocks are formed when molten rock, called **magma**, cools and solidifies. Nearly all igneous rocks are formed of *crystals*. The crystals grow as the molten rock cools. The more slowly the rock cools, the bigger the crystals grow. You can see the crystals in the granite in picture 5. Notice that the crystals are *interlocking*.

Molten rock is less dense than solid rock, and so it tends to rise very slowly towards the surface of the Earth. If the molten magma reaches the Earth's surface and is erupted from a volcano, it is called **lava**. When the lava cools and solidifies it becomes rock. **Basalt**, a smooth black rock, is the most common type of lava (picture 4(a)). There are many less common types of lava, and sometimes volcanoes throw out ash (see topic K2). Rocks formed by eruption from volcanoes are called **extrusive** igneous rocks.

With the naked eye, basalt looks smooth and black. But under the microscope, crystals of several different minerals can be seen. These are different kinds of **silicate** minerals. Picture 4(b) was taken through a special microscope which uses polarised light. This gives some of the minerals bright colours which makes them easier to see.

Sometimes magma contains dissolved gases. When the magma reaches the surface, where the pressure is lower, the gases come out of solution to form gas bubbles. You can see the same effect when you open a bottle of fizzy drink. When the lava cools, the bubbles are preserved in the rock. **Pumice** is a type of lava with more gas bubbles than rock. If you've used pumice stone in the bath, you'll know it can float.

Very often magma gets trapped inside the crust and never reaches the surface. Rocks formed from this kind of magma are called **intrusive** igneous rocks. Because the magma is insulated by the surrounding rocks, it takes a very long time to cool – sometimes millions of years.

Granite is probably the most common intrusive igneous rock. It is different from basalt in that it cools very slowly from molten magma deep in the Earth's crust. Because it takes a long time to cool, the crystals have longer to grow, so they are larger. They are easy to see with the naked eye and are much lighter in colour than basalt (picture 5).

Many of the sea cliffs and high moors in Cornwall are made from granite. It has resisted weathering and erosion for many millions of years.

The size of crystals in an igneous rock gives us clues about how the rock was formed (table 1).

Picture 5 Granite.

Table 1 The size of rock crystals gives us clues about how the rock formed.

Large crystals
- Formed by molten rock which cooled slowly
- Usually intrusive
- E.g. granite

Small crystals
- Formed by molten rock which cooled quickly
- Usually extrusive
- E.g. basalt.

Picture 6 Layers of sedimentary rock, Burton Bradstock, Dorset.

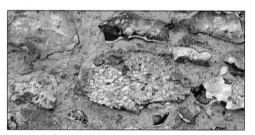

(a) Conglomerate.

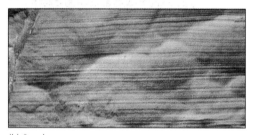

(b) Sandstone.

(c) Mudstone.

(d) Shale.

Picture 7

SEDIMENTARY ROCKS

One way to think of sedimentary rocks is as 'second-hand' rocks. They are made up either of fragments of older rocks or from the remains of living organisms.

Sedimentary rocks often occur in layers, or **beds**. The older rocks are in the lower layers. Picture 6 shows the cliffs at Burton Bradstock in Dorset. These cliffs are made of beds of sandstone which were laid down in the sea about 190 million years ago. Most sedimentary rocks are laid down in the sea, but they may also form in rivers, lakes, and even in deserts.

■ Sedimentary rocks from particles or fragments

Even the hardest rock will start to crumble and weather as thousands of years go by. Fragments of rock fall down hillsides due to gravity, or get washed down by rain. Rivers will carry the fragments down into deltas, lakes, or the sea. Waves beat against cliffs and knock fragments away. (More about this **weathering** and **erosion** is in topic K4.)

Look again at picture 6. You can see where the cliff has fallen to make a pile of boulders on the beach. The action of the waves will eventually break them up into pebbles and sand. These pebbles and sand could become the sedimentary rocks of the future.

Sedimentary rocks are named according to the size of the fragments that they're made of. A rock made of pebbles is called a **conglomerate** (sometimes called a 'pudding stone' because it looks a bit like an old-fashioned steamed plum pudding). A rock made of sand is called simply a **sandstone**. A rock made of fine mud is usually called a **mudstone**, but if it's flaky and breaks easily into layers, it's called a **shale**. Some of these rocks are shown in picture 7.

Conglomerates and sandstones are made mainly of fragments of the hard, resistant mineral **quartz**. In many cases this will have been weathered from granite. Quartz is one of the commonest minerals found in rocks. Quartz comes in many colours, from transparent bright purple (amethyst) to opaque grey or brown flint. This can make it tricky to identify.

Mudstones and shales are made from clay minerals. These vary in colour from creamy white, to reddish brown, grey, and black. The individual grains are too small to be seen even with a hand lens.

HOW DO SAND, PEBBLES AND MUD TURN INTO ROCK?

There are two ways that loose sediment can be turned into rock. First, as more sediment accumulates on top, everything gets squashed and compressed into rock. Second, other minerals sometimes seep between the fragments in the rock, and 'glue' them together. You can see this in the conglomerate in picture 7(a). The spaces between the pebbles are filled with brown quartz.

ORGANIC SEDIMENTARY ROCKS

Most limestones are made of the shells and skeletons of organisms that lived in the water. Sometimes the shells are so small, or broken up into such small fragments, that you can't see them with the naked eye, or even with a hand lens.

Shells and skeletons are almost always made of calcium carbonate, so limestone is made of calcium carbonate too.

Some limestones are formed chemically when calcium carbonate precipitates out of a solution. The solution of calcium carbonate could be in sea water, in lake water, or in a hot spring. Picture 8 shows a chemical limestone, called travertine. It's used as an ornamental stone on the front of shops.

The limestone in picture 2 is a mixture of a chemical limestone and shells. It was formed, around 100 million years ago, in very warm tropical seas.

Evaporites are another group of sedimentary rocks. They are formed by the evaporation of sea water, leaving behind a mixture of salts.

FOSSILS

Normally when an animal dies, the soft parts of its body decay, leaving only the hard parts, such as the bones and teeth. Given enough time even a bone will decay completely, but occasionally something else happens. As the organic matter decays, the bone becomes full of tiny holes and spaces. If the bone is buried in mud, the mineral particles work their way into it and gradually replace it. As a result, the bone becomes rock-hard and turns into a **fossil** (picture 9).

Fossils are common in sedimentary rocks. They give scientists useful clues about the way life evolved on Earth.

METAMORPHIC ROCKS

Rocks may be changed or **metamorphosed** in two ways: by heat alone or, more usually, by a combination of heat and pressure. In both cases, the solid rock gradually changes, without melting. New minerals form in the rocks. The texture of the rocks is changed too, and any fossils in sedimentary rocks are often obliterated.

■ Heat only

When lava spills out of a volcano onto older rocks, the older rocks get hot, and literally 'cook'. When intrusive igneous rocks get trapped inside the crust they heat the rocks around them. This time the 'cooking' effect is longer and slower, but more pronounced (see picture 10).

The heat of the magma tends to make the surrounding rocks harder. The grains in sandstones stick together tightly and form a hard, sugary-looking rock. Limestone changes to a sugary-looking rock too – marble. Mudstones and shales turn into hard splintery rocks at high temperatures, but at lower temperatures they develop spots – a sort of geological heat-rash!

■ Heat and pressure

The most common types of metamorphic rock are formed by heat *and* pressure deep in the crust at subduction zones or collision zones. (See topic K1, pictures 5 and 6. Look at them again before you read on.)

Picture 8 Travertine is often used on the facing of shop fronts, particularly Macdonald's.

Picture 9 This sea scorpion became fossilised in sedimentary rocks about 400 million years ago.

Picture 10 Metamorphic rocks being formed by heating.

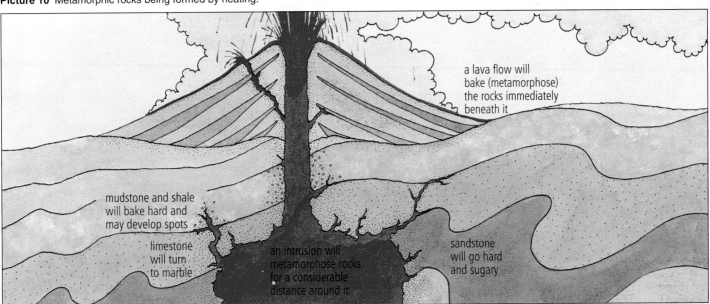

a lava flow will bake (metamorphose) the rocks immediately beneath it

mudstone and shale will bake hard and may develop spots

limestone will turn to marble

an intrusion will metamorphose rocks for a considerable distance around it

sandstone will go hard and sugary

Slate is one of the commonest rocks formed in this way. It is a metamorphosed mudstone or shale. Slate can be split very easily along **cleavage** planes. The cleavage is caused by the effect of pressure.

Limestone will also turn into marble under the effects of heat and pressure. Most limestone is impure. It is these impurities that form the coloured bands and swirling patterns that make marble so attractive.

ROCK DETECTIVE WORK

Table 1 gives you some clues to help you decide whether a rock is igneous, sedimentary or metamorphic.

Table 1 Clues to rock types.

Igneous rocks	Sedimentary rocks	Metamorphic rocks
■ have no fossils, ■ have an interlocking crystalline structure, ■ are likely to be hard.	■ may have layers (bedding) visible, ■ will have separate grains (not interlocked), ■ may be quite soft (you may be able to rub grains off), ■ may have fossils, ■ if calcium carbonate is present, will fizz with dilute HCl.	■ may be able to be split along a cleavage plane, ■ may be banded or streaked, ■ may be hard, ■ may have sparkling mica flakes, aligned in streaks or layers, ■ may have a 'sugary' texture, or be noticeably crystalline, ■ if marble, will fizz with dilute HCl.

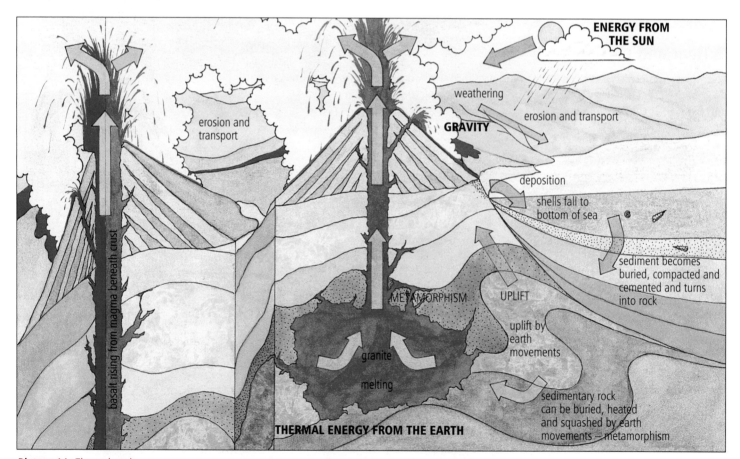

Picture 11 The rock cycle.

THE ROCK CYCLE

We've already seen that older rocks can be worn away to provide fragments to make newer sedimentary rocks. We've seen how rocks can be changed by heat and pressure into metamorphic rocks. In fact if rocks get heated enough (to about 700 °C to 800 °C), they can melt to form an igneous magma. So, one kind of rock can be re-cycled to form another type.

Look at picture 11 on the previous page. If you follow the arrows from the top of the volcano in the foreground, you can see igneous rock being formed from magma, then eroded. The fragments are deposited in the sea as sediment. The sediments harden into rock, and can then be buried and metamorphosed. The metamorphic rock may get so hot as to melt and form magma which will cool to form igneous rock. Then the cycle can start all over again. There are many other ways around the **rock cycle**. A summary of the rock cycle is shown in picture 12.

In the next topic, K4, we'll learn more about how rocks weather and about erosion and transport.

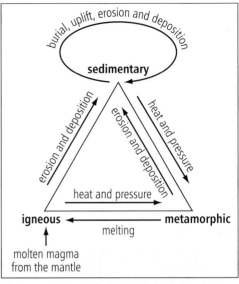

Picture 12 A simplified view of the rock cycle.

Activities

A Looking at gravestones

Work in groups. Make a study of your local graveyard. Try to identify the rocks the gravestones are made of, or at least if they are igneous, sedimentary or metamorphic. Don't try to use acid or damage the stones in any way – treat the graveyard with respect. Note the date on each stone. Look for signs of weathering – give each stone a score of one to ten for its state of preservation. Try to decide which rocks are least resistant to weathering.

B The matchstick/cleavage analogy

Empty a box of matches onto a table, with the matches pointing in all different directions. Then push the matchsticks. The matchsticks will tend to line up at right angles to the direction in which they're being pushed. The same thing happens to the minerals in slate – tiny flakes of mica (too small to be seen with the naked eye) align themselves at right angles to the pressure in the Earth's crust. These lines of mica flakes form lines of weakness in the rock – the cleavage planes (see picture 13).

Picture 13

Questions

1 Classify the following as igneous, sedimentary or metamorphic rocks:

limestone, basalt, slate, conglomerate, marble, sandstone, granite, mudstone, shale.

2 Picture 14 shows a rock which is used as a facing stone in many high streets. It's called **blue pearl larvikite** and comes from Norway. Is it igneous, sedimentary or metamorphic? Say why you have made your choice.

3 Picture 15 shows a rock from the North Pennines. It fizzes when put in hydrochloric acid. Can you suggest what it might be? Write down as much evidence as you can for your answer.

4 Look at picture 6. Which process in the rock cycle do you see taking place? What evidence can you see that some of the beds of rock in the cliff might be harder than others?

5 Look at pictures 5, 6 and 7 in topic K1. Which sort of plate boundaries are likely to produce: (a) basaltic rocks, (b) granitic rocks?

Picture 14

Picture 15

Shaping the landscape

We think of the landscape as unchanging. But it is slowly and continually being re-shaped.

Picture 1 A faulted landscape.

PUSHING AND PULLING – HOW THE BASIC SHAPES ARE FORMED

Topics K1 and K2 explain how the crust of the Earth is divided into plates. These plates move the lithosphere about, pushing together in some places and tearing apart in others. Volcanoes erupt lava and ash, and can build up into high mountains. Sometimes the rocks in the crust snap, causing earthquakes, and leaving behind cracks or **faults** (picture 1).

Sometimes the rocks don't fault – they bend. Sudden forces tend to cause faults, but forces that act slowly can cause gradual bending. If the rocks in the crust are pushed slowly they bend and form **folds** (picture 2). This can happen when two plates push together and collide (look back to picture 6, page 266).

About 50 million years ago, Africa started to move towards Europe. The rocks were compressed and folded into a mountain chain – the Alps. The ripples spread many hundreds of miles away, as far away as the south of England (see picture 3). The upward, humped shaped fold is called an **anticline** and the downward, basin-shaped fold is called a **syncline**. The top of the anticline cracked, and the rocks wore away along the line of weakness. This has left lines of chalk hills (called **escarpments**) which form the North and South Downs. The line of chalk hills formed by the northern limb of the syncline forms the Chiltern Hills.

Picture 2 A folded landscape.

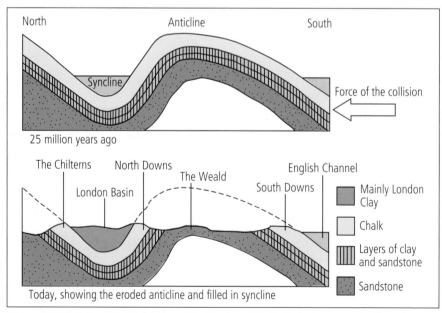

Picture 3 The hills of the Chilterns and the North and South Downs were pushed into shape at the time the Alps were formed.

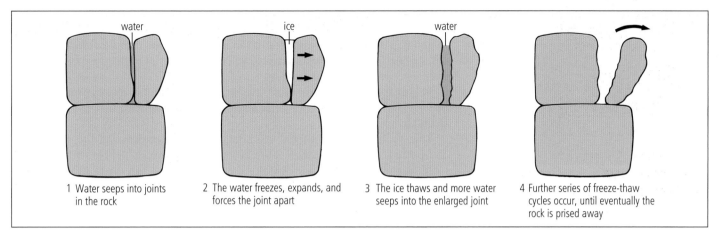

1 Water seeps into joints in the rock

2 The water freezes, expands, and forces the joint apart

3 The ice thaws and more water seeps into the enlarged joint

4 Further series of freeze-thaw cycles occur, until eventually the rock is prised away

Picture 4   Frost shattering.

The energy that produces folding and faulting comes from within the Earth. It comes from the internal energy of the Earth which drives the convection currents in the mantle, which in turn drive the movements of the tectonic plates.

WEATHERING AND EROSION

When rocks are exposed to the weather – to wind, rain and frost – they will start to disintegrate and crumble. This is called **weathering**. There are three main types of weathering. They often act together, rather than by themselves.

■ Physical weathering

This is the loosening of fragments of rock by physical means. There are two important ways that this can happen:

a   Some rocks absorb water. If water absorbed in a rock freezes, it expands and pushes the grains of rock apart. When the rock warms up again, the ice will melt. Picture 4 shows what will happen if this freezing and thawing is repeated time and time again in a jointed rock.

b   The minerals that make up a rock will expand at different rates on heating and contract again on cooling. If this happens time and time again – for example heating up during the day and cooling at night, for months and years on end – the resulting stresses will cause the rock to crack.

■ Chemical weathering

This can happen in two ways. First, the minerals which compose the rock can break down and change. Often they change into clay which is then easily washed away by rain. Picture 5 shows a china clay pit in Cornwall. In the hot wet climate of the past, the feldspar in the granite reacted with warm water to form clay.

Second, some minerals will react with **impurities** dissolved in rainwater. Rainwater is often slightly acidic and so will react with limestone. (See topic D2.)

■ Biological weathering

Plants and animals can cause rocks to break up. Roots can be very forceful in exploiting any weaknesses in the rock as the photograph in picture 7 shows.

Biological weathering is important in the formation of soil. Weathered rock fragments form the basis of all soils.

Picture 5   A china clay tip in Cornwall.

Picture 6   Rievaulx Abbey, North Yorkshire. Weathering has made the stone crumble.

Picture 7 Tree roots splitting rocks.

Picture 8 A pothole in the bed of a stream.

■ Transport and erosion

Sometimes the material weathered from rocks is carried (transported) away. This can happen in several ways. **Gravity** will cause material to fall down slopes – for example down the side of a valley.

Water in the form of rain and rivers can wash material away. Wind can blow loose material away. In cold climates and mountainous areas, material can be carried by ice.

This removal of weathered material is called **erosion**. As the material is transported, it can itself cause more erosion. For example, pebbles bumping and shuffling their way along the bottom of a stream will slowly wear away the rocks on the stream bed (picture 8).

■ Deposition

Eventually the eroded material is deposited as pebbles, sand or mud. This happens when whatever is carrying it – water, wind or ice – slows down. For example, when a gust of wind dies down, any sand or dust it was carrying is dropped. You are quite likely to be able to see this happening on a windy day in your school grounds. Gravity is the important force here. When the force of the moving wind or water supporting the load stops, gravity takes over and pulls the load downwards towards the Earth.

Questions

1 Imagine you have a party of primary school children visiting your school. Using what you have learnt in both K3 and this topic, write a short story for them entitled 'the adventures of a grain of quartz'. Perhaps it could start off in some granite, and eventually end up in a sandstone, or in a desert. Make it as eventful as you can.

2 Explain the following: weathering, erosion, transport, deposition.

3 Explain how the following sources of energy have shaped the landscape on the crust of the Earth:
   a thermal energy from inside the Earth
   b the Sun
   c gravity

4 a What evidence can you find or think of to support the theory that the landscape around where you live hasn't changed very much in i) the last 100 years ii) the last 1000 years.

   b Do you think it has changed much in the last million years? Give reasons for your answer.

Disaster at Izmit

Read the following newspaper articles, which have been adapted from reports that appeared in the Daily Telegraph in August 1999.

Earthquake deaths will top 40,000

Fatma Tandogan, a 51 year-old survivor, weeps at a collapsed house in Golcuk, Turkey.

The estimate of the number of people killed in the Turkish earthquake rose beyond 40,000 yesterday, making it the worst natural disaster to strike the country in its history.

Inadequate sanitation could lead to outbreaks of disease among the homeless. Rescue workers are being immunized against cholera and dysentery, and the Turkish government warned that bodies pulled from the wreckage could have to be buried in mass graves.

Turkey gave its first estimate of the cost of the earthquake to the country's economy, warning that the damage inflicted upon its industrial heartland could take up to £6 billion to repair. Some analysts suggested the figure could be double that.

Daily Telegraph, 21 August 1999

Predictions of the enormous death toll were borne out in Goluck, where are least 10,000 people are thought to be buried under hundreds of buildings.

A young Kurdish couple, Ahmet and Sema Bulte, were pulled alive from the ruins of a seven-storey building by a French rescue team after being trapped for almost 90 hours. They

Worst quakes

Place	Date	Magnitude	Deaths
Afghanistan	1998	7.1	5,000
Afghanistan	1998	6.4	4,000
Iran	1997	7.1	1,613
Japan	1995	7.2	6,424
India	1993	6.4	7,601
Iran	1990	7.7	40,000
Armenia	1988	6.9	25,000
Mexico	1985	8.1	8,000
China	1976	n/a	242,000
Japan	1923	n/a	142,807

emerged, with only a few scratches, through a hole carved by rescuers.

Mrs Bulte said: "There must be many people still down there, we could hear them moaning for help." Mr Bulte had managed to contact his brother just before his mobile phone's battery ran out and almost at the moment telephone lines were restored.

Shocks may go on for months, say scientists

By Roger Highfield, Science Editor

The Earth's outer layer is like a jigsaw puzzle of unevenly shaped rigid plates that are constantly chafing, squeezing and separating from each other.

The Turkish land mass is a small tectonic plate, the Anatolian plate, which is being squeezed between the African and Arabian plates, from the south, and the Eurasian plate, from the north. As a result, the Anatolian plate is moving westwards, towards the Aegean, which is shrinking as one part of the sea floor is being thrust under another.

Yesterday's quake struck at Izmit, which is at the boundary between the Eurasian and the Anatolian plates. This is called the north Anatolian fault. This is a strike/slip fault in which tectonic plates slide past each other horizontally. The San Andreas Fault in California is a well-known example.

A spokesperson for the British Geological Survey said: "Our experience of large earthquakes in this region is that the aftershocks continue for weeks or months. This fault is very much prone to aftershocks, because it doesn't make a clean break when it moves." Further movements, or tremors, were needed to release the remaining stress that had built up in the fault. Small aftershocks might still be taking place a year from now, he added.

Daily Telegraph, 18 August 1999

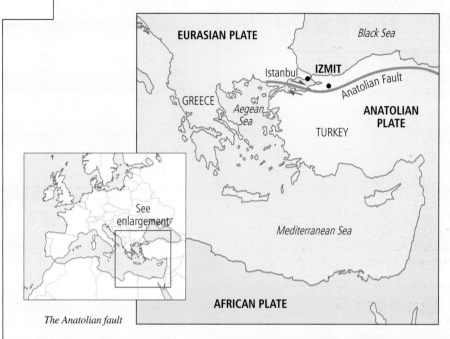
The Anatolian fault

Now answer the following questions.

1 a What are the names of the tectonic plates that are nearest to Izmit?

   b According to the science editor of the Daily Telegraph, what was the cause of the earthquake of August 1999?

   c Plate movements similar to those at Izmit have produced earthquakes along the line of the San Andreas Fault in California (see picture 4 on page 269). Suggest why the death toll in recent Californian earthquakes has not been as high as that in Turkey.

2 How does the newspaper article explain the cause of the aftershocks that followed the earthquake at Izmit?

3 a Quoting the newspaper report, describe how the lives of one Turkish couple were saved by a mobile phone.

   b Describe one advantage and one disadvantage of using a mobile phone in a city that has just been devastated by an earthquake.

4 In heavily populated areas such as Izmit, the risk of death from diseases such as cholera and dysentery increases after a major earthquake. Explain why.

5 Look at the table of Worst quakes in the newspaper article.

   Notice that the death toll in Iran was about 30 times as great as that in the Philippines, although the magnitude (size) of the earthquakes was the same in both countries.

   Working in groups, discuss possible reasons for this. What steps can be taken to reduce the devastation that a major earthquake can cause?

K5

How old is the Earth?

This topic explores ways of finding out the answers.

A bishop once used evidence in the Bible to work out that the Earth was made in the year 4004 BC. But, over the last two centuries, scientists have collected evidence from rocks that suggests that the Earth is considerably older.

■ Counting the layers

In some newer rocks it is possible to distinguish lighter and darker layers, laid down in different seasons of the year. So the layers can be counted just like the rings on a tree. Picture 1 shows a rock formed in a Tyneside coal mine during the 1800s. A white mineral, barium sulphate, settled out in a water trough. During working days it was blackened by coal. So, you can see how many days were worked during the week, and count the number of weeks. The rock is artificial, of course. Natural banded rocks like this do occur. But they are very rare and very young compared with the age of the Earth. We couldn't date the whole Earth with them.

HOW CAN WE TELL IF ONE ROCK IS OLDER THAN ANOTHER?

We can use common sense. The positions of different rocks give plenty of evidence about the order in which things happened. Look at picture 2. In a pile of sedimentary rocks, the ones at the bottom must be the oldest—sediment is always added to the top.

The fragments in any sedimentary rock must be older than the rock itself, so pebbles in a conglomerate are obviously older than the rock that contains them.

An igneous rock must be younger than the rocks into which it has intruded.

If unfolded beds of rock lie on top of folded ones, then the unfolded ones must be a lot younger than the folded one. Think of what must have happened. Some time after being deposited and turned into solid rock, the older rocks were squashed and folded. Then they were eroded, and then, after that, the younger set of rocks was laid down.

■ Using fossils

The remains of living organisms found in the rocks also give information about which rocks are older and which are younger. If we know the time when certain fossils lived, using evidence from one kind of rock, then we can use those fossils to date other rocks that contain the same fossils.

The methods described so far enabled the geologists of the nineteenth century to unravel the story of the Earth. But they could only work out the order in which

Picture 1 The Sunday Stone was formed in a Tyneside coal mine in the 1800s.

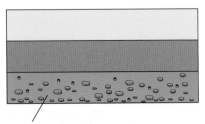

Pebbles in a conglomerate must be older than the rock they're in.

The bottom layers of sedimentary rock must be older than the top.

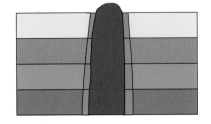

The sedimentary rocks must be older. An igneous rock is cutting across layers of sedimentary rock.

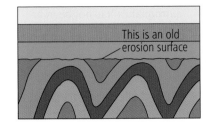

This is an old erosion surface

The lower beds were once flat layers. Then they were squashed and folded. The upper layers were later deposited on top.

Picture 2 How we can tell the age of rocks by looking at them.

things happened. They gave names to the various stages and events in the Earth's history (see the time chart on page 282). But no-one was able to give reliable dates to these events. It was not until the early part of this century that scientists discovered that **radioactive elements** could be used to date rocks.

■ Radioactive dating

Radioactive elements decay into lighter elements. They decay at a known rate. So, using a special machine called a mass spectrometer, scientists can measure how much of the original radioactive element is left and how much of the new, lighter elements are present. The ratio of the two gives a fairly accurate estimate of the age of the rock.

The oldest rock so far found in the world, was found in a remote region of northern Canada and is 3.96 billion years old (picture 3).

Radioactive dating has been used to measure the age of meteorites and moonrocks. These measurements suggest that the whole Solar System, Earth, meteorites and the Moon were formed at the same time—4.6 billion years ago. For the first 4 billion of those years, there was no life as we know it, and people have only been on the Earth for the last 0.003 billion years.

Picture 3 Samuel Bowring of Washington University, St Louis, USA, with the oldest rock so far discovered. It is estimated to be 3.96 billion years old.

Activities

A The geological history of your area

ICT See if you can collect enough information to write a short geological history of your area. (You may find the time chart, page 282 useful for this.)

1 Find a geological map of Britain in an atlas in your library. Use it to find out the approximate ages of the rocks in your area.

2 Try to find out if there is a collection of fossils available nearby, perhaps in a local museum, or in your school. Find out if any of these have been useful in dating the rocks nearby.

3 If there are igneous or metamorphic rocks nearby, try to work out if they are older, younger, or the same age as any sedimentary rocks.

B Be a geological detective

(You may prefer to work in groups for this.) Picture 4 shows the rocks exposed in two cliffs, 200 km apart.

1 Try to work out the order of the ages of the labelled rocks in each cliff.

2 Looking at the fossils, decide which beds in the two cliffs are the same age.

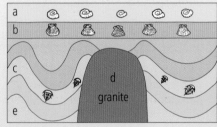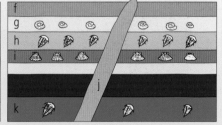

Picture 4

3 For both cliffs together, try to work out the order of the rocks labelled (a) to (k).

4 How do you think the skills of being able to work out ages of rocks in different areas helps geologists looking for coal or oil?

Questions

1 Why must the pebbles in a rock be older than the rock itself?

2 a Explain what you understand by radioactive half-life.

b Uranium-238 has a half-life of 4.5 billion years (4.5 x 10⁹ years). By a remarkable coincidence, the Earth is believed to be about 4.5 billion years old. How much of the original uranium-238 is still on Earth, unchanged?

c Uranium decays, eventually, to a stable form of lead (lead-206). A rock sample was analysed, which showed that the proportion of uranium-238 atoms to lead-206 atoms was 3 to 1.

i) What fraction of the uranium had decayed?

ii) Explain why a reasonable estimate of the age of this rock is about 2.25 billion years.

iii) Would you expect to find a rock in which the ratio of uranium to lead was 1 to 3? Explain your answer.

3 Why is radioactive dating quite accurate for igneous rocks, but no use for sedimentary rocks?

The history of the Earth: a geological time-chart

Millions of years ago

CENOZOIC The Earth's climate became colder, resulting in Ice Ages	**QUATERNARY**	Holocene **0.01** Pleistocene **2**	**0** — Early Egyptian cities, etc Many Ice Ages Humans migrate over Asia
This is the age of the mammals, but also of insects and flowering plants Opening of the North Sea	**TERTIARY**	Pliocene **7** Miocene **26** Oligocene **38** Eocene **54** Palaeocene **65**	First human beings (Africa) India meets Asia, Himalayas form First deer, monkeys, dogs, cat Africa, Europe and Asia collide, Alps form First rodents, elephants, horses Extinction of dinosaurs
MESOZOIC This was the age of the dinosaurs	**CRETACEOUS** **136**		Final break-up of Pangaea Sea flooded to cover more land Formation of chalk over much of what is now Europe First flowering plants and modern types of insect
The great southern continent of Pangaea broke up, forming most of our modern continents	**JURASSIC** **190**		Beginning of the Atlantic Ocean First birds and mammals
The Earth's climate was warm and pleasant almost everywhere	**TRIASSIC** **225**		Many new species Sea levels fall all over the world
PALAEOZOIC	**PERMIAN** **280**		Rise of the reptiles Formation of Pangaea
At the beginning, most life was in the sea. Plants colonised the land in the Silurian era, followed after a few million years by amphibians. Towards the end of this period the first reptiles appeared, as land animals	**CARBONIFEROUS** **355**		Britain at the Equator; coal laid down in many parts of the world. Age of amphibians. First reptiles
	DEVONIAN **395**		Age of the first amphibians First fish, first flying insects Animal life moves on to the land
	SILURIAN **440**		Plants move on to the land
	ORDOVICIAN **500**		} Sea covers many continents Most life in the sea, as shellfish and floating plants
	CAMBRIAN **570**		
PRECAMBRIAN	**PROTEROZOIC** **2500**		— First multicellular organism
This covered a huge period of time – over 4000 million years. It began with the formation of the Earth and ended with the first many-celled organisms The first green plants appeared in the sea – and began to put oxygen into the atmosphere	**ARCHAEAN** **4600**		? First free oxygen in atmosphere ? First living organisms — single-celled plants and animals 3960 — Age of oldest known rocks Earth cooling down; formation of tectonic plates

GCSE exam questions

SECTION A **Materials (pages 1–21)**
SECTION B **Air and water (pages 23–51)**

1 One definition of an element is:

"A substance that cannot be broken down into simpler substances by chemical methods."
The table below shows some of the 'substances' which Antoine Lavoisier thought were elements. He divided the 'substances' into four groups. He published these groups in 1789.
The modern names of some of the 'substances' are given in brackets.

Acid-making elements	Gas-like elements	Metallic elements		Earthy elements
sulphur	light	cobalt	mercury	lime (calcium oxide)
phosphorus	caloric (heat)	copper	nickel	magnesia (magnesium oxide)
charcoal (carbon)	oxygen	gold	platina (platinum)	barytes (barium sulphate)
	azote (nitrogen)	iron	silver	argilla (aluminium oxide)
	hydrogen	lead	tin	silex (silicon dioxide)
		manganese	tungsten	
		zinc		

a Name **one** 'substance' in the list which is **not** a chemical element or compound. *[1]*

b i Name **one** substance in the list which is a compound. *[1]*

  ii Suggest why Lavoisier thought that this substance was an element. *[1]*

Total 3 marks

(NEAB)

2 John Dalton was a famous chemist who lived 200 years ago.
He made a list of substances he thought were elements. He gave symbols to these elements. There is a copy of his table at the top of the next column.

a We now know that some substances (such as hydrogen, carbon, oxygen and zinc) are elements. Write down the names of two other substances in his list that we now know are elements. *[2]*

b Here are three compounds shown using Dalton's symbols.
Write down the names of the compounds.
One has been done for you. *[2]*

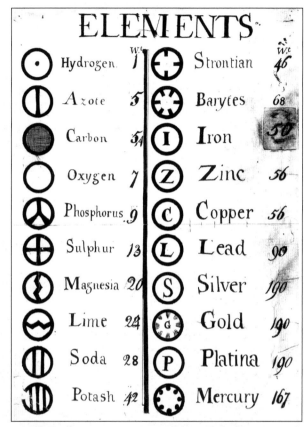

From Dalton's notebook.

c Dalton stated that:
1 All elements are made up of atoms.
2 Atoms cannot be split up into simpler particles.
We now know that atoms contain smaller particles.
Describe the structure of an atom such as carbon. *[4]*

Total 8 marks

(OCR)

3 This question is about the composition of the atmosphere.

a Finish the table to show the composition of the atmosphere.
Use all the names from the list.

argon
carbon dioxide
nitrogen
oxygen

About 80%	About 20%	Traces

[3]

b Millions of years ago the atmosphere of the Earth had a different composition.

   i How have the amounts of carbon dioxide and oxygen changed since then? **[1]**

   ii Suggest how the evolution of plants has helped to produce the present composition of the atmosphere. **[3]**

c The composition of the atmosphere is also affected by the weathering of vast amounts of igneous rocks containing iron compounds.
Some of the iron compounds are changed into iron(II) carbonate.
This is readily oxidised, on contact with air, to form iron(III) oxide.
The equation for this reaction can be represented by

$$4FeCO_3(s) + O_2(g) \rightarrow 2Fe_2O_3(s) + 4CO_2(g)$$

How does this process affect the composition of the atmosphere? **[2]**

Total 9 marks

(OCR)

SECTION C What are things made of? (pages 53–93)

4 The diagram below shows an experiment using concentrated ammonia solution and concentrated hydrochloric acid.

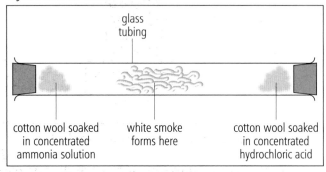

a The label shown below was on the bottle of concentrated ammonia solution.

What does the label tell you about the concentrated ammonia solution? **[1]**

b Concentrated hydrochloric acid is corrosive.
Suggest two precautions that should be taken when putting the cotton wool soaked in concentrated hydrochloric acid into the tube. **[2]**

c Ammonia and hydrogen chloride gases both quickly escape from the solutions.

   i The gases meet and react to form the white smoke as shown in the diagram. Explain, in terms of particles, why the gases meet. **[2]**

   ii The bonding in a molecule of ammonia is shown in the diagram below.
Draw a similar diagram to show the bonding in a molecule of hydrogen chloride (HCl). You need only to show the outer energy level (shell) electrons.

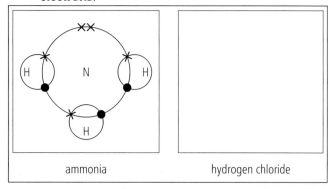

ammonia   hydrogen chloride

[2]

   iii Explain why both ammonia and hydrogen chloride gases escape from solution very quickly at room temperature. **[2]**

Total 9 marks

(NEAB)

5 a The diagrams show the particles present in four samples of gas. Each circle represents an atom. Circles of the same size and shading represent atoms of the same element.

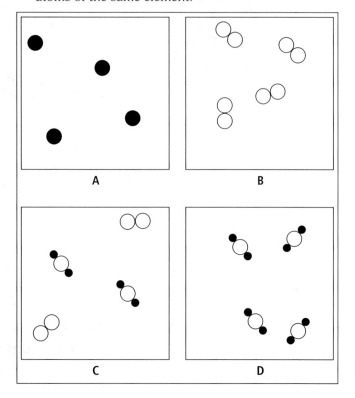

Which diagram represents:

i oxygen, O_2; [1]

ii steam, $H_2O(g)$; [1]

iii a mixture of gases; [1]

iv a monatomic gas. [1]

b Copy the box below and draw circles to represent the arrangement of particles in a solid element. One particle has been drawn for you.

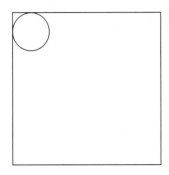

[2]

c Describe how the arrangement and movement of particles in a solid change when it is heated until it is a liquid. [3]

Total 9 marks

(Edexcel)

6 Look at the diagrams. They show two forms of carbon.

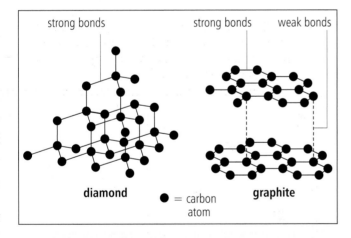

c Diamond tips are used on drills. What property of diamond makes it suitable for this use? [1]

b Graphite is soft and slippery. It is also a good conductor of electricity. Suggest a use for graphite. [1]

c There are strong bonds between the carbon atoms in diamond. What name is given to this type of bond? [1]

d Graphite conducts electricity. Explain how. [1]

Total 4 marks

(OCR)

7 Limestone is an important raw material.

a The main compound in limestone has the formula $CaCO_3$.
Name the elements in this compound. [2]

b Limestone has many uses. Select from the list below **two** important materials made from limestone.

cement diesel oil glass poly(ethene) sodium hydroxide sulphuric acid [2]

c The diagram shows a lime kiln. The limestone is heated by the burning coal.

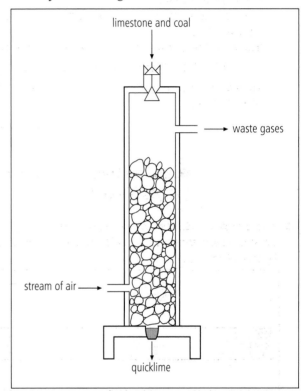

i Suggest why hot air is blown into the lime kiln. [1]

ii Give two reasons why carbon dioxide is produced in the lime kiln. [2]

d i Quicklime (calcium oxide) can be converted to slaked lime (calcium oxide) by adding water. Write a word equation to represent this reaction. [1]

ii Why do farmers sometimes add slaked lime to acidic soil? [1]

iii Use these relative atomic masses:
H = 1; O = 16; Ca = 40
to calculate the relative formula mass (M_r) of:
1 quicklime CaO
2 slaked lime $Ca(OH)_2$ [2]

Total 11 marks

(NEAB)

8 The flow chart on the next page shows the main stages in the production of ammonium nitrate.

a i Name two raw materials shown in the flow chart as **A** and **B** by choosing words from the list.

  air coke limestone natural gas   *[2]*

  ii Give the word equation for the reaction which makes ammonia.   *[1]*

  iii What is the purpose of the iron in the reactor? *[1]*

  iv What is the purpose of pipe **C**?   *[1]*

b Look at the flow chart again. Give the name of the acid **D** which is added to the ammonia to make ammonium nitrate.   *[1]*

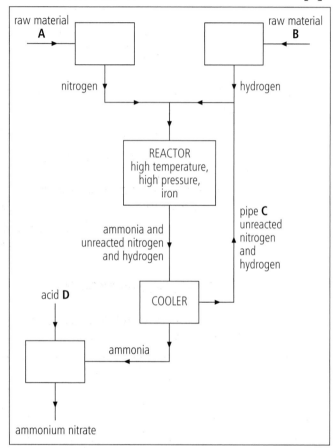

c i Explain why farmers add ammonium nitrate to the soil.   *[2]*

  ii Explain how ammonium nitrate can cause pollution.   *[2]*

Total 10 marks

(NEAB)

9 This question is about ammonia and fertilisers.
Ammonia is made from nitrogen and hydrogen in the Haber process.
The equation is:

$$N_2 + 3H_2 \rightleftharpoons 2NH_3$$

a Write down the name of the catalyst in this process.   *[1]*

b The diagram shows the energy changes when ammonia is made.

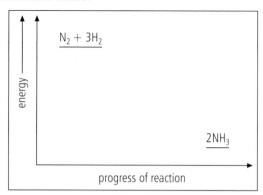

What can you conclude from this energy level diagram?   *[1]*

c Ammonium nitrate is a fertiliser made from ammonia and nitric acid.
Nitric acid is made from ammonia in three stages.

Stage 1
ammonia + oxygen → nitrogen monoxide + steam

Stage 2
nitrogen monoxide + oxygen → nitrogen dioxide + steam

Stage 3
nitrogen dioxide + water → nitric acid

  i Ammonia is a raw material in this process. What are the other two raw materials?   *[1]*

  ii In Stage 1, the platinum has to be heated to 900 °C to start the reaction.
Then the temperature of the catalyst stays at 900 °C without the need for further heating.
What does this tell you about the first stage? *[1]*

Total 5 marks

(OCR)

10 Ammonia (NH_3) is manufactured from hydrogen and nitrogen in the Haber Process.

a i Write a balanced equation for the formation of ammonia in the Haber Process.   *[2]*

  ii Draw a dot and cross diagram to show the bonding in a molecule of ammonia.   *[2]*

  iii Explain, in terms of the bonds broken and formed, why the formation of ammonia from nitrogen and hydrogen is exothermic.   *[3]*

b The manufacture of methanol from carbon monoxide and hydrogen requires similar conditions to those used in the Haber process.
The equation for the manufacture of methanol is

$$CO(g) + 2H_2(g) \rightarrow CH_3OH(g)$$

The reaction is exothermic.
The reaction conditions are a pressure of 200 atm and a temperature of 400 °C.

i State ONE advantage of using a pressure higher than 200 atm.
Explain your answer. **[3]**

ii State ONE disadvantage of using a pressure higher than 200 atm. **[1]**

iii State ONE advantage of using a temperature lower than 400 °C.
Explain your answer. **[3]**

iv State ONE disadvantage of using a temperature lower than 400 °C.
Explain your answer. **[2]**

Total 16 marks

(Edexcel)

11 The electrolysis of sodium chloride is an important industrial process. Three useful substances are produced:
- chlorine gas is formed at the positive electrode;
- hydrogen gas is formed at the negative electrode;
- an alkali is left in the solution.

The reactions which take place at the electrodes are represented by the equations shown below:

$$2Cl^- - 2e^- \rightarrow Cl_2$$
$$2H^+ + 2e^- \rightarrow H_2$$

a Name the alkali which is left in solution. **[1]**

b State why the chloride ions move towards the positive electrode. **[1]**

c Why is the formation of chlorine at this electrode said to be an oxidation reaction? **[1]**

d i Calculate the mass of chlorine produced when 10 kg of hydrogen are made. (Relative atomic masses: H = 1; Cl = 35.5). **[3]**

ii A cylinder contains 71 kg of chlorine gas (Cl_2). Calculate the volume that 71 kg of chlorine gas would have at 25 °C and 1 atmosphere pressure. (The relative formula mass of any gas, (M_r) in grams, has a volume of 24 dm³ at 25 °C and 1 atmosphere pressure.) **[3]**

Total 9 marks

(NEAB)

12 Chlorine, hydrogen and sodium hydroxide are produced by the electrolysis of sodium chloride solution.
A student passed electricity through sodium chloride solution using the apparatus shown in the diagram at the top of the next column.

a Name gas **A** and gas **B** **[3]**

b Describe and give the result of a test you could do in a school laboratory to find out which gas is chlorine. **[2]**

c Chlorine is used for treating water for drinking and in swimming pools. Why? **[1]**

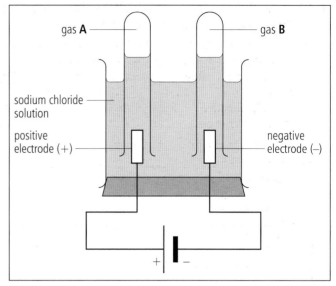

d i Balance the half equation for the production of hydrogen at the electrode.

$$H^+ + e^- \rightarrow H_2$$ **[1]**

ii Which word, from the list, best describes the reaction in part (d)(i)?
decomposition cracking neutralisation oxidation reduction **[1]**

Total 6 marks

(AQA)

SECTION E Metals (pages 115–133)

13 Four powdered metals **A**, **B**, **C** and **D** are placed in dilute acid. The diagram shows what happens.

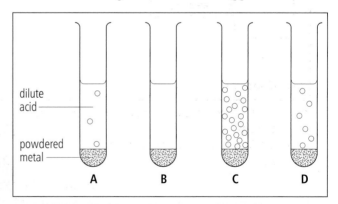

a Use the information in the diagram to put the metals **A**, **B**, **C** and **D** in order of reactivity (most reactive first). **[1]**

b A test tube of the gas produced was collected. What test could you do to show that the gas is hydrogen? Give the result of this test. **[2]**

c Another student placed the same four powdered metals in dilute acid, but measured the temperature rise in each tube. The student forgot to make a note of which metal was used in the tube. Put metals **A**, **B**, **C** and **D** in the correct place in the table.

Metal	Temperature rise (°C)
0	
16	
32	
25	

[2]

Total 6 marks

(NEAB)

14 The use of most metals depends on their reactivity.

a Reactivity of metals can be compared by using displacement reactions. The reactions of four metals **R**, **S**, **T** and **U** with their salt solutions are shown. (These letters are not the chemical symbols for the metals.)

Metal salt solution	Metal			
	R	S	T	U
R		✗	✗	✓
S	✓		✗	✓
T	✓	✓		✓
U	✗	✗	✗	

✓ = reaction ✗ = no reaction

i Use the information to arrange the metals **R**, **S**, **T** and **U** in order of reactivity, with the most reactive first. **[2]**

ii Metal **R** was zinc and metal **T** was copper. State what causes the colour changes that you see when zinc reacts with copper sulphate solution. **[3]**

b The alkali metals, in Group 1, are the most reactive metals. The symbols and atomic numbers for the first three alkali metals are shown here.

$_3$Li $_{11}$Na $_{19}$K

i Describe what you see when sodium reacts with water. **[3]**

ii Write a balanced chemical equation for the reaction of sodium with water. **[3]**

iii If the reaction is repeated using lithium it is much slower, but with potassium it is much faster. Give the reasons for the similarities and differences in the reactions of lithium, potassium and sodium with water. **[4]**

Total 5 marks

(SEG)

15 Choose words from the list to copy and complete the passage about the extraction of aluminium. Words may be used **once** only.

carbonate	chloride	chlorine	cryolite
electrolysis	graphite	negative	neutralisation
oxide	oxygen	positive	steel

The main ore of aluminium is bauxite. This is an impure form of aluminium .... and has the formula Al_2O_3. The ore is purified and then dissolved in molten .... Aluminium is extracted by the process of .... The electrodes are made of .... which is a form of carbon. Aluminium is produced at the .... electrode. The gas called .... is produced at the other electrode.

[6]

Total 6 marks

(NEAB)

16 Iron is extracted from haematite (Fe_2O_3) and aluminium is extracted from bauxite (Al_2O_3).

a The method used to extract iron from haematite is different from the method used to extract aluminium from bauxite.
Name the raw materials used and describe what happens during each process. (Diagrams, details of industrial equipment or details of purification are **not** required.) **[8]**

b Explain why different methods are used for iron and aluminium. **[2]**

Total 10 marks

(NEAB)

17 The diagram below shows the blast furnace used to extract iron from its ore.

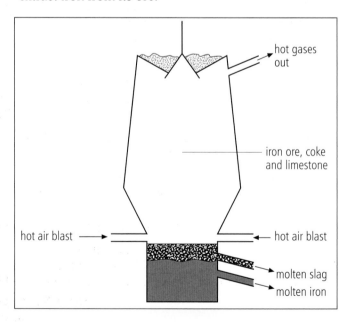

i What is meant by the word **ore**? *[2]*

ii Describe the part played by coke, hot air and limestone in the blast furnace. *[3]*

iii One of the main reactions in the furnace is:

iron(III) oxide + carbon monoxide
$\rightarrow$ iron + carbon dioxide

Which compound is reduced during the reaction? Give a reason for your answer. *[2]*

iv Most of the iron produced in the blast furnace is converted into steel. Give one reason for this conversion. *[1]*

Total 8 marks

(WJEC)

SECTION F Families of elements
(pages 135–155)

18 Part of the Periodic Table which Mendeléev published in 1869 is shown below.

	Group 1	Group 2	Group 3	Group 4	Group 5	Group 6	Group 7
Period 1	H						
Period 2	Li	Be	B	C	N	O	F
Period 3	Na	Mg	Al	Si	P	S	Cl
Period 4	K	Ca	*	Ti	V	Cr	Mn
	Cu	Zn	*	*	As	Se	Br
Period 5	Rb	Sr	Y	Zr	Nb	Mo	*
	Ag	Cd	In	Sn	Sb	Te	I

Use the Periodic Table in the Data Section to help you answer this question.

a Name two elements in Group 1 of Mendeléev's Periodic Table which are not found in Group 1 of the modern Periodic Table. *[2]*

b Which group of elements in the Periodic Table is missing in Mendeléev's table? *[1]*

c Mendeléev left several gaps in his Periodic Table. These gaps are shown as asterisks (*) on the table above.
Suggest why Mendeléev left these gaps. *[1]*

d Copy and complete the following sentence:
In the **modern** Periodic Table the elements are arranged in order of their ………….. numbers. *[1]*

Total 5 marks

(AQA)

19 a The table gives the energy required to break some bonds. The number of bonds broken is the same in each case.

Bond	Energy required (kJ)
C—H	435
Cl—Cl	243
H—Cl	432
C—Cl	346

The energy required to break a bond is the same as the energy given out when the bond forms.
In the presence of sunlight, methane will react with chlorine as in the equation.

$$
\begin{array}{ccc}
\quad\ H & \quad Cl & \quad Cl & \quad H \\
\quad\ | & \quad | & \quad | & \quad | \\
H-C-H\ +\ Cl & \longrightarrow & H-C-H\ +\ Cl \\
\quad\ | & & \quad | \\
\quad\ H & & \quad H
\end{array}
$$

Calculate the energy transfer in the reaction. You **must** show your working. *[3]*

b Chlorine, bromine and iodine are halogens. They are in Group 7 of the Periodic Table.
If chlorine is bubbled through a solution of potassium bromide, the solution turns orange-red.
If iodine is mixed with potassium bromide solution, no colour change is seen.

i Write a balanced equation for the reaction between chlorine and potassium bromide. *[2]*

ii Put the elements, bromine, chlorine and iodine in order of reactivity (most reactive first). *[1]*

Total 6 marks

(OCR)

20 The label below was on a bottle of bromine.

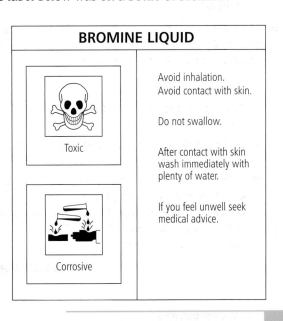

BROMINE LIQUID

Toxic

Corrosive

Avoid inhalation.
Avoid contact with skin.

Do not swallow.

After contact with skin wash immediately with plenty of water.

If you feel unwell seek medical advice.

a Describe one safety precaution you would take when using bromine. Give the reason for your choice. *[2]*

b Bromine can be made from sea water. in 1000 g of sea water there is 0.065 g of bromine. What mass of sea water would be needed to make 1000 g of bromine? *[2]*

c In sea water the bromine is present as bromide ions (Br^-). The equation below shows how chlorine can be used to displace bromine from sea water.

$$Cl_2(g) + 2Br^-(aq) \rightarrow Br_2(aq) + 2Cl^-(aq)$$

Explain, as fully as you can, why chlorine can displace bromine from sea water. To obtain full marks, your answer should refer to electronic structure. *[3]*

Total 7 marks

(AQA)

SECTION G Acids and ions (pages 158–177)

21 This label has been taken from a bottle of *Johnson's pH 5.5 Liquid Soap*.

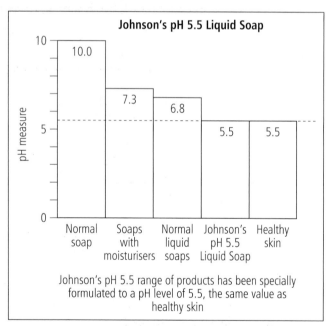

a Describe a test you could do in a school laboratory to find out if *Johnson's Liquid Soap* does have a pH of about 5.5. Give the results of this test. *[2]*

b Which soap mentioned in the bar chart is (i) most acidic and (ii) nearest to neutral? *[2]*

c Suggest why *Johnson's pH 5.5 Liquid Soap* may be better than normal soap for the skin. *[1]*

Total 5 marks

(NEAB)

22 Dilute hydrochloric acid was added slowly to dilute sodium hydroxide solution in a beaker. The graph below shows how the pH of the solution in the beaker changed as the acid was added.

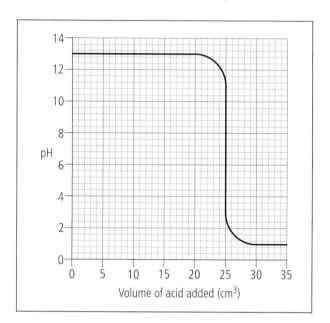

a What is the pH of the solution in the beaker when 30 cm³ of dilute hydrochloric acid has been added? *[1]*

b The dilute sodium hydroxide solution in the beaker contained Universal Indicator. What colour was the solution in the beaker when the following volumes of dilute hydrochloric acid had been added?
  i 30cm³
  ii 10 cm³ *[2]*

c i What is the pH of a neutral solution? *[1]*
  ii What volume of dilute hydrochloric acid was added to neutralise the sodium hydroxide solution in the beaker? *[1]*
  iii The neutral solution was evaporated to leave a solid salt.
    What is the name of the salt which is formed? *[1]*
  iv Describe what the salt looks like. *[1]*
  v State the type of bonding that is present in this salt. *[1]*
  vi Copy and complete the word equation for the reaction of sodium hydroxide with hydrochloric acid.
    sodium hydroxide + hydrochloric acid →
    .... + ... *[3]*

Total 9 marks

(Edexcel)

23 a i A student added a few drops of Universal Indicator to some sodium hydroxide solution. The indicator turned purple.
What was the pH of the sodium hydroxide solution? *[1]*

ii The student added an acid until the solution was neutral.
What is the colour of Universal Indicator when the solution is neutral? *[1]*

b i Which acid should the student add to sodium hydroxide solution to make sodium sulphate? *[1]*

ii Use the table of ionic symbols in the Data Section of your textbook to write the formula of sodium sulphate. *[1]*

c The student noticed that the solution in the beaker got warm when the acid reacted with the alkali.
The energy diagram at the top of the next page represents this reaction. *[1]*

i In terms of energy, what type of reaction is this? *[1]*

ii Use the energy diagram to calculate a value for the amount of energy released during this reaction. *[1]*

iii Explain, in terms of bond breaking and bond forming, why energy is released during this reaction. *[3]*

iv The reaction takes place very quickly, without the help of a catalyst. What does this suggest about the activation energy for the reaction? *[1]*

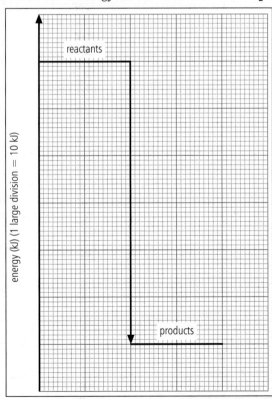

energy (kJ) (1 large division = 10 kJ)

reactants

products

Total 10 marks
(AQA)

24 In an experiment an alkali is added to an acid.

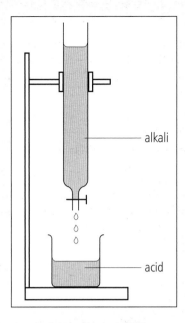

alkali

acid

a The acid is slowly added to the acid.
i How does the pH of the acid change while the alkali is being added? *[1]*

ii Copy and complete the word equation to show the **type** of substance made during the reaction.
acid + alkali → .... + water *[1]*

b Ammonium sulphate is a fertiliser.
It can be made by reacting ammonia with sulphuric acid.
Look at the table. It shows the formulas and the formula masses (M_r) of two fertilisers.

Name	Formula	Formula mass (M_r)
urea	$CO(NH_2)_2$	60
ammonium sulphate	$(NH_4)_2SO_4$	_____

Use the relative atomic mass (A_r) values given below to calculate the formula mass of ammonium sulphate.
N = 14; H = 1; O = 16; S = 32; C = 12 *[1]*

c Copy and complete the following word equations.
sodium hydroxide + nitric acid
→ .... + water

potassium hydroxide + sulphuric acid
→ .... + water *[2]*

d i Write down the formula of the ion which is present in solutions of all acids. *[1]*

ii Write down the formula of the ion which is present in solutions of all alkalis. *[1]*

Total 7 marks
(OCR)

25 a Copy and complete the table of results below which shows how sodium hydroxide reacts with some salt solutions.
M represents a metal.

Salt solution	Colour of the salt solution	Colour of precipitate formed with sodium hydroxide solution
iron(III) chloride	....	....
copper(II) sulphate	blue	....
M sulphate	colourless	white

[3]

b Is element **M** a transition metal? Give your reasoning. *[2]*

c Copy, complete and balance the symbol equation for the reaction between iron(III) chloride solution and sodium hydroxide solution.

$FeCl_3 +$ .... $\rightarrow$ .... $+ 3NaCl$

[2]

Total 8 marks

(WJEC)

26 Soap does not form a good lather when the tap water is hard.
Scum is formed instead.
The map shows where the water is soft, hard, or very hard.

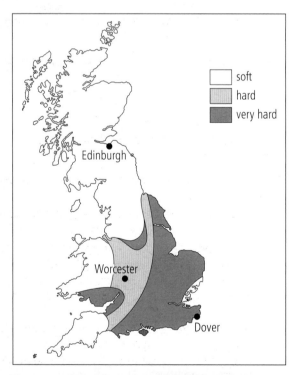

soft
hard
very hard

Edinburgh
Worcester
Dover

a There are three places named on the map.
Which of these is likely to have tap water which is very hard? *[1]*

b i This list contains the symbols for some ions. Choose from the list the two ions most likely to be found in hard water but not in soft water.
Ca^{2+} H^+ OH^- Mg^{2+} K^+ Na^+ *[2]*
ii Suggest how these two ions get into water to cause hardness. *[2]*

c 'Lime scale' is a problem in hard water areas.
Lime scale forms inside kettles.
This lime scale can be removed in a number of ways.
The table compares three liquid removers of lime scale.

Scale remover	Price per kettle cleaned	Suitable for	Speed of action	Ease of use	Effectiveness
Easykleen	£1.00	CIMPRW	fast	3	3
Scale-Out	£0.65	CP	slow	1	1
citric acid solution	£0.65	CMP	slow	3	2

Key:
Suitable for
C – coffee makers, I – steam irons, M – metal kettles,
P – plastic kettles, R – car radiators, W – washing machines

Ease of use – on a scale of 1 to 3.
1 means difficult to use, 3 means easy to use

Effectiveness – on a scale of 1 to 3.
1 means poor, 3 means good

i Citric acid solution is better for removing lime scale than Scale-Out.
Give reasons for this. Use the information in the table. *[3]*
ii As an advertising manager you are asked to write a leaflet to encourage people to buy the new scale remover Easykleen.
What are the advantages of this product? *[3]*

Total 11 marks

(OCR)

27 Analysis of a water supply produced the following data.

Analysis		
Ion		**Concentration (mg per dm³)**
calcium	(Ca^{2+})	104.0
magnesium	(Mg^{2+})	1.4
sodium	(Na^+)	8.0
potassium	(K^+)	1.0
iron	(Fe^{3+})	0.02
hydrogencarbonate	(HCO_3^-)	293.0
chloride	(Cl^-)	15.0
sulphate	(SO_4^{2-})	12.0
nitrate	(NO_3^-)	5.0
fluoride	(F^-)	0.1

a **i** Which **two** elements in this water supply are in Group 2 of the Periodic Table? *[1]*

  ii Write down the name of a transition metal which is present in the water supply. *[1]*

  iii Write down the names of two ions in this water supply which can combine together to form a compound of formula XY_2 where X is a metal. *[2]*

b Sana tests for the ions found in this water supply. She concentrates the ions by evaporating some of the water before doing the tests.
Give the words and symbols that would correctly complete the **four** gaps that have been left in the table.

	Test	What is seen	Ion present
(i)	Add dilute hydrochloric acid. Test the gas given off with limewater.	It fizzes, and the gas given off turns the limewater	HCO_3^-
(ii)	Add dilute nitric acid and silver nitrate solution	A white precipitate is formed.	
(iii)	Add dilute nitric acid and barium chloride solution.	A .... precipitate is formed.	SO_4^{2-}
(iv)	Add sodium hydroxide solution.	A brown precipitate is formed	....

[5]

c A hospital process has to let 30 dm³ of water flow through pipes in 24 hours.
If more than 120 mg per hour of calcium flows through the pipes, the process becomes damaged.
Decide whether this supply is suitable for use in the process.
You **must** show how you work out your answer. *[2]*

d **All** the hardness in this water has to be removed before the water is used in a steam-iron.
Which **two** of the methods in the list below could be used successfully?
Boil the water, cool it and then filter it.
Distil the water.
Trickle the water down a zeolite ion-exchange column.
Treat the water with calcium hydroxide then filter it. *[2]*

e Glyn always makes the tea using this water supply. He boils the water in an electric kettle.
Describe and explain the problem caused by the frequent use of this water supply in the kettle. *[3]*

Total 16 marks

(OCR)

SECTION H **Chemicals from oil**
(pages 179–207)

28 The table gives the names and formulas of four **alkanes** in crude oil.

Name	Formula
methane	CH_4
hexane	C_6H_{14}
decane	$C_{10}H_{22}$
hexadecane	$C_{16}H_{34}$

a Copy and complete the formula of the alkane containing 8 carbon atoms.
C H *[3]*

b Cracking of hexane can produce two hydrocarbons each containing two carbon atoms. One compound has a molecular formula C_2H_6 and the other C_2H_4.

  i Copy and complete a balanced equation for this cracking reaction.
$C_6H_{14} \rightarrow$ .... + ... *[2]*

  ii Suggest two conditions for this cracking reaction. *[2]*

  iii Explain why the cracking of long chain alkanes from crude oil is important commercially. *[2]*

  iv The graphical (displayed) formulae of the two hydrocarbons are:

ethane   ethane

How can the two compounds be distinguished by a simple chemical test? *[3]*

c Chloroethene is produced from a hydrocarbon. The formula of chloroethene is *[3]*

Draw a graphical (displayed) formula for poly(chloroethene). *[3]*

d This list includes some of the products formed when methane burns.

  carbon   carbon dioxide   carbon monoxide
  hydrogen   water

  i Write down the names of **two** products formed by the **complete** combustion of methane. *[2]*

  ii Some water heaters use methane as a fuel. These water heaters need to be checked and serviced regularly.
Some people die from breathing the fumes from heaters which have not been serviced.
Explain how these fumes are produced and why they are dangerous. *[3]*

Total 18 marks

(OCR)

29 a Ethene is the starting material for two plastics, poly(ethene) and PVC.
Give **one** use for each of these plastics. **[2]**

b Ethene is produced from crude oil. Crude oil is obtained by drilling into the Earth's crust. The diagram shows a section of the Earth's crust. Copy the diagram and choose words from the list to label this diagram.

gas oil petrol non-porous rock porous rock

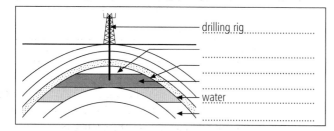

[4]

c Crude oil is a mixture of many compounds. Most of the compounds consist of molecules made of only carbon and hydrogen. Choose one word from the list below to complete the sentence.

carbohydrates carbonates hydrocarbons
hydrogencarbonates

Compounds made only of carbon and hydrogen are called .... **[1]**

d The crude oil is separated into fractions. The diagram shows a column used for this process.

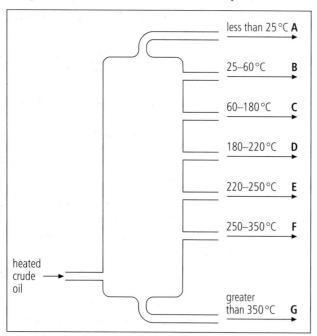

i Complete the name of the process used to separate the fractions. **[1]**
ii Explain, as fully as you can, how this process of separation works. **[3]**

iii The fraction used to make ethene is called naphtha. It is a liquid which boils between 100 °C and 150 °C.
Which of the letters **A** to **G** on the diagram above shows where the naphtha leaves the column? **[1]**

e The fractions contain molecules with similar numbers of carbon atoms. The main fractions are shown in the table below.

Name of fraction	Number of carbon atoms in molecules
petroleum gases	1 to 4
gasoline	4 to 12
naphtha	7 to 14
kerosene	11 to 15
diesel oil	14 to 19
lubricating oil	18 to 30
residue	more than 30

Naphtha burns more easily than diesel oil.
Explain why. **[1]**

Total 13 marks

(NEAB)

30 Crude oil is a mixture of chemicals called hydrocarbons.

a Which two elements are present in hydrocarbons. **[2]**

b The diagram shows part of an oil refinery where hydrocarbons are separated from each other.

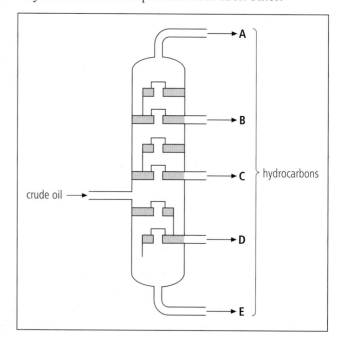

i Name the process used to separate the hydrocarbons.
Choose from:

combustion
cracking
fractional distillation
reduction
reforming
[1]

ii **A, B, C, D** and **E** are hydrocarbons produced in this process.
Which of these hydrocarbons is most likely to be a **gas** at room temperature?
Which of these hydrocarbons is most likely to be a **solid** at room temperature? *[2]*

c Some of the hydrocarbons, such as propane gas, are used as fuels.
Some houses which do not have natural gas use propane.
i Propane gas tanks have the following symbol on them.

What does this symbol mean? *[1]*
ii Propane gas tanks should be outside the house, in a shady place.
Explain why. *[2]*
iii For safety, a substance with a strong smell is added to the propane gas.
Explain why this is a good idea. *[1]*
iv What should people in the house do if they smell gas? *[1]*
v What should people in the house **not** do if they smell gas? *[1]*

Total 11 marks

(OCR)

31 a Copy and complete the sentences about oil by choosing the **best** words from this list:

air
carbohydrates
hydrocarbons
impermeable rocks
paraffin
permeable rocks
sea creatures

Crude oil is mixture of ....
It was made when high temperatures and high pressures acted on the remains of .... in the absence of .... It was trapped in the Earth between .... *[4]*

b Petrol is a mixture of alkanes.
People must not smoke near petrol pumps.
Why is this? *[1]*

c The table gives some information about four alkanes in crude oil.

Name	Formula	State at room temperature and atmospheric pressure	Time to pour 250 cm³ from a bottle in seconds
methane	CH_4	gas	
hexane	C_6H_{14}	liquid	1
decane	$C_{10}H_{22}$	....	3
hexadecane	$C_{16}H_{34}$	liquid	5

i Give the state at room temperature and atmospheric pressure of decane. *[1]*
ii The time taken to pour the alkanes changes as the number of carbon atoms changes.
Copy and complete the sentence by choosing the best word from this list.

decreases   increases   stays the same

As the number of carbon atoms in the alkane increases, the time taken to pour the alkane
.... *[1]*
iii Copy and complete the formula of the alkane containing 8 carbon atoms.

C H

[1]

d This list includes some of the products formed when methane burns.

carbon   carbon dioxide   carbon monoxide
hydrogen   water

i Write down the names of **two** products formed by the **complete** combustion of methane. *[2]*
ii Some water heaters use methane as a fuel.
These water heaters need to be checked and serviced regularly.
Some people die from breathing the fumes from heaters which have not been serviced.
Explain how these fumes are produced and why they are dangerous. *[3]*

e Burning large amounts of fossil fuels is changing the composition of the atmosphere.
Write down the name of a gas which is increasing in concentration. *[1]*

f The list gives four processes which involve oxygen.
combustion   photosynthesis
respiration   rusting
Which process in the list removes carbon dioxide from the atmosphere and replaces it with oxygen? *[1]*

Total 15 marks

(OCR)

32 Poly(ethene) is a plastic.
Poly(ethene) can be made from ethene.
Look at the diagram. It shows an ethene molecule.

Ethene is a member of a group of hydrocarbons.
All the group have a carbon–carbon double bond.

a What is the name of this group of hydrocarbons? *[1]*

b Ethene is made from the large molecules in crude oil.
Write down the name of this process. *[1]*

c When ethene reacts, the molecules join together to make a long chain known as poly(ethene).
Write about the conditions needed for ethene molecules to join together to make poly(ethene). *[2]*

d Poly(chloroethene) is a plastic used to make water pipes.
What properties of poly(chloroethene) make it suitable for making water pipes? *[2]*

e Poly(ethene) is a polymer.
Look at the table. It shows some information about other polymers.

Monomer	Name of polymer	Repeat unit of polymer
	poly(ethene)	
	poly(chloroethene)	
	poly(tetrafluoroethene)	

Draw the structures that should go into the empty boxes in the table. *[2]*

f Ethene can be made into ethane.

ethene   ethane

What substance does ethene react with to make ethane? *[2]*

g Ethane is an example of a **saturated** hydrocarbon.
Explain what is meant by '**saturated**'. *[1]*

h Ethene will undergo an **addition** reaction with bromine.
Draw the structure of the compound that is formed in this reaction.

[1]

Total 11 marks

(OCR)

33 The table contains some data about a series of alcohols.

Name	Molecular formula	Boiling point (°C)	Difference in boiling point between adjacent alcohols (°C)
ethanol	C_2H_5OH	78	
propan-1-ol	C_3H_7OH	98	20
butan-1-ol	C_4H_9OH	117	
pentan-1-ol	$C_5H_{11}OH$	138	

a i Calculate the difference in boiling points between adjacent alcohols.
Give the figures that would go in the **two** spaces in the table.
The difference in boiling point between the first two alcohols has been done for you. *[1]*

ii The boiling point of another alcohol in the same series is 177 °C.
Suggest its molecular formula. Give your reason. *[2]*

b The displayed (graphical) formula of ethanol and propan-1-ol are shown below.

Draw the displayed formulae of **two** isomers which have the molecular formula **C_4H_9OH**. *[2]*

c Ethanol can be used as a fuel.
Write a balanced equation for its complete combustion in oxygen. *[2]*

Total 7 marks

(OCR)

34 The table shows information about some alcohols.

Name	Formula	Boiling point in (°C)
methanol	CH_3OH	65.1
ethanol	C_2H_5OH	78.6
propan-1-ol	C_3H_7OH	97.5
butan-1-ol	C_4H_9OH	117.3
pentan-1-ol	$C_5H_{11}OH$	138.1

a Draw the structure of propan-1-ol and of another alcohol with the formula C_3H_7OH. **[2]**

b The alcohols in the table form an homologous series.

  i What is the general formula of an alcohol in this series? **[1]**

  ii What is the connection between boiling point and molecular mass of these alcohols? **[1]**

c Some alcohols can be oxidised to carboxylic acids. Copy and complete the equation for the oxidation of butan-1-ol to show the structure of the butanoic acid produced.

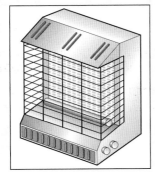

butan-1-ol   from oxidising agent

butanoic acid   water **[1]**

Total 5 marks

(OCR)

SECTION I Energy and chemistry (pages 210–235)

35 The gas used as a fuel for heating in most homes is methane, CH_4.

a It is very important to have a good air supply when methane burns. Explain why. **[2]**

b The word equation when methane burns in a good air supply is:

    methane + oxygen → carbon dioxide + water

  i Balance the chemical equation for this reaction.

    $CH_4(g) + O_2(g) \rightarrow CO_2 + H_2O(g)$ **[1]**

  ii Why is this reaction called an exothermic reaction? **[1]**

c The experiment shown was used to test the gases formed when methane burns in a good air supply.

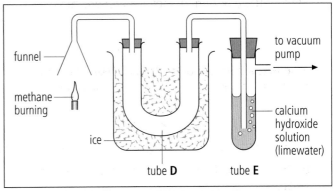

funnel

methane burning

ice   tube **D**   tube **E**

to vacuum pump

calcium hydroxide solution (limewater)

  i Explain why the water formed in tube **D**. **[2]**

  ii Give a chemical test for water, giving details of the test and the result. **[2]**

  iii The reaction that happens in tube **E** is:

    $Ca(OH)_2(aq) + CO_2(g) \rightarrow CaCO_3(s) + H_2O(l)$

    Describe and explain the change you would see in tube **E**. **[2]**

Total 10 marks

(SEG)

36 The recipe below is for home-made yoghurt.

> **Home-made yoghurt**
>
> 1. Heat 600 cm^3 of milk to 48 °C.
>
> 2. Stir in 60 g of dried milk powder and 1 tablespoon of natural yoghurt.
>
> 3. Pour the mixture into a vacuum flask and leave for 7 hours.
>
> 4. Tip the yoghurt into a bowl and cool it quickly by standing the bowl in cold water. Whisk the yoghurt from time to time as it cools.
>
> 5. Cover the yoghurt and refrigerate for 3 to 4 hours until it is thicker.

a Why is the small amount of natural yoghurt added to the milk? **[1]**

b Why is it important not to heat the mixture of milk and bacteria above 48 °C? **[1]**

c Suggest why the mixture is kept in a vacuum flask. **[2]**

d A chemical reaction takes place when the milk changes to yoghurt. The pH of the mixture gets lower as the reaction takes place.

  i What type of substance makes the pH lower? **[1]**

  ii How could you show that the pH of yoghurt is lower than milk? **[1]**

e The bacteria in the yoghurt produce a catalyst.
  i What effect does this catalyst have on the chemical reaction in the milk? **[1]**
  ii Which of the following words describe this type of catalyst?

   acid   alkali   enzyme   metal   sugar **[1]**

Total 8 marks

(AQA)

37 At room temperature, hydrogen peroxide decomposes very slowly to form water and oxygen. The decomposition is speeded up when a catalyst is added.

a The following equation represents the decomposition of hydrogen peroxide.
The structural formulae of the chemicals involved are shown.

$$2 \left(\begin{array}{c} O\text{---}H \\ | \\ H\text{---}O \end{array} \right) \longrightarrow 2 \left(\begin{array}{c} O \\ / \ \backslash \\ H \quad H \end{array} \right) + O{=}O$$

Use the following information about bond energies to answer this part of the question.

Bond	Bond energy (kJ)
O=O	498
O—O	146
H—O	464

  i Calculate the energy needed to break all the bonds in the reactants. **[2]**
  ii Calculate the energy released when new bonds are formed in the products. **[2]**
  iii Calculate the energy change for this reaction. **[1]**
  iv Is the reaction exothermic or endothermic? Explain why. **[1]**
b i What is meant by 'activation energy'? **[1]**
  ii The energy level diagram for the decomposition of hydrogen peroxide into water and oxygen is shown below.

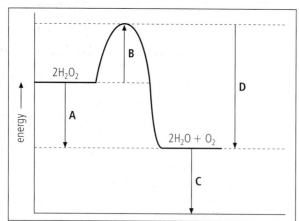

Which energy change, **A**, **B**, **C** or **D**, is the activation energy? **[1]**

  iii Explain, in terms of energy, how a catalyst makes hydrogen peroxide decompose more quickly. **[1]**

Total 9 marks

(NEAB)

38 Soap can be made by reacting fats with sodium hydroxide solution.

   fat + sodium hydroxide → soap + glycerol

The diagram shows a laboratory experiment to make soap.

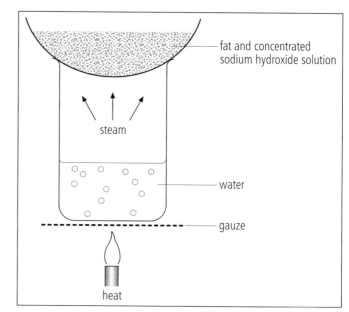

From the information in the diagram, give **two** factors which increase the rate of this reaction.
In each case, explain, in terms of particles, why the rate of reaction increases. **[7]**

Total 7 marks

(NEAB)

39 Sue studied the reaction between calcium carbonate and hydrochloric acid.
The equation for the reaction is:

$CaCO_3(s) + 2HCl(aq) \rightarrow CaCl_2(aq) + H_2O(l) + CO_2(g)$

Sue carried out three experiments to study the effect of the surface area of the calcium carbonate.
She used calcium carbonate in the form of small lumps or medium lumps or large lumps.
In each experiment she used the same mass of calcium carbonate.
She measured the volume of gas collected in a gas syringe at intervals.

a Write down **two** other things she should keep the same in each experiment. **[2]**

b In each experiment all the calcium carbonate had reacted within five minutes.

Sue's graph line for medium lumps is shown on the grid.
Sketch graph lines for small lumps and large lumps.
Label your lines S for small lumps and L for large lumps.

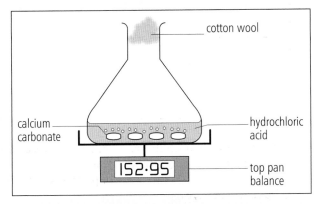

[3]

c Sue measured the rate of this reaction in a different way.
This is the apparatus she used.

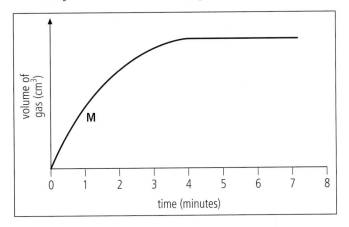

i How could she use the measurements of mass to follow the rate of the reaction? [2]
ii Why did she put cotton wool in the neck of the flask? [1]

Total 8 marks

(OCR)

40 The Haber process is used to make ammonia NH_3.
The table shows the percentage yield of ammonia at different temperatures and pressures.

Pressure (atmospheres)	Percentage (%) yield of ammonia at 350 °C	Percentage (%) yield of ammonia at 500 °C
50	25	5
100	37	9
200	52	15
300	63	20
400	70	23
500	74	25

a i Use the data in the table to draw two graphs on the grid below. Draw one graph for a temperature of 350 °C and the second graph for a temperature of 500 °C. Label each graph with its temperature. [1]
ii Use your graphs to find the conditions of temperature and pressure needed to give a yield of 30% ammonia. [1]
iii On your graph sketch the line you would expect for a temperature of 250°C. [1]

b i This equation represents the reaction in which ammonia is formed. [1]

$$N_2(g) + 3H_2(g) \rightleftharpoons 2NH_3(g)$$

What does the symbol $\rightleftharpoons$ in this equation tell you about the reaction? [1]
ii Use your graphs and your knowledge of the Haber process to explain why a temperature of 450 °C and a pressure of 200 atmospheres are used in the industry. [5]

c i Ammonium nitrate is one type of artificial fertiliser.
Calculate the relative formula mass of ammonium nitrate NH_4NO_3.
(Relative atomic masses:
H = 1; N = 14; O = 16.) [1]
ii Use your answer to part (c)(i) to help you calculate the percentage by mass of nitrogen present in ammonium nitrate NH_4NO_3. [2]

Total 16 marks

(AQA)

SECTION J Electricity and chemistry
(pages 237–261)

41 The diagram shows how pure copper can be made.

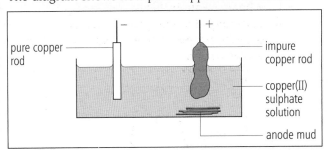

a Here is a list of statements about this process. Write down the statements from this list that are **true**.
Copper(II) sulphate solution is the electrolyte.
During electrolysis, copper(II) sulphate solution turns colourless.
The pure copper rod is the cathode.
The mass of the impure copper rod increases during electrolysis.
Impurities, such as silver, collect in the anode mud.

[4]

b Copper is used for making electricity cables and water pipes in your home.
What are the physical and chemical properties of copper which make it suitable for:
  i electricity cables
  ii water pipes? **[4]**

Total 8 marks

(OCR)

42 This question is about atomic structure and bonding.
Use the Periodic Table in the Data Section to help you answer this question.
Look at the table below. It gives some information about atoms.

Atomic	Atomic number	Mass number	Electronic structure
sodium	11	23	2.8.1
fluorine	9	19	2.7
chlorine	17	35	2.8.7
chlorine	17	37	2.8.7
argon	A	40	2.8.8
sulphur	16	32	B

a Write down the numbers that should be placed in boxes **A** and **B** of the table. **[2]**

b Chlorine appears twice in the table. **[1]**
Each of these atoms is an isotope of chlorine.
Explain what is meant by the word **isotope**. **[1]**

c Argon is a noble gas. It is very unreactive.
Explain why. Use ideas about atomic structure. **[1]**

d Look at the diagrams.
They show the electronic structure of a sodium atom and a fluorine atom.

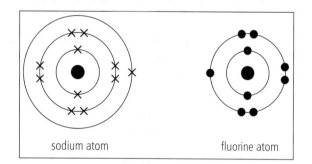

sodium atom   fluorine atom

A sodium ion and a fluoride ion are formed when sodium reacts with fluorine.
Draw a dot and cross diagram to show the electronic structure of a fluoride ion. **[1]**

Total 5 marks

(OCR)

43 Sodium and potassium are both in Group 1 of the Periodic Table.

a Explain, by reference to their electronic structures, why both elements are placed in Group 1. **[1]**

b Use the Periodic Table in the Data Section to help you answer this question.
The diagrams below represent the electronic structures of some atoms and ions.

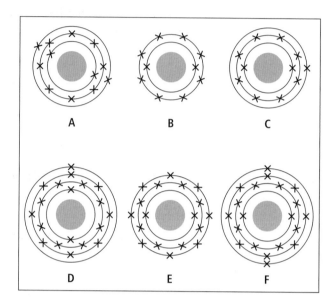

Which one of the structures, **A–F**,
  i represents a sodium **atom** **[1]**
  ii represents a potassium **ion**? **[1]**

c Sodium and potassium both react with cold water.
  i The word equation represents the reaction of sodium with water.

  sodium + water → sodium hydroxide + hydrogen

  Copy and complete the symbol equation for this reaction.

  ……….. + ……….. → 2NaOH + ……….. **[2]**

  ii How does the reactivity of potassium with water differ from that of sodium with water?
  Explain this difference in reactivity by reference to the electronic structures of the potassium and sodium atoms. **[4]**

Total 9 marks

(NEAB)

44 a Magnesium reacts with chlorine to form an ionic compound.
The atomic numbers of the two elements can be found on page 302 of your book.
  i State the electronic arrangements of the two elements. **[2]**

ii Explain, by means of a diagram or otherwise, how atoms of the two elements are changed into ions. Include the charges on the ions in your answer. **[4]**

iii I Give the name and formula of the compound formed during the reaction. **[2]**

II Would you expect the compound to be a gas, a liquid or a solid at room temperature? Give an explanation for your answer. **[2]**

b Chlorine also forms a compound with hydrogen. By means of a labelled diagram, show how the atoms are bonded together. Name this type of bonding. **[3]**

Total 13 marks

(WJEC)

SECTION K Earth (pages 263–282)

45 The Earth's crust is cracked into a number of large pieces which are moving very slowly.

a Give the name for these large pieces. **[1]**

b State the result of these large pieces slowly moving
i apart, **[1]**
ii towards each other. **[1]**

Total 3 marks

(WJEC)

46 In a volcano, molten rock (magma) flows to the surface up a central tube.
This magma can solidify in the tube to form a plug.
The photograph shows the remains of a plug from a volcano.

a What sort of rock makes up this plug? Choose one of the following:

igneous   metamorphic   sedimentary **[1]**

b The diagram shows the volcano.

Copy the diagram and write an **X** on the diagram of the volcano to show where the plug is formed. **[1]**

c The plug shown in the photograph was originally surrounded by other rocks which have now worn away.
Suggest a reason why the other rocks have worn away faster than the plug. **[1]**

d Which part of the Earth does the magma come from?
core   crust   mantle **[1]**

e The magma that formed the plug cooled slowly. What would you expect the rock in the plug to look like?
Choose one of the following:
a powder   small crystals   large crystals **[1]**

f It is dangerous to live near volcanoes. Suggest two reasons why it is dangerous. **[2]**

Total 7 marks

(OCR)

47 This question is about different types of rocks.

a The lists show the names of some rocks and descriptions of them.
Match each name to the correct description and then write down a sentence to describe each rock shown in the table.
Each name must be matched with a different description.
One has been done for you.

Name of rock	Description of rock
basalt	grains arranged in layers of dark and light bands
conglomerate	crystals smaller than 0.5 mm, mainly dark in colour
gneiss	small stones bound together by cementing material
granite	hard, brittle, grey rock that splits into sheets
slate	crystals bigger than 0.5 mm, mainly light in colour

[3]

b Write down the name of an example of each of the following rock types.
Choose your answers from this list.

basalt
conglomerate
gneiss
granite
slate

i a sedimentary rock **[1]**
ii a metamorphic rock **[1]**
iii an extrusive igneous rock **[1]**
iv an intrusive igneous rock **[1]**

Total 7 marks

(OCR)

Data section

Contents

Table 1   The elements. In this table, we have left out elements 58 to 71, which are very rare. We have given structures only for the most important elements.

Atomic number	Element	Symbol of element	Relative atomic mass	Melting point	Boiling point (°C)	Type of structure (°C)	Date of discovery
1	hydrogen	H	1	−259	−253	simple molecular (H_2)	1766
2	helium	He	4	−270	−269	simple molecular (He)	1868/1895
3	lithium	Li	7	181	1331	giant metallic	1818
4	beryllium	Be	9	1283	2487	giant metallic	1798
5	boron	B	11	2027	3927		1808
6	carbon	C	12				
	– diamond			3550	4827	giant covalent	ancient
	– graphite			3650 (sublimes)		giant covalent	ancient
7	nitrogen	N	14	−210	−196	simple molecular (N_2)	1772
8	oxygen	O	16	−219	−183	simple molecular (O_2)	1774
9	fluorine	F	19	−220	−188	simple molecular (F_2)	1887
10	neon	Ne	20	−248	−246	simple molecular (Ne)	1898
11	sodium	Na	23	98	890	giant metallic	1807
12	magnesium	Mg	24	650	1117	giant metallic	1808
13	aluminium	Al	27	659	2447	giant metallic	1827
14	silicon	Si	28	1410	2677	giant covalent	1824
15	phosphorus (white)	P	31	44	281	simple molecular (P_4)	1669
16	sulphur (monoclinic)	S	32	119	445	simple molecular (S_8)	ancient
17	chlorine	Cl	35.5	−101	−34	simple molecular (Cl_2)	1774
18	argon	Ar	40	−189	−186	simple molecular (Ar)	1894
19	potassium	K	39	63	766	giant metallic	1807
20	calcium	Ca	40	850	1492	giant metallic	1808
21	scandium	Sc	45	1400	2477	giant metallic	1879
22	titanium	Ti	48	1677	3277	giant metallic	1825
23	vanadium	V	51	1917	3377	giant metallic	1830
24	chromium	Cr	52	1903	2642	giant metallic	1797
25	manganese	Mn	55	1244	2041	giant metallic	1774
26	iron	Fe	56	1539	2887	giant metallic	ancient
27	cobalt	Co	59	1495	2877	giant metallic	1735
28	nickel	Ni	59	1455	2837	giant metallic	1751
29	copper	Cu	64	1083	2582	giant metallic	ancient
30	zinc	Zn	65	419	908	giant metallic	1746
31	gallium	Ga	70	30	2237		1875

continued

Atomic number	Element	Symbol of	Relative atomic element mass	Melting point (°C)	Boiling point (°C)	Type of structure	Date of discovery
32	germanium	Ge	73	937	2827		1886
33	arsenic	As	75	613			1250
34	selenium	Se	79	217	685		1817
35	bromine	Br	80	−7	58	simple molecular (Br_2)	1826
36	krypton	Kr	84	−157	−153	simple molecular (Kr)	1898
37	rubidium	Rb	86	39	686	giant metallic	1861
38	strontium	Sr	88	769	1384	giant metallic	1808
39	yttrium	Y	89	1522	3338	giant metallic	1843
40	zirconium	Zr	91	1852	4377	giant metallic	1824
41	niobium	Nb	93	2467	4742	giant metallic	1802
42	molybdenum	Mo	96	2610	5560	giant metallic	1778
43	technetium	Tc	99	2172	4877	giant metallic	1937
44	ruthenium	Ru	101	2310	3900	giant metallic	1844
45	rhodium	Rh	103	1966	3727	giant metallic	1803
46	palladium	Pd	106	1554	2970	giant metallic	1803
47	silver	Ag	108	962	2212	giant metallic	ancient
48	cadmium	Cd	112	321	765	giant metallic	1817
49	indium	In	115	156	2080	giant metallic	1863
50	tin	Sn	119	232	2260	giant metallic	ancient
51	antimony	Sb	122	631	1750		ancient
52	tellurium	Te	128	450	990		1783
53	iodine	I	127	114	184	simple molecular (I_2)	1811
54	xenon	Xe	131	−112	−107	simple molecular (Xe)	1898
55	caesium	Cs	133	29	669		1860
56	barium	Ba	137	725	1640		1808
57	lanthanum	La	139	921	3457		1839
72	hafnium	Hf	179	2227	4602		1923
73	tantalum	Ta	181	2996	5427		1802
74	tungsten	W	184	3410	5660		1783
75	rhenium	Re	186	3180	5627		1925
76	osmium	Os	190	2700	>5297		1803
77	iridium	Ir	192	2410	4130		1803
78	platinum	Pt	195	1772	3827		1735
79	gold	Au	197	1064	3080		ancient
80	mercury	Hg	201	−39	357		ancient
81	thallium	Tl	204	304	1457		1861
82	lead	Pb	207	328	1740		ancient
83	bismuth	Bi	209	271	1560		1753
84	polonium	Po	210	254	962		1898
85	astatine	At	210	302	337		1940
86	radon	Rn	222	−71	−62		1900
87	francium	Fr	223	27	677		1939
88	radium	Ra	226	700	<1137		1898
89	actinium	Ac	227	1050	3200		1899
90	thorium	Th	232	1750	4787		1828
91	protactinium	Pa	231	<1597	4027		1917
92	uranium	U	238	1132	3818		1841

Table 3 The reactivity series of metals.

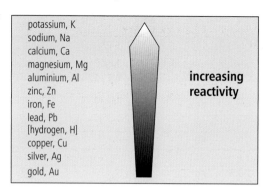

potassium, K
sodium, Na
calcium, Ca
magnesium, Mg
aluminium, Al
zinc, Zn
iron, Fe
lead, Pb
[hydrogen, H]
copper, Cu
silver, Ag
gold, Au

increasing reactivity

Table 3 The alkanes.

Name	Formula	Melting point (°C)	Boiling point (°C)
methane	CH_4	−182	−161
ethane	C_2H_6	−183	−88
propane	C_3H_8	−188	−42
butane	C_4H_{10}	−138	−1
pentane	C_5H_{12}	−130	36
hexane	C_6H_{14}	−95	69
heptane	C_7H_{16}	−91	99
octane	C_8H_{18}	−57	126
nonane	C_9H_{20}	−51	151
decane	$C_{10}H_{22}$	−30	174
dodecane	$C_{12}H_{26}$	−10	216
eicosane	$C_{20}H_{42}$	37	344

Table 4 Charges on some ions.

Positive ions (cations) Usually metals		Negative ions (anions) Usually non-metals	
ammonium	NH_4^+	bromide	Br^-
hydrogen	H^+	chloride	Cl^-
copper(I)	Cu^+	iodide	I^-
potassium	K^+	hydroxide	OH^-
sodium	Na^+	nitrate	NO_3^-
silver	Ag^+	carbonate	CO_3^{2-}
calcium	Ca^{2+}	oxide	O^{2-}
magnesium	Mg^{2+}	sulphate	SO_4^{2-}
copper(II)	Cu^{2+}	sulphite	SO_3^{2-}
iron(II)	Fe^{2+}	sulphide	S^{2-}
zinc	Zn^{2+}	phosphate	PO_4^{3-}
aluminium	Al^{3+}		
iron(III)	Fe^{3+}		

Name	Other name	Formula
aluminium oxide	alumina	Al_2O_3
ammonia		NH_3
ammonium chloride		NH_4Cl
ammonium nitrate	'NITRAM'	NH_4NO_3
calcium carbonate	limestone, chalk	$CaCO_3$
calcium chloride		$CaCl_2$
calcium hydroxide	slaked lime	$Ca(OH)_2$
calcium oxide	quicklime	CaO
carbon monoxide		CO
carbon dioxide		CO_2
cobalt(II) chloride	cobalt chloride	$CoCl_2$
copper(II) chloride	copper chloride	$CuCl_2$
copper(II) oxide	copper oxide	CuO
copper(II) sulphate	copper sulphate	$CuSO_4$
hydrogen chloride		$HCl(g)$
hydrochloric acid		$HCl(aq)$
hydrogen fluoride		$HF(g)$
hydrogen peroxide		H_2O_2
hydrogen sulphide		H_2S
iron(II) chloride		$FeCl_2$
iron(III) chloride		$FeCl_3$
magnesium carbonate		$MgCO_3$
magnesium chloride		$MgCl_2$
magnesium oxide	magnesia	MgO
manganese(IV) oxide	manganese dioxide	MnO_2
nitric acid		HNO_3
nitrogen monoxide		NO
nitrogen dioxide		NO_2
potassium chloride		KCl
potassium hydroxide	caustic potash	KOH
potassium manganate(VII)	potassium permanganate	$KMnO_4$
potassium nitrate	saltpetre	KNO_3
silicon(IV) oxide	silicon dioxide, silica	SiO_2
sodium carbonate	soda ash, washing soda	Na_2CO_3
sodium chloride	salt	$NaCl$
sodium hydrogencarbonate	sodium bicarbonate	$NaHCO_3$
sodium hydroxide	caustic soda	$NaOH$
sodium nitrate		$NaNO_3$
sodium sulphate		Na_2SO_4
sulphur dioxide		SO_2
sulphur trioxide		SO_3
sulphuric acid		H_2SO_4
zinc oxide		ZnO
water		H_2O

Table 5 The formulas of some inorganic compounds.
This table shows the formulas of some of the compounds you are likely to meet quite frequently in your study of chemistry. It gives the proper chemical names, and also other names that are sometimes used.

Table 6   Testing for gases.
The table summarises the tests for some common gases.

Gas	Test	Positive result
Oxygen	Insert a glowing splint into gas	Splint relights
Hydrogen	Insert a burning splint into gas	Gas explodes with a squeaky 'pop'
Chlorine	Put damp indicator paper into gas	Indicator paper is bleached
Ammonia	Put damp indicator paper into gas	Indicator paper turns blue
Carbon dioxide	Bubble gas through lime water	Lime water forms milky precipitate

Table 7   Flame test colours.
The table gives the characteristic flame colours of some metal ions.

Metal ion	Flame colour
Lithium, Li^+	Brilliant red
Sodium, Na^+	Yellow-orange
Potassium, K^+	Lilac (pink-mauve)
Calcium, Ca^{2+}	Brick red
Strontium, Sr^{2+}	Crimson red
Barium, Ba^{2+}	Pale green
Copper, Cu^{2+}	Green

Table 8 The Periodic Table.

	group 1	group 2													group 3	group 4	group 5	group 6	group 7	group 0
period 1								hydrogen H 1												helium He 2
period 2	lithium Li 3	beryllium Be 4													boron B 5	carbon C 6	nitrogen N 7	oxygen O 8	fluorine F 9	neon Ne 10
period 3	sodium Na 11	magnesium Mg 12													aluminium Al 13	silicon Si 14	phosphorus P 15	sulphur S 16	chlorine Cl 17	argon Ar 18
period 4	potassium K 19	calcium Ca 20	scandium Sc 21	titanium Ti 22	vanadium V 23	chromium Cr 24	manganese Mn 25	iron Fe 26	cobalt Co 27	nickel Ni 28	copper Cu 29	zinc Zn 30	gallium Ga 31	germanium Ge 32	arsenic As 33	selenium Se 34	bromine Br 35	krypton Kr 36
period 5	rubidium Rb 37	strontium Sr 38	yttrium Y 39	zirconium Zr 40	niobium Nb 41	molybdenum Mo 42	technetium Tc 43	ruthenium Ru 44	rhodium Rh 45	palladium Pd 46	silver Ag 47	cadmium Cd 48	indium In 49	tin Sn 50	antimony Sb 51	tellurium Te 52	iodine I 53	xenon Xe 54
period 6	caesium Cs 55	barium Ba 56	Lanthanides see below	hafnium Hf 72	tantalum Ta 73	tungsten W 74	rhenium Re 75	osmium Os 76	iridium Ir 77	platinum Pt 78	gold Au 79	mercury Hg 80	thallium Tl 81	lead Pb 82	bismuth Bi 83	polonium Po 84	astatine At 85	radon Rn 86
period 7	francium Fr 87	radium Ra 88	Actinides see below	Rf 104	Db 105	Sg 106	Bh 107	Hs 108	Mt 109									

Lanthanides

La 57	Ce 58	Pr 59	Nd 60	Pm 61	Sm 62	Eu 63	Gd 64	Tb 65	Dy 66	Ho 67	Er 68	Tm 69	Yb 70	Lu 71

Actinides

Ac 89	Th 90	Pa 91	U 92	Np 93	Pu 94	Am 95	Cm 96	Bk 97	Cf 98	Es 99	Fm 100	Md 101	No 102	Lr 103

Index

P

Pacific Ocean 266
painting for rust protection 31, 33c
paper chromatography 20
Papua New Guinea 133
particles 54–61, 62
    see also atoms; ions; molecules
percentage composition 77–8
Periodic Table 136–41, 151c
    and electronic structure 256–7
    full table 307
    see also alkali metals; alkaline earth metals;
halogens; noble gases; transition metals
periods (Periodic Table) 137, 140–1, 256, 257
permanent hard water 176
pesticides 47, 109c
petrol 38c, 187, 215
pH 160
    of acid rain 34
    and tooth decay 162, 163
phases 17
phosphates for softening water 175
phosphorus 77, 128, 141
    in fertilisers 78, 107
photographic film 149
photosynthesis 24, 25, 210, 218
physical properties 5, 124, 140
physical weathering 277
pipettes 80
plants 25, 104, 145, 220
    photosynthesis 24, 25, 210, 218
    polysaccharides in 201, 202
plastics 201, 202, 204, 205a
    as addition polymers 206
    costs of 180
    uses 5, 6
plate tectonics 266–7
plating 31, 33c, 240–1, 241a
platinum catalysts 108, 155, 227
pollution 38a
    air see air pollution
    by oil 180, 184
    thermal pollution 45
    water pollution 46–51, 49a, 175
polyester 203, 204
poly(ethene) see polythene
polymerisation 200, 206–7
polymerising glues 191c
polymers 200–7, 205a
polypropene 202, 203, 206
polysaccharides 201–2
polystyrene 203, 206
polystyrene cement 191c
polytetrafluoroethene (PTFE) 204
polythene 7c, 200, 202, 206
    chains in 203, 204
    degradability 205
    manufacturing costs 96, 97
polyvinyl acetate (PVA) 197
polyvinyl chloride (PVC) 180, 203, 205, 206–7
poor metals 137
position of equilibrium 235
potassium 142, 143, 238, 239, 256
    in fertilisers 78, 107
potassium hydroxide 238, 239
pottery 2, 90

power stations 40, 99, 225
    and pollution 34, 35, 38, 39c
precipitation 42, 43, 164, 170–3
    for softening water 174–5
pressure 5
    inside the Earth 264, 273–4
    in reactions 105–6, 226, 235
prices see costs
products 3, 68
proteins 10, 200, 202, 203, 205
    in cooking 225
protons 250, 251, 252
PTFE see polytetrafluoroethene
pumice 271
pure substances 14, 20–1, 40
PVA (polyvinyl acetate) 197
PVC (polyvinyl chloride) 180, 203, 205, 206–7

Q

quarrying 101
quartz 84–5, 272
    see also silicon oxide
quenching 92
quicklime see calcium oxide

R

radiation, solar 35, 37
radioactive elements 265, 281
radium 261c
radon 152
Ramsay, Sir William 153
rates of reaction 105–6, 224–31
raw materials 96–7, 101
    for the Haber Process 106
    limestone 101, 103c
    ores 126
    salt 112
rayon 197, 202
reactants 3, 68
reacting masses 72–4, 76–7
reactions, rates of 105–6, 224–31
reactive metals 137
    see also alkali metals; alkaline earth metals
reactivity 140–1, 147
    of halogens 146, 147–8
    of metals 123–4, 142, 143, 144, 245
    of noble gases 152, 153
reactivity series 120–2, 124, 126, 304
recycling 128, 130–1, 131a, 205
    in natural cycles 25, 41
redox reactions 28, 248–9
    see also oxidation; reduction
reducing agents in metal extraction 126–7
reduction 28, 248–9
    in metal extraction 126, 128, 130
refrigerators 56
relative atomic masses 70, 71, 138, 253
relative formula masses 70–1
respiration 27, 218
reversible reactions 168–9, 234–5
    Contact Process 111
    Haber Process 105–6
Ring of Fire 269
rock cycle 274–5
rocks 270–5, 277–8, 280–1

rubber 200
rusting 27, 30–2, 32a, 33c
Rutherford, Ernest 250, 261c

S

salt, common see sodium chloride
salts 150c, 166
    ethanoates 197–8
    making 123, 163–5, 169, 171
sand 11, 84–5
sandstones 103c, 176, 272, 273
saturated compounds 188, 189
saturated solutions 42
sea, chemicals from 150c
sea-floor spreading 266
sedimentary rocks 270, 272–3, 274–5
separating funnels 19
separating mixtures 18–21, 21c
sewage 41, 46–7
shales 272, 273
shells, electron 254–5, 258–60
silicon 10–11, 84, 90, 140
silicon oxide 11, 84–5, 141
    see also quartz
silver 118, 122, 124, 249
    in photography 149
    plating with 240–1, 245
slaked lime see calcium hydroxide
slate 270, 274, 275a
smoke 36, 37, 60c
soap 174
    see also detergents; washing powders
sodium 142–3, 251, 256
    from electrolysis 238, 243
    reactions 27, 121
        with alcohols 194
    reactivity 122, 123, 140
    salts 163, 164
    in sodium chloride 8, 64, 258
    for softening water 175
sodium carbonate 101, 170–1, 174, 197
sodium chloride (salt) 8, 9, 164
    bonding in 258, 259
    chemicals from 112–13, 242, 244, 247c
    dissolving 168
    effect on boiling point of water 21
    electrolysis 242–3, 244
    from the sea 150c
    ions 64, 92, 165, 166
sodium hydrogencarbonate 162, 163, 210
sodium hydroxide 90, 162–4
    chlor-alkali process forms 112–13, 244
    reaction with acids 80–1, 169, 197
        tests for ions in solution 172
sodium oxide 27, 121
sodium stearate 174
sodium sulphate 164, 165
sodium thiosulphate 231
softening water 174–5
solder 21
solid foams 16
solids 4, 54–6, 59
    in mixtures 14, 15, 18–19
solubility 43–5, 171
solubility curves 44
soluble salts, making 164–5

soluble substances 18–19, 42
solutes 19, 42
solution mining 112
solutions 42–5, 79–81, 172–3
 electrolysis in 244–6
 as mixtures 14–15, 16, 17, 18–19
solvent glues 191c
solvents 18–19, 42, 45, 192
space-filling models 82, 83
spectator ions 169, 170, 249
spectra, atomic 255
spectrometers 75c, 145, 253
stainless steel 31, 32, 33c
stalactites and stalagmites 170
Stanton, Dr William 103c
starch 200, 201–2, 225
state symbols 63
states of matter 4–5, 54–7, 63
 see also gases; liquids; solids
Staudinger, Hermann 200
stearate ions 174
steels 7c, 116, 128, 155
 stainless steel 31, 32, 33c
Strassmann, Fritz 250
structural formulas 183
structure 65, 82–93, 203–4
 trends across periods 140, 141
subduction zones 266, 269, 273
sublimation 4, 5
substances 3
substrates, enzyme 232
sugars 10, 19, 65, 88
 dissolving 42, 57
 in fermentation 193, 194, 233
 reaction with sulphuric acid 111
 see also glucose
sulphates 122, 171, 173, 176
 from sulphuric acid 163, 164
sulphur 39c, 63
 burning 27, 79, 110, 216
 in the Contact Process 111
 reaction with iron 71, 72
sulphur dioxide 99
 in the Contact Process 111
 and pollution 30, 39c, 162
 in acid rain 34, 35, 37
 sulphur burning forms 27, 79, 110, 216
 volcanoes give out 110, 269
sulphur trioxide 34, 111
sulphuric acid 90, 110–11, 159

 in acid rain 34
 ions from 168
 reactions 163, 164, 165
 with ammonia 105
 with metals 122, 158
superglue 191c
supply and demand 113, 186
surface area 225–6
suspensions 14, 15, 16
swimming pools 146
symbols 8, 63
synclines 276
synthesis 9

T

taxation and pollution 38a
tectonics 266–7
teeth 5, 40, 145, 162, 163
temperature
 and biological washing powders 229a
 and enzymes 232
 inside the Earth 264–5
 and reactions 105–6, 225, 235
 and solubility 44–5
temporary hard water 175–6
tennis racquets, materials for 7c
Thames, River 46, 47, 50c
thermal pollution of water 45
thermoplastics 207
thermosets 207
Thomson, Sir J.J. 250
time-chart, geological 282
tin 31, 118, 240
titrations 80–1, 165
trace elements 10
transition metals 137, 154–5
 see also chromium; copper; iron; nickel
troposphere 37
trout in Loch Fleet 167c
Turkey, earthquake in 278–9c

U

universal indicator 160
unsaturated compounds 188, 189
uranium 252, 261c
urea fertilisers 109a
UV radiation 35, 37

V

vanadium pentoxide catalyst 111
vinegar 15–16, 80, 158, 160, 193
volcanoes 24, 25, 110, 269, 271
volume 78–9

W

washing powders 175, 229a, 233
 see also detergents; soap
washing soda see sodium carbonate
waste 47, 129
water 10, 62, 63, 83, 244, 260
 boiling point 21
 in clay 90
 combustion produces 27, 64, 194, 214–15
 disinfection with chlorine 146
 drinking see drinking water
 hardness 43, 99, 174–7, 177a
 hydration of ethene 193
 reactions with metals 121–2, 142–3
 in rusting 30–1
 as a solvent 42–5
 testing for 43, 154
 in weathering and erosion 277, 278
water cycle 41
water pollution 45, 46–51, 49a, 175
water supplies 40–1, 51c
 see also drinking water
water vapour 24, 25, 41
weathering 270, 272, 277
word equations 3, 68

X

X-ray diffraction 83, 87c
xenon 55, 152

Z

zinc 118, 119
 in corrosion 31, 33c, 132c
 plating with 240
 reactions 121, 122–3, 228, 249
zinc sulphate 123, 249

Acknowledgements

The authors and publisher are grateful to the following for permission to reproduce photographs. While every effort has been made to trace copyright holders, if any acknowledgement has been inadvertently omitted, the publisher will be pleased to make the necessary arrangement at the first opportunity.

AFRC: 16.7;
ALFED: 131;
Ann Ronan: 161.1;
Associated press: 278 (bottom) (Murad Sezer);
Atomic Energy Research Establishment, Harwell: 250.2;
Axon Images: 118.7, 222, 273.8;
BOC: 21 (photo courtesy of BOC);
BP Amoco: 187;
Bridgeman Art Library: 54.1, 126.1;
British Coal: 225.4;
British Gas: 68, 222;
British Geological Survey: 129.8;
British Museum: 12;
Bruce Coleman: 129.7 (M Kahl);
CEGB: 122;
Chris Ridgers: 2.1, 2.2, 2.3, 8.2, 20, 42.1, 49, 58, 63, 69, 70, 72, 90, 98.2, 117.6, 119, 124, 136, 158.2, 162.1, 171, 174, 175, 180.1, 180.2, 206, 207, 210.2, 224, 225.2, 270.2, 270.3;
Copper Development Association: 246;
Corel (NT): 7, 115, 120.3, 135, 145.3, 157, 263;
De Beers: 265;
Derby Museum and Art Gallery: 140 (*The Alchemist* by Joseph Wright);
Didier Barrault: 170.1;
Digital Stock (NT): 34, 95;
Digital Vision (NT): 26.1, 40.2, 250.1;
DVLA: 38;
Ecoscene : 103.3 (John Farmer), 104 (Sally Morgan), 154.3, 194.5 (Joel Creed);
ESB, Eire: 216;
Express Newspapers: 47.3;
Frank Lane Picture Agency: 270.1 (S McCutcheon);
Friends of the Earth: 48.7;
Geoscience Features Picture Library: 1, 11 (W Higgs), 42.2, 98.1, 99.3, 129.9, 165, 269.6;
Getty Images: 62.1;
Greg Evans: 120.1;
Hitachi: 62.2;
ICI: 107, 109.1, 111, 168, 242;
Image Bank: 76;
J Allen Cash: 30, 39, 80, 170.2, 202.7, 248.1;
John Urling Clark: 47.4, 61.3, 61.4, 67.1, 67.2, 73, 83, 88.2, 116.3, 159.4, 191, 204.13, 238.1, 239, 241, 254, 261;
Johnson Matthey: 227.9;
Kemira Agro (UK) Ltd: 108 (photo courtesy of Kemira Agro);
Leslie Garland Picture Library: 36, 116.1, 259.6 (Andrew Lambert);
Maldon Crystal Salt Company: 150;
Manchester City Council: 220;
Mary Evans Picture Library: 5.5;
Martyn Chillmaid: 4, 8.1, 16.6, 16.8, 17, 18.1, 24, 26.3, 45.8, 56.8, 57.10, 71, 109.2, 112.2, 117.5, 121, 142, 155, 194.4, 196, 197.3, 198.5, 198.6, 200, 227, 233.3, 233.4, 255.4;

Michael Marten: 47.5;
Military Picture Library: 77;
New Media: 256;
NHPA: 158.1;
Novosti UK: 138.2;
Oxford Scientific Films: 277.5 (Terry Middleton);
Photo Co-op: 146 (Gina Glover);
Photodisc (NT): 27;
Photri: 46.1;
Pilkington plc: 209;
Rex Features: 145.4, 154.4, 183.9 (Nahassia SIPA Press), 218.1, 237;
Robert Harding Picture Library: 82.2, 214, 259.4 (Jason Burns, Dr Ryder, Photo take NYC);
Robert Opie Collection: 54.2, 235;
Royal Holloway and Bedford College, London University: 87.1 (Dr Martin Moore);
Royal Mail: 87.3;
Science and Society Picture Library: 138.1, 139, 238.2;
Science Museum: 283;
Science Photo Library: 13 (J L Charnet), 18.3 (Biophoto Associates), 53 (Alfred Pasieka), 57.11 (Andrew McClenaghan), 84 (Roberto de Giuliemo), 85.7, 85.8 (Sinclair Stammers), 93 (John Walsh), 110, 161, 162.2 (Maximilian Stock Ltd), 179 (Mehan Kulyk), 210.1 (Vaughan Fleming), 232 (J C Revy), 249, 251 (US Department of Energy), 255.5 (Department of Physics, Imperial College);
Shell Photographic Library: 181, 183.10;
Shuttleworth Collection: 117.4;
SNV: 99.4;
Stockbyte (NT): 14, 15, 45.7, 82.1, 153, 197.4, 245, 277.6;
Stone: 23 (Ron Dahlquist), 118.7 (right) (Mark Harwood), 130;
Stuart Boreham: 78.5, 78.6, 141, 176.6;
Sylvia Pitcher Photolibrary: 5.4 (Nik Milner);
Telegraph Colour Library: 192 (Elke Hesser);
Thames Water: 40.1;
Thomas Photos: 226.5;
Tiger Exhausts: 33.2;
Topham Picturepoint: 87.2, 99.5, 269.4;
TRIP: 33.1 (J Ellard), 185 (H Rogers), 195 (Ask Images), 248.2 (R Belbin);
University of Leicester: 148 (Professor J Holloway)

Picture research by johnbailey@axonimages.com

Thanks are also due to the following awarding bodies for kind permission to reproduce examination questions:

Assessment and Qualifications Alliance (AQA)
Edexcel
Oxford Cambridge and RSA Examinations (OCR)
Welsh Joint Education Committee (WJEC)